The Aesthetics and Ethics of Copying

Also available from Bloomsbury

Aesthetic and Artistic Autonomy, edited by Owen Hulatt
Aesthetics, Arts, and Politics in a Global World, Daniel Herwitz
The Bloomsbury Companion to Aesthetics, edited by Anna Christina Ribeiro
The Bloomsbury Companion to Ethics, edited by Christian Miller
The Cultural Promise of the Aesthetic, Monique Roelofs
Introducing Aesthetics and the Philosophy of Art, Darren Hudson Hick
Philosophy of Law, Jeffrey Brand

The Aesthetics and Ethics of Copying

Edited by

Darren Hudson Hick and Reinold Schmücker

Bloomsbury Academic
An imprint of Bloomsbury Publishing Plc
B L O O M S B U R Y
LONDON • OXFORD • NEW YORK • NEW DELHI • SYDNEY

Bloomsbury Academic
An imprint of Bloomsbury Publishing Plc

50 Bedford Square
London
WC1B 3DP
UK

1385 Broadway
New York
NY 10018
USA

www.bloomsbury.com

BLOOMSBURY and the Diana logo are trademarks of Bloomsbury Publishing Plc

First published 2016
Paperback edition first published 2017

British Library Cataloguing-in-Publication Data
A catalogue record for this book is available from the British Library.

ISBN: HB: 978-1-4742-5451-9
PB: 978-1-3500-5607-7
ePDF: 978-1-4742-5453-3
ePub: 978-1-4742-5452-6

Library of Congress Cataloging-in-Publication Data
Names: Hick, Darren Hudson, editor. | Schmücker, Reinold, editor.
Title: The aesthetics and ethics of copying / edited by Darren Hudson Hick and Reinold Schmücker.
Description: New York : Bloomsbury, 2016. | Includes bibliographical references and index.
Identifiers: LCCN 2016016216 (print) | LCCN 2016027810 (ebook) | ISBN 9781474254519 (hardback) | ISBN 9781474254533 (epdf) | ISBN 9781474254526 (epub)
Subjects: LCSH: Arts--Reproduction--Moral and ethical aspects. | Aesthetics.
Classification: LCC NX635 .A39 2016 (print) | LCC NX635 (ebook) | DDC 701/.17--dc23
LC record available at https://lccn.loc.gov/2016016216

Cover design: Catherine Wood
Cover image © Darren Hudson Hick

Typeset by Fakenham Prepress Solutions, Fakenham, Norfolk NR21 8NN

Contents

List of Figures

List of Tables

Notes on Contributors

Mark Alfino is a philosopher at Gonzaga University in Spokane, Washington, USA, and specializes in information ethics and applied ethics. He is co-editor of the *Handbook of Intellectual Freedom* (Litwin Press, 2014) and *McDonaldization Revisited: Critical Essays in Consumer Culture* (Greenwood Press, 1998) and co-author of *Information Ethics for Librarians* (Macfarland, 1997).

Jan Bäcklund is an Associate Professor in the Schools of Fine Arts at the Royal Danish Academy of Fine Arts in Copenhagen, Denmark, where he focuses on issues of forgery, art history, and art theory. He is currently working on a research project with the title "Ready-made and Fake: Rudiments of a Quantified Art Theory."

Amrei Bahr is a PhD student at the Westfälische Wilhelms-Universität Münster, Germany. Her research focuses on artifact copies and artifact functionality in the overlap between the philosophy of art and philosophy of technology. She is the co-editor of *Ernest Sosa: Targeting his Philosophy* (Springer, 2016). In 2015–16, she was a fellow of the research group *The Ethics of Copying* at the Center for Interdisciplinary Research (ZiF) in Bielefeld, Germany.

Lionel Bently is the Herchel Smith Professor of Intellectual Property at the University of Cambridge, U.K., and Director of the Centre for Intellectual Property and Information Law. He is co-author of *Intellectual Property Law* (Oxford University Press, 4th edn, 2014), editor of the *Cambridge Intellectual Property and Information Law* series, co-editor of *Trade Marks and Brands: An Interdisciplinary Critique* (Cambridge University Press, 2008) and co-author of *The Making of Modern Intellectual Property Law* (Cambridge University Press, 1997). In 2015–16, he was the chair of the European Copyright Society and a fellow of the research group *The Ethics of Copying* at the Center for Interdisciplinary Research (ZiF) in Bielefeld, Germany.

Dieter Birnbacher is a Professor of Philosophy at the Heinrich-Heine-Universität Düsseldorf, Germany, where he focuses on ethics and applied ethics. Among other works, he is the author of *Verantwortung für zukünftige Generationen* [Responsibility for Future Generations] (Reclam, 1988), *Tun und Unterlassen* [Acting and Omitting] (Reclam, 1995), *Natürlichkeit* (de Gruyter, 2006; English translation under the title *Naturalness. Is the "Natural" Preferable to the "Artificial"?*, University of America Press, 2014), and *Bioethik zwischen Natur und Interesse* [Bioethics Between Nature and Interest] (Suhrkamp, 2006). He is the co-editor of *Giving Death a Helping Hand: Physician-Assisted Suicide and Public Policy. An International Perspective* (Springer, 2006) and *The Politics of Sustainability. Philosophical Perspectives* (Routledge, 2015).

Massimiliano Carrara is an Associate Professor of Logic and Philosophy of Language at the University of Padua, Italy. In addition to his work on logic, he has an ongoing research project on artifact kinds and counterfeits. Among other works, he is co-editor of *Unity and Plurality: Philosophy, Logic, and Linguistics* (Oxford University Press, 2016). In 2015–16, he was a fellow of the research group *The Ethics of Copying* at the Center for Interdisciplinary Research (ZiF) in Bielefeld, Germany.

Thomas Dreier is Director of the Institute for Information and Economic Law and the Center for Applied Legal Studies at the Karlsruhe Institute of Technology in Karlsruhe, Germany, and honorary professor at the Albert-Ludwigs-Universität Freiburg, Germany. He specializes in copyright, in particular as regards digital technologies, information law, and art law. A guest professor at New York University, the University of Haifa, Israel, and the National University of Singapore, he has authored and edited numerous books and articles on copyright, information, and art law. In 2015–16, he was a principal investigator of the research group *The Ethics of Copying* at the Center for Interdisciplinary Research (ZiF) in Bielefeld, Germany.

Charles Ess is Professor of Media Studies in the Department of Media and Communication at the University of Oslo, Norway. He works at the intersections of philosophy, computing, applied ethics, comparative philosophy, and media studies, with specific focus on research ethics, Digital Religion, and virtue ethics in media and communication, specifically social robots. Recent publications include *Digital Media Ethics* (Polity Press, 2009, 2nd edn, 2013), (co-editor) *The Handbook of Internet Studies* (Wiley-Blackwell, 2012), and "What's Love Got to Do with It? Robots, Sexuality, and the Arts of Being Human," in M. Nørskov (ed.), *Social Robots: Boundaries, Potential, Challenges*, 57–79 (Ashgate, 2015).

In 2015–16, he was a fellow of the research group *The Ethics of Copying* at the Center for Interdisciplinary Research (ZiF) in Bielefeld, Germany.

Annette Gilbert is a Lecturer at the Friedrich-Alexander-Universität Erlangen-Nürnberg, Germany. She works in comparative literature, focusing on experimental and avant-garde literature as well as on issues of appropriation and the ontology of literary works. She is the editor of *Wiederaufgelegt. Zur Appropriation von Texten und Büchern in Büchern* [Republished. The Appropriation of Texts and Books in Books] (transcript, 2012), *Reprint. Appropriation (&) Literature* (Luxbooks, 2014), and *Publishing as Artistic Practice* (Sternberg, 2016). She was Head of the Junior Research Group, "In & Out & Between: Framing in the Arts of the 20th Century" at the Peter Szondi Institute of Comparative Literature at the Freie Universität Berlin, Germany, and in 2015–16 a fellow of the research group *The Ethics of Copying* at the Center for Interdisciplinary Research (ZiF) in Bielefeld, Germany.

Darren Hudson Hick is a philosopher of art at Texas Tech University (Lubbock, Texas, USA), where he specializes in philosophical problems in intellectual property, the ontology of art, and related matters. As well as numerous articles on these subjects, he is the author of *Introducing Aesthetics and the Philosophy of Art* (Bloomsbury, 2012) and *Artistic License: The Problems of Copyright & Appropriation* (University of Chicago Press, forthcoming). In 2015–16, he was a fellow of the research group *The Ethics of Copying* at the Center for Interdisciplinary Research (ZiF) in Bielefeld, Germany.

Wybo Houkes is an Associate Professor in the Philosophy of Science and Technology at Eindhoven University of Technology in Eindhoven, Netherlands, where he focuses on the philosophy of technical artifacts, analyses of technical knowledge, and applications of evolutionary theory to technology. He is the co-author of *Technical Functions: On the Use and Design of Artefacts* (Springer, 2010). In 2015–16, he was a fellow of the research group *The Ethics of Copying* at the Center for Interdisciplinary Research (ZiF) in Bielefeld, Germany.

Lisa Jones is a Principal Teaching Fellow in Philosophy at the University of St Andrews, Scotland. She teaches in the philosophies of art and literature, and also in moral philosophy. Her research interests are in aesthetics, philosophy of art, and philosophy of literature, with a focus on the values of literature (cognitive and ethical), the intersection between ethics and aesthetics, and the nature of narrative. In 2015–16, she was an associate member of the research group *The Ethics of Copying* at the Center for Interdisciplinary Research (ZiF) in Bielefeld, Germany.

Jakub Macek is an Assistant Professor in the Department of Media Studies and Journalism and a researcher at the Institute on Research of Children, Youth and Family, both at Masaryk University, Brno, Czech Republic. His research focuses on the sociology of new media and media audiences. He has recently finished a research project entitled "New and old media in everyday life: media audiences at the time of transforming media uses."

Hans Nieswandt is a DJ, music producer, journalist, and Artistic Director of the Masters program in popular music at the Institute of Popular Music at Folkwang University in Bochum, Germany. In addition to several albums, he is the author of *DJ Dionysos Geschichten aus der Diskowelt* [DJ Dionysus: Stories from the Disco World] (Kiepenheuer & Witsch, 2010), *Disko Ramallah und andere merkwürdige Orte zum Plattenauflegen* [Disco Ramallah and Other Strange Places to DJ] (Kiepenheuer & Witsch, 2006), and *plus minus acht: DJ Tage, DJ Nächte* [Plusminuseight: DJ Days, DJ Nights] (Kiepenheuer & Witsch, 2001). In 2015–16, he was an associate member of the research group *The Ethics of Copying* at the Center for Interdisciplinary Research (ZiF) in Bielefeld, Germany.

David Oels is Headmaster of SchuleEins in Berlin, Germany, and former Assistant Professor of Book Studies at the Johannes Gutenberg-Universität Mainz, Germany, specializing in literary forgeries and the distinction between fiction and nonfiction. He is the co-author of *Sachbuch und Populäres Wissen im 20. Jahrhundert* [Nonfiction and Popular Knowledge in the 20th Century] (Peter Lang, 2007) and co-editor of the journal *Non Fiktion. Arsenal der anderen Gattungen* [Non Fiction: Arsenal of the Other Genres] (Wehrhahn).

Eberhard Ortland is the Assistant to the research group *The Ethics of Copying* at the Center for Interdisciplinary Research (ZiF) in Bielefeld, Germany, where he focuses on issues in aesthetics and copyright. In addition to several articles on the subject, he is the editor of Theodor W. Adorno's posthumously edited lectures on Aesthetics, *Nachgelassene Schriften*, Bd. IV, 3: *Ästhetik* [Posthumous Writings, vol. IV, 3: Aesthetics] (Suhrkamp, 2009), co-editor of *Geistiges Eigentum und Originalität* [Intellectual Property and Originality]

(Turia + Kant, 2011) and managing co-editor of the encyclopedia *Original & Kopie* [Original & Copy] (Felix Meiner Verlag, forthcoming 2018).

Maria Elisabeth Reicher is a Professor of Philosophy at RWTH Aachen University in Aachen, Germany, where her work focuses on ontology and the philosophy of art. In addition to many articles on these subjects, she is the author of *Einführung in die Philosophische Ästhetik* [Introduction to Philosophical Aesthetics] (WBG, 2005; rev. edn, 2015) and *Referenz, Quantifikation und ontologische Festlegung* [Reference, Quantification and Ontological Commitment] (Ontos, 2005), the editor of *Fiktion, Wahrheit, Wirklichkeit. Philosophische Grundlagen der Literaturtheorie* [Fiction, Truth, Reality. Philosophical Fundamentals of Literary Theory] (mentis, 2007, 2nd edn, 2010) and co-editor of the journal *Grazer Philosophische Studien* (Brill). In 2015–16, she was a fellow of the research group *The Ethics of Copying* at the Center for Interdisciplinary Research (ZiF) in Bielefeld, Germany.

Reinold Schmücker is a Professor of Philosophy at the Westfälische Wilhelms-Universität Münster, Germany, working on fundamental problems in aesthetics, ethics, and political philosophy. In his recent research, he has been particularly interested in the philosophy of artifacts, meta-ethics, and applied ethics. As well as numerous articles, he has authored *Was ist Kunst? Eine Grundlegung* [What Is Art? A Groundwork] (1998; rev. edn, Vittorio Klostermann, 2014). He is the editor of *Identität und Existenz. Studien zur Ontologie der Kunst* [Identity and Existence. Studies in the Ontology of Art] (mentis, 2003, 4th edn, 2014) and has co-edited *Wozu Kunst?* [Why Art?] (WBG, 2001), *Gerechtigkeit und Politik* [Justice and Politics] (Akademie Verlag, 2002), *Kunst und Kunstbegriff* [Art and the Concept of Art] (mentis, 2002, 3rd edn, 2013), and *Vorrang der Moral?* [Overridingness of Morality?] (Vittorio Klostermann, 2016). In 2015–16, he was a principal investigator of the research group *The Ethics of Copying* at the Center for Interdisciplinary Research (ZiF) in Bielefeld, Germany.

Aram Sinnreich is an Associate Professor of Communication Studies at the American University School of Communication in Washington, DC, USA. He is the author of *The Piracy Crusade: How the Music Industry's War on Sharing Destroys Markets and Erodes Civil Liberties* (University of Massachusetts Press, 2013) and *Mashed Up: Music, Technology and the Rise of Configurable Culture* (University of Massachusetts Press, 2010). In 2015–16, he was a fellow of the research group *The Ethics of Copying* at the Center for Interdisciplinary Research

(ZiF) in Bielefeld, Germany; currently, he is working on a critical course book on copyright and intellectual property for Yale University Press.

James O. Young, Fellow of the Royal Society of Canada, is Professor of Philosophy at the University of Victoria, BC, Canada. He is the author of *Global Anti-realism* (Avebury, 1995), *Art and Knowledge* (Routledge, 2001), *Cultural Appropriation and the Arts* (Blackwell, 2008), and *Critique of Pure Music* (Oxford University Press, 2014). He has edited *Aesthetics: The Critical Concepts* (Routledge, 2005) and (with Conrad Brunk) *The Ethics of Cultural Appropriation* (Wiley-Blackwell, 2009). He has translated, introduced, and annotated Batteux's *Fine Arts Reduced to a Single Principle* (Oxford University Press, 2015) and is the author of over fifty articles in refereed journals as well as many chapters.

Pavel Zahrádka is an Assistant Professor of Sociology and Philosophy at Palacký University in Olomouc, Czech Republic, where he focuses on intersections between philosophical aesthetics and cultural sociology. He is the editor of *Estetika na přelomu milénia* [Aesthetics at the Turn of the Millennium] (Barrister & Principal, 2011) and *Spotřební kultura: Historie, teorie a výzkum* [Consumer Culture: History, Theory and Research] (Academia, 2014) and the author of the book *Heteronomie estetické hodnoty* [Heteronomy of Aesthetic Value] (Host, 2015). In 2015–16, he was a principal investigator of the research group *The Ethics of Copying* at the Center for Interdisciplinary Research (ZiF) in Bielefeld, Germany.

Preface

Prada Marfa

On the cover of this book is a photograph of *Prada Marfa*, located on a lonely stretch of highway, about twenty minutes outside of Marfa, Texas, deep in the Chihuahuan Desert. Through the windows, you can see an array of shoes and handbags from Prada's 2005 collection, the year that *Prada Marfa* was built. But you can't get any closer than the windows. The items aren't for sale, and, in any event, the door doesn't open. *Prada Marfa* isn't a store; it's a *copy* of a store, brought to life by Berlin-based artists Michael Elmgreen and Ingar Dragset.

For eight years, aside from some incidents of vandalism (including a break-in where thieves discovered that the high-end Italian bags on display had no bottoms, and that the shoes were all right-footed), the work didn't attract any trouble from the residents of West Texas, or the travelers who took a side-trip through the desert to see it—that is, until *Playboy* decided to install a 40-foot neon Playboy bunny logo a ways down the same highway. The sign was a part of *Playboy Marfa*, a 2013 work by New York artist Richard Phillips. Local residents, it seems, weren't too keen on the idea of being associated with a giant, glowing symbol of pornography.

Residents found a way to get rid of *Playboy Marfa*. The U.S. Highway Beautification Act of 1965 requires highway advertising to have a permit. The glowing Playboy logo qualified as advertising, and permits are not available for that particular stretch of U.S. Route 90 on which *Playboy Marfa* sits. The work was, indeed, commissioned and owned by Playboy Enterprises, and the Texas Department of Transportation (TxDOT) ordered it removed. Unfortunately, *Prada Marfa* sits on the same stretch of highway, and its awnings are adorned with Prada logos (used, incidentally, with the permission of Prada). TxDOT reluctantly determined that it, too, constituted illegal outdoor advertising. In the eyes of Texas, the artwork had become an advertisement for the very thing it copied.

While *Playboy Marfa* was being carted up and moved 500 miles to its new home in Dallas (where, apparently, residents are less concerned about associations with *Playboy*), defenders of *Prada Marfa* (including, as it turns out, TxDOT) were brainstorming for ways to protect and retain the now-iconic work. In September of 2014, a solution was reached: the Ballroom Marfa Foundation, which maintains the site, worked with TxDOT to have the building reclassified as an art museum, and *Prada Marfa* as its only exhibit. The copy had become its own museum: a representation of itself.

The aesthetics and ethics of copying

Although the Highway Beautification Act isn't usually the legislation at issue, copying has for centuries been tied up with the law. Most often, when copies (and copyists) run into legal troubles—especially when either the copy or the thing being copied is art—it is because they have violated intellectual property laws: copyright, trademark, or patent. While *Prada Marfa* is something of a unique case, however, this isn't because it grabbed headlines. Indeed, rarely a week goes by without a case of copying garnering national or international attention.

Copyright infringement, plagiarism, forgery, and cultural appropriation are all forms of what might be called *copying-wrongs*, either moral or legal. Copying—of artworks and otherwise—has always been a widespread human practice, and normative and legal lines have been drawn and redrawn over the centuries, separating allowable from illicit copying. Claims of illicit copying have been levied against the emulation of a style, the "copying and pasting" from one text into another, the duplication of electronic data, sampling and mash-ups of pre-existing musical works, and countless other activities. But what qualifies as a copy, and which copies are illicit (and why) remain open, surprisingly complex questions crossing the boundaries between philosophy, the law, art history, and other fields.

In the short history of contemporary aesthetics—the field in which we both work—questions of copying have largely focused on the problems of forgery (particularly growing out of Nelson Goodman's *Languages of Art* and Denis Dutton's collection, *The Forger's Art*). In recent years, however, philosophical questions of copying have expanded into a larger arena of aesthetic, ethical, and legal concern, especially as conflicts have arisen between new artistic practices and the often strict demands of intellectual property law. From movable type to photography to digitization, advances in technology have made the copying of artworks and other artifacts exponentially easier—but more than this, have allowed for the easy recombination and re-presentation of others' creative products as *new* works. Such practices have been bolstered by apparent changes in attitudes and intuitions among artists and the public at large regarding the appropriation of ideas, styles, and fully realized artworks. But there are still apparent lines to be drawn between appropriation and *mis*appropriation, and artists, lawyers, courts, and scholars struggle to find—and at times, shift or erase—these lines. In recent years, researchers from a number of fields, and from around the globe, have been drawn to questions about the aesthetics and ethics of copying, and this volume collects new essays by some of the leading scholars in this burgeoning topic.

The contributions

The collection is broken into four main parts and a coda. Part 1 ('The Copying Animal: Exploring the Cultural Value of Copying') focuses on the role that copying plays in human culture. Dieter Birnbacher, Mark Alfino, and Wybo Houkes each confront the fundamental question of how—and why—copying fits into our broader system of values. Birnbacher (Chapter 1) opens this part with the ancient story of Amphitryon (itself copied, adapted, and recopied over millennia) to frame the question of whether originals—of artworks or other artifacts, of natural objects, of persons—hold any inherent value over and above their copies. Alfino (Chapter 2) then looks to the deep roots of a copying ethics in our human development and the cultural and evolutionary importance of copying (both perfect and imperfect), placing the burden on the moralist to establish grounds for restricting copying. Finally, Houkes (Chapter 3) looks to the social and material preconditions of copying—and specifically to digital file-sharing—to analyze both the "right-making" and "wrong-making" features of imitative behavior. *Replication* of artifacts, Houkes contends, may contain wrong-making features that *rational imitation* does not.

The chapters in Part 2 ('What is a Copy? Conceptual Perspectives') set a groundwork for understanding the nature of copies and copying—a necessary prerequisite for any subsequent discussion of the subject—teasing out the several factors and conceptual distinctions that must be accounted for in an ontology of copying, and showing how these interweave with ethical and legal concepts. As becomes clear, a simple distinction between an *original* and a *copy* will not do the necessary work. Instead, we must account for an array of copy-kinds, including *fakes*, *counterfeits*, *replicas*, and *genuine instances*, as well as such distinctions as the *authentic* or *inauthentic* copy, the *legitimate* or *illegitimate* copy, and the *permitted* or *illicit* copy. Maria Elisabeth Reicher (Chapter 4) begins this part by analyzing the core concepts embedded in copyright law, working to establish an ontology of "works"—primarily but not exclusively *art*works—consistent with this complex institutional structure. Amrei Bahr (Chapter 5) focuses on understanding the nature of copies. To build grounding for answering ethical and legal questions in the domain of copying, she provides an ontological analysis, untangling important distinctions between four kinds of "artifact copies." In contrast, Massimiliano Carrara (Chapter 6) seeks to refine a long-accepted definition of a "counterfeit" (or "fake" or "forgery") as a copy of an original falsely presented as the original, showing that this analysis quickly runs into a number of difficulties, and offering in its stead a more nuanced definition. Finally, in order to tease out the ways in which the ontology of artistic copying is inextricably embedded in cultural practice, Darren Hudson Hick (Chapter 7) analyzes the possibility of a literary work that, as a matter of authorial fiat, does not allow for further genuine copies, suggesting that what counts as a copy is always open to change.

Part 3 ('The Copying Artist: Aesthetic and Ethical Challenges') focuses on special concerns in the domain of artworks. Annette Gilbert, James O. Young, and David Oels each look at unique issues in the overlap between aesthetics and ethics in literary works. Analyzing the reach of an author's authority and the role that a literary work's extratextual materiality plays in its authenticity, Gilbert (Chapter 8) examines a peculiar sort of copy in the literary world: the published work that, while produced by the authorized publisher, nevertheless violates the author's wishes regarding the work's form. Next, Young (Chapter 9) looks to the copying of fictional characters, arguing that, for the purposes of intellectual property, such characters should be treated more like patentable inventions than copyrightable works. As such characters are built from the public domain, Young argues, so too should they swiftly return. Oels (Chapter 10) looks to cases in which authors of fiction are accused of infringing on works of nonfiction, arguing that our deeply embedded distinctions of "fact" and "fiction," and "original" and "copy," should be treated as gradations rather than absolutes, and that it is therefore questionable whether nonfictional works in general should be understood—as they had been—as mere collections of facts.

In the second half of Part 3, Lisa Jones, Jan Bäcklund, and Eberhard Ortland further expand the art discussion. Jones (Chapter 11) focuses in her chapter on appropriation art—in which one or more artworks are incorporated into some new work—to argue that (issues of ownership and permission aside) such a form of copying may on occasion constitute an *aesthetic* wrong that rises to the level of a *moral* wrong. Bäcklund (Chapter 12) next looks to the copying of artistic style, a practice with a unique place in art history: on the one hand necessary, and on the other forbidden. Style, Bäcklund argues, is a sort of code *requiring* copying to enact meaning. Perhaps the most famous recent case of stylistic copying is Pharrell Williams and Robin Thicke's 2013 hit, "Blurred Lines," found in 2015 to have infringed the copyright in Marvin Gaye's 1977 classic, "Got to Give it Up." Ortland (Chapter 13) closes this section using the "Blurred Lines" case (and its divisive decision) to argue that ethical (and legal) judgments about artistic copying require first aesthetic judgment of both the original and its copy.

Part 4 ('Freedom for All? Towards an Ethics of Copying for the Digital Age') turns to the moral dimensions of copying in the twenty-first century. Thomas Dreier (Chapter 14) opens this section with an analysis of the relationship between copyright, its European variant of *droit d'auteur*, and their relationship with the ethical foundations underlying the law, once severed from the legal discussion, but recently revived as a fundamental topic of inquiry. Next, Lionel Bently (Chapter 15) uses a peculiar sort of case in the law—self-plagiarism—to investigate how the law treats copying and self-copying, and how it reflects our ethical intuitions, analyzing the three most prominent justifications for copyright: autonomy, natural rights, and utilitarianism. Charles Ess (Chapter 16) argues that recent developments point to an ethical perspective generally excluded from the standard justifications for copyright—virtue theory—but which he contends better captures a growing notion of selfhood that is strongly relational rather than individualistic. Aram Sinnreich (Chapter 17) next offers empirical analysis to suggest that the proliferation of participatory artistic practices—including mash-ups, remixes, and machinima—are accompanied with increasingly complex ethical frameworks operating across a spectrum of morally relevant criteria, and which are increasingly at odds with the state of intellectual property laws. In another empirical study, Jakub Macek and Pavel Zahrádka (Chapter 18) analyze the case of Czech "post-TV" audiences, suggesting that those who illicitly download films and TV series are generally neither amoral pragmatists nor cultural revolutionaries, but rather share a nuanced ethical framework that content providers have yet to adapt to. Finally in this part, Reinold Schmücker (Chapter 19) takes on Macek's and Zahrádka's results and infers from the growing gap between the norms of copyright law and widespread normative intuitions regarding licit and illicit copying that we are in need of an ethics of copying that could be used as a normative framework for the moral evaluation of copying practices as well as laws restricting acts of copying. To set groundwork for such an ethics of copying, he outlines a normative basis for it and suggests five exemplary domain-specific principles which it might include.

The collection closes with a 'Coda': a chapter by Hans Nieswandt (himself a practicing DJ and music producer) reflecting on the history and practice of music editing. Nieswandt argues that, rather than harming the original, the edit is a celebration of it, reviving the dead for a new generation.

Certainly, we cannot hope to *settle* debates about the aesthetics and ethics of copying with this collection of essays. Far from it: the contributors whose works are collected herein often disagree with each other, often wildly so. But it is through the lively (and occasionally tempestuous) study of copying—in all its aesthetic, ethical, legal, and cultural respects—that we begin to make clear what makes the subject both fascinating and important, and we begin to chart a path for continued discussion.

Darren Hudson Hick
Reinold Schmücker

Acknowledgments

First and foremost, we want to thank our contributors, who have made this collection everything that it is. Although speaking from a fantastically diverse set of perspectives, all of the authors represented in this volume have now worked together for years in a true spirit of collaboration, and we have all learned a great deal from each other. This has been made possible by the inspiring atmosphere at the Center for Interdisciplinary Research (Zentrum für interdisziplinäre Forschung: ZiF) in Bielefeld, Germany, who funded and hosted not only a series of workshops and conferences but also a one-year research group on *The Ethics of Copying* (2015–16), giving rise to the essays making up this unique collection. We owe a great deal in particular to Britta Padberg, the executive secretary of ZiF, who has supported us on the long road from the first idea of this project to its realization with bountiful sympathy and useful advice, to Marina Hoffmann's experienced conference organization, and to the whole team of the ZiF who shepherded the fellows of the research group so warmly.

We also want to give special thanks to the Centre for Advanced Study in Bioethics at the Westfälische Wilhelms-Universität Münster for their co-funding of the international conference, *The Ethics of Copying* (July 2014), the German Research Foundation (Deutsche Forschungsgemeinschaft: DFG) for their co-funding of the international conference, *Towards an Ethics of Copying* (October 2015), to Claudia Güstrau for her inestimable support in overseeing so many organizational and accounting issues, to Kerstin Gregor for her great help in preparing the index, and in particular to translator Michael Weh, who provided invaluable assistance throughout the process of building this volume.

We want to thank the team at Bloomsbury, including Colleen Coalter, Andrew Wardell, Catherine Wood, and Fakenham Prepress Solutions, who believed in our project and worked closely with us to help bring this volume to fruition.

Finally, we need to thank our endlessly supportive wives, Delaina Pearson and Andrea Rössler, true originals for whom there can be no substitutes, no copies.

Darren Hudson Hick
Reinold Schmücker

Part One

The Copying Animal: Exploring the Cultural Value of Copying

1

Copying and the Limits of Substitutability

Dieter Birnbacher

1. Introduction: An unusual case of copying

Perfect copies, the analogue of Nelson Goodman's "perfect fakes" (Goodman 1976: 99) have their own fascination, not only in philosophy, but also in literature and popular imagination. One of the most fascinating literary examples of copying is the story of *Amphitryon,* retold by a long series of playwrights in dramatic form, among them Plautus and Molière, of which the play by Heinrich von Kleist is acknowledged to be the deepest and psychologically most complex development. As with many works of Kleist, the core of the play is a tragic irritation, a disconcerting dialectic that shatters the coordinate system of our habitual ways of thinking. In *Amphitryon* the object of irritation is the impossibility of distinguishing between original and copy and the breakdown of the usual criteria of identification. Alcmene is caught in the contradiction between the strict identity requirements inherent in her love for her husband Amphitryon and his apparent reduplication. On the one hand, Alcmene is adamant in maintaining that she loves only one of the copies, the authentic Amphitryon. On the other hand, she is unable to tell which of the two Amphitryons is the authentic one and goes so far as to identify the false Amphitryon as the real one in the presence of the real one. The following is the climax of the scene in which this happens:

> First commander: Speak!
> Second commander: Talk to us!
> Third commander: Tell us!
> Second commander: Lady, one word!—
> First commander: We are lost if she goes on saying nothing.
> Jupiter: Give truth your voice, dear.

> Alcmene: This one here is Amphitryon, dear friends.
> Amphitryon: That man over there is Amphitryon! Almighty Gods!
>
> Act 1, Scene 2

The fact that Alcmene mistakes the false Amphitryon for the real one is what manifestly happens on stage. What looks, at first sight, as a purely farcical gag, has, however, a deeper meaning. It can be interpreted as the expression of an unconscious feeling that, in some way, her love is not as strictly individual as she thinks and that, given that the false Amphitryon is a perfect copy of the true Amphitryon, identity, to use Parfit's phrase, does not, after all, matter. Another interpretation is that Alcmene is so much impressed by Jupiter's passion for her that she instinctively attributes this quality to her beloved husband, i.e. by dissonance reduction, the tendency to bring valuations and perceptions into harmony, even at the cost of illusion.

One of the comical turns of Kleist's play is that the dialectic within Alcmene's heart is mirrored by an analogous dialectic in the heart of Jupiter, who is by no means satisfied with his role of a perfect copy. This god may be sufficiently perfect to act as a perfect copy of Amphitryon, but he is not perfect enough to leave it at that and to keep his vanity at rest. His ambition is to be a *more than perfect* copy. He insists on individuality and irreplaceability no less than Alcmene. He prides himself that though indistinguishable from Amphitryon in order not to betray himself, he is slightly more perfect in surpassing Alcmene's legitimate husband in passionate love-making. He attempts the impossible, to be numerically identical with Amphitryon and to be qualitatively different from him at the same time. He urges Alcmene to promise that she will never lose the vivid memory of the "day with a god" in her future marriage and of its exceptional pleasures, incomparably superior to those of her marital love life.

2. What is it for a person to be a "copy"?

Under what a conditions can a person legitimately be imagined to be a "copy" of another person in the first place? There are a number of conditions that a personal copy shares with other, non-personal, copies.

One condition is that there is an O (the original) with which C (the copy, which is numerically distinct from O) shares a broad range of qualitative features. Which of these qualitative features have to be identical depends largely on context. Jupiter obviously intends to copy Amphitryon to the extent that Alcmene is unable to notice any relevant difference. In the case of Amphitryon, this condition should be more perfectly fulfilled than in non-mythical cases. After all, Jupiter is a god, even the supreme god. But in fact, the copy is far from perfect. Jupiter's all-too-human arrogance makes him enact a less than perfect copy by striving to be more perfect than the original.

A second condition is that C is the result of an intentional replication of O. A qualitatively identical replica would not be a copy unless intentionally produced *as a copy*. As Wollheim mentions in the context of his discussion of the identity criteria for works of art, there might be what *prima facie* might be called an *involuntary* copy: a naïve poet of the nineteenth century might have written a short poem that proves later to be identical with a poem of the sixteenth century. In this case, the later poem could not be called a *copy* of the older one. Nor would it be the *same* poem as the older one (Wollheim 1980: 170). This kind of case must be distinguished from "involuntary copies" where the author has prior experience of the original. Thus, the only piece of music I ever composed (in early youth) soon proved to be an exact replica of a part of a composition of Bartók that I had heard but forgotten about. Something similar often takes the form of *involuntary plagiarism* by what in psychology is known as *kryptomnesia*: an author writes a text that is identical with the text of an author of a book he has read before but which he does not remember. Though this may not necessarily hold in legal cases, it seems counterintuitive to say that, in cases such as these, the author *copied* the older text. Copying seems to presuppose awareness that one is copying.

In the case of *Amphitryon*, there are, however, some features that distinguish it from other, more normal kinds of copying and which seem inseparable from the fact that the copy is imagined to be a person rather than a material object. The most important is, no doubt, that a personal copy, however perfect a copy it may be as seen from the outside, has, in addition, an inner life which may be completely different from that of the original, both in its phenomenal and in its intentional dimension. In particular, a person, in contrast to a material object, is able to make assertions about its own authenticity. In the case of Jupiter, Jupiter-alias-Amphitryon is a fake. But whereas fakes are normally declared to be authentic by some other person (e.g. its author or its devotees), Jupiter himself declares himself to be the authentic Amphitryon.

Claims of this kind are common enough, but they do not normally go together with perfect qualitative identity. Even world views, religious or philosophical, that assume that a person has more than one life, in virtue of metempsychosis or resurrection for example, do not generally assume that the re-embodied person is qualitatively identical with the former person in all respects. It is true that we sometimes say of a non-personal fake or of a piece of plagiarism that it *makes a false claim* to authenticity, but this is only a metaphorical way of speaking. A material copy does not literally say anything, even if we are strongly tempted to speak in this way if, for example, a piece of plagiarism betrays itself so blatantly as a BA thesis in my faculty did some years ago, by omitting to erase from the title page the name of the university to which the original had been submitted.

Is a "perfect" personal copy imaginable that exemplifies all qualitative features of the original including its inner states and mental acts? The answer obviously depends on how the term "qualitative" is interpreted, and especially if "qualitative" is taken to refer only to *observable* or also to *unobservable* properties, and whether it is taken only to *manifest* or also to *dispositional* properties. In an idealized world of "series persons"—a science fiction world in which a great number of persons are indistinguishable from each other in bodily aspects—a person C may behave exactly like another person O, so that it is behaviorally indistinguishable from C, without however having the same thoughts and feelings. Obviously, this would not suffice for being qualitatively indistinguishable. Comprehensive qualitative identity, as required by a "perfect copy," has to include unobservable properties along with observable ones. Take, for example, the case of an original of a painting and a copy that differ only in the fact that under the observable surface of the original there are hidden layers of color that have become invisible but which have to be assumed in order to explain certain phenomena revealed by X-ray analysis (cf. Wollheim 1980: 174). Even if C reproduces only the observable surface of the painting it might be termed a copy. It cannot, however, be termed a perfect or qualitatively identical copy. Qualitative identity requires that O and C have the same qualitative properties irrespective of whether these are observable or detectable or epistemically accessible in any other way.

The same holds for dispositional properties such as tendencies, liabilities, and potentials. An object can count as a perfect copy of another object only if it shares with it not only its manifest but also its dispositional properties. Also in this respect, Jupiter, being immortal rather than mortal, cannot be a perfect copy of Amphitryon. A subclass of dispositional properties, relevant for authenticity questions in art, are those that refer to properties that are unobservable now but will become observable in the future due to scientific and technical progress, thereby opening up new avenues to tests of authenticity. Because of the openness of the future in this respect and the impossibility of exhaustive verification, it seems hardly possible to assert of any copy that it is perfect with perfect certainty. The same holds, *a fortiori*, for any personal copy. Any person that claims to be a perfect copy of another person might reveal itself as a less than perfect copy by the detection of a piece of memory that it does not (or could not) share with the original. But a perfect personal copy is not thereby a matter of impossibility. There do not seem to be any *logical* limits to the idea of a personal perfect copy. A personal perfect copy must, of course, be thought to think that it is the original, in spite of the fact that this thought is necessarily false. This, however, does not imply that the copy can share *all* descriptive properties with the original. Qualitative features represent only a small subclass of descriptive properties. Though qualitatively identical, A and B may differ in their *relational* properties, and that is how O and C usually differ, over and above the relation of identity in which they differ necessarily.

Even if Jupiter is far from being a perfect copy of Amphitryon, a perfect *doppelgänger* of Amphitryon does not seem beyond imagination. One condition is that his inner life, including his apparent memories, is identical with that of the original and that he shares all of the original's dispositions. There would be logical limits to the identity of their thoughts only as far as relations enter their content. If C and O meet, C perceives O and vice versa, so that the content of their perceptions of each other differ, just as the direction of their perceptions of each other differ.

3. Identity and value

Why do singularity and authenticity make such a difference to emotional attitudes such as love? In the case of Amphitryon, Alcmene holds fast to her expressed conviction that there is a world of axiological difference between the true and the false Amphitryon, or between the original and the copy. For her, her love is strictly dependent on the singularity of its object. From the perspective of her love, this object is strictly non-substitutable: all possible value belongs to the original, none to the copy. In point of value, original and copy are at the extreme ends of the spectrum. And this would be so, it seems, even in the case that Jupiter were a truly perfect copy of her husband.

Does Alcmene have a point? What kind of value is present in the original that is not to be found in the perfect copy? And if there is such a value, why should it make so much of a difference to the overall value of the object?

Prima facie there seem to be reasons to doubt whether there can be values that differentiate between O and C. One is that axiological value generally resides in properties and not in individuals. Whenever an individual is valuable, it is, as a rule, valuable *qua* being the bearer of certain general properties. It is characteristic of general properties that they are indifferent to the identity of the individuals that have them. It is not the individuality or singularity of the individual as such, its *haecceitas,* in which value resides, but the specific constellation of values to be found in it. Even if this individual is the only one to exhibit this specific constellation of values, there might in principle be others that exhibit the same constellation.

Another way to express the same is by means of the concept of *supervenience.* Value properties are generally *supervenient* on certain descriptive properties. If an individual entity is valuable, this is in virtue of some descriptive property the individual possesses. It follows that if two individuals are descriptively indistinguishable and among their properties is at least one on which a value property supervenes, then the two indistinguishable individuals should have the same kind and the same degree of value.

It follows that if O and C differ in value, this difference must depend on corresponding differences in descriptive properties. These descriptive properties must be general properties, i.e. they must not be strictly bound to the individuals that possess them. If an individual A has it, it must be logically possible that another individual B has it, instead of A or in addition to A.

There are, therefore, two conditions that have to be fulfilled to establish a value difference between A and B: (1) A and B must differ in at least one descriptive property P; (2) P must make a difference to the overall value of A and B.

Let's examine the first condition. When is this condition fulfilled in two qualitatively identical individuals, A and B?

There are three properties that are sometimes proposed as characteristic of the original–copy relation and at the same time as constitutive of value differences between both: (1) the specific *aura* the original is said to possess in contrast to its copies; (2) the *singularity* of the original in contrast to the potential multiplicity of its copies; and (3) its *uniqueness.* All three purported properties, I suggest, are insufficient to establish a value gradient between original and copy.

The concept of aura is well known from the writings of Walter Benjamin, where it is used in more than one context and bears a number of related but clearly different meanings. One meaning, however, is to shed light on the essential difference of the original and its reproductions: "That which withers in the age of mechanical reproduction is the aura of the work of art" (Benjamin 2010: 16). The problem of the *auratic* conception of the peculiar value of the original, as I see it, is that it puts the cart before the horse and mistakes what results from the *knowledge* that A is the original and B the copy for a quasi-qualitative property of A not shared by B. As soon as we know or believe that A is the original and its qualitatively identical replica B (a copy of A), A and B are easily perceived as no longer qualitatively identical because the perception of A is unavoidably tinged by the belief that it is the original and the perception of B by the belief that it is "merely" a copy. What is in this way added to the perception of A may well be called "aura." But this kind of aura is dependent on the belief that A is the original and not on anything in A itself.

Think of the exposition of the treasures of the tomb of Tut-anch-Amun that is at present traveling around the world, consisting exclusively of copies of the originals. However impressive these works of art may be, it is practically impossible to separate the aesthetic satisfaction they yield from the thought that what we see are "only" copies and merely *represent* the glory of the original treasures. If there were, contrary to what everyone believes, an original among the pieces of the exposition, it would be perceived in exactly the same way. If it had an aura the other pieces lack nobody would notice it.

Museums sometimes replace originals that have gone on tour by declared copies. What if someone exchanged the copy for the original but declared it to be only a substitute? No doubt there would be a significant loss in aura. If the Nefertiti of the *Neues Museum* in Berlin were in reality a qualitatively identical copy but were *believed* to be the original it would have the same aura as the original. Nothing would have changed, as far as the perception of the work is concerned. Aura is a *projective* property. It can be possessed both by O and by C, in dependence of what is believed about their respective histories. It can neither justify these beliefs nor serve as a basis of any kind of surplus value O may have as compared with C.

Analogous reservations apply to the property of being *singular* where that is proposed as a distinctive feature of the original. As soon as a *copy* of O exists, O is no longer singular. As soon as a *perfect copy* of O exists, as in the mythical world of science fiction, O is no longer *unique*. But not every original is singular or unique. The original of a copy can just as well be the token of a type of which there are an indefinite number of tokens, such as multiples in art like novels or photographs. The relation between original and copy is not reserved for objects that are the only token of their type. O can itself be one of the many copies of some other O, as quite a number of popular sculptures are because they are copied from Roman sculptures that are in turn copies of Greek originals. The original from which the copy comes need neither be singular nor unique.

What is necessary, however, to make C a copy of O is that O and C differ in their respective *histories*. What distinguishes O and C is primarily that O has a history that is different from C's history. These histories differ at least in *temporal* respects: C necessarily comes into existence later than the original O. They often differ also in *genetic* respects: C's way of coming about often differs from the way O came about; C necessarily involves intelligent action whereas O can have originated without human intervention. Interestingly, it was, among others, the specific history of the production of a work of art that was associated by Benjamin with the concept of aura: what is singular about the original of a work of art is the fact that it was generated in an extended, careful, and reflexive process of creation, in contrast to its mechanical reproduction by a machine, but also to the productions of the Dadaists whose idea was exactly to destroy this kind of aura by declaring quasi-mechanical collocations of objects to be works of art, thereby replacing the traditional way of production of a work of art by a quasi-mechanical way of reproduction (cf. Benjamin 2010: 41). What we "see" in the original (or, rather, project into it) is the peculiar way it has come about or how it had been before it was made the original of a copy. The identity of Amphitryon, for Alcmene, is constituted by his history: he is the one she married, long before the copy entered the scene.

It follows that if O is *ceteris paribus* of greater value than C, the value difference must be explained by some form of *historical* value taken in its widest possible sense, including properties such as age, authenticity, authorship and causal role. Various kinds of values can be associated with historical properties, though historical value is hardly self-sufficient. The value of historical *authenticity*, for example, is dependent on the possession of other qualities. In general, the authentic is worthy of preservation only if it is valuable in other respects, such as its documentary value, scientific interest, artistic importance, or causal role. For example, there might be some value in the historical prototype of a technical machine or appliance that played an important role in the causal history of the multitude of copies that were derived from it. Nevertheless, this value may be negligible in view of the value of the long series of exemplars for which it served as a model. The same is true for the criterion of *age*, for example in the context of the valuation of natural items. The fact that an element of nature is extremely old is in general a reason to preserve it only if there are further values that go with it such as irreplaceable ecological functions, aesthetic attractiveness, or symbolic value. If it is at the same time harmful or dangerous, it will be better to eliminate it for good—*pace* the views of some ecological extremists like Ehrenfeld (1978: 208) who go as far as to ascribe a right to continued existence even to the smallpox virus.

Generally it can be said that if O is held to be intrinsically more valuable than C this is not because O is the original and C the copy *simpliciter* but because of particular historical values possessed by O and not possessed by C. These values are heterogeneous, causal, documentary, symbolic, or sentimental. They change with context and perspective, and the value gradient between original and copy varies widely. From the perspective of one valuation system the value difference between the original and one of its qualitatively identical copies may be near infinite whereas from the perspective of another it may be null or even negative.

4. The surplus value of the original—overestimated?

Copies are generally, and rightly, welcomed if they have the character of a reconstruction of something that has been lost and is brought to new life. The value of the copy then depends both on the value that is attributed to the original and the fidelity of the reconstruction. Thus, the value of copying old towns or buildings destroyed by war or natural degradation seems to depend both on the value (aesthetic, historical, or sentimental) attached to the original, and the extent to which the substance of the old buildings is reconstructed in detail, e.g. in accordance with surviving plans, descriptions, or photographs. See, for example, the impressive reconstruction of the old town of Danzig which today seems as completely "original" as it can be and which breathes, as it were, the breath of its glorious past.

A similar situation obtains in the axiology of nature, for example, in relation to attempts to "reconstruct" species lost by human destructive activities or by the overall impact of civilization, and in the restoration of landscapes and vegetations after exploitation. Species that have gone extinct can be reconstructed by reactivating preserved genetic material, or by "back-breeding" extinct species by gradually breeding their original features into their domesticated forms. In this way, the Tarpan wild horse has been revived by deliberately reversing the breeding efforts of over thousands of years of livestock cultivation. In future, the same may be achieved, possibly more effectively, by gene technology and synthetic biology. Apart from that, landscapes and vegetations that have been lost by cultivation (like certain forms of wetland) can be revived, and even copied, by systematic restitution of the ecological factors from which they originated. In this case, too, the value of the reconstruction depends on the value attributed to the "original" and the degree to which the "copy" reproduces the essential features of the original. It furthermore depends on the extent to which the reconstruction adds to the aesthetic quality of the landscape of which it is a part and to the overall biodiversity of the respective region.

Apart from that, reconstruction—and in this sense "copying"—of lost originals has become increasingly important in science. The most well-known attempts to "copy" former stages of historical developments that have been irretrievably lost have been made in particle physics, in evolutionary biology, and in experimental archaeology. In particle physics, stages of cosmic evolution are reconstructed in order to test theoretical models of "the first three minutes" (Weinberg 1977) in the evolution of the cosmos. In evolutionary biology, experiments with former stages in the evolution of the natural conditions on earth, on the line of the famous Stanley Miller experiments with primeval atmosphere, are crucial for understanding the origins of life. One of the problems of this kind of research is that some conditions have been irreversibly lost. According to at least one theory, the early environment contained, among others, one factor necessary for the evolution of primitive bacteria that cannot be reconstructed: a radioactive isotope of iron that transmuted into radiation millions of years ago. In experimental archaeology, finally, the conditions are reconstructed under which former civilizations modified their environment with the aim of a better understanding of their technologies.

In general, copies are welcomed whenever the original has been irretrievably lost. The copy then functions as a *substitute*. By sharing the essential features of the original, it takes the place of the original in a given network of relations and shares some or most of the relational properties of the original by being as close as possible to the lost original in qualitative respects. An example from everyday life is the substitution of pet animals: the original is replaced, following its death, by a qualitatively identical animal which then is made to perform the same functions as the original and to serve as the object of the same emotions as its predecessor. As a *copy* of the original it functions as a close or near-perfect substitute. A well-known case from the history of philosophy is Schopenhauer's poodle, which in fact was a series of different poodles that bore the same name and were treated as if they were identical—in spite of the fact that Schopenhauer was one of the first philosophers to note that higher animals have their own individual character.

Where the original and the copy are both available, however, it is common to value the original more highly than the copy, to grant it, as it were, a considerable *surplus value*. In some contexts, this surplus is hardly more than what might be called the *curiosity value* of a rare and causally important specimen, like, for example, the authentic Gutenberg Bibles in Mainz or natural monuments like old trees in old villages. For this kind of curiosity value, it is not even necessary to be particularly old—if we think, for example, of the prototype of the Moon Vehicle in the Space Museum in Washington, DC, or the items of the Computer Museum in Southern California. For other fields of application it is much less clear whether there is what has been coined "origin value" (Basl 2010: 36) in the original over and above the values inherent in the qualitatively identical copy. In some cases it seems that the occasionally enormous *economic* value of originals—for example in art, musical instruments, or manuscripts of prominent writers—is taken at face value and interpreted as the real value of these originals. The economic value, however, can hardly serve as an indicator of the "real" or intrinsic value of these originals. It is primarily based on *extrinsic* valuations such as the prices collectors or investors are prepared to pay for them, either because of their singularity or rarity or because of their attractiveness as an investment.

5. Three unconventional cases of copying

Let me briefly discuss the value gradient between original and copy in three unconventional cases, each of them coming from an area in which this gradient plays a certain role: in the *human sphere*, in *nature*, and in the sphere of *personal relations*. The last example brings us back to Amphitryon's and Alcmene's quandary.

1. Plants and animals can be copied, in a sense, by *cloning*. With animals, including humans, clones are far from perfect copies because (at least as long as the cloning is by nuclear transfer) they only share the nuclear DNA and not the full genome that contains the additional DNA of the mitochondria. Even from a purely genetic point of view, they are less perfect copies than identical twins. But an artificially produced human clone of a past person comes as near as possible to what was defined above as a copy; it is a deliberately produced reproduction of the qualitative features of a temporally prior item.

In the case of a potential clone, we are confronted with the perhaps most radical devaluation of the copy one can think of: the German Embryo Protection Law declares no less than a *war* on human clones. Section 6 of this law enjoins anybody who might come across a cloned human foetus to see to it that it will not be born. Thus, the potential human clone is literally a *persona non grata*. Though the prohibition of cloning primarily aims at condemning the *procedure* of cloning humans and not the *result* of the procedure, the law makes it clear that it insists, apart from natural twinning, on the genetic singularity and uniqueness of each human being. This insistence has its counterpart in one of the arguments that used to be put forward by conservatives against all forms of destruction of the human embryo, whether by abortion, research cloning, or embryo research. Apart from the arguments of *species membership*, *continuity*, *identity*, and *potentiality*, *uniqueness* of the human embryo used to be appealed to for some time by ethicists and lawyers as an argument for embryo protection. In the meantime, this argument has only rarely been put forward. The reason is obvious: the argument is too weak to be convincing. Nearly everything in the mesocosmic world is unique, so it is hard to see why this property should be able to add value to the unborn human individual. Uniqueness plays a part, too, in the traditional explication of the principle of *human dignity*. In German constitutional law, the so-called "object formula" has been frequently used to elucidate the content of the inherently vague concept of human dignity. According to it, human dignity should be regarded as violated whenever the concrete human individual "is demeaned as an object, as a mere means or as an exchangeable item" (Dürig 1954: 127). This can be understood as the principle that the individual should be respected as something unique and non-exchangeable. It should be respected as a being for which there can be no substitute.

Cloning of a child that a couple has lost by an accident in order to have a substitute is, in a certain way, the substitution of one individual by a copy, analogous to the replacement of Schopenhauer's poodle by a poodle resembling the former as much as possible in order to ease the transition. There are no doubt good reasons for a prohibition of the *procedure* of cloning humans since this is, to all appearances, an excessively risky undertaking. But one wonders what the reasons are to prevent a cloned foetus from seeing the light of the world in case it happens to exist in spite of the prohibition. It is not clear why, in this case, the copy should have less value than the original from which it is derived. The fact that it is a kind of a temporally delayed artificial twin of a former or a living person seems insufficient to deprive it of the right to existence the law ascribes to normal foetuses.

2. Copying *nature* has become a controversial issue in nature ethics, especially in the context of the restoration of landscapes after phases of intense exploitation such as strip mining. The questions raised in this context were called the "substitution problem" in nature ethics (Katz 1987; Birnbacher 2004). Representatives of the so-called "anti-restoration thesis" like Elliot (1997: 80) argue that the loss

in value caused by the historical discontinuity of the existence of a landscape or ecosystem cannot be fully compensated by reconstituting the respective piece of nature elsewhere ("type restoring"), nor by restoring the piece of nature in the same place ("token restoring"). Even fully restored nature lacks the value of originality and continuity. Elliot does not, however, want to exclude that this loss of value may be offset by a possible man-made qualitative *improvement*, at least as far as the destruction of originality from a purely axiological perspective is concerned. However, such a view would be, according to Elliot, grossly unreasonable. For him, the destruction of originality is morally negative, regardless of the axiological balance of value (Elliot 1997: 113–14). As is the case for assaults in criminal law, damage to nature cannot be completely compensated by subsequent restitution. What applies in the social world, namely that we are, as a rule, not prepared to judge a theft to be less problematic if the thief later refunds the victim in kind, should also apply to offences against nature. Even if nature is destroyed with the promise that it will then be restored in an "improved" form, and then is in fact recreated in an "improved" form, the destruction is not as such excusable.

This position implies that substitution of a former piece of nature by an exact copy means *ceteris paribus* a loss of value over and above the loss of value incurred by the non-availability of the piece of nature during exploitation. Is this plausible?

The least that can be said is that the analogy Elliot draws between the destruction of parts of nature by exploitation on the one hand and theft and assault on the other is unconvincing. The fact that theft and assaults are prohibited depends not only on the fact that both leave victims in a worse state than they have been previously, but also on the fact that people's safety from injury is compromised because they have to fear further harmful attacks. The assurance that we will, at a later point in time, be "compensated" for bodily harm with so much extra well-being, or for a theft by returning the stolen objects or by financial compensation, provides little comfort. Even then it remains a fact that we are involuntarily harmed. This kind of reasoning, however, is not applicable to nature. At most, higher animals are potential subjects of threats.

Another open question is to what extent categories familiar from aesthetics can or should be transferred to the natural environment. In a work of art, the historical circumstances of its creation are often, and rightly, relevant to its valuation. However, categories such as originality, creativity, and innovative content that go with the historical features of works of art do not seem to be applicable to nature. It is true that historical concepts like authenticity are sometimes applied to natural objects. But even then it is not universally with the positive value component that is inseparable from them when applied to art and historical documents. A stretch of stony desert may be authentic to the same degree as a lush oasis, in the sense that both are qualitatively identical with a historical state that is contextually taken as reference point. Authenticity, used in this way, can have evaluative overtones, but need not.

My conclusion is that there may be deontological limits to the substitution of natural items by copying former stages of nature, but no axiological ones. The destruction or spoliation of parts of nature by exploitation for human purposes can be inherently problematic, especially if relatively trivial purposes are assumed to compensate the losses. But the reasons for such a deontological norm are different from a possible axiological relevance of authenticity.

3. Probably the strongest reservations against substitution of the "original" by a copy are to be found in the sphere of *personal* values rooted in affective ties like love and friendship. Personal ties seem to transcend axiological value because they are related to their objects not via general *properties* (including historical properties like "origin value") but are more directly bound to their objects. The objects of love and friendship are inexchangeable precisely because these emotions are directed at individuals *qua* individuals and not *qua* possessors of general properties. That is why love, more clearly than friendship, is not an object of why-questions. It also explains why in personal relations we rightly speak of bonds, bonding, etc. What connects us to the objects of our personal relations are ties that are not mediated by general attributes. Remember Henry de Montherlant's perspicacious dictum "On aime d'amitié parce que, on aime d'amour tandis que."

As a corollary of this, the absence of substitutability in affective relations is strictly *relative*. An object of love or friendship is irreplaceable not in the impersonal sense of a philosophical axiology but only with respect to the individual emotionally related to it. This, at least, is the accepted view. The question opened up by Kleist's version of the story of Amphitryon is whether this absence of substitutability is possibly an illusion. The famous sigh of Alcmene that concludes the play ("Ach") may be a hint that she, too, is not quite sure.

References

Basl, J. (2010), "Restitutive Restoration, New Motivation for Ecological Restoration," *Environmental Ethics* 32 (2): 135–47.

Benjamin, W. (2010), *The Work of Art in the Age of Mechanical Reproduction*, Scottsdale, AZ: Prism Key Press.

Birnbacher, D. (2004), "Limits to Substitutability in Nature Conservation," in M. Oksanen (ed.), *Philosophy and Biodiversity*, 180–95, Cambridge: Cambridge University Press.

Dürig, G. (1956), "Der Grundrechtssatz von der Menschenwürde," *Archiv des öffentlichen Rechts* 81 (2): 117–57.

Ehrenfeld, D. (1978), *The Arrogance of Humanism*, New York: Oxford University Press.

Elliot, R. (1982), "Faking Nature," *Inquiry* 25 (1): 81–93.

Goodman, N. (1976), *Languages of Art. An Approach to a Theory of Symbols*, 2nd edn, Indianapolis, IN: Hackett.

Katz, E. (1985), "Organism, Community, and the Substitution Problem," *Environmental Ethics* 7 (3): 241–56.

Weinberg, S. (1977), *The First Three Minutes. A Modern View of the Origin of the Universe*, New York: Basic Books.

Wollheim, R. (1980), *Art and its Objects*, 2nd edn, Cambridge: University of Cambridge Press.

2

Deep Copy Culture

Mark Alfino

When philosophers and ethicists have wanted to reflect philosophically on the problem of copyright and the nature and justification of intellectual property, they have naturally gravitated toward a few key developments in the modern history of copyright, especially the movement in the United Kingdom away from copyright as a monopoly right granted in perpetuity by the crown and toward the modern proprietary author with limited rights in copies. This shift was one of the most important changes in the way humans have thought about and controlled knowledge, cultural artifacts, and intellectual work in general, and it reflects the general values of the Enlightenment period regarding the public exercise of reason. These values also found their way into the U.S. Constitution's treatment of intellectual property in copyright and patents as part of a social system that both secures the rights of authors and "promotes the progress of science and the useful arts" (U.S. Constitution, art. I, § 8, cl. 8). The naturalness of focusing on this sea change in cultural values is reflected in the fact that the history of political and moral thought about copyright has moved within this Enlightenment matrix of values through two centuries of intellectual property legislation in most modern states.

Without denying the importance of the Enlightenment paradigm, this essay investigates possibilities for a deeper and more fundamental retrieval of the place and importance of "copy behavior" in human history and identity. This will involve a radical change in orientation from the modern period, with its timescale of decades and centuries, to an anthropological, archeological, and evolutionary orientation, with a time frame measured in tens to hundreds of thousands of years. The premise of the investigation is that many of the modern and contemporary moral and policy challenges of intellectual property have deeper roots than the modern tension between an author's statutory property right and the society's claim to the collective benefits of knowledge and innovation.

There are certainly reasons to be skeptical that this kind of investigation could produce useful insights into modern copyright ethics and aesthetics. How much can we really know about early and ancient human cultures and the role of copying and learning in evolution? Even if such a journey yields some insights, how can they be brought back to the present landscape of problems in law, ethics and aesthetics raised by copying, especially in its new and technologically advanced forms?

The answer to these questions will only be found in the results of the investigation, but we should not assume that the "Enlightenment matrix" of values handles contemporary problems better simply because it is more proximate in time. In fact, many copyright intellectuals, such as Lawrence Lessig and Julie Cohen, argue that Enlightenment categories of rights and markets do not adequately frame the wide range of problems raised by contemporary aesthetics and ethics. When we wonder about the nature of contemporary forgery or plagiarism, whether someone can own a "style," whether a DJ is violating someone's rights by freely mixing copyrighted material, the nature and extent of fair use, and myriad public policies issues about the freedom of individuals to engage in non-commercial use of "propertied culture," we are certainly working within a set of values that are familiar to us and which might guide us as we move from standard cases to novel ones. To the extent that the handling of contemporary copyright problems is a matter of negotiation of rights, the proximate resources of the legal tradition and the work of "normal" copyright ethics will be useful. But it does not follow that the patchwork of solutions from within the Enlightenment tradition will comprehend the changes that new technologies and new aesthetic and intellectual practices are creating. For this we might need a new kind of analysis which reaches beyond the current paradigm.

The adoption of an anthropological perspective can move philosophical reflection on the nature of the copy beyond the Enlightenment model, not by setting the last two hundred years of theorizing about intellectual property aside, but by treating the contemporary history as part of a larger pattern of human behavior in which copies, learning, and identity are at stake. Two broad patterns emerge. On the one hand, anthropologists, especially those working from within an evolutionary model, have new and interesting things to tell us about the role of copying behaviors in the growth of human culture, especially learning and management of social status. This direction of the investigation concerns adaptive, maladaptive and non-adaptive uses of copy behavior and the cognitive "intellectual toolkit" that it is part of. On the other hand, the same set of social and intellectual capacities helps humans establish identities within human societies. The philosophical retrieval of "deep copying" in human evolution places copy behavior at the heart of the cognitive and emotional capacities that lead to both the growth of culture and knowledge and the formation of our identities. Stated as a thesis: Copying as a cognitive and social behavior is central to distinctively human modes of being and underlies evolutionary processes that both shape culture and allow culture to shape us. Most of this paper is devoted to establishing this thesis, but at the end I will try to identify the implications of the "deep copy culture" viewpoint to practical problems in copy ethics.

As mentioned above, one standard frame of reference for modern copyright ethics is the period within which modern copyright law was established in English law. The 1709 Statute of Anne was the first modern copyright law to set statutory limits to copyright. This posed a direct conflict to the interests of the Stationers' Company, a group of primarily London-based publishers who controlled much of the print market. The cultural background to this legal dispute is the key to seeing the Statute of Anne as part of a revolutionary process that established so many parameters of modern copyright, with influences from eighteenth-century ideas about the author as a proprietor of his or her work, creative genius, and the unity of a print "work," from stories to scientific treatises. Also at stake is the influence of social class and royalty in maintaining the old system of production and markets. Much artistic and academic work in seventeenth- and eighteenth-century England had been done under patronage or by members of the ruling class. The initial control of copyright was established as a privilege from the crown. These are some aspects of the cultural milieu within which the Stationers enjoyed their monopoly as the eighteenth century began. So, when the Statute of Anne appeared to strictly limit copyright to fourteen to twenty-eight years, the Stationers argued—through court cases throughout the central decades of the century—that the statutory limits did not override a common law justification for perpetual copyright.

The competing arguments came to a head in the celebrated case of *Donaldson v. Beckett,* heard over a three-week period in the House of Lords in 1774. Luminaries such as Edmund Burke were in attendance, and Samuel Johnson, who had strong views against perpetual copyright, must have followed the proceedings closely (Rose 1988: 52). *Donaldson* reversed the last case in which the Stationers' argument was upheld. After *Donaldson*, the modern conception of copyright, in the U.S. and U.K., establishes copyright as a statutory monopoly, not a property interest governed primarily by a natural property right.

But the cultural significance of *Donaldson* was at least as great as its legal significance. In the status quo prior to the Statute of Anne, copyright made relatively limited mention of authors. But as polemics grew over the justice of perpetual copyright, Rose argues, the Stationers found it useful to appeal to the public's sympathy for the creative work of the author (59). In many ways, our modern conception of the author and the work was formed during this period, along with some of the first arguments, Johnson's among them, that society ultimately had a collective interest, if not right, to the innovations and creative work of its members.

In this summary we can see both one of the limiting conditions of the modern view, as well, perhaps, as a way to reframe copyright in terms of deeper cultural forces. Because of the cultural forces in play during its creation, modern copyright treats the production of ideas worth copying as an economic asset of an individual or corporation of individuals. The right to exploit a resource of one's own creation, especially with the proviso of "enough, and as good left" (Laslett 1970) (as the "Lockean proviso" stipulates and as intellectual and creative production usually does), still holds a central focus of modern copyright, with the burden of proof falling on those who would argue for the value or importance of ideas to the society as a whole.

Modern media monopolies still exist and if anything they are proportionally stronger than the Stationers' Company, with a global reach protecting a huge array of profitable intellectual property assets. Many regard the public interest as being served by the diffusion of intellectual property through a market, and, arguably, a market-based approach to authorship and authors' rights has enabled many millions of people to create careers and livelihoods within the knowledge and entertainment industries. But as we shall see when we return to the practical problems of the copy in contemporary aesthetics and ethics, the cultural consolidation of the intellectual or creative work as an economic product to be exploited through statutory monopolies may pose a problematic limiting condition to rethinking the problems presented by the copy in light of the information technology revolutions of the last thirty years.

At a deeper level, one could argue that modern copyright represents a culturally negotiated resolution of a tension at least as old as agriculture: the relationship between the relative advantages that a member of a group receives from an innovation vs the advantage to a group or society from sharing an innovation. Also in play in the shift from a patronage model to a commercial model is the question of who in the society is in a position of power to say what counts as innovative or worthy of publishing. These issues, of course, are also in play in contemporary discussions. The fight over the Statute of Anne was, perhaps only in hindsight, as much about letting markets and democracies drive publishing as it was about the justice of the specific privilege held by the Stationers.

Before we turn to some of the general and theoretical resources of anthropological and evolutionary thought on copying and learning, we ought to compare the cultural moment (really six decades) of modern copyright leading to *Donaldson*, with another, somewhat distant cultural moment in copy behavior and technology: the transition from the Oldowan toolkit to the Acheulean toolkit for making hand axes. Importantly, this "moment" was a transition of several hundred thousand years (starting about 1.8 million years ago) during which humans developed a variety of stone working tools and methods for creating more effective, double-beveled hand axes with longer cutting edges. While we have no newspaper or court records to follow in this transition, we do know that, unlike the *Donaldson* case, this earlier transition correlates with more than a doubling of brain size. Recent research has linked the capacities for the Acheulean toolkit to neural correlates of speech and language (Stout 2008), suggesting that those capacities preceded and may have enabled the "cognitive toolkit" that made the actual technology possible. But theories are still speculative in this area.

Ultimately, we do not know the extent to which the spread of the Acheulean toolkit was effected through cultural transmission (such as learning) as opposed to an individual or cultural selection process. Given the completeness with which the newer toolkit spread it is unlikely that it was effected solely through cultural learning. Because the new axe technology would have allowed its user to capture more energy than its competitors, a more plausible (though still speculative) hypothesis is that the Acheulean transition is an example of gene culture co-evolution. As brain size grew and we developed relatively advanced capacities, such as social cognition and modeling, people with capacities (both cognitive and motor skill) to produce more effective tools enjoyed a selective advantage over those with fewer such advantageous and heritable capacities. A general premise of cognitive archeology is that our "cognitive architecture" may have developed through selection in ways parallel to our morphology. As with language, at some point we are unfolding capacities that we seem oddly "prepared for."

What should interest us from the standpoint of developing a deep theory of copying is that, as in the transition leading to modern copyright, our ancestors experienced changes that gave them the ability to exploit, by copying, a new technology. There was no "public interest" to serve 1.8 million years ago, but the selective transmission of capacities that allowed early humans to make incrementally better hand axes occurred during a time of significant growth of human populations. Of course, by contrast, modern copyright law and values were experienced as a consequence of self-reflective discourse over the relative rights of creators and producers vs the public. But in both cases we have an explosion of copy behavior relevant to human flourishing. Like the linguistic and artistic capacities that allow us to create copyrighted works, the capacities for imitation, copying, and replication that underlie artifactual creation are in some ways innate to our normal cognitive abilities and in other ways elicited by our environment and by learning. In both cases—literally in the older case and figuratively in the modern one—it is plausible that our copying behaviors altered the direction of our own replication as a species. Of course, the less literal recent changes have profound literal effects nonetheless. Today, in developed countries, the knowledge and entertainment industries have clearly increased the relative fitness of people with the requisite capacities for this kind of work.

So far I have been using the concept of a "copy" rather loosely. As we turn from illustrative examples such as modern copyright law and ancient stone tool technology to the theoretical resources needed to support our thesis, we should make a brief analytical review of the concept of copying. A narrow but rigorous and intuitive way to think about a copy is that it bears a logical relationship to a prior original or artifact. As a copy becomes increasingly "faithful," it moves toward being a "duplicate."

But the breadth of theoretical resources needed for our thesis requires a broader definition than this. I will follow the approach of Marcus Boon in *In Praise of Copying* (2010), which brings forward a much richer, but less stable meaning of copy. Boon thinks about the nature of the copy through several registers of cultural meaning: 1) *mimesis* in the Greek philosophical tradition (18); 2) the postmodern critique of origins, which undermines the "original/copy" distinction (24); and, ultimately, 3) a Buddhist critique of the ultimate reality of appearances (26). For Boon, copying is "a matter of 'presenting and producing something in a manner which is typical of something else.' All copies are made—they are produced—and the making involves an attempt to turn something into something else, so that that which is produced is now 'like' something else" (19). This is a useful, if broad, definition of copying, which links copying activity to the bringing forth of an appearance or representation. You could say that Boon places copying at the heart of a process of semiosis that brings forward characteristic appearances', appearances that are part of a symbolic order because they are "like" something. Much of Boon's argument is made from within the history of human culture of copying, with fascinating discussions of many related cultural topics including the Roman goddess Copia, Renaissance manuals of rhetoric, hip hop, and more Buddhism. This gives his use of the concept an "intentionalist" orientation in practice, but the process of copying and replication that brings forth appearances does not strictly require intentional awareness of the copying. Therefore, we will broaden Boon's definition a bit to encompass natural processes (both intentionally directed and non-intentional) that bring forward characteristic appearances, from genetic processes to the cognitive and cultural processes that led to so many copies of hand axes and Beatles records.

Two other features of copying at this level of description bear mention. First, copying is not just a single act, but often part of a production process, whether of Hollywood movies or hand axes. Copying over time involves repetition—the repetition of the artifact as product, but also feedback processes which come into play as imperfect copying produces variation. Evolutionary selection processes have a similar structure in which natural variation (in both genotypes and phenotypes) is exposed to selection pressure from an environment. Second, when we link copying to intentionality, we naturally include moral categories of evaluation. A forgery is a morally bad use of the ability to copy because of its producer's intent to deceive. But throughout nature and within human social life, we find so many instances of copying or imitating to conceal and deceive that we ought to include it in our analytic of copying without presuming only the intentionalist or moralist articulation. We copy both to convey and to conceal. Those capacities seem prior to and separate from their employment in representing values. From the camouflage of animals to the ways in which we allow others to dissemble or otherwise maintain their privacy in social life, copying to conceal ought to be kept in mind as a parallel phenomenon with copying to convey intent or communicate directly and faithfully. The biologist Robert Trivers makes this point with extensive examples in *The Folly of Fools* (2011).

While this way of extending the notion of a copy as single artifact bearing a logical relation to an original to a more open-ended production of likenesses may seem unduly broad, our goal, like Boon's, is to assemble theoretical resources that support the view that copying is central to human being. Our focus on the anthropological and archeological record avoids privileging the most recent—intentional and articulate—history of *Homo sapiens*. As we shall see, copying was essential to our evolution and identity long before we knew what it was.

1. Theoretical resources for a theory of "deep copy culture"

In order to defend the thesis that copying as a cognitive and social behavior is central to being human and part of evolutionary and social processes that shape our identity, it will be helpful to look beyond specific cultural moments and turn toward theoretical resources. Four in particular—three in evolutionary anthropology and one in cultural anthropology—stand out. Theories of gene culture co-evolution, theories of the effect or power of learning in evolution, and theories of multi-level selection all support the idea of a deep role of copying behavior and process in becoming the sorts of humans we are. The fourth theoretical resource, from cultural anthropology, draws on Dan Sperber's concept of an "epidemiology of representations."

We have already seen how the parallels between stone tool development and brain size lead to speculation that the Acheulean axe may have evolved in tandem with specific cognitive capacities (Stout et al. 2008). This hypothesis can be researched by studying the physical and mental skills and capacities needed to produce an artifact such as an Acheulean axe, matching that with our knowledge of contemporary neurology and neural development from the fossil record. As cited earlier, Stout et al. present evidence, for example, suggesting that Stone Age tool making draws on neural activity that presupposes language. It may be that both language and stone tool production require a level of social cognition which allows for instruction and copying through learning. We will explore the learning process more in the next section. Here we have not only the broad hypothesis that artifacts are part of the evolutionary landscape, but that copies of them can exert a selection pressure on the creatures that produce them, favoring those with capacities related to superior knowledge of stone, tools, eye–hand coordination, and the ability to imitate experts (hence, those with advanced social cognition). Thus, it is not so much the ability to make a particular kind of axe that is selected for, but rather the capacities—differentially distributed in a population—that allow the next improvement in axes to be adopted. Crucially, it is the relentlessness of the copy/selection process over time that produces both artifact and artificer.

A second area for theoretical support comes from theories of learning and evolution. The idea that the new traits and behaviors acquired by an organism can be passed along to its offspring is correctly associated with Jean-Baptiste Lamarck, a pre-Darwinian evolutionist. Lamarckism is a famous example of a fallacious evolutionary hypothesis. Giraffes that stretch a lot to reach food on trees do not pass on longer necks to their progeny. A more promising approach, with its own history of controversy, has been the so-called "Baldwin Effect," which has many forms, but generally claims that learning or the capacity to learn can influence evolution. A range of skeptical and supportive positions on the Baldwin effect have been advanced since James Mark Baldwin suggested the idea in "A New Factor in Evolution" (1896), and since the 1950s when the effect was revived and named by George Gaylord Simpson (Weber 2003).

The genetic focus of the modern synthesis in evolutionary theory had little place for the Baldwin effect. Also, our understanding of brain evolution, developments in forensic archeology, game theory, and artificial intelligence all contributed to its revival. Prior to the emergence of these fields it would have been hard to frame and test hypotheses about learning and evolution. The crucial contribution to the revival of the Baldwin effect was the famous 1987 paper by computer scientists Geoffrey Hinton and Steven Nolan, "How Learning Can Guide Evolution." By looking at learning as a search strategy and making some assumptions about the search environment, Hinton and Nolan developed one of the first computer simulations that showed the potential magnitude of the effect of learning on adaptation, especially in environmental landscapes which contain so-called fitness "spikes" (hard-to-find adaptive responses which accelerate evolution by creating opportunities for rapid increases in fitness). An example of a fitness spike might be a new way to increase energy uptake.

While Hinton and Nolan's original simulation is simple compared to evolutionary algorithms today, most theorists take their work and the field of artificial intelligence to have opened a large area of theoretical modeling of learning and evolution. For our purposes, the important insight of neo-Baldwinian theories of learning is that they give a large theoretical space to copy behaviors and capacities in the learning process. Whether the learning is individual trial and error or social learning through imitation, learning requires the capacity to track instances of behaviors and their results, and to mimic and model behavior. In some recent modeling of social learning, copying others was found to be the most effective strategy (Rendell 2010; Richerson 2005: 124). Moreover, the density of a human population can affect its ability to share learning (Powell 2009). In the famous case of Tasmanian culture, we have an example of loss of cultural learning through separation from a larger culture (Henrich 2004).

While theories of learning and evolution have controversial pasts in Lamarck and Baldwin, we now have both theoretical and empirical research which suggests how basic capacities for learning are, especially given our big-brained evolutionary path, and how important the underlying capacities for imitation and copying are to these processes.

The possibility of gene culture co-evolution and the likely role of learning in evolution suggest that copying, imitation, and modeling played crucial roles in our evolution. From these approaches we are likely to learn more about how our selection environment includes both our artifacts and us and the role of social learning. As complex and long-developing as this process has been in our history, new levels of complexity enter the scene with Neolithic societies of the past 12,000 years. With increased brain size and the advent of social cognition, the ability to store, organize, and make inferential use of a wide range of information about members of our groups and goal-directed behavior, our copy lives became dramatically more complex. Living in a human society with social structure, such as occurred as agricultural societies supported increasingly larger towns and cities, requires individuals to manage and update representations of their status and identity constantly and in minute detail. Every interaction from dress to forms of address carries social meanings and codes that must be understood and observed. Humans living in agricultural society embraced social hierarchy as a natural consequence of the risks and rewards of that approach to energy capture (Morris 2015). Social hierarchy brings with it an explosion of copy behavior because it is maintained in part through its persistent representation of status and self.

Multilevel selection theories are well positioned to capture this complexity because they make theoretical room for the possibility that natural selection operates at many levels, defining even the very identity of an organism. A major focus within this category of theories is explanations of human behaviors in terms of both individual and group fitness. If human groups, and not just individuals, do compete in an evolutionary sense, then our capacities for social cognition and management of hierarchy are important because they affect the performance of the group. From theoretical models for how group-fitness-enhancing values become stable in a population (Boyd and Richerson 2005) to empirical work on the conditions and variables affecting stable cooperative schemes (such as we find in research on public-goods games, for example), we are starting to appreciate the function that our self-representations (e.g. trustworthiness) and collectively enforced rules and values have in social life. In addition to managing the processes of learning that are crucial to our individual flourishing, we manage (largely unconsciously) the social meanings of our behaviors and statements to enable complex human organizations like modern states and corporations.

With this more complex picture of human society in mind, we can see the importance of capacities for symbolic representation and interpretation, and with that, the importance of theoretical resources in cultural anthropology. In symbolic anthropology, as Geertz famously argued, social meanings are not captured simply by behaviors, but by the way actors cite and use social codes and meanings. Participants in human cultures create social meanings through a process of copying, citation and expression. We do not just signal a few specific messages such as our trustworthiness or capacity for altruism in this way. We use social meaning processes to construct and express many aspects of our identity and to build coalitions with others.

Using a more structuralist model, Dan Sperber famously suggested thinking of cultural representations using an epidemiological metaphor. Culture is an "epidemiology of representations." We talk easily now about images, ideas, and texts going "viral," but this metaphor has also been theoretically powerful in work on cultural transmission and in thinking about how cultural representations spread and mutate. Underlying this way of thinking is a fundamental intuition that producing representations is a major function of symbolic social processes. Without exaggeration, one could say that we are not only the products of our interactions with our environments and artifacts, but we spend a great deal of energy producing and reproducing social meanings through citation, expression, and consumption. We are copy creatures.

The breadth and scope of this conclusion is no doubt related in part to breadth of the concept of "copy" with which we began. Following Boon, we have made the copy more than an isolated instance of reproduction, but rather a process of producing representations, both symbolic and artifactual, which have the character of being "like" something. Copying is an activity that is implicitly or explicitly inscribed in a symbolic order. Our use of evolutionary theory paints a picture of the emergence of this symbolic order and its increasingly self-conscious and self-reflective use to do the heavy work of culture—maintaining stable and functional human societies.

2. A phenomenology of the copy self

So far we have been identifying and interpreting theoretical resources and research projects that would support the thesis that copy culture is distinctively human culture and that the underlying activity of copy behavior—from imitation to expressions—both represents and shapes our nature. At this level copying is a bodily and organismic activity. Selection operates on the individual phenotype expressed through genes and in interaction with an environment.

Alongside this general pattern, we have theoretical evidence that human culture is tied to the expansion of human cognitive ability throughout the Pleistocene period. The capacities that emerge during this period, and which are reflected in artifactual production of tools and implements as well as the ability to model human behavior and goals, communicate intentions, and make inferences, take the copying of both artifacts and mental states to extraordinary new levels of complexity. Today, in both the practical and social domains, we manage representations and appearances both to achieve immediate personal goals and to signal our social status and commitments to group goals. We use copying behaviors both to signal our identities and intentions and to conceal them. Copying and representation are fundamental to these processes and these are the processes that have led to us.

But what is the phenomenal experience of the self in relation to the copy? A phenomenology of the "copy self" (here indicated briefly and only in relation to contemporary post-industrial cultures) might corroborate our thesis by suggesting that the dynamics of copy behavior today are prominent structures of our lived experience, especially as it relates to the goal of establishing a mature individual self and facing our finitude.

The family is the most typical, even universal, structure for the development of our sense of self. Within family life, children are typically valued uniquely and given to understand themselves as unique individuals (still for most religious believers as divine "gifts") who share deep connections, especially in the case of biologically related siblings, with other family members. The traditional family structure with multiple siblings and multigenerational households foregrounds family resemblances. Our experience of ourselves as both "unique" and "copy" is already present at some level in our experience of family life.

But the focal point for a phenomenology of the copy self will naturally be the universal cultural experience of the passage into adulthood. It is in this experience, whether in a modern or traditional society, that the self confronts the range of cultural identities available to it. These possibilities are not experienced exactly as a choice of items on a shelf, but as a process of self-discovery or destiny. We grow into our mature identities through a process of taking on or rejecting the styles and aesthetic choices that somehow express our emerging self-understanding.[1] Fashion, body art, social networks, work, and personal pursuits are all familiar features of the culture through which individuals create identities by adopting and adapting cultural representations (copies) of ways of being a self. These possibilities vary across cultures and within them, ranging from conformism and maintenance of a high degree of fidelity and success in the transmission of behaviors, beliefs, and attitudes to more individualistic social and family cultures, such as in the U.S., which place more emphasis upon the individual pursuit of personal liberty and economic opportunity than upon geographic proximity of family members. One finds a similar range of behaviors among traditional societies (Diamond 2013).

What should concern us here is less the specific ways that these choices work themselves out for individuals in particular cultures than the fact that a crucial way that we experience the growth of identity is through selection and imitation of role models, tastes, and preferences that come to define our identity. This is a process of working with "copies"—representations available in the culture—to create an original self. The phenomenon is so ubiquitous that it can be observed at almost any level of a modern society, especially among adolescents who are given some latitude to experiment with style and identity. Young adults experiment with a "look" by accepting, fashioning, or rejecting the representations available to them and within their awareness.

But the problematic of creating a unique identity from representations available in one's culture (along with the ways we can play, alter, and adapt them) can also be seen in very sophisticated reflections on the nature of the self in and beyond adolescence, in which the concern for being a "mere" copy is more prominent. Years ago, Harold Bloom identified the poet's "anxiety of influence" as "the horror of finding himself to be only a copy or a replica" (Bloom 1973). The problem of the development of a personal style, whether as a poet or a contemporary artist, is still quite real and the assessment of style itself is still a matter of great discussion in contemporary aesthetics. Both problems concern a somewhat culturally specific parallel desire for originality and statement. The challenge for the strong poet, as for the strong intellectual or any individual in a modern liberal copy culture, is to be influenced deeply by the best knowledge and representations of one's culture and yet to make an original appropriation, expression, or statement from that influence. A key aspect of the phenomenology of the copy self in such cultures is to avoid becoming one.

Another feature of the phenomenology of the copy self is the anxiety of discovering that one's life is merely an instantiation of pre-existing patterns, choices, and preferences. This feeling was captured well in the Philip Larkin poem, "Continuing to Live," and discussed in a famous essay by Richard Rorty, "The Contingency of Self" (1989: 23). Larkin's poem is a reflection on aging and death in which the narrator comes to worry about the perishability of his unique lived experience—his "lading-list." The concluding stanzas capture this existential concern about the illusion of an identity built up from "copies" or "blind impresses":

And once you have walked the length of your mind, what
You command is clear as a lading-list.
Anything else must not, for you, be thought
　To exist.

And what's the profit? Only that, in time,
We half-identify the blind impress
All our behavings bear, may trace it home.
　But to confess,

On that green evening when our death begins,
Just what it was, is hardly satisfying,
Since it applied only to one man once,
　And that one dying.

Larkin 2004

As Rorty put it, Larkin identifies a fear of the loss of the uniqueness of our sense of ourselves. In original expression we have the possibility of demonstrating that we are not a copy or replica (Rorty 1989: 24). In its absence, a creative person might wonder whether their life was merely an experience of already-created possibilities—pre-existing copies and patterns.

Admittedly, these are highly culturally specific reflections of a specific contemporary copy culture. But they move us closer to a description of the way individuals work with copies (and influences), both consciously and intuitively, in making identities and in creating original statements. This description also moves our reflection closer to aesthetics in general. Without reducing the aesthetic to a function of identity making, it is reasonable to say that the cultural production of images, sounds, words, ideas, artifacts, and ways of living comprise some of the media within which we construct the meaning of an individual life. As we shall see when we try to draw some practical conclusions from the investigation, it is important to see copies of cultural products as material that we *work with*—whether we are strong poets or anxious teenagers—to construct a life that is not merely a copy.

3. Practical conclusions

The larger goal in arguing for the deep naturalness of copy processes and behaviors is to highlight ways that our current copyright practices fit or fail to cohere with the general picture that this deep history paints. I will follow two lines of thought which connect our investigation to contemporary issues.

First, the deep copy culture of humans is not confined to the "progress of science and the useful arts." Rather, it is a phenomenon that exists at many levels of scale and experience. It is not just present in artistic statements of great originality, but part of our everyday social life and problem solving. One advantage of the timeframe of our investigation is that it helps us see copy culture as part of a repertoire of natural behaviors that run deep in our natural history and seem independent of the very recent emergence of commercial culture.

However, when we look at advanced post-industrial cultures such as the U.S., we find the transformation (or colonization) of traditional culture into "propertied culture" (cultural expressions in which someone owns copyright, patent, or trademark) and traditional forms of culture into commercial culture. Thus, it is increasingly common for casual and non-commercial use of propertied culture to trigger rights violations. Seen from the standpoint of modern copyright, this is a completely welcome outcome because it extends the market for profitable cultural representations (books, movies, theatre), promoting economic growth.

From the perspective of our investigation, however, the uncritical extension of propertied culture is problematic if it distorts natural symbolic behaviors or constrains access to adaptive resources. People naturally use the representations and cultural images and identities available to them to construct and revise their identities and expression, from the great poet to a man or woman trying to get a date. In a highly commercialized culture, a higher percentage of those representations are propertied and will require payments to rights holders. But conditioning access to culture on economic status is problematic if working with cultural representations is both crucial to identity formation and a wide range of social and evolutionary processes; that is, if the deep copy culture hypothesis is correct.

To see why, consider the following thought experiment. Imagine a future in which an indigenous people lacks the financial resources to access archives of its own culture's history. Of course, many existing indigenous peoples do in fact lack the resources to travel to the urban locations where universities and states often archive and display their cultural artifacts. So this part of the thought experiment is not so unrealistic. But to make the thought experiment more vivid, imagine also—and contrary to recent experience—that research archives in the future become less transparent, with fewer resources online at no charge, and that more institutions charge for access to collections. Further, imagine that the cultural group seeking access to its own cultural archives (of art, personal records, traditional practices, history) has undergone a profound dislocation in its cultural experience, perhaps due to war and genocide or an oppressive regime that criminalized its practice, so that the project of recovering cultural knowledge is particularly immediate and relevant.

What would be wrong with simply denying the group access to the archive? If we are imagining propertied culture as meeting Locke's proviso of leaving "enough, and as good left," then the answer could be "nothing." But clearly this misses something vital about the role of culture. As I have been arguing, culture does "work" for us that we did not appreciate or understand well in the eighteenth century, when we were opening up new markets for copyright with decisions like *Donaldson*.

If we are participants in a deep copy culture, one which has consequences for our flourishing both individually and as a group, then the denial of the group's access to its own culture is a perverse and unnatural act, akin to a violation of a human right. Cultural representations are the medium and reference points for identity. Like education, which takes us deeper into complex cultural representations, the denial of access to one's own culture, like the desecration of cultural artifacts, is an act of profound aggression. When cultures have been disrupted in deep ways, such as in the transatlantic slave trade or genocides, people typically develop new culture around the disruption, treating it as the crisis of history and identity that it is.

Our thought experiment represents an extreme limit condition to dramatize the unnaturalness of a fully propertied copyright culture. But it is not so far-fetched to connect access to one's culture to a fundamental human right. It is similar, for example, to Article 9 of the European Convention on Human Rights, which governs freedom of thought, conscience, and religion (European Court of Human Rights 2010) and protects broad ranges of cultural practice from intimidation and fear.

In *Configuring the Networked Self* (2010), Julie Cohen makes a similar critique of a fully propertied copyright system (one without fair use, for example). She highlights the deep incoherence in such a system by showing how it ignores the need for, among other things, creators who can work freely with copies and instances of propertied culture. Modern copyright law focused on works as economic products and externalizes all of the processes, such as education and access that involve freely and playfully working with copies. The current trend toward longer and longer copyright periods (from fourteen to twenty-eight years, to now seventy years beyond the life of the author) necessarily entails a weaker claim by society for the importance of access to cultural representations of all kinds. An appreciation of deep copy culture should serve as a counterweight and source of skepticism about this trend.

A second practical line of thought follows specifically from the ways in which copying and imitation are connected to learning, adaptive behaviors, and human flourishing. Not all copying is valuable and knowing that imitation of others is often our primary strategy is sobering. We have to remember that the inhabitants of Easter Island were probably engaging in faithful cultural transmission and copying behavior as they cut down the last tree on the island, leading to the decimation of their culture by cannibalism. In principle, copy behaviors can be part of a social epistemology in which reliable and useful knowledge promote human flourishing as easily as they can be part of a system of deception and self-deception about the human good. Appreciating deep copy culture naturally leads to concern about the quality of the cultural system in producing both reliable practical knowledge which facilitates growth and flourishing and a challenging critical culture which reviews and revises values with the same goal in mind.

And here, after casting suspicion on it in the thought experiment, we should acknowledge the effectiveness of commercial culture in creating markets for creators and works and in promoting technology which has dramatically reduced the costs of at least digital culture. But commercialization can also have distorting effects on knowledge production and dissemination. Often publishers create property in works that were already paid for by government or university research. Licensing agreements for public library and research library resources have institutionalized a dramatic division between the portion of the population that can access specialized research information—often research that the public library patron has already paid his state government to produce—and the portion that cannot. The commercialization of government information, such as laws and court cases,[2] is another big example of the distorting effect of the market on the quality of a collective "social epistemology." The combination of the market and copyright protection played a big historic role in creating the modern proprietary author and the modern intellectual property industry. While that is generally agreed to have been a good thing because it has motivated the creation and dissemination of information, we should be alert to places where we have created artificial markets for copies in existing social resources (thus re-privatizing them), which serve only the narrow interests of their owners and actually retard the growth of an epistemically reliable social network of information.

We are products of a deep history of replication and imperfect copying which has, improbably, created a creature with a passion and capacity for managing appearances, representations, and images symbolically. We have put this to good use not only in managing the social hierarchy necessary for modern societies, but in imagining ourselves and in posing deep questions about ourselves through more cultural production—books, films, art—that we make from copies and in order to copy. Respecting deep copy culture does not require us to oppose the commercialization of culture unilaterally, but retrieving a sense of the complexity, ubiquity, and naturalness of copy behaviors might alert us to moments in which our commitment to the commercial strategy for creating more and more copies undermines the goal of creating the kind of access to culture that our copy-hungry minds crave.

Notes

1 Of course, the process varies along many dimensions predicted by personality and features of cultural transmission. In highly biased cultural transmission contexts, children with conservative personalities are more likely to make choices about identity that are more consistent with their parents' choices (Richerson and Boyd 2005: 68).

2 Dramatically played out, for example, in the career of Aaron Swartz, who called attention to these issues.

References

Bloom, H. (1973), *The Anxiety of Influence*, Oxford: Oxford University Press.

Boon, M. (2010), *In Praise of Copying*, Cambridge, MA: Harvard University Press.

Boyd, R. and P. J. Richerson (2005), *The Origin and Evolution of Cultures*, New York: Oxford University Press.

Boyd, R. and P. J. Richerson (2009), "Culture and the Evolution of Human Cooperation," *Philosophical Transactions of the Royal Society B* 364 (1533): 3281–8.

Cohen, J. (2012), *Configuring the Networked Self*, New Haven: Yale University Press.

Diamond, J. (2013), *The World Until Yesterday*, New York: Penguin Books.

Geertz, C. (1973), "Thick Description: Toward an Interpretive Theory of Culture," in *The Interpretation of Cultures*, New York: Basic Books.

Henrich, J. (2004), "Demography and Cultural Evolution: How Adaptive Cultural Processes Can Produce Maladaptive Losses—the Tasmanian case," *American Antiquity* 69 (2): 197–214.

Hinton, G. E. and S. J. Nowlan (1987), "How Learning Can Guide Evolution," *Complex Systems* 1 (3): 495–502.

Larkin, P. (2004), "Continuing to Live," in *Collected Poems*, 177, New York: Farrar, Straus and Giroux.

Laslett, P. (1970), *Locke's Two Treatises of Government*, London: Cambridge University Press.

Mesoudi, A., A. Whiten, and K. N. Laland (2004), "Perspective: Is Human Cultural Evolution Darwinian? Evidence Reviewed from the Perspective of the Origin of the Species," *Evolution* 58 (1): 1–11.

Morris, I. (2015), *Farmers, Foragers, and Fossil Fuels: How Human Values Evolve*, Princeton: Princeton University Press.

Powell, A., S. Shennan, and M. G. Thomas (2009), "Late Fleistocene Demography and the Appearance of Modern Human Behavior," *Science* 324 (5932): 1298–301.

Rendell, L., R. Boyd, D. Cownden, M. Enquist, K. Eriksson, M. W. Feldman, L. Fogarty, S. Ghirlanda, T. Lillicrap, and K. N. Laland (2010), "Why Copy Others? Insights from the Social Learning Strategies Tournament," *Science* 328 (5975): 208–13.

Richerson, P. J. and R. Boyd (2005), *Not by Genes Alone*, Chicago: The University of Chicago Press.

Rorty, R. (1989), *Contingency, Irony, and Solidarity*, Cambridge: Cambridge University Press.

Rose, M. (1988), "The Author as Proprietor: Donaldson v. Beckett and the Genealogy of Modern Authorship," *Representations* 23: 51–85.

Sperber, D. (1985), *On Anthropological Knowledge*, Cambridge: Cambridge University Press.

Stout, D., N. Toth, K. Schick, and T. Chaminade (2008), "Neural Correlates of Early Stone-age Toolmaking: Technology, Language and Cognition in Human Evolution," *Philosophical Transactions of the Royal Society B* 363 (1499): 1939–49.

Trivers, R. (2011), *The Folly of Fools: The Logic of Deceit and Self-Deception in Human Life*, New York: Basic Books.

Weber, B. and D. Depew (2003), *Evolution and Learning: The Baldwin Effect Reconsidered*, Cambridge, MA: The MIT Press.

3

Imitation and Replication of Technologies: The Prospects for an Evolutionary Ethics of Copying

Wybo Houkes

Widespread, frequent use of file-sharing services, facilitated by broadband internet connections, has led to a social phenomenon that appears to call for urgent ethical reflection. Attitudes towards the copying practices enabled by current information and communications technology diverge, to put it diplomatically. Some condemn them as "internet piracy" or "freeloading" (Ruen 2012); for others, they signal the start of an era of "free content" and "distributed creativity." Efforts are made—by legislative bodies, lobby groups, and many others—to restrict file-sharing practices, such as "digital rights management," "voluntary copyright-alert programmes," or "educational notices," followed by lawsuits against individual downloaders.[1] For some, these are a welcome correction to a "Decade of Dysfunction" (Ruen 2012); for others, a necessary evil; and still others regard them as an attack on civil liberties (Sinnreich 2014). Meanwhile, *Game of Thrones* is making media headlines worldwide, not as a sex-and-gore-filled TV series, but perhaps primarily because of how often episodes are downloaded.[2]

This chapter looks at contemporary copying practices from a moral perspective, which is different—but not disconnected—from a legal, sociological, or practical perspective: it primarily addresses the question of what, if anything, makes copying (or, more specifically, file-sharing) right or wrong—not the question of how it works, how it arose or continues to develop as a social phenomenon, or how it can be legally or effectively restricted.

In developing this moral perspective, I take a broad view of copying, in two respects. First, I consider a larger scope of targets for copying than *Game of Thrones* and other digital content, namely, technologies broadly conceived, i.e.

any designed item, knowledge, or course of action that may be used in pursuit of practical purposes (Mitcham 1978; Houkes and Vermaas 2010). This first, "synchronic" broadening enables a second, "diachronic" broadening: I look at contemporary copying practices in a very wide historical context, namely in the light of human evolution. A broad evolutionary perspective can reveal some of the morally relevant features of contemporary copying practices, precisely because this perspective at first abstracts away some of the specifics and sidesteps most of the current controversy. For the same reason, it may reveal contextual factors in our assessment of what is morally relevant about copying practices. Still, deep-historical perspectives like the one chosen here should be treated with caution, not only because of the risk of evolutionary storytelling, but also because every such perspective highlights some historical continuities while ignoring others.

In this chapter, contemporary copying is initially put in a favorable historical light—namely, as a contemporary expression of a characteristic form of human behavior: that of imitating others. It seems fair to say that human beings are natural born copyists. Little of our behavioral repertoire is self-taught: the songs we sing, the food we cook, and the papers some of us write, all consist of elements taken from the work of others. Some of this imitative behavior is deeply ingrained into our daily lives, or almost automatic, like mirroring the body language of a conversation partner; other imitation is extremely costly, like apprenticeships, or risky, like industrial espionage. In Section 1, I review the results of cultural-evolutionary models of social learning that suggest that there is nothing objectionable about imitation. On the contrary, human flourishing is impossible without so-called cumulative cultural traits, and our uniquely human forms of imitative behavior explain why we possess such traits with unparalleled scope and depth. Then, in Section 2, I argue how these results might be used as ingredients in an "evolutionary ethics" of copying, i.e. an attempt to either ground our general moral sense or specific judgments in human evolutionary history, or to show that some moral judgments are, in this respect, groundless. I sketch two different strategies against the background of evolutionary ethics more generally, and identify some of the main challenges for both strategies. Finally, in Section 3, I argue that contemporary copying practices—both legal and illegal—have morally relevant characteristics that distinguish them within the broad class of imitative behavior. I characterize them as *replications* of technologies, and argue that this form of imitation lacks some of the right-making features of imitative behavior, that it has specific wrong-making features, and yet that it also lacks a wrong-making feature of other, historically important forms of imitation.

1. Imitation in human cultural evolution

In this section, I review two insights[3] on imitative behavior, drawn from studies of human cultural evolution. These appear, at first glance, to offer a powerful corrective to negative moral sentiment about and attempts at restricting copying practices; the next section studies problems and possibilities for developing these evolutionary insights into an ethics of copying practices.

Cultural-evolutionary theory is a research program that spans across many disciplines, including archaeology, palaeontology, anthropology, and psychology. It takes the capacity to acquire and pass on cultural traits,[4] through social learning, as a pivotal adaptation in human evolution. It reconstructs how our capacity for cultural transmission arose, and seeks to explain several stylized facts in the history of humankind and of technology (Boyd et al. 2015), as well as specific events, such as the so-called "Tasmanian tool loss" (Henrich 2004) and the appearance of "modern" human behavior in the late Pleistocene (Powell et al. 2009). Many have criticized cultural-evolutionary theory and its explanatory potential *vis à vis* alternatives (e.g. Read 2006; Claidière and Sperber 2007; Vaesen 2012). Here, I focus only on two relatively uncontroversial, general insights.

One insight, which cultural evolutionists share with a larger community of behavioral and life scientists, concerns the distinctive character of human imitative behavior. The other is more specific to cultural-evolutionary theory, and concerns an analysis of why human imitation is adaptive and how it may lead to cumulative cultural traditions. I review each insight in turn.

First, regarding human imitative behavior. Apes and parrots have a reputation when it comes to imitation; yet there is an impressive amount of evidence, gathered by ethnologists and developmental psychologists, that distinguishes human imitative behavior from similar behavior of non-human animals. There is no generally accepted taxonomy of these forms of behavior, nor is there a uniform terminology to characterize commonly recognized forms. However, three forms of imitative behavior roughly capture the major varieties as well as what are, to the best of our current knowledge, distinctively human forms.

The first form, *end-state emulation*—also called "stimulus enhancement," "goal emulation," or just "emulation"—is an attempt to reproduce the end state of some observed behavioral pattern. It is easy enough to see why this form of behavior might be adaptive: paying attention to the successful outcomes of the behavior of conspecifics, say the acquisition of some berries, and striving for similar success is beneficial, unless the rewards are trivial to obtain anyway (there are berries everywhere) or the emulated behavior is or has become extremely risky (the only berries left are in a snake pit). In this light, it is far from surprising that primates, corvids, and other non-human animals have been observed regularly to engage in end-state emulation.

A second form, *task mimicry*—also known as "task imitation" or just "imitation"—seems to be less widespread. It involves reproducing the exact same behavioral pattern that was observed. To illustrate the difference with end-state emulation, suppose that you observe Lionel Messi scoring a particularly beautiful goal, after passing three defenders. When this prompts you to go and play soccer in order to score a goal yourself, this counts as end-state emulation, unless you attempt to go through Messi's exact series of motions. As the example makes clear, this form of behavior is not obviously fitness-enhancing: in terms of contribution to fecundity or viability, only the goal matters, not the way of scoring it. However, task mimicry and end-state emulation may be thought of as complementary strategies: one is sensible in circumstances in which the other is unwise. Task mimicry might be preferable in case the route to the reward is difficult, so that only something very much like the original behavioral pattern will work.

Another thing that the example might show is that emulation and mimicry are difficult to tell apart. Suppose that you see me stumbling about on a soccer field, attempting some tricks on equally clumsy defenders, and managing to score a goal in the end. Did you witness a rather unsuccessful mimicry of Messi's latest solo and goal, or an end-state emulation? More improbably, suppose that you observe me slaloming past the defenders and scoring a goal in exactly the same way as Messi did: was this deliberate mimicry or improvisation in an unpredictable situation? Without knowing my intentions, it is impossible to say: end-state emulation and task mimicry are not just types of behavior, but *action types*. Therefore, it is not surprising that every purported observation of animals engaging in task imitation rather than end-state emulation is contested. Only observations of similar sequences of behavior would appear to be good candidates for attempted task mimicry, and those observations can always be alternatively explained as convergences in pursuit of the same goal—in particular, if the goal is difficult to obtain. Thus, task mimicry in animals is hard to attribute univocally in exactly those conditions under which we would expect to see it.

Even if it is difficult to distinguish two types of imitative behavior in animals, we can distinguish a third type in ourselves, which might be understood as a hybrid of the two types already described. Often, when we imitate some successful routine, we deliberately go through something much like the observed motions: we do more than end-state emulate. Yet we—again deliberately—do not mimic the exact behavioral pattern. We might, for instance, know that some finger twist is unnecessary, or that an extra step is required in our current circumstances, and adjust our behavior accordingly. I call this type of action "rational imitation." This may suggest that we know exactly what goes on in this form of behavior, and that it is evidently superior to the other forms. However, there are all kinds of complexities from the cognitive perspective, such as mindreading or "intention guessing," causal knowledge and the capacity for planning, and neither these capacities nor their joint operation in imitative behavior is well-understood. We should be able to discern the goal-directedness of another's behavior, parse the behavioral pattern, interpret this pattern in terms of the other person's mental states (knowledge, desires, etc.), mark any differences with our own mental states, adjust the pattern to these differences, and execute it. Thus, it may well be possible to distinguish various actions that share one or more—but not all—elements of rational imitation. This would make the notion less tied to (a particular conception of) humankind and thus more amenable to comparative animal ethnology. It would also show that we might seldom—if ever—engage in full-blown analysis of another's and our own actions, in order to achieve a similar goal with optimal efficacy and minimal effort.

Still, we can sometimes retrospectively analyse our behavior as if it were the product of rational imitation. Furthermore, there is some evidence that human children are capable of mimicking complicated action sequences *and* gradually removing those actions that are redundant for achieving the overall goal (e.g. Flynn and Whiten 2006; Flynn 2008; but also see Horner and Whiten 2005 for evidence of "over-imitation"). Conversely, it has been shown that in relatively simple but non-trivial tasks, failures are weeded out, that redundancies survive some generations but fail to be transmitted at some point, and that successes are seldom lost in transmission (e.g. Caldwell and Millen 2008). Thus, rational imitation is recognizable in human actions, even if it is ill understood and easily over-idealized. Given how complicated it is to interpret behavior in terms of the first two types of imitation, it is even less surprising that no instances of rational imitation in non-human animals have been reported as such in the literature. The notion sets us apart from other species, virtually by construction.

That we are, in our biased "insider" perspective, unique in our capacity for rational imitation is—despite the name—no reason to congratulate ourselves. As sketched above, it would seem that, in combination, end-state emulation and task mimicry are satisfactory strategies for achieving any reward worth having, in all realistic circumstances. Rational imitation might be a clever way of weeding out costly redundancies, but it comes at a high cost itself: the huge brain required for mindreading, planning, and other cognitive functions consumes vast amounts of energy. If all it does is fine-tune behavioral repertoires that would be largely successful otherwise, our brain would be like an all-terrain vehicle that never leaves suburbia or a concert piano used only to play "Twinkle Twinkle Little Star"; evolution would have scrapped it in favor of some leaner, more fit-to-purpose tool long ago. Why is rational imitation worth having?

The answer—and here I move from the first, broader insight to the second, more exclusively cultural-evolutionary insight—may be found in how rational imitation fosters so-called cumulative cultural traditions. Very few, if any, great achievements are the result of an individual effort. The history of technology, for instance, is better understood in terms of gradual modification, substitution, and recombination than of great inventions by some individual genius (Basalla 1988; Arthur 2001). Indeed, most current technologies are so complicated that they cannot result from some individual effort: no single person could successfully reconceive or recreate a smartphone or aircraft from scratch.[5]

It is easy enough to guess how such complexity is possible despite limitations in individual time, effort, or cognitive capacities: if, at every point in time, a few modifications could be tried out, if none would undo all progress made so far, and if a few modifications would be added and passed on to the next stage, a "ratchet" effect is created by which technologies become more complicated (and, arguably, more effective in some way or another). According to cultural evolutionists, most of humanity's scientific, technological, and artistic achievements may be attributed to these ratchet effects; and rational imitation would be just the process that creates these effects. The key is faithful transfer of information, combined with strong sensitivity to success—or "high-fidelity transmission" with strong "success bias" in the cultural-evolutionist jargon. Suppose that an instrument maker shows all her apprentices a particular way of making, say, a compass; that they are, at some point, all capable of reproducing this behavioral pattern, and that each of them goes on to add some modifications, either deliberately or by making a few small errors. This will lead to a variety of compass-making routines, with varying success: probably, many will be worse than the original; but possibly, a few are even better. Then, if the apprentice compass maker who comes up with the best second-generation routine has a larger chance of becoming the mentor of the third generation, a miniature ratchet effect occurs.

Efforts to investigate under which conditions these social learning processes lead to cumulative traditions are still ongoing, and typically take the form of population-dynamic or agent-based models of cultural change (see Dean et al. 2014 for a recent overview). One provisional result is that end-state emulation is unlikely to lead to cumulative traditions. Another is that rational imitation does so, but that it requires a combination of success bias, high-fidelity but imperfect transmission, and a sizeable population of imitators. The first condition is the most obvious: if success bias would be replaced by random copying, no cumulative effect would occur, since improvements would be as often ignored as they are imitated. The second is slightly more involved; roughly, the idea is that low-fidelity transmission would increase the chance that any improvement made in the previous generation is lost when a new generation of instrument makers learns the tricks of the trade. That some copying errors may in fact be improvements is acknowledged, but becomes increasingly unlikely the more generations have passed: at some point, random reinvention destroys more than it creates. More straightforwardly, *perfect* transmission would stop progress altogether, because it eliminates variation. The third and final condition concerns the number of imitators. If imperfect transmission has a higher chance to decrease performance than to increase it, making further progress requires an ever larger population of apprentices.[6]

In combination, these two insights suggest that humans have a unique capacity to engage in imitation, with an elaborate (and costly) mental underpinning, and that this capacity has served us well: the cumulative cultural traditions that it makes possible have led to a broad repertoire of sophisticated technologies, which have allowed—and continue to allow—human beings to flourish virtually everywhere, and that has made us resilient to all kinds of environmental changes. To sum up: if we are distinctively good at anything, it is at imitation; and if anything has been good for us, it has been imitation.

2. A corrective evolutionary ethics of copying?

The insights described in the previous section might look like they put in perspective any attempt at formulating ethical restrictions on copying. In fact, however, they need to be put into perspective themselves before their impact can be established. For although (cultural) evolutionary theory is seldom used in debates concerning file-sharing and digital rights, there is a recent surge of interest in the role of evolution in ethical debates. This has revealed several ways of doing so, all of which come with their own complications, and some of which seem generally unsuccessful. Roughly, the use of evolutionary insights in ethics comes in two pairs: it can be constructive or corrective, and specific or general. I briefly introduce each category, before discussing how the results described in Section 1 can be used.

The *constructive* use of evolutionary insights is supposed to provide explanatory underpinnings for human morality in general, or for specific moral intuitions or judgments. As evolutionary explanations go, this focuses on what may be called "moral traits," and explains either the origin of these traits, or their changing distribution over time under particular selection pressures. Thus, one might explain how a capacity for particular (i.e. non-global) altruism could have fitness-enhancing effects through group selection (e.g. Sober and Wilson 1998), or one could reconstruct the role in human evolution of ever more elaborate and generally applicable forms of "normative guidance" (e.g. Kitcher 2011). The latter can be taken as a general-constructive evolutionary ethics, the former as a specific-constructive. Other specific uses concern explanations of sexual taboos or our resentment of cheaters, which will be discussed later.

As the examples make clear, there is a strong descriptive element to these constructive uses: they provide explanations how or why, in the light of evolution, we came to be moral creatures of a particular kind. It is controversial whether such an evolutionary ethics could also be prescriptive, i.e. justify our moral beliefs. Less, but still more than a little, controversial is whether an evolutionary ethics can play a negative prescriptive role, i.e. whether it can undermine or "debunk" existing justifications for moral beliefs. Many critics seem to agree, however, that if evolutionary arguments can play any role in normative or meta-ethics, it is negative (e.g. Kahane 2011; FitzPatrick 2014).

This *corrective* role of evolutionary considerations can, again, be either general or specific. In the literature, a general-corrective use has received most attention, in the form of so-called global debunking arguments (e.g. Joyce 2006; Street 2006). The upshot of these arguments is that none of our moral beliefs are justified since they are the products of our evolutionary history, and evolution by natural selection does not track the moral truth. Critics have rightfully targeted both the cogency of this argument and the sketchiness of its causal claim. Whether these objections can be satisfactorily addressed is irrelevant here, because the insights of Section 1 are insufficiently general to cast doubt on all our moral beliefs; they can at most target beliefs about imitative behavior.

However, use of these insights must take a different form than most debunking arguments, which supply an account of how our beliefs are the products of evolutionary history. One example is Greene's (2007) evolutionary debunking of differential responses to equivalent scenarios. Most respondents believe that it is morally problematic to push someone from a footbridge to save innocent trolley occupants, while it is acceptable to pull a switch that has the same net effect in lives saved and lost. According to Greene, this is not because a deontological analysis is correct for one form of the trolley dilemma and a utilitarian for the other, but because our evolutionary history has equipped us with strong sentiments about direct violence, whereas we (presently) lack such sentiments about indirect violence. So, the debunking argument goes, the differences in responses do not reflect a genuine moral difference between the scenarios, but rather differential selection pressures in our evolutionary history. By contrast, the insights of Section 1 do not concern the evolutionary history of some of our moral beliefs regarding file-sharing and other specific copying practices. Rather, they point out that such beliefs cannot have an evolutionary history, given the prevalence of imitative behavior in humans.

This might clarify how *not* to construct an evolutionary ethics of copying, but it leaves open how one may construct an evolutionary ethics of copying on the basis of the previous section. Here, I sketch two strategies: one that is primarily corrective, in arguing that resentment of file-sharing is groundless; another that is more constructive, in emphasizing a particular right-making feature of imitative behavior.

For developing the corrective strategy, evolutionary debunking arguments are best taken as a variant of a more traditional form of moral scepticism. Showing how human evolution might have given rise to moral beliefs is one way of bringing out the historical antecedents of these beliefs. To these antecedents, some arguments add the observation that different moral beliefs were maintained in a different age, to conclude a form of moral relativism; but debunking is possible even if we do not have access to historical contrasts with our own moral beliefs.

One can use this intellectual kinship between evolutionary and historical debunking arguments to infer from the lack of an evolutionary explanation of "downloader resentment" that there must be another historical explanation. For, one might submit, *any* belief has a historical cause; and if the cause cannot be found in evolutionary history, it must have more recent origins. From here, it is a small step—especially if one has strong prior convictions concerning the matter—to proposing candidates for the relevant historical circumstances: the rise and further development of copyright law, its extension to ever more products, internationalization and corporatization. To put it roughly: if resentment of copying is not the result of the relentless force of natural selection, it is a product of corporate indoctrination. Alternatively, one might assume that only moral beliefs for which there is an evolutionary history can legitimately be held to be universal, or connected to "human nature" (Nichols 2004). Beliefs for which there is no such history must, by contrast, be the product of particular historical or social circumstances—and here, the usual suspects may be listed. In these two ways, one may conclude that beliefs about the moral inadmissibility of file-sharing are misguided, because the adaptivity of imitative behavior means that such beliefs lack an evolutionary grounding.

Another strategy is more constructive. For the insights of Section 1 do more than—or something different from—showing that there is no evolutionary explanation for moral resentment of copyists. Rather, there is a specific right-making feature of imitative behavior: it enables cumulative cultural traditions that make possible or enhance human life in a wide variety of environments. Thus, imitating others is, by and large, and highly defeasibly, a good thing to do: if we would collectively refrain from imitation, the consequences would—again, on a collective level—be disastrous. Misgivings about imitation would stimulate an excessive reliance on individual learning, whereas average group fitness is highest when there is a mixture of learning strategies in the population with a heavy emphasis on imitation (e.g. Kameda and Nakanishi 2003), and whereas, individually, hybrid strategies that use social learning where they can and individual learning where they must, have the highest payoff (Rendell et al. 2010). Thus, imitative behavior has a specific right-making feature: in the long run, it has highly beneficial consequences. Conversely, negative attitudes towards imitative behavior, or any institution aimed at restricting it, undermine these consequences and must therefore be morally misguided or even wrong.

This constructive strategy might be more promising than the corrective, because it does not rest on questionable assumptions about historical explanations of moral beliefs. However, it is not self-evident that one can conclude that imitative behavior is generally justified, merely on the basis that it features in a possible explanation of some highly general good. For the remainder of this chapter, I shall accept that the insights of Section 1 reveal a right-making feature of imitation—but this single feature is a small basis for an ethics of contemporary copying practices.

Both strategies, however, seem dangerously narrow in their use of human evolution. Our evolutionary history has, according to many, not just equipped us with advanced imitative capacities, but also with sophisticated mechanisms for detecting cheaters.[7] No appeal to human evolution can be complete without at least considering the repercussions of these detection mechanisms. Just as file-sharing might be a contemporary expression of evolved capacities for imitative behavior, attempts to curtail such copying practices might express evolved instincts to resent or punish "free-riders," i.e. those who profit from social institutions without paying the corresponding costs. Enriching the idyllic imitation-focused insights with those that concern the harsher aspects of social interactions should be a first priority for those who seek an evolutionary justification of all forms of copying—especially those that are low on costs.[8]

3. From rational imitation to indiscriminate replication

In the remainder of this chapter, I choose another way to enrich—or complicate—an evolutionary ethics of copying than considering free-riding and cheater detection. Reviewing the evolutionary history of imitative behavior does not only reveal deep continuities, but also important differences between specific imitative practices. Learning from a parent or master artisan how to produce a technological artifact is, in many ways, a different practice than downloading digital media. The question is, of course, whether at least some of these differences are morally relevant: whether some of the features that made imitation, historically, a "good thing" are missing in current copying; and/or whether copying has specific features that make it, now, a "bad thing."

In distinguishing current copying practices from imitative behavior in general, I avoid the typical philosophical strategy of offering explicit definitions. Rather, I focus on prototypical examples of either type of activity: knapping stone tools in the context of a long-term apprenticeship and downloading the latest *Game of Thrones* episode. For these examples, I attempt to find moral difference-makers, i.e. distinguishing features that are morally relevant.[9] Furthermore, I avoid focussing on *illegal* downloading and thus possibly prejudging the issue. The four features identified below apply to any form of downloading, and could therefore be ingredients for a general ethics of copying, rather than merely a justification for punishing illegal downloading.

3.1 Replication: Product-centered, fixed-process imitation

Consider downloading *Game of Thrones* and learning how to knap a stone axe. One conspicuous difference seems to be that the former leads to acquisition of a product, whereas the latter leads to acquisition of a productive technique.

Thus, if your ultimate desire is for a (digital or material) product, it is immediately satisfied by the copying activity. However, on closer inspection, it is also satisfied, albeit indirectly and conditionally, by the second activity: provided that you have the time and materials needed to exercise your newly learned technique, any desire that you have for stone axes can be satisfied. Furthermore, downloading can be straightforwardly characterized as exercising a productive technique: by taking a certain sequence of actions, such as installing a torrent client, using the search function on a tracker, and selecting a file, you acquire the desired product. Downloading is, in its own way, a form of production.[10] It makes more copies of an item, rather than, for instance, transferring control over existing copies. This might happen without permission of the owner of the original—but so might imitation of a productive technique, in industrial espionage.

A better way to capture the intuitive difference is that the productive technique used in downloading is of a different kind than that used in producing the original, whereas it is approximately the same in the stone-knapping case. Thus, in the typology of Section 1, downloading is not task mimicry or rational imitation. Neither, however, can it be cast as emulation: it does not involve some individual, spur-of-the-moment sequence of actions in pursuit of an observed desirable outcome, but faithfully follows an entrenched sequence.[11] It might be unclear what counts as "producing the original" in the case of digital media, since there are several non-trivial techniques that convert an initial idea or story into the *Game of Thrones* episode available for your viewing pleasure. However, none of these techniques essentially involves file-sharing via a torrent site.

This first difference is not necessarily a *moral* difference, but it serves to distinguish imitative behavior of the "file-sharing" kind from that of the "stone-knapping" kind, and to set apart the former within the more general class of imitative behavior. To give it a distinctive name—without defining it or indicating (at this stage) a moral difference—I call the product-centered, fixed-process imitative behavior exemplified by downloading *Game of Thrones* "replication."

3.2 Digital scaffolding: Incomplete artifacts

A second difference between the prototypes is that downloading is an activity in a digital "online" environment, whereas stone-knapping happens "offline." Thus, the former is impossible without various social and technological support systems, such as a computer, power grids, and internet providers.

Downloading is heavily "scaffolded" or technologically "mediated," to the point of being "enabled" by technologies. Stone-knapping does not require this social and technological scaffolding. Yet it would be naive to conclude that it requires no scaffolding: as investigations by anthropologists and (experimental) archaeologists have shown, stone-knapping is impossible without access to the right sites, and such access may be heavily institutionalized (Stout 2002). More generally, many non-digital productive techniques require the use of pre-produced and reusable instruments, as well as divisions of labor and other social institutions.

What is more distinctive is that digital items are *incomplete* artifacts. Without particular other artifacts they cannot be used even if they have been produced flawlessly. Downloading is not only enabled by power stations and internet providers, but also by the software that is required to enjoy whatever was obtained by this particular productive technique: .pdf and .mp4 files do not (dis)play themselves. Thus, these copying practices are at best partial expressions of autonomy, and also affirm dependence on particular technologies and the corporations that supply them; and changing dependences does not make you a crusader for freedom.[12] One might rightfully object that many non-digital objects are similarly incomplete. A can opener is useless if there were no cans, and so are many specialized components if the devices that they are part of were scrapped. However, as any user of software that fails to be "backwards compatible" has experienced, digital objects can become entirely useless, and it is typically much easier to find alternative purposes for material objects than for digital objects. One cannot even make a doorstop or a paperweight—to give the stock examples of reuse in the philosophical literature—out of .wp5 files or Fortran-77 routines. This particular dependence means that downloading might lack the right-making feature of affirming or furthering end-user autonomy, which is sometimes attributed to it; rather, it might have a specific wrong-making feature of covertly restricting this autonomy, or of expressing indifference to one's own autonomy in seeking entertainment.

3.3 Digital scaffolding: Flawless replication

Because downloading takes place in a digital environment, it has another feature that distinguishes it from the stone-knapping case. Human imitative behavior was described in Section 1 as "high-fidelity": attempts at reproducing a conspecific's behavioral pattern typically lead to a similar but non-identical behavioral pattern, because of small errors and deliberate modifications. That there is no guaranteed identity is not a flaw, but the key to (the cultural-evolutionists' explanation of) cumulative cultural traits: if there were only perfect copies, technological change would stop after just one generation. From a cultural-evolutionary perspective, copies can be too true to be good.

By contrast, if there would be no guaranteed identity in downloading, you would regard the reproductive technique as flawed: you would not be pleased if other characters would be killed in your copy of *Game of Thrones*—even if, from a narrative perspective, this might be an interesting innovation. Thus, if we would only engage in downloading and other flawless replicative techniques, there could be no cumulative cultural traditions—although, of course, there can still be creative reuse, by recombination and other techniques, of downloaded material, just as there can be creative use of flawlessly sampled pieces of music. Yet here, the possibility of new (steps in) cultural traditions resides not in the process of replication itself, but in what is done with the replicated material afterwards. In a sense, this requires that the replicated product is not the intended end result, but only the raw material with which new products will be created through further productive techniques.

That downloading involves flawless replication rather than high-fidelity transmission means that it lacks the right-making feature attributed to imitative behavior in the constructive evolutionary ethics of Section 2. As indicated there, this is a defeasible feature; and of course, a file-shared digital item is not guaranteed to be a perfect copy—but still, in comparison with stone-knapping, a specific opportunity for acting for the long-term collective good is lost in downloading.

3.4 Indiscriminate replication

A fourth and final feature of file-sharing is that it is, in comparison with stone-knapping, an almost non-committal activity. Learning how to knap flint, or acquiring any artisanal capability, requires a large investment of time and effort and, at least traditionally, maintaining a long-term social relation with a cultural or biological parent. Indeed, it has been suggested that our biologically remarkable imitative and pro-social capacities developed in tandem to facilitate this acquisition of adaptive cultural traits through apprenticeships (Sterelny 2012). By contrast, file-sharing combines a small social bandwidth with an enormous information bandwidth.

This difference in commitment is, intuitively, morally relevant, but difficult to assess. First, of course, saving effort is not blameworthy in general; efficiency is neither a virtue nor a vice. Secondly, traditional imitation is not necessarily very time-consuming. It may be an exaggeration that "[f]ive minutes with a wheel, a snowshoe, a bobbin, or a bow and arrow may allow an artisan of one culture to capture a major achievement of another" (Gould 1987: 70), but only imitation of traits with a large "tacit" or "personal" component, in Polanyi's (1964) terms, requires long-term exposure and effort. Thirdly, apprenticeship is a morally ambiguous institution at best: the long-term dependencies characteristic of apprenticeships (or, nowadays, internships) often lead to exploitation. Fourthly and finally, if acquisition of cultural traits would generally become less time-consuming, the demographic effect on cumulative cultural change could be strengthened, since more people could make an effort at imitating a mentor trait. Thus, if facilitating cultural accumulation is a right-making feature, indiscriminate replication has it to a larger degree than traditional, labor-intensive imitation. Only because it is virtually flawless, as pointed out above, replication loses this right-making feature.

What, then, might make indiscriminate replication morally wrong? One intuition is that it is a form of overindulgence, in which one acquires a larger number of commodities than one can reasonably expect to enjoy to their fullest. Presumably, it would only take days or weeks to download more TV series than one would want to see in a lifetime—let alone to appreciate them with the care that would lead (some of) them to enrich one's character. Indiscriminate replication may therefore be regarded as expressing or furthering habits that do not encourage human flourishing. Developing this intuition requires a virtue-ethical perspective. This is a marked shift from the broadly consequence-based perspective that was earlier used to identify the right-making features of imitative behavior, and also from the autonomy-centered argument given earlier. Moreover, like every application of virtue ethics, it risks arbitrarily proclaiming as a general principle a form of (perceived) human flourishing preferred by a particular sociocultural elite. Possibly, re-reading *War and Peace* is a better activity than participating in a *Game of Thrones* binge-a-thon—but I will not argue the point here.

Surveying all four features, downloading may be characterized as indiscriminate, flawless replication of incomplete artifacts, in contrast with the careful, high-fidelity imitation of (sustenance) tool production exemplified by stone-knapping. Comparatively, downloading lacks the right-making feature of facilitating cumulative cultural change; and it may possess the additional wrong-making features of increasing technological dependence and of facilitating overindulgence; but it also lacks the wrong-making feature of facilitating exploitative social relations. This makes it at least sufficiently *different* in morally relevant respects, and may very well make it morally more problematic. Each of the four features is in need of closer analysis, especially with regard to its moral relevance. Moreover, it needs to be investigated how the various right-making and wrong-making features balance out for the types of imitative behavior surveyed here.

4. Conclusions

This chapter considered contemporary copying practices in the light of evolution. After reviewing work on the importance and uniqueness of imitative behavior in humans, it explored two strategies for developing an evolutionary ethics of copying. One was a largely corrective position, which discredits moral resentment of copying behavior as misguided, because this resentment lacks an evolutionary explanation. The other was a more constructive view, which focuses on cumulative cultural traits, a long-term collective good, which are enabled by human imitative behavior, and which would be undermined if copying were restricted or morally discredited. Furthermore, an inventory was made of specific right-making and wrong-making features of contemporary copying, in contrast with those of traditional forms of imitative behavior.

Both the two strategies and the inventory are prospective only. They need to be developed in much more detail before they offer strong arguments rather than suggestive hints in the debate about digital rights and internet piracy. Some of the largest challenges to be addressed have been identified in passing. Overall, I hope to have made clear, first, that many parties in this debate can profit from looking at copying in the light of human evolution; and, secondly, that a richer evolutionary light could be cast by considering the contrast between copying and other imitative practices (especially apprenticeships) in more detail, and by including evolutionary theorizing about the detection and punishment of cheaters.

Notes

1 See computer.howstuffworks.com/drm.htm, copyrightinformation.org/the-copyright-alert-system/what-is-a-copyright-alert and riaa.com/index.php for more information about these three countermeasures.

2 In the first three months of 2015 alone, episodes of *Game of Thrones* were downloaded 7 million times (hollywoodreporter.com/news/game-thrones-piracy-soars-season-787594). For comparison: the compilation *1962–1966* by the Beatles sold roughly as many copies in the U.S. in forty-two years.

3 Throughout, I refer to these and other claims about (human) evolution as "insights." This is not to be read as a claim about their truth value.

4 "Cultural traits" are understood, in this research tradition, as all pieces of information that may be acquired by social learning and that may affect observable behavior. Culture includes knowledge, skills, technologies, languages, legal and religious systems. See Mesoudi (2011: 2–3) for this definition and for an overview of the central ideas and results in cultural-evolutionary theory.

5 An amusing case in point is Thomas Thwaites's "Toaster Project," an attempt to build an electric toaster from scratch (www.ted.com/talks/thomas_thwaites_how_i_built_a_toaster_from_scratch). It took him roughly five months, and the toaster self-destructed within five seconds.

6 This is the "demographic effect" in cultural change: a change in population size can explain the loss of tool traditions (Henrich 2004) or the emergence of improved technologies (Powell et al. 2009).

7 The need for such cheater detection mechanisms is central to the "Machiavellian Intelligence" or "Social Brain" hypothesis for the large brains of primates (Byrne and Whiten 1988; Dunbar 2003).

8 One might wonder why insights regarding cheater detection are not more central to this chapter. This has two reasons. First, because cheating and free-riding are parasitic phenomena, they are most appropriately studied against the background of what they are parasitic on. Here, (part of) this background is developed in the form of socially beneficial imitative practices. Second, detection and especially punishment of cheaters is less obviously adaptive than one might think: often, punishment comes at a cost to the punishers, creating a riddle that evolutionary game theorists have not yet solved; see Sigmund (2007) for an authoritative description of the problem and the many attempts to address it. A proper discussion of this debate, and its possible repercussions for an ethics of copying, are therefore best left for another paper.

9 This can be understood as a tentative construction of a "conceptual space" (Gärdenförs 2000) of imitative practices, with a specific eye to dimensions that make the prototypes morally (rather, say, than economically or technologically) different.

10 In the terminology introduced in Houkes and Vermaas (2009), it involves execution of a *make plan* and counts as a *making* activity, just as stone-knapping.

11 In Houkes and Vermaas's (2009) terminology, downloading does not involve *construction* of a make plan and therefore does not count as *manufacturing*.

12 One does, of course, have the freedom to seek or develop alternative software; but this is a freedom seldom used by downloaders of *Game of Thrones*.

References

Arthur, W. B. (2009), *The Nature of Technology: What It Is and How It Evolves*, New York: Free Press.

Basalla, G. R. (1988), *The Evolution of Technology*, Cambridge: Cambridge University Press.

Boyd, R., P. J. Richerson, and J. Henrich (2015), "The Cultural Evolution of Technology: Facts and Theories," in P. J. Richerson and M. H. Christiansen (eds), *Cultural Evolution: Society, Technology, Language, and Religion*, 119–42, Cambridge, MA: MIT Press.

Byrne, R. W. and A. Whiten (eds) (1988), *Machiavellian Intelligence: Social Expertise and the Evolution of Intellect in Monkeys, Apes, and Humans*, Oxford: Oxford University Press.

Caldwell, C. A. and A. E. Millen (2008), "Experimental Models for Testing Hypotheses about Cumulative Cultural Evolution," *Evolution and Human Behavior* 29 (3): 165–71.

Claidière, N. and D. Sperber (2007), "The Role of Attraction in Cultural Evolution," *Journal of Cognition and Culture* 7 (1–2): 89–111.

Dean, L. G., G. L. Vale, K. N. Laland, E. Flynn, and R. L. Kendal (2014), "Human Cumulative Culture," *Biological Reviews* 89 (2): 284–301.

Dunbar, R. I. M. (2003), "The Social Brain: Mind, Language, and Society in Evolutionary Perspective," *Annual Review of Anthropology* 32: 163–81.

FitzPatrick, W. (2014), "Morality and Evolutionary Biology," *The Stanford Encyclopedia of Philosophy* (Fall 2014 edn), E. N. Zalta (ed.). Available online: http://plato.stanford.edu/archives/fall2014/entries/morality-biology/

Flynn, E. (2008), "Investigating Children as Cultural Magnets," *Philosophical Transactions of the Royal Society B* 363 (1509): 3541–51.

Flynn, E. and A. Whiten (2008), "Cultural Transmission of Tool Use in Young Children," *Social Development* 17 (3): 699–718.

Gärdenförs, P. (2000), *Conceptual Spaces: The Geometry of Thought*, Cambridge, MA: MIT Press.

Gould, S. J. (1987), *An Urchin in the Storm: Essays about Books and Ideas*, New York: Norton.

Greene, J. (2007), "The Secret Joke of Kant's Soul," in W. Sinnott-Armstrong (ed.), *Moral Psychology, Volume 3: The Neuroscience of Morality*, 35–66, Cambridge, MA: MIT Press.

Henrich, J. (2004), "Demography and Cultural Evolution: How Adaptive Cultural Processes can Produce Maladaptive Losses: The Tasmanian Case," *American Antiquity* 69 (2): 197–214.

Horner, V. and A. Whiten (2005), "Causal Knowledge and Imitation/Emulation Switching in Chimpanzees (*Pan troglodytes*) and Children (*Homo sapiens*)," *Animal Cognition* 8 (3): 164–81.

Houkes, W. and P. E. Vermaas (2009), "Contemporary Engineering and the Metaphysics of Artefacts," *The Monist* 92 (3): 403–19.

Houkes, W. and P. E. Vermaas (2010), *Technical Functions: On the Use and Design of Artefacts*, Dordrecht: Springer.

Joyce, R. (2006), *The Evolution of Morality*, Cambridge, MA: MIT Press.

Kahane, G. (2011), "Evolutionary Debunking Arguments," *Noûs* 45 (1): 103–25.

Kameda, T. and D. Nakanishi (2003), "Does Social/Cultural Learning Increase Human Adaptability?" *Evolution and Human Behavior* 24 (4): 242–60.

Kitcher, P. (2011), *The Ethical Project*, Cambridge, MA: Harvard University Press.

Mesoudi, A. (2011), *Cultural Evolution: How Darwinian Theory Can Explain Human Culture and Synthesize the Social Sciences*, Chicago: The University of Chicago Press.

Mitcham, C. (1978), "Types of Technology," *Research in Philosophy and Technology* 1: 229–94.

Nichols, S. (2004), *Sentimental Rules: On the Natural Foundations of Moral Judgment*, Oxford: Oxford University Press.

Polanyi, M. (1964), *Personal Knowledge: Towards a Post-Critical Philosophy*, London: Routledge.

Powell A., S. Shennan, and M. Thomas (2009), "Late Pleistocene Demography and the Appearance of Modern Human Behavior," *Science* 324 (5932): 1298–301.

Read, D. (2006), "Tasmanian Knowledge and Skill," *American Antiquity* 71 (1): 164–84.

Rendell, L., R. Boyd, D. Cownden, M. Enquist, K. Eriksson, M. W. Feldman, L. Fogarty, S. Ghirlanda, T. Lillicrap, and K. N. Laland (2010), "Why Copy Others?" *Science* 328 (5975): 208–13.

Ruen, C. (2012), *Freeloading: How Our Insatiable Hunger for Free Content Starves Creativity*, Brunswick: Scribe.

Sigmund, K. (2007), "Punish or Perish? Retaliation and Collaboration among Humans," *Trends in Ecology and Evolution* 22 (11): 593–600.

Sinnreich, A. (2014), *The Piracy Crusade: How the Music Industry's War on Sharing Destroys Markets and Erodes Civil Liberties*, Amherst: University of Massachusetts Press.

Sober, E. and D. S. Wilson (1998), *Unto Others: The Evolution and Psychology of Unselfish Behavior*, Cambridge, MA: Harvard University Press.

Sterelny, K. (2012), *The Evolved Apprentice: How Evolution Made Humans Unique*, Cambridge, MA: MIT Press.

Stout, D. (2002), "Skill and Cognition in Stone Tool Production," *Current Anthropology* 43 (5): 693–722.

Street, S. (2006), "A Darwinian Dilemma for Realist Theories of Value," *Philosophical Studies* 127 (1): 109–66.

Vaesen, K. (2012), "Cumulative Cultural Evolution and Demography," *PLoS ONE* 7 (7): e40989.

Part Two

What Is a Copy? Conceptual Perspectives

4

What Is the Object in Which Copyright Can Subsist? An Ontological Analysis

Maria Elisabeth Reicher

1. Copyright and ontology—a complex relationship

The topic of this paper is the ontology of works and its relation to copyright law. An ontology of works is, roughly, a theory of what kind of object a work is. Although many copyright issues concern works of art and science (and the examples given in what follows shall be taken primarily from the realm of art), the term "work" is used here in a wider sense, which includes also objects of design and life style (like pieces of furniture, garments, and dishes), objects of utility (such as a garlic press or a tea bag), tools, and instruments. One might summarize the concerns of an ontology of works by means of the following three questions:

1. To which ontological category (or categories) do works belong?
2. In what relationships do works stand to other objects? For instance, in what relations does a musical work stand to sound-carriers, to copies of scores, to particular interpretations, to the goings-on in the mind of the composer, to the experiences of the audience?
3. What is the internal structure of a work? Which parts or components can be distinguished within, say, a novel, a play, a symphony?

There are two sorts of relations between ontology and copyright: On the one hand, copyright issues might prove relevant for the discussion of ontological problems. On the other hand, ontological considerations might prove relevant for the discussion of copyright issues.[1] I shall consider the matter from both sides, starting with the ontological point of view.

Many professional philosophers hold a view that I call "ontological neutralism." Its core thesis is that only ontologists have ontological views, i.e. only ontologists have opinions on what kinds of things there are, on whether a work of music is a material object, or on whether a poem is identical to something in the mind of the poet, etc.[2]

But ontological neutralism is wrong. *Everybody* has ontological views. They reveal themselves in *utterances* on the one hand and in *practices* on the other. Thus, the search for an ontology of works should be started with a careful examination of the various discourses about works and the various practices connected with them. Discourses about works comprise scientific discourse as well as art criticism, art history, literary theory, and last, but not least, copyright law, but they also comprise our everyday talk about movies and actors, pop songs, novels, theater productions, food, fashion, and furniture. Practices connected with works concern their production as well as their reception and use, but also the things that are done by publishers, translators, dealers, collectors, and curators, and again last, but not least, the decisions that are taken in juridical practice with respect to copyright cases.

An adequate ontology of works should be consistent with these discourses and practices, but, in addition, it should also help us to gain a better understanding of them, and, perhaps, rid them of internal inconsistencies and make them more coherent.

Copyright law and jurisdiction provide a considerable amount of data that should be taken into account by an ontology of works. If such an ontology were in conflict with relevant and widely accepted parts of copyright law and/or approved jurisdiction, this would be a *prima facie* reason against it, since, as has been stated above, copyright law and the related jurisdiction are important parts of our practices concerned with works of all kinds. Thus, if, for instance, an ontological theory that implied that works are material objects were in conflict with copyright law and jurisdiction, this would be a *prima facie* reason to reject such a "materialist" ontology. Therefore, copyright law and jurisdiction are relevant to ontology. On the other hand, at least some experts in copyright law explicitly state the relevance of ontology for their field. Alois Troller, for instance, writes:

> Science cannot do without philosophical thinking. Scientists make use of philosophical insights, even if they are not aware of this. This holds for natural scientists as well as for scientists in the field of law.
>
> Also those lawyers who form their opinions on men and on material as well as on intellectual things without taking care of ontological problems make use of ontological insights on the basic elements of the system of laws; in the same way proceed those who consciously reject any ontology and allegedly determine the legal ought autonomously.
>
> Troller 1967: 385–6[3]

Copyright law is full of strong ontological assumptions. One might summarize the most fundamental ones as follows:[4]

1. Works are *intellectual objects*[5].
2. Works have to be distinguished from their *occurrences*.
3. Works are *created* through mental acts.
4. Works have to be distinguished from that which can be perceived by the senses.
5. One has to distinguish the *form* of a work from its *content*.

The first ontological question that is raised by copyright law is "What exactly is an 'intellectual object'?" In order to clarify the concept of an intellectual object, I distinguish the following three categories:

a. The category of material objects, i.e. objects that are extended and located in space, accessible to the senses, and exist independently of any consciousness.
b. The category of mental objects, i.e. objects that are not extended and located in space, not accessible to the senses, and belong to a particular consciousness at a particular time.
c. The category of abstract objects, i.e. objects that are not extended and located in space, not accessible to the senses, but can be apprehended by different persons at different occasions.

It is plain that intellectual objects cannot be material objects. It is, however, less clear, whether they are mental or abstract objects. The question of which interpretation should be preferred will be discussed in Section II. For the time being, it should be noted that even many of those philosophers who believe that there are such things as abstract objects must find the legal work concept to be highly problematic. For, in the philosophical tradition, it was almost a dogma that abstract objects are necessary and eternal objects, i.e. objects that neither have a beginning nor an end and do not owe their existence to any contingent processes.[6]

In Austrian copyright law, works are defined as "characteristic intellectual creations in the fields of literature, music, the fine arts, and the art of film."[7] If this definition were sufficiently clear and adequate for the purposes of copyright, it would be superfluous from the lawyer's point of view to engage in further investigations about the nature of this concept. As Max Kummer wrote:

> A lawyer who deals with the concept of a work almost is in danger of dealing with something anachronistic. Even more: one might even accuse him of doing

> something superfluous, for the juridical practice has always found its way after a fashion, along the lines of the concept of a work (or so it seems, at least). Why stir up problems, where the instinctive feeling of the judge was sufficient until today!
>
> Kummer 1968

Kummer, however, goes on to point out that the last word has not yet been spoken on the concept of the work, since certain developments in contemporary art require further refinements. Kummer had in mind, among other things, *objets trouvés* (like Duchamp's *Bottle Rack*), aleatoric music and poetry, optical art, and abstract painting in general. Kummer's observation (although several decades old by now) seems hardly to have lost anything of its relevance to the current situation, especially in the light of recent developments in what is called "conceptual art" or "appropriation art" in the fine arts, and "sampling" in music.

Thus, the concept of a work in copyright law is not as clear, adequate, and unproblematic as one might wish. In the rest of this paper, I shall try to clarify and refine it. In Section II, I shall delineate the basic elements of an ontology of works and explain what I take to be the most important difference between the philosophical work concept and the legal work concept of copyright law. In Section III, I shall discuss two problems of copyright connected with contemporary developments in art and answer the questions raised by these problems in the light of the ontology of works delineated in Section II.

2. A philosophical ontology of works

In what follows, I am going to delineate an ontology of works that is supposed to do justice to copyright discourse and related practices. I will do this by answering the three questions formulated at the beginning of this paper.

2.1 To which ontological category do works belong?

Given the simple categorial scheme introduced above, the question may be stated as follows: Are works material, mental, or abstract objects? The legal work concept is certainly correct insofar as works are not material objects. Among other things, the material object hypothesis (as one might call it) does not do justice to the fact that one and the same piece of music may be performed twice, that one and the same piece of drama may be produced twice, etc. In fact, talk about performances or productions of a work doesn't even make sense against the background of the material object hypothesis. A material object (say, a particular piece of paper with marks of ink on it) is just not the kind of object of which one can sensibly say that it is *performed*. A piece of paper may be archived, burned, crumpled, copied, exhibited in a showcase—but it is not the kind of thing that can be performed.

Are works, then, mental objects, in the sense explicated above? If this were the case, they would be private and subjective. It would be impossible that you and I have heard the same piece of music or have read the same poem. Even for a particular single subject, it would be impossible to hear the same piece of music twice or to read the same poem twice. We couldn't say, truthfully: "I have read this novel twice." We could say only: "I have had two reading experiences that were alike in many respects and have common causal origins" (where a common causal origin may be, among other things, a particular copy of a book or a particular series of processes in the mind of an author).

Furthermore, if we identified the work with the mental goings-on in the mind of the author[8] during the process of creation, the work would cease to exist in that very moment in which it was finished. Consequently, there would never exist anything that could be protected by copyright.

In what follows, I take it for granted that works are abstract objects that can be *realized* in concrete material or mental objects. I call objects of this kind *types*.[9] According to this hypothesis (which I call the "abstractness hypothesis," for short), works are not dependent on a particular consciousness, and thus they are not subjective and private. The abstractness hypothesis also allows that one and the same piece of music can be performed many times, that there may be many productions of one and the same piece of drama, etc.

Nevertheless, the abstractness hypothesis is controversial among philosophers. One might object, for instance, that abstract objects cannot be perceived. This is one of the defining features of abstract objects. Yet, isn't it one of the basic facts about works that we can perceive them? The answer to this objection is included in the answer to our second question:

2.2 In what relationships do works stand to other objects?

In what relations do works stand to material objects on the one hand and mental objects on the other? Let me start with material objects. I distinguish three basic relations between works and material objects:

1. The realization relation.
2. The notation relation.
3. The "production artifact" relation.

A musical work or a work of drama may be realized in particular performances, i.e. in particular events at a particular theater or concert hall on a particular evening. Similarly, a film work may be realized in particular showings, i.e. in a particular event in a particular movie theater, namely, the changing patterns of light on a particular screen (plus the sounds that go with them). Works of architecture may be realized in concrete buildings, works of poetry in concrete recitations, works of painting in concrete pieces of canvas with paint on them.

Note that the term "realization" is used here in a somewhat technical sense. Realizations, in this sense, must not be confused with *productions* or *interpretations*. A production of a work of drama is itself an abstract object that can be realized in many particular performances; the same holds for a musical interpretation.[10]

On the other hand, realizations must not be confused with notations and production artifacts. A notation of a musical work is a score. A notation of a work of drama is a script that contains the dialogues plus the author's stage directions. Notations of works of architecture are blueprints. Blueprints and sketches may also serve as notations for works of painting, sculpture, and furniture, and even for works of photography and film.

Intuitively, the difference between realizations and notations may be explained as follows. A realization of a work is the goal and final point of a creative process. A notation, by contrast, is only a *means* to this end.

The function of notations is (at least) a twofold one. First, a notation may save the work from falling into oblivion. This is particularly important in the case of works whose performances are extremely ephemeral, like works of music (and it was, of course, much more important before the invention of sound-recording technologies). Second, a notation is a convenient (and often indispensable) device in all those cases where the production of a realization is not in the hands of the author herself, or at least not in the hands of the author alone (as, for instance, with works of symphonic music, most film works, and most works of architecture). That is, the notation is not only a means for the *conservation* of the work; it also provides a set of *instructions for the production of a realization*. Some philosophers think that there is a third function of notations, namely to establish *identity conditions* for works. It is argued that by writing a score, for instance, a composer lays down the limits within which a performance may count as a performance of this particular work.[11]

Let me now turn to what I call "production artifacts." A production artifact is a thing that may serve as a means for the production of a realization. For instance, a sound-carrier (e.g. a CD, a vinyl record) may be a production artifact of a work of music. A strip of celluloid may be a production artifact of a film work. A negative or a computer chip can be a production artifact of a work of photography.

The main difference between notations and production artifacts is the following: The author of a notation makes use of a *notation system*, i.e. a system of symbols, a sort of language, which is based on conventions. Thus, notations require competent "readers," i.e. persons who are acquainted with the conventions that constitute the notation system. Not so with production artifacts. The patterns on a CD are not symbols within a notation system, and thus they do not require competent readers. All they require is the right technical device (i.e. a CD player).

Thus far I was talking about the works' relationships to material objects of various kinds. Let me now turn to mental objects. There are two classes of mental objects that are obviously relevant in the present context: first, the mental goings-on in the authors' minds while they create their works; and second, the mental goings-on in the minds of the recipients.

Again, copyright law is right in claiming that authors are *creators* of their works in a literal sense, i.e. they *bring works into existence*. Works can be created in various ways: by writing down words, by playing notes on a piano, by drawing a blueprint, by putting paint on a canvas, etc. But there is an essential ingredient to every process of creation, namely a certain kind of *mental* process, which can be described, in a very general way, as a process of *making decisions*.[12] This process consists essentially in *determining the essential features of realizations* of the work. Thus a composer determines which properties a particular musical performance must have in order to count as a performance of her piece, an architect determines which properties a particular building must have in order to count as a realization of his work of architecture, etc. Metaphorically speaking, the author determines the boundaries of the class of possible realizations of her work.

In certain circles, especially among postmodernist literary theorists, it became fashionable to proclaim the "death of the author." Though the exact meaning of this slogan is often left unclear, there is at least one interpretation that is clearly in conflict with my account of what authors are doing. According to this interpretation, works are not created by authors but rather by recipients (if there is such a thing as work creation at all); there are either no works at all or, at least, no works prior to processes of reception. A poet may put down words on paper, but in doing so she does not create a literary work. She just produces an artifact that might serve as a starting point for a creative process within another person's mind. The author has no particular authority; she cannot declare certain interpretations of "her" work as correct or as incorrect. For the idea of the correctness of an interpretation presupposes a sort of correspondence between the interpretation and something to be interpreted, namely a *work*; and it is exactly the existence of such an object of interpretation that is denied by those who claim that "the author is dead."

It is obvious that such a denial flies in the face of discourse about works and practices within art and sciences, including not the least discourse and practices concerning copyright. For if there were no authors and no works, copyright would just lose its subject.

The doctrine of the death of the author is a bizarre exaggeration of the role of the recipients, at the expense of the authors. This doctrine must be rejected; but this should not lead one to overlook the relevance of the mental goings-on within the recipients' minds. Earlier I characterized a realization of a work as the goal and final point of the creative process. A creative process starts with certain mental goings-on within the author's mind. At least in standard cases, the aim of authors is to induce particular mental processes within other minds. Normally, the production of certain patterns of ink is not an end in itself. Nor is the point of putting words on paper just to have somebody else use the written symbols as instructions for the production of sounds—or, more exactly, the resulting sound event is not an end in itself either. Rather, it is a means to induce a particular series of thoughts, images, feelings, moods, etc. within the audience.

This point can be generalized to all kinds of creative processes, especially in the arts. The composer's final goal is not just to produce musical sounds but to bring it about that people (perhaps among other things) have certain kinds of musical experiences. The painter's final goal is to bring it about that people (perhaps among other things) have certain visual experiences. This aspect of artistic creation and artists' intentions seems to be particularly salient for much of what is categorized as so-called "conceptual art," especially for those works which are intended to trigger reflections on the nature of art and related concepts (such as the concepts of artist, creativity, etc.). Thus, the mental processes within the recipients' minds may be considered to be realizations of works in their own right.

2.3 What is the internal structure of works?

Most works are highly complex objects, i.e. we may distinguish many different parts in them. Remember: I am not talking about material things (like concrete book copies, musical performances, etc.), but about *abstract* objects. What kind of parts can we distinguish within abstract objects? In what follows, I am going to sketch a very general and rough outline of a mereology of works.[13]

An adequate mereology of works has to be multidimensional, i.e. one must distinguish more than one way to "cut" a work into pieces—or, less metaphorically, the analysis of works has to proceed along various different lines. I distinguish five "mereological dimensions":

i. The vertical dimension: "quasi-temporal" and "quasi-spatial parts." A quasi-temporal part of a symphony is one of its movements; a quasi-temporal part of a drama is one of its scenes. A quasi-spatial part of a work of architecture may be a roof or the front of a building. A quasi-temporal part of a novel may be one of its chapters.

ii. The horizontal dimension: "strata." A stratum of a string quartet is the cello part, another the viola part, etc. Strata of a film work may be the pattern of changing light on the screen, the pattern of sounds, the dialogues, the music.

iii. The dimension of inclusion: "logical parts." The skins of an onion may serve as a model of this mereological dimension. Imagine, for example, a character of a play (let's call it "Mr. C") that is characterized as follows: "Man in a dark, long coat who is standing in front of the house on the other side of the street and staring at the illuminated window on the second floor." Suppose that this is all the author tells us about this character. Now, we may distinguish parts of Mr. C in the following way:

male human being wearing a dark coat
male human being wearing a coat
male human being
human being
being

We may say that there is a character, *male human being wearing a dark coat*, and this is a proper logical part of Mr. C. It is determined as being human, being male, and wearing a dark coat—and that's it. The character *male human being* is also a proper logical part of Mr. C, and in addition it is a proper logical part of the character *male human being wearing a dark coat*. And so forth. Just as the skins of an onion include each other, characters include less and less determinate characters as their logical parts.

I used a character in order to illustrate the concept of a logical part since it provided both a natural and easily describable example. However, not only characters but all kinds of constituents of works may be divided into logical parts. In general, the various mereological dimensions are not mutually exclusive, i.e. one and the same thing may be a part in more than one mereological dimension. A *musical motif*, for instance, may be a logical part of one or more quasi-temporal parts of one or more strata of a musical work: it is part of a stratum, insofar as it is part of one (or more) of several voices of a work; it is a quasi-temporal part, insofar as it occupies, say, just two bars of a musical work that consists of hundreds of bars; it is a logical part, insofar as one and the same motif may occur in variations, for instance in different instrumentations and different keys.

iv. The dimension of constitutive types: mental processes, material objects, and imaginary worlds. What has been said so far suggests that a work is a type of mental process. Authors determine the essential features of a series of mental goings-on, and in doing so they create types of mental goings-on, and these types may be realized (and, in cases of successes, are realized) in the audience's minds.

This is true; but it is not the whole story. Unfortunately, a beautiful, sensitive mind is not yet a great artist. The ability to see the world through an artist's eyes, to have deep impressions under circumstances that strike us normal people as trivial and boring is perhaps a necessary condition for being an artist, but it is surely not a sufficient one. Thus, the determination of essential features of mental goings-on cannot be everything there is to the creation of a work, at least not in the arts. A work of art must be more than just a type of mental goings-on.

What is more to the creation of an artwork (and probably to the creation of many works in other fields as well) *is the determination of essential features of some material object* that may function as a means to trigger the intended mental processes in the audience. Therefore, many works consist both of a mental object type and a material object type.[14] Thus, the poet has to determine a structure of words, the composer a structure of sounds, the painter a structure of colors and lines, etc.

Some works, however, have still another constituent, which may be called the *work's world*. In the case of fictional works this is an *imaginary world*. The work's world may be realized, in principle, in "real" states of affairs (unless the world's work is contradictory, but in this case at least parts of the world may be realized).

v. The dimension of the "content": stories, plots, and characters. Within what is often called the "content" of a work, one may distinguish at least three different kinds of objects, which I call characters, plots, and stories. I use the term "character" here in a somewhat technical sense, such that it denotes not only fictitious persons and animals, but also things and places. Thus, characters in this wide sense are not only Hamlet and Winnie the Pooh, but also the uncanny house from Hitchcock's *Psycho* and the town of Springfield from the series *The Simpsons*.

The "plot" of a work is the totality of events that is described or depicted within it. What I call "the story" is *the totality of events depicted or described in a certain way*. That is, the story is determined not by the plot alone, but also by a particular *narrative structure*. The narrative structure involves, among other things, the *perspective* from which something is described or depicted as well as the *temporal structure*: For instance, is an event (or a series of events) described from the perspective of one (or more) of the characters or from the perspective of an omniscient narrator? Is the succession of events described in the order of their taking place, or perhaps in the opposite order, or by means of flashbacks?

2.4 The work concept in ontology and in copyright law

What, in general, is the relation between the ontological work concept and the work concept of copyright? The most important difference is that copyright law demands a certain amount of "individuality" or "creativity"—a condition that is not involved in the ontological work concept. From an ontological point of view, a work may be completely mundane. What makes something a work *per se* is just that it is the product of particular intentions and decisions. It is not required that the respective intentions and decisions have any minimal degree of individuality, creativity or originality (in the sense of novelty, uniqueness, and inventiveness) or that they somehow mirror the author's personality or innermost essence.

Exactly this requirement of individuality, creativity, or originality is part and parcel of the work concept of many (though not all) copyright laws.[15] It is not hard to understand the intention behind this restriction: A copyright law that would protect everything that is a work in the ontological sense seemingly threatens to open the door to a flood of legal actions that are intuitively unjustified but hard to dismiss (or only after lengthy investigations that bring to light that the plaintiff's alleged "creations" themselves in fact resulted from plagiarism), and such a development is potentially harmful to the society as a whole, since it might lead to drastic limitations of creativity.

On the other hand, the requirement of individuality seems to be the Achilles' heel of copyright law. For the notion of individuality (or any analogous notion that might be used with the same intention in this context) is notoriously vague and unclear.[16]

3. Copyright and contemporary art—two problems

3.1 Appropriation art

"Appropriation art" means, roughly, "[t]he reuse of pre-existing material in new contexts," especially in the visual arts.[17] A similar phenomenon outside the field of the visual arts is the practice of "sampling" in music. Parody may be considered to be a special case of appropriation art.

Very diverse things are subsumed under the heading "appropriation art." At one end of the scale, one may find collages that make use of one line of a pre-existing poem or a small piece of a pre-existing drawing or photograph but consist in the largest part of new (or at least unprotected) material and/or are highly original in the combination of the various pre-given elements. At the other end one finds exact replicas of pre-existing works which are taken *as a whole* out of their original contexts and put in new ones, without any substantial change in their visual appearance. Examples of the latter are Sherrie Levine's replicas of photographs by Walker Evans, which she entitled "After Walker Evans" and exhibited under her name.

It is obvious that appropriation artists may come into conflict with copyright law, even though copyright law includes "fair-use exemptions," which allow, for the sake of artistic creativity and freedom of artistic expression, the use of protected works within certain limits.

From an ontological point of view, the most radical cases are the most interesting ones. They pose the question of whether one may create a new work by mere "recontextualization." Is, for instance, the photo series "After Walker Evans" a new work created by Sherrie Levine, or did Levine just produce another realization of Evans's work?

In the light of the ontology of works delineated above, the answer is clear: Levine indeed created a new work. Although her work has the material object type (or, more exactly, the biggest part of the material object type) in common with the work of Walker Evans, it contains a new type of mental process. Levine probably intended the recipients to reflect on notions such as authorship and originality and to become aware of the fact that a picture may have different meanings in different contexts. Most probably, none of these intentions are constitutive for Evans's work.

It must be noted, however, that the difference between the two works is not just a matter of Levine's private intentions. Rather, she managed to communicate these intentions in a quite successful way, partly by means of the new title ("After Walker Evans"), partly by the particular setting in which the pictures were exhibited (namely an exhibition which was announced as an exhibition of works by Levine). In this particular case, title and exhibition context are clearly parts of the work as a whole; thus, even the material type element of the work is not exactly identical to the original one.

Therefore, Levine's work is clearly distinct from Evans's, despite the similarity of its constitutive material object types. Furthermore, Levine's work is a work of *art*, since she pursues her specific communicative intentions (to make the recipient reflect on or to question the notions of authorship, originality, context, meaning, etc.) by aesthetic means. However, neither the claim that Levine created a new work nor the claim that it is a work of art is supposed to be a value judgment. Both the concept of a work and the concept of art are understood here in a (value) neutral sense. There are surprising, witty, highly original works of art as well as boring and epigonic ones, and I leave it to the experts in the field to judge where in this range Levine's work falls.

3.2 Popular music: Shall sound be protected by copyright?

It has been argued that copyright rests on too narrow a concept of a musical work (with a strong bias in favor of Western "classical" music) and as a consequence of this it is "systematically misrepresenting and under-privileging popular music as a field of creative practice" (Barron 2006: 25). In particular, the criticism goes, contemporary legislation tends to consider only those musical features to be parts of the work which can be notated in a traditional score, notably melody and harmony. Consequently, other musical features, which are of high importance, especially in popular music, are completely ignored, or at least their importance is grossly underestimated. This holds in particular for the musical quality of *sound*.

Barron cites the following case (ibid.). Several members of the pop band Spandau Ballet claimed co-authorship for the songs recorded under the band's name, but Gary Kemp, the band's principal songwriter, claimed exclusive authorship for them. Kemp was indeed the author of the basic melodic and harmonic scaffolding of the songs in question. He had played them to the other band members on the guitar; afterwards, however, the band developed the final sound of the songs (as they were recorded) through a collective process that lasted for several months. The final versions sounded remarkably different from the original versions played on the guitar. Also, the final versions included elements such as a saxophone solo, which were not parts of Kemp's original guitar outline.

The judge decided in favor of Kemp; the action of the other band members was dismissed. The judge explained his decision by arguing that the work that Kemp had played on the guitar *is identical with* the work that was finally recorded (in spite of the obvious differences). He argued that the original version was just *another performance of the same work* as the final version and that copyright needs to make a strict distinction between a work and its performances.

From an ontological point of view, the judge was right, in principle, to point out that a work is to be strictly distinguished from its performances (i.e. realizations) and that different performances of one and the same work may sound different. Nevertheless, he applied a too "thin" concept of a musical work in this particular case. In the mereological terms introduced above, one might say that the judge considered only one or two strata of the piece in question (the stratum of the main voice and, perhaps, the stratum of the guitar) but ignored the others (the stratum of the saxophone, for instance, probably also the drums stratum, the bass stratum, perhaps a stratum of background singing, etc.). Furthermore, most probably, the judge ignored a variety of logical parts of the work in question. To use the onion metaphor, what the judge considers as "the musical work" under discussion are just the "innermost skins" of the onion (the melody, in the first place); the "outer skins," such as instrumentation, "mix," etc.—that is, all those features that are responsible for the peculiar sound of a piece—are not acknowledged as parts of the work.

However, this privileged treatment of a limited number of elements of the work at the expense of others seems arbitrary, both from an ontological and from an aesthetic point of view. The ontology of musical works does not provide any reason to exclude *a priori* certain features of music from those that constitute a musical work's identity. The judge's remark that a work is to be distinguished from its performances may be, though true, off the point in this context. If those features that constitute the sound of a piece are taken to belong to the work, one may still distinguish the work from its performances. For one and the same work (*including* the sound) may be multiply performed—just as one and the same melody may be multiply performed.

Neither is the exclusion of sound features justified from an *aesthetic* point of view. For those features of a piece that constitute its sound may be just as (or even more) relevant for its aesthetic properties, aesthetic value, and the arousal of aesthetic feelings in the recipients as the bare melody.

Furthermore, it is unjustified, both from an ontological and from an aesthetic point of view, to privilege those features of music that can be easily laid down in the notation system of classical music (i.e. in a "score" in the traditional sense). Some philosophers—erroneously—think that the score (and the score only) determines a musical work's identity (see Goodman 1976). According to this view, all and only those features that are explicitly laid down in the score belong to the work, and, consequently, a particular musical event P is a performance of a particular work W if, and only if, P exemplifies all of the features laid down in W's score.

The notation system of classical music has been designed for the needs of composers in a particular musical tradition, which does not imply that it is appropriate for all kinds of music, in particular for contemporary popular music. Even in the context of classical music, however, scores function more like *recipes* than like *definitions*, i.e. they are (usually) not designed to provide strict identity criteria for musical works but rather to provide instructions for the production of performances, according to the composer's intentions. Just as recipes usually presuppose a certain amount of pre-given knowledge, experience, and sensitivity on the part of the cooks, scores usually presuppose a certain amount of pre-given knowledge, experience, and sensitivity on the part of the performing musicians. It is unlikely that the author of a recipe explicitly and unambiguously lays down all the features that are relevant for the work's identity. For instance, normally recipes do not tell us how much salt we should add to the meal; nevertheless, we know that the meal should not be oversalted (and we know quite well when a meal is oversalted), even if the recipe does not explicitly say so. In the same vein, it is unlikely that a composer lays down in a score all those features that she decided to be essential for the work's identity. Rather, the composer relies to a certain extent on the knowledge, experience, and sensitivity of the performing musicians that should enable them to grasp even those of her intentions that are not explicitly and unambiguously laid down in the score.

Just as the languages in which recipes are written are very limited means to express what a certain meal should *taste* like, the classical notation system for music is quite a limited means to express what a certain piece of music should *sound* like. This holds for classical music and probably even more for contemporary avant-garde and popular music. Thus, even if the songwriter of Spandau Ballet had produced a score of the original version of his song (which he seemingly did not), this would not have provided sufficient reason to deny the co-authorship of his fellow band members.

4. Concluding remarks

After having shown that copyright is of high relevance for those philosophers who deal with questions concerning the ontology of works, I have sketched an ontological theory of works and their parts which does justice to the data provided by copyright. Finally, I have applied this ontology to cases that play a certain role in contemporary debates about copyright.

I did not intend to show, however, that difficult copyright cases can or should be resolved by philosophers. This is not the task of ontology (nor the task of aesthetics). Thus, the above discussion of the Spandau Ballet case was not intended to show that the judge's decision was wrong; it was only intended to show that some of the ontological assumptions underlying the decision are questionable. This does not rule out that the decision might be sensible for other reasons.

Copyright issues are often a matter of a difficult weighing up of diverse (and sometimes opposite) interests (for instance, the interest of authors to receive a fair reward for their efforts and achievements and the interest of other authors or society as a whole that material and ideas can be used freely for creative purposes). It is the task of lawyers to find solutions that do justice in the best possible way to all the diverse interests involved in these issues.[18]

On the other hand, lawyers who are dealing with copyright make a lot of more or less explicit ontological assumptions, which arise partly from common sense, partly from proven legal practice. Though I am confident that there is a considerable amount of wisdom both in common sense and in proven legal practice, I am also convinced that a conceptually rigorous systematic investigation may sometimes be a corrective to common sense, and perhaps even legal practice may benefit from it.[19]

Notes

1 Darren Hick stresses the first of these relations when he, after having observed that it is important to understand what the object of copyright is, states that copyright law seems "to provide the foundation necessary to build such an understanding" (Hick 2011: 186).

2 A *locus classicus* for such a position is Carnap 1950. For more recent work in a similar spirit, see Jackson 1980 and Horgan 1986.

3 This and all other English translations in this paper are mine.

4 For a characterization of the basic ontological assumptions in various copyright laws in quite similar terms see also Hick 2011: 186–7. Hick is well acquainted with U.S. and British copyright law, but he also mentions the German and the Italian. It seems that, as far as the above-mentioned ontological presuppositions are concerned, there are no essential differences between these diverse national laws.

5 In German "*geistige Gegenstände*." For the problem of the interpretation of "intellectual" (or "*geistig*") in this context, see below.

6 For a detailed and well-argued platonist ontology of artworks see Wolterstorff 1980. But there are also philosophers who advocate ontologies that are quite consistent with copyright law. In this field, pioneering work has been done by the Polish phenomenologist Roman Ingarden. See in particular Ingarden 1931 and Ingarden 1962. For more recent work in a similar spirit see Reicher 2003, Wilson 2010, and Hick 2011.

7 Austrian "Urheberrechtsgesetz" §§1–9; similarly in Swiss copyright. See Swiss "Bundesgesetz über das Urheberrecht und verwandte Schutzrechte" Art.2. Differently German "Urheberrechtsgesetz" §2.

8 Here and in what follows, I use the term "author" in a wide sense, such that it denotes any subject who is the creator of a work of whatever kind.

9 A type ontology for objects of copyright is advocated also in Wilson 2010, Hick 2011, and (arguably) in Wreen 2010 (although it seems that Wreen wishes to avoid a definite commitment). However, type ontologies may differ in relevant details. For instance, while I take a type's identity to be constituted exclusively by its internal properties, Hick considers the context of creation as well to be constitutive for a type's identity (see Hick 2011: 190–2). Accordingly, in contrast to Hick (cf. ibid.: 192–5), I would claim that there need not be a causal connection between two instances of one and the same type.

10 Thus, a musical interpretation is to be considered, from an ontological point of view, as a work in its own right, though as one that is based upon the original work.

11 I shall discuss this claim in Section III below.

12 Hick describes the process of type creation, a bit more specifically, in terms of selection and arrangement of pre-existing elements (Hick 2011: 188–9).

13 A mereology of works is *prima facie* relevant for copyright issues, since copyright protects not only works as a whole but also their parts.

14 The distinction between mental object types and material object types as distinct constituents of works may be taken as an ontological interpretation of the much-discussed *idea-expression dichotomy* in copyright. I agree with Hick that the concept of an "idea," as opposed to "expression," should be interpreted as the "content of a thought, feeling, emotion, desire, and/or other cognitive state or event" (Hick 2009: 402). I take the "idea" (content) to be a mental object type (i.e.

an abstract object that may be realized in mental states and/or processes) and the "expression" to be a material object type (i.e. an abstract object that may be realized in material objects). By contrast, Hick suggests that "ideas are a class of entities *internal* to the mind, while expressions are a class of entities *external* to the mind" (ibid.). Despite this difference, Hick comes very close to my view when he states that "[a]lternatively, we might say that ideas are entities instantiated in the mind, while expressions are entities instantiated outside the mind" (Hick 2009: 407 n.21).

15 In German, Austrian, and Swiss *Urheberrecht*, the requirement of originality is deeply entrenched and is referred to as *Schöpfungshöhe*, *Gestaltungshöhe*, or *Werkhöhe*. For a detailed comparative treatment of this requirement (in the context of notions of authorship in various copyright laws), see Ginsburg 2003.

16 For a thorough criticism of this notion see Kummer 1968.

17 Okpaluba 2002. Regarding the concept of appropriation art, its theoretical roots, its history, and some prominent copyright lawsuits in which appropriation artists were involved, see also Hick 2013.

18 That ontological investigations alone are not sufficient for resolving the normative problems involved in copyright issues is also (in a detailed and convincing way) argued in Wilson 2010. There, the author also outlines how normative considerations using concepts from political and social philosophy might provide a theoretical grounding of legislative regulations of intellectual property.

19 Preliminary versions of this chapter have been presented at the conferences *Copyright & Art. Aesthetical, Legal, Ontological, and Political Issues* and *Towards an Ethics of Copying* at the Zentrum für interdisziplinäre Forschung (ZiF) in Bielefeld in 2005 and 2015 respectively. An earlier version has been published in Czech language in Zahrádka 2011. I thank the participants of the above-mentioned conferences as well as Reinold Schmücker and Darren Hick for numerous helpful comments, and the latter also for drawing my attention to a number of recent publications.

References

Barron, A. (2006), "Copyright Law's Musical Work," *Social & Legal Studies* 15 (1): 101–27.

Carnap, R. (1950), "Empiricism, Semantics, and Ontology," *Revue Internationale de Philosophie* 4: 20–40.

Ginsburg, J. C. (2003), "The Concept of Authorship in Comparative Copyright Law" (January 10, 2003). Columbia Law School, Pub. Law Research Paper No. 03-51. Available online: SSRN: http://ssrn.com/abstract=368481 or http://dx.doi.org/10.2139/ssrn.368481

Goodman, N. (1976), *Languages of Art. An Approach to a Theory of Symbols*, Indianapolis, IN: Hackett.

Hick, D. H. (2009), "Making Sense of the Copyrightability of Plots: A Case Study in the Ontology of Art," *Journal of Aesthetics and Art Criticism* 67: 399–407.

Hick, D. H. (2011), "Toward an Ontology of Authored Works," *British Journal of Aesthetics* 51: 185–99.

Hick, D. H. (2013), "Appropriation and Transformation," *Fordham Intellectual Property, Media & Entertainment Law Journal* 23: 1155–95.

Horgan, T. (1986), "Psychologism, Semantics, and Ontology," *Noûs* 20: 21–31.

Ingarden, R. (1931), *Das literarische Kunstwerk*, Tübingen: Niemeyer. [English translation: *The Literary Work of Art*, Evanston, IL: Northwestern University Press, 1973.]

Ingarden, R. (1962), *Untersuchungen zur Ontologie der Kunst. Musikwerk—Bild—Architektur—Film*, Tübingen: Niemeyer. [English translation: *Ontology of the Work of Art. The Musical Work, The Picture, The Architectural Work, The Film*, Athens, OH: Ohio University Press, 1989.]

Jackson, F. (1980), "Ontological Commitment and Paraphrase," *Philosophy* 55: 303–15.

Kummer, M. (1968), *Das urheberrechtlich schützbare Werk*, Bern: Stämpfli.

Okpaluba, J. (2002), "Appropriation Art: Fair Use or Foul?" in D. McClean and K. Schubert (eds), *Dear Images. Art, Copyright and Culture*, 197–224, London: Ridinghouse.

Reicher, M. E. (2003), "Eine Typenontologie der Kunst," in R. Schmücker (ed.), *Identität und Existenz. Studien zur Ontologie der Kunst*, 189–99, Paderborn: mentis (4th edn, 2014).

Troller, A. (1967), "Urheberrecht und Ontologie," *UFITA* 50: 385–419.

Wilson, J. (2010), "Ontology and the Regulation of Intellectual Property," *Monist* 93 (3): 450–63.

Wolterstorff, N. (1980), *Works and Worlds of Art*, Oxford: Clarendon.

Wreen, M. (2010), "The Ontology of Intellectual Property," *Monist* 93 (3): 433–49.

Zahrádka, P. (ed.) (2011), *Estetika na prelomu milénia*, Brno: Barrister & Principal.

5

What Is an Artifact Copy? A Quadrinomial Definition

Amrei Bahr

The domain of copies contains a variety of heterogeneous phenomena, including paper copies produced by Xerox machines, digital copies of software or music, counterfeit commercial products, and many art forgeries,[1] but also the results of molecular cloning as well as the duplicates of cells that evolve in natural replication. This chapter aims at defining one such phenomenon, namely the kind of copies that I call "artifact copies," i.e. copies that are both copies of artifacts and artifacts themselves (and, what is more, are not genuine instances—I will get back to this point in due course). The production of artifact copies poses a number of problems, most of which are of an ethical or legal kind—e.g. when the demands of authors clash with the interests of recipients or users. My study of artifact copies is intended to provide both a conceptual and an ontological basis for discussing ethical and legal questions of copying that are connected with copyright issues.[2]

The chapter is in two parts. First, I propose a definition of the concept ARTIFACT[3] and add some remarks on aspects of the ontology of artifacts that are relevant for my project: I note that the class of artifacts comprises both concrete and abstract entities. Abstract artifacts are considered to be intentionally created *design plans* which are the bases for creating concrete artifacts. Concrete artifacts that genuinely instantiate these design plans are referred to as *exemplars*. In the second part, I give a definition of ARTIFACT COPY. From my previous remarks on artifact ontology, I derive a distinction between four different kinds of artifact copies: a) exemplar copies, i.e. concrete artifact copies of concrete artifacts; b) design plan based copies, i.e. concrete artifact copies based on abstract artifacts; c) design plan copies, i.e. abstract artifact copies of abstract artifacts; and d) exemplar based copies, i.e. abstract artifact copies based on concrete artifacts.[4] I first give a definition of EXEMPLAR COPY by arguing that an object *y* has to meet four individually necessary and jointly sufficient conditions to justifiably be called an exemplar copy of *x*, namely the *intention condition*, the *similarity condition*, the *causal connection condition*, and the *authorized creator exclusion condition*. The definition of EXEMPLAR COPY then serves as a basis for my definitions of the other three kinds of artifact copies that I develop subsequently. Taken together, the four definitions form a complete[5] definition of the concept ARTIFACT COPY.

Before I pursue my definitional enterprises, some preliminary remarks are required. First, I will briefly say something about the scope of this chapter. Initially, I would like to guard against a possible linguistic misunderstanding that is linked to a peculiarity of the English word "copy"—in contrast to, for example, the German word "*Kopie*": If the English word "copy" is used, sometimes a genuine instance (i.e. an exemplar of something) is meant, as in the sentence: "I have sent you a copy of my recent book." This sense of "copy" will not be relevant in this chapter. Instead, I will focus on the sense of "copy" that becomes vivid in the sentence: "The painting in my office is not the real *Mona Lisa*; it is only a copy." But not all of the phenomena that are covered by the word "copy" in this sense fall into the scope of this chapter. Rather, it is limited to what I call "artifact copies," i.e. entities that are both artifacts themselves and copies of artifacts. Outside the scope of this chapter lie three other phenomena: first, artificial copies of natural entities (e.g. the results of molecular cloning); secondly, natural copies of artificial entities (e.g. the naturally evolving replica of an artificial cell); and thirdly, natural copies of natural entities (e.g. the copy of a gene that is the result of genetic transcription). The reason for bracketing out artificial copies of natural entities, as well as natural copies of natural and of artificial entities, lies in my aim to provide a basis for ethical and legal discussions that involve authors' rights: I aim at preparing the ground for answering questions more or less directly related to issues of copyright. Human-induced copying processes that copy natural entities—for instance, the cloning of natural cells—are unrelated to these issues, because, in these cases, no one has copyrights in the copied items. And if the copying processes are naturally evolving ones where the copied item is artificial and so, perhaps, subject to copyright, these too are irrelevant in terms of copyright issues, as here, no one can be blamed for copyright infringement. In the case of naturally evolving copying processes where the copied item is a natural entity, we neither have a copyrighted (or even copyrightable) entity, nor someone to blame for potential copyright infringement.

An additional reason for leaving out natural copies of both natural and artificial entities lies in the nature of these copies. Naturally evolving copies differ in an important aspect from artificial copies: the latter require intentions, whereas the former don't (which is analogous to the difference between biological functions and artifact functions as I conceive of these). We do indeed have one and the same term here, but it is linked to two different concepts, and therefore it would not make much sense to try to reconcile both concepts in one definition. With these preliminary considerations in mind, let us now turn to our first subject, namely artifacts.

1. My definition of ARTIFACT

In what follows, I will briefly give a definition of the concept ARTIFACT, and then add a few remarks on my understanding of the ontology of artifacts as required to grasp the distinction between the four different kinds of artifact copies that I want to suggest later on. I will not give a detailed argument to prove the adequacy of my definition of ARTIFACT, as artifacts are not themselves—or at least not explicitly—the main focus of this chapter. My definition is as follows:

> *(A)* *x* is an artifact if and only if *x* is an intentionally created, finished object,[6] whereas the intention is directed towards both the creation of the object and some, but not all of its features.[7]

The class of artifacts comprises both concrete and abstract entities: the table that I am now sitting at to write this chapter is an example of a concrete artifact—but there are also abstract artifacts,[8] namely artifact types, e.g. the type this particular table is an instance of. This type is both an abstract entity and an artifact, as it is an intentionally created *design plan* for tables which was the basis for constructing this particular table. Whereas the creation of concrete artifacts requires physical work, the creation of abstract artifacts demands intellectual work. The relationship between abstract and concrete artifacts can be put as follows: for every concrete artifact, there is a design plan, whereas a design plan can either have one artifact as its instance, which for example is the case with most paintings, or it can have several artifacts as its instances, which holds for most technical artifacts, or it can even have no instance at all, which is the case when a design plan is never or has not yet been implemented (for whatever reason).[9] The design plans themselves can be written or laid down in the form of sketches, scores, descriptions, prototypes, models and so on. But we should be aware that these are only concrete manifestations of the design plan that are supposed to *visualize* the abstract plan—they are not identical to the plan. The concrete manifestations of the design plan are mostly to be distinguished from the concrete exemplars which are genuine realizations of the plan. For example, my table is an *exemplar* of its design plan, while there is presumably also a sketch or something similar that was the basis of creating tables of that particular kind, which is the *manifestation* of the plan. Most of the time, an item is either a manifestation of a design plan or a realization of it (or neither of the two). An important exception which will be of central concern later on are prototypes: they are both manifestations of the design plan and genuine realizations of it. In what follows, I will call the genuine concrete artifacts that instantiate a design plan *exemplars*[10] and the abstract artifacts *design plans*. With these remarks about artifacts and their ontology in mind, let us now turn to the second question that has to be answered: How are we to define the concept ARTIFACT COPY?

2. My definition of ARTIFACT COPY

As I have stated above, artifacts can be either concrete or abstract entities. Therefore, copies of artifacts can either have concrete artifacts or abstract artifacts as their reference. Furthermore, the copies themselves can also be either concrete or abstract. This results in four different variants of artifact copies in total—hence, I will propose four different definitions. The first one concerns copies of concrete artifacts that are themselves concrete entities; I call these "exemplar copies." The second takes into account copies that are themselves concrete and trace back to abstract artifacts, i.e. design plans; those I call "design plan based copies." The third definition I will propose applies to copies that are copies of abstract artifacts and are also themselves abstract; I call them "design plan copies." Finally, the fourth kind of phenomena I will define are copies of concrete artifacts that are themselves abstract; these I call "exemplar based copies." The adjunct "based" always indicates an ontological transition: in the case of design plan based copies, it indicates the transition from the abstract design plan to the concrete copy; in the case of exemplar based copies, the transition goes from the concrete exemplar to the abstract copy. In contrast, design plan copies are abstract copies of an abstract design plan, and exemplar copies are concrete copies of a concrete exemplar. I start with defining the concept EXEMPLAR COPY, taking this as a basis for my definitions of the other three concepts in question.

2.1 Exemplar copies: Concrete artifact copies of concrete artifacts

In which cases are we justified in saying that *y* is an exemplar copy of an exemplar *x*? I will argue that an object *y* has to meet four necessary conditions to justifiably be called an exemplar copy of *x*: the *intention condition*, the *similarity condition*, the *causal connection condition*, and the *authorized creator exclusion condition*. I will discuss each of these conditions, showing for each why it should be considered necessary. As the intention condition and the similarity condition are linked to each other, and fairly uncontroversial, I will start with these.

2.1.1 The similarity condition and the intention condition

If an artifact *y* is a copy of *x*, it resembles *x*—I believe this much is uncontroversial.[11] The claim finds expression in what I call the *similarity condition*. A first tentative version of this condition can be stated as follows:

If *y* is an exemplar copy of an exemplar *x*, then
(SC) *y* is similar to *x*.

As we will see in a moment, this formulation of the similarity condition is in dire need of revision—but before we get to that, we will first have to look at the intention condition. Similarity is an essential aspect of all copies; it plays an important role not only in terms of actual similarity, but also as regards the *intentions* that are central for copying. When it comes to artifacts in general, intentions play a crucial role, as we have seen in the definition of the concept ARTIFACT: in order for an object *x* to be an artifact, there has to be a certain intention that has guided its creation. I have limited the scope of this chapter to copies that are themselves artifacts. These copies share this important artifact characteristic: they owe both their existence and some of their features to the intentions of their creator. In the case of exemplar copies, at least some of these features are strongly determined by an intention referring to the exemplars of which they are copies, insofar as the copies are—at least in part—intended to be similar to the exemplars. This idea is captured in the intention condition *(IC)*:

If *y* is an exemplar copy of an exemplar *x*, then
(IC) *y* was produced with the intention to create something that is similar to *x*.

We now have two conditions for exemplar copy status, the similarity condition and the intention condition. But the similarity condition in its tentative formulation *(SC)* is too weak: the things surrounding us resemble each other in myriad ways.[12] When it comes to artifacts, a couple of the intended similarities are crucial, and not every artifact *y* with an intended similarity to an exemplar *x* should be considered a copy of *x*. Imagine that a conscious agent, Vince, wants to make a copy of his hair dryer. And indeed, he manages to make an object that resembles his hair dryer, namely regarding its weight: both the hair dryer and the object Vince has created weigh 987 grams. However, the object Vince has created is not a hair dryer itself, but a block of wood, and besides the weight, it bears little resemblance at all to the hair dryer. In this case, both the intention condition and the similarity condition are fulfilled: the hair dryer and the block of wood are similar, and Vince has intended this similarity. Nevertheless, it would be absurd to claim that the block of wood is a copy of the hair dryer. Even if we concede to Vince that he has tried very hard to create a copy of his hair dryer, I believe that we would not say that he has succeeded in doing so. Intended similarities between artifacts can occur in several respects and also in several amounts, but not all respects and not all amounts are sufficient or even relevant for something to be a copy.[13] Therefore, we should reformulate the similarity condition and add two restrictions, one regarding the *degree* of similarity and one regarding the *respect* of similarity required for a copy.

Regarding the degree of similarity, I suggest that we delegate the decision whether or not something is a copy to those who are experts in the domain the respective exemplar belongs to: If an expert of the relevant sort, who is familiar with an exemplar, *x*, is confronted with an alleged copy, *y*, and recognizes *y* as strongly resembling *x*, then the amount of similarity necessary for *y*'s being a copy of *x* is in place. This has an obvious advantage: someone who is not familiar with a domain of artifacts might not recognize similarities that are obvious for an expert. An expert in jazz music will have knowledge about the standard forms of jazz music, about motifs, and about the rules for playing a solo, for example. Of course, this knowledge will qualify the expert to discover similarities that someone having no knowledge about jazz music might never find.[14]

But of course, we might nevertheless be confronted with cases in which an artifact strongly reminds an expert of a certain exemplar, but where we would not want to call the artifact a copy of that exemplar. Consider the following example: I take a photo of the sculpture *Kirschensäule* by Thomas Schütte which is situated in Münster. Of course, this photo would strongly remind an expert in contemporary art of the statue itself—but still, we would not want to call my photo a copy of the statue. This leads us to the *respect* of similarity needed for a copy. To account for the proper respect of similarity, I suggest the following specification: for *y* to be an exemplar copy of a certain exemplar *x*, *y* must belong to the same material and perceptual kind as *x*. If the respective exemplar is audible, the copy has to be audible as well; if the exemplar is, as in the *Kirschensäule* case, a three-dimensional visibly receivable object, the copy has to be of the same kind. Taken together, these thoughts on the required amount and respect of similarity lead to the following, modified version of the similarity condition:

> If *y* is an exemplar copy of an exemplar *x*, then
> *(SC′)* *y* is similar to *x* to the degree that experts confronted with *y* recognize *y* as strongly resembling *x*, and in the respect that *x* and *y* belong to the same material and perceptual kind.

I believe that it is indisputable that neither *(IC)*, nor *(SC′)* is individually sufficient for exemplar copy status: *(IC)* can be fulfilled although someone fails to create a copy due to incompetence or other reasons; *(SC′)* can be fulfilled if we have two genuine exemplars realizing one and the same design plan, although obviously, neither is a copy of the other, as in the case of two Technics 1210 MKII turntables, both being instances of the same type. But are *(IC)* and *(SC′)* taken together sufficient for exemplar copy status? I do not believe this is the case, either—an important condition is still missing: the *causal connection condition.*

2.1.2 The causal connection condition

Let me illustrate the necessity of the causal connection condition with the help of a thought experiment. From October 2007 until April 2008, the Colombian sculptor Doris Salcedo exhibited her installation *Shibboleth* in the main entrance hall of Tate Modern in London. The installation consisted of a long crack in the concrete floor of the entrance hall—the crack had a length of 167 metres. Now let us imagine that someone, Howard, intends to make a copy of that installation. Howard starts with building a hall similar to the entrance hall of Tate Modern, with a similar concrete floor. He then tries out several tools to create a crack similar to the *Shibboleth* crack, but does not succeed: the floor does not even show the faintest sign of his efforts. But, all of a sudden, Howard's hall is shaken by an earthquake that tears the hall floor—with a crack, as it happens, that looks significantly similar to the *Shibboleth* crack. If *(IC)* and *(SC′)* taken together were sufficient, we would have to say that we are now faced with a copy of *Shibboleth*: Howard had the intention to create something similar to *Shibboleth*, therefore the *intention condition* is fulfilled. Also, the crack in Howard's hall and the *Shibboleth* crack are significantly similar in the strong sense required by *(SC′)*: art experts will surely be reminded of *Shibboleth* when confronted with the crack in Howard's hall, and both are undoubtedly of the same material and perceptual kind.

But the similarity between the crack in Howard's hall and the *Shibboleth* crack is not a result of Howard's intention to create something similar to the *Shibboleth* crack, but is rather due to two lucky coincidences: the coincidence that there was an earthquake that created a crack, and the even more unlikely coincidence that the crack turned out to resemble the *Shibboleth* crack. Howard's intention was not causally effective for this result.[15] Should we say that Howard has created a copy in this case? It seems to me that we should not say so: although we do have an intention and a similarity of the required sort, these two aspects are not connected in the way that is necessary for copies. Therefore, a third condition is required, namely the causal connection condition:

> If *y* is an exemplar copy of an exemplar *x*, then
> *(CCC)* among the causes of the similarity that *y* bears to *x* is that the creator of *y* has intended *y*'s similarity to *x*.

Notably, *(CCC)* presupposes that both *(IC)* and *(SC′)* are fulfilled.

Are *(IC)*, *(SC′)*, and *(CCC)* taken together sufficient for exemplar copy status? If they were, every genuine exemplar of an artifact type that was created using a prototype that manifests the design plan would also be a copy: here, we also have a similarity in the required way, the intention to create something similar, and the similarity is due to this intention. But we would not want to call all realizations that are derived from a prototype and whose creator was at the time of creation authorized[16] to create genuine exemplars that realize this design plan "copies" in the sense set out earlier in this chapter, as these are clearly not mere copies, but paradigmatic cases of genuine exemplars. Therefore, we have to add the *authorized creator exclusion condition*.

2.1.3 The authorized creator exclusion condition

The *authorized creator exclusion condition* reads as follows:

> If *y* is an exemplar copy of an exemplar *x*, then
> *(ACEC)* the creator of *y* is not an authorized exemplar creator at the time of the creation of *y* or whose creation of *y* is outside the bounds of such authorized creation.

Taken together, the four conditions form the definition of EXEMPLAR COPY *(EC)*:

(EC) *y* is an **exemplar copy** of an exemplar *x* if and only if

(IC) *y* was produced with the intention to create something that is similar to *x*; and

(SC') *y* is similar to *x* to the degree that experts confronted with *y* recognize *y* as strongly resembling *x*, and in the respect that *x* and *y* belong to the same material and perceptual kind; and

(CCC) among the causes of the similarity that *y* bears to *x* is that the creator of *y* has intended *y*'s similarity to *x*; and

(ACEC) the creator of *y* is not an authorized exemplar creator at the time of the creation of *y* or whose creation of *y* is outside the bounds of such authorized creation.

Let us now turn to the three remaining kinds of artifact copies—their definitions can be derived from the one just given.

2.2 Design plan based copies: Concrete artifact copies based on abstract artifacts

Design plan based copies are concrete artifact copies that are based on a certain design plan. If I want to create a concrete copy of Apple's iPhone 6, two possibilities are at hand: either I take an exemplar of the iPhone 6 and copy it—this would be an exemplar copy, being subject to the aforementioned definition; or I use a manifestation of Apple's respective design plan to create a copy of the iPhone 6, howsoever I may get hold of that. The result would then be a design plan based copy. To get to the definition of the concept DESIGN PLAN BASED COPY, we will have to slightly modify some of the conditions we have developed in the course of defining the concept EXEMPLAR COPY. First, the relevant intention in the case of design plan based copies differs slightly from the relevant intention in the case of exemplar copies: To create a design plan based copy *y*, one has to intend the realization of the design plan *x*—which will result in a certain similarity that also differs from the one required for exemplar copies: instead of being similar to *x* itself, *y* must be similar to genuine exemplars realizing *x*—to a degree and in a respect analogous to *(IC)* in the definition of exemplar copies. The causal connection condition *(CCC)* here connects the similarity to genuine exemplars realizing *x* with the intention to realize *x*. Finally, condition *(ACEC)* stays without any modification: authorized exemplar creators of course produce genuine exemplars instead of copies also in this case. Hence, we get the following definition of DESIGN PLAN BASED COPY:

(DPBC) *y* is a **design plan based copy** based on a design plan *x* if and only if

(IC′) *y* was produced with the intention to realize *x*; and

(SC″) *y* is similar to genuine exemplars realizing *x* to the degree that experts confronted with *y* recognize *y* as strongly resembling genuine exemplars realizing *x*, and in the respect that *y* and genuine exemplars realizing *x* belong to the same material and perceptual kind; and

(CCC′) among the causes of the similarity that *y* bears to genuine exemplars realizing *x* is that the creator of *y* has intended *y* to realize *x*; and

(ACEC) the creator of *y* is not an authorized exemplar creator at the time of the creation of *y* or whose creation of *y* is outside the bounds of such authorized creation.

2.3 Design plan copies: Abstract artifact copies of abstract artifacts

Next in line are copies that differ from the two copies already considered insofar as they are themselves not concrete, but instead abstract entities—namely, design plan copies, abstract artifact copies of an abstract artifact, i.e. a design plan.[17] We do not have any ontological transition here, therefore the condition *(IC)* remains the same: to create a design plan copy *y* of a design plan *x*, one has to create something similar to *x*. *(SC)* should be slightly modified; whether or not the amount of similarity is sufficient for *x* to be a design plan copy of a design plan *y* is decided by experts who, confronted with a *manifestation* of *y*, should recognize the manifestation as strongly resembling manifestations of *x*. Additionally, as abstract entities are not directly perceptually accessible, we need to remove this part of the condition; we can replace it by referring to the fact that both the copy and its reference must be abstract entities. *(CCC)* does not require modification—here, the similarity also needs to be causally dependent on the intentions of the creator of *y*. Lastly, the fourth condition, *(ACEC)*, must be modified: in the case of design plan copies, we do not deal with exemplars at all, but only with design plans—both the copy and its reference are design plans. Therefore, it does not matter whether or not the creator of *y* is an authorized exemplar creator; instead, it is of importance if the creator of *y* is also the creator *x* or the current rights holder of *x*. If she is, I believe that we would not call her creation a copy, but rather a further development of *x*. This yields the following definition of the concept DESIGN PLAN COPY:

(DPC) *y* is a **design plan copy** of a design plan *x* if and only if

(IC) *y* was produced with the intention to create something that is similar to *x*; and

(SC''') *y* is similar to *x* to the degree that experts confronted with manifestations of *y* recognize these as strongly resembling manifestations of *x*, and in the respect that *x* and *y* are both abstract entities; and

(CCC'') among the causes of the similarity that *y* bears to *x* is that the creator of *y* has intended *y*'s similarity to *x*; and

(ACEC') the creator of *y* is not the creator of *x* and/or the rights holder of *x* at the time of the creation of *y*.

2.4 Exemplar based copies: Abstract artifact copies based on concrete artifacts

The final kind of artifact copies still remaining to be considered are exemplar based copies. Here, we have an ontological transition again: whereas the basis of the copy is a concrete exemplar, the copy itself is an abstract design plan. *(IC)* has to be modified, as what is relevant here is that realizations of the copy *y* are similar to the exemplar *x*. Also, *(SC)* requires reformulation to factor over the similarity between *y*'s realizations and *x*. *(CCC)*, too, needs to be put differently as the relevant intention must be causally linked to the similarity between *y*'s realizations and *x*. And, last but not least, we need to alter condition *(ACEC)* to rule out cases in which the creator of the design plan *y* is also the creator (or rights holder) of the design plan that *x* is a realization of. In these cases, as in the case of design plan copies, we would rather say that *y* is a further development of the design plan that *x* has realized, rather than being a copy. The following definition of the concept EXEMPLAR BASED COPY is the result of these considerations:

(EBC) *y* is an **exemplar based copy** of an exemplar *x* if and only if

(IC'') *y* was produced with the intention to create something whose realizations are similar to *x*; and

(SC'''') *y*'s realizations are similar to *x* to the degree that experts confronted with realizations of *y* recognize these as strongly resembling *x*, and in the respect that *x* and realizations of *y* belong to the same kind of perceptually accessible things; and

(CCC''') among the cause of the similarity that *y*'s realizations bear to *x* is that the creator of *y* has intended *y* to be created in a way that *y*'s realizations are similar to *x*; and

(ACEC'') the creator of *y* is not the creator of the design plan *x* is a

realization of and/or the right holder of the design plan that *x* is a realization of at the time of the creation of *y*.

Taken together, the four definitions of the four different kinds of artifact copies constitute the following definition of ARTIFACT COPY:

(AC) *y* is an artifact copy if and only if
y is an **exemplar copy** of an exemplar *x*, that is

- *(IC)* *y* was produced with the intention to create something that is similar to *x*; and
- *(SC′)* *y* is similar to *x* to the degree that experts confronted with *y* recognize *y* as strongly resembling *x*, and in the respect that *x* and *y* belong to the same material and perceptual kind; and
- *(CCC)* among the causes of the similarity that *y* bears to *x*is that the creator of *y* has intended *y*'s similarity to *x*; and
- *(ACEC)* the creator of *y* is not an authorized exemplar creator at the time of the creation of *y* or whose creation of *y* is outside the bounds of such authorized creation

or

y is a **design plan based copy** based on a design plan *x*, that is

- *(IC′)* *y* was produced with the intention to realize *x*; and
- *(SC″)* *y* is similar to genuine exemplars realizing *x* to the degree that experts confronted with *y* recognize *y* as strongly resembling genuine exemplars realizing *x*, and in the respect that *y* and genuine exemplars realizing *x* belong to the same material and perceptual kind; and
- *(CCC′)* among the causes of the similarity that *y* bears to genuine exemplars realizing *x* is that the creator of *y* has intended *y* to realize *x*; and
- *(ACEC)* the creator of *y* is not an authorized exemplar creator at the time of the creation of *y* or whose creation of *y* is outside the bounds of such authorized creation

or

y is a **design plan copy** of a design plan *x*, that is

- *(IC)* *y* was produced with the intention to create something that is similar to *x*; and
- *(SC‴)* *y* is similar to *x* to the degree that experts confronted with manifestations of *y* recognize these as strongly resembling

manifestations of *x*, and in the respect that *x* and *y* are both abstract entities; and

(CCC'') among the causes of the similarity that *y* bears to *x* is that the creator of *y* has intended *y*'s similarity to *x*; and

(ACEC') the creator of *y* is not the creator of *x* and/or the rights holder of *x* at the time of the creation of *y*

or

y is an **exemplar based copy** of an exemplar *x*, that is

(IC'') *y* was produced with the intention to create something whose realizations are similar to *x*; and

(SC'''') *y*'s realizations are similar to *x* to the degree that experts confronted with realizations of *y* recognize these as strongly resembling *x*, and in the respect that *x* and realizations of *y* belong to the same kind of perceptually accessible things; and

(CCC''') among the cause of the similarity that *y*'s realizations bear to *x* is that the creator of *y* has intended *y* to be created in a way that *y*'s realizations are similar to *x*; and

(ACEC'') the creator of *y* is not the creator of the design plan *x* is a realization of and/or the right holder of the design plan that *x* is a realization of at the time of the creation of *y*.

3. Conclusion

Due to quickly emerging new possibilities to produce copies (and further development of established copying techniques), copying a wide range of items is today possible for almost everyone, often being an easy, inexpensive practice resulting in incredibly exact copies hardly distinguishable from the items they are copies of, even by experts. As a result of this development, ethical and legal questions raised by copying increase in number and become more and more pressing. At the same time, current copyright regulations are often stretched to their limits: it is frequently far from clear how to trade off against each other the interests of the different parties involved, including authors, copyists, users, and recipients, but also commercial enterprises and states, especially if one also tries to do justice to the moral intuitions shared by many of the participating actors, which often clash with the legal status quo. This calls for ethical considerations of the questions raised, as well as for scrutiny and most probably for a subsequent revision of copyright laws. Convincing ethical and legal regulations of copying activities likewise require both conceptual and ontological groundwork: it is not only a prerequisite to state which objects copyright (at least potentially) encompasses; it is also essential to get insight regarding the features of these objects. The objects in question include both copyrightable objects[18] and objects that potentially infringe copyrights. In this chapter, I have placed a special focus on the latter ones—hence, the definitions just stated are supposed to clarify which results of copying practices we can distinguish and how these can be characterized. I hope to thereby contribute to providing a first basis for discussing and evaluating practices of copying from both an ethical and a legal point of view.[19]

Notes

1 It is a common view in aesthetics that not all forgeries are copies—the most popular example of a forgery that is not taken to be a copy is the famous *Supper at Emmaus*, painted by van Meegeren and often regarded as imitating the style of the old master Vermeer.

2 Although ethical and legal problems regarding the practice of copying are mostly connected with copyright and questions regarding intellectual property, this does not hold for all of these problems. Consider, for instance, cases of copying weapons of mass destruction that do not primarily raise problems regarding intellectual property: these cases would nonetheless obviously raise problems of an ethical and a legal kind.

3 In what follows, I will indicate that I talk about concepts by using capital letters (e.g. ARTIFACT); this indication convention is used by Sainsbury and Tye (2012), among others. When I talk about words, I will indicate this by using quotation marks (e.g. "artifact").

4 This quadrinomial typology is a further development of the binominal typology I have presented earlier (cf. Bahr 2013), and which only includes exemplar copies and design plan based copies. I have extended my typology because it recently occurred to me that the binominal distinction fails to capture the class of artifact copies in a reasonable manner, as it takes into consideration only copies which are themselves concrete entities, and neglects copies with an abstract nature.

5 I take the definition to be complete in the sense that it includes every entity that can reasonably be subsumed under the concept ARTIFACT COPY in the context of ethical and legal debates.

6 As Laycock points out, "the concept of *object* – that concept of object which is of fundamental interest within philosophy – is among the most general concepts (or

categories) which we possess" (Laycock 2014: 1). The concept I have in mind here is indeed a very general one: As suggested by Künne and Tugendhat, I take the category of objects to include all (possible) referents of singular terms (cf. Künne 2007: 43; Tugendhat 1982: 23).

7 There has been some effort in philosophy to present a convincing definition of what it is to be an artifact. The four necessary conditions most prominently offered include: 1) the (most often only implicitly stated) requirement that the entities in question are objects; 2) the requirement that these entities are in a certain sense made or created; 3) the requirement that this creation is guided by the intentions of an author; and finally 4) the requirement that the things in question have functions. Definitions including these four conditions can be found in, among others, Hilpinen 1993, Dipert 1995, Baker 2007, and Jansen 2013. My definition entails the first three conditions, but I have excluded the fourth one here as a more general requirement that makes reference to *features* instead of functions seems to me to be much more reasonable: I do not see why in principle there should be no non-functional artifacts. In a similar vein, Reicher (2013) proposes only the first three requirements, but not the fourth one—also, she argues for adding the claim that artifacts should be finished products, which I have supplemented my definition with as I too consider it to be of importance to demarcate artifacts from soon-to-be artifacts which are still in their preliminary stages.

8 The thesis that there are such things as created abstract objects certainly is a highly controversial one among philosophers: according to the standard philosophical account of abstract objects, these objects exist outside time (and space)—they are eternal objects, i.e. there is no point in time when they begin (or cease) to exist, and hence, they cannot be created (see e.g. Kivy 1987). On additional grounds, van Inwagen denies that abstract objects can be subject to creation by making reference to the claims that creation is a causal relation and that abstract objects cannot enter into causal relations as they are causally inefficacious (van Inwagen 2009). Nevertheless, I take it to be utterly commonsensical that there are a number of objects—e.g. musical and literary works—which are both created and abstract, multiply instantiable objects, and to me it is far from obvious why ontology should depart from that commonsensical view. For a defense of embracing this commonsensical view in ontology see Thomasson 1999, Sainsbury 2009, and Reicher 2013.

9 Note that there is no chronology implied here: An author can produce a design plan either by solely thinking it up—a procedure which we could call "armchair invention"—or by directly working with the material that will in the end form the basis for the first material realization of the respective design plan.

10 Of course, exemplars do not necessarily have to be well-formed—malformed exemplars likewise count as exemplars (provided that they display a sufficient number of the features required by the design plan).

11 The aspect of similarity appears to me to be an essential aspect of what it is to be a copy; this point of view is also put forward by Carrara and Soavi (2010: 424). In contrast, in a reply to Kennick, Goodman expresses doubts in the necessity (and also the sufficiency) of a (specific) similarity as holding between an original and its copy (Goodman 1986: 291). He argues against the relevance of similarity by making reference to Holbein's portraits: "Two Holbein portraits of the same person, or indeed all Holbein's painted portraits, may be more like each other than a pencil copy of any of them by another artist is like the original" (ibid.). This may well be true—nevertheless, it only illustrates that genuine portraits painted by Holbein might exhibit greater similarity to each other than one Holbein portrait and its copy by another artist, but not that similarity is altogether irrelevant for copies. If the pencil sketch of the other artist did not resemble the respective Holbein portrait (that is, to a certain amount or in a certain respect), we would most probably not call the sketch a copy of the portrait. Nevertheless, Goodman's doubts regarding the relevance of similarity for the question of what it is to be a copy (which most probably result from his doubts regarding the concept of similarity in general, cf. Goodman 1972) point to an additional problem which I will address in due course, namely the problem of how to specify the amount or respect in which similarity has to hold between a copy and the copied object.

12 As Putnam (1981) famously notes, stating that two things are similar is most often both incredibly uninformative and irrelevant, as "[e]verything is similar to everything else in infinitely many respects" (64).

13 It might seem that we could drop the problematic talk of similarities here and instead refer to design plans by saying that in order for an object *y* to be an exemplar copy of an exemplar *x*, it should instantiate the same design plan as the exemplar does. But this would gloss over the fact that the class of exemplar copies comprises also copies of exemplars that are indeed sufficiently similar to the respective exemplars, but nevertheless do not display a sufficient amount of features required in the design plan the exemplars instantiate.

14 By making reference to experts, I want to include not only those copies laypersons would easily recognize as such, as their similarity to their copied object is apparent, but also copies which display similarities of a rather subtle kind that can be spotted by experts only.

15 To be more precise, Howard's intention was not causally relevant for the *Shibboleth*-shaped crack in the concrete floor—his intentions did of course feature prominently in creating the preconditions for something to emerge which is similar to *Shibboleth*, by designing both the hall and the floor based on the design of the Tate Modern hall and floor.

16 Note that apart from exemplars authorized as such, we have to distinguish authorized and unauthorized copies: For one thing, the author of a design plan is

able to decide on potential exemplar authors. This ability consists in being able to determine who can create *genuine* instances of the design plan and under what conditions. For another thing, an additional ability that solely the author of a design plan has is the ability to determine who is legitimated to create copies with the intention to distribute them: who—if anyone—is allowed to create copies that are intended to be distributed is at the author's discretion.

17 Design plan copies potentially pose serious problems for industrial development. Many enterprises suffer from industrial espionage, where third parties illegally get hold of design plans for the products these enterprises have developed. An example is the turntable company, *clearaudio electronic*, from Bavaria: their plan for an innovative turntable was stolen by hackers and the plan was then implemented by a Chinese company (cf. Kappel and Wolf 2013).

18 In the course of this chapter, I have dealt with copyrightable objects by most generally referring to them as *abstract artifacts*, i.e. design plans. For an account doing more justice to these objects by dedicating an illuminating, in-depth discussion to them, see Hick 2011.

19 I thank Wybo Houkes for helpful comments on a previous version of this chapter.

References

Bahr, A. (2013), "Was heißt 'ein Artefakt illegitim kopieren'? Grundlagen einer artefaktbezogenen Ethik des Kopierens," *Deutsche Zeitschrift für Philosophie* 61 (2): 283–99.

Baker, L. R. (2007), *The Metaphysics of Everyday Life. An Essay in Practical Realism*, Cambridge: Cambridge University Press.

Carrara, M. and M. Soavi (2010), "Copies, Replicas, and Counterfeits of Artworks and Artifacts," *The Monist* 93 (3): 414–32.

Dipert, R. (1995), "Some Issues in the Theory of Artifacts: Defining 'Artifact' and Related Notions," *The Monist* 78 (2): 119–35.

Goodman, N. (1972), "Seven Strictures on Similarity," in *Problems and Projects*, 437–446, New York: Bobbs-Merrill.

Goodman, N. (1986), "A Note on Copies," *Journal of Aesthetics and Art Criticism* 44 (3): 291–2.

Hick, D. H. (2011), "Toward an Ontology of Authored Works," *British Journal of Aesthetics* 51 (2): 185–99.

Hilpinen, R. (1993), "Authors and Artifacts," *Proceedings of the Aristotelian Society* 93: 155–78.

Inwagen, P. van (2009), "God and other Uncreated Things," in K. Timpe and E. Stump (eds), *Metaphysics and God: Essays in Honor of Eleonore Stump*, 3–20, London: Routledge.

Jansen, L. (2013), "Artifact Kinds Need Not Be Kinds of Artifacts," in C. Svennerlind, J. Almäng, and R. Ingthorsson (eds), *Johanssonian Investigations. Essays in Honour of Ingvar Johansson on His Seventieth Birthday*, 317–37, Heusenstamm: ontos.

Kappel, B. and S. Wolf (2013), "Tatort Internet: Deutscher Mittelstand im Visier von Industriespionen," *Blickpunkt Wirtschaft*, January 2013. Available online: http://www.ihk-trier.de/p/Tatort_Internet_Deutscher_Mittelstand_im_Visier_von_Industriespionen-13-12518.html

Kivy, P. (1987), "Platonism in Music: Another Kind of Defense," *American Philosophical Quarterly* 24 (3): 245–52.

Künne, W. (2007), *Abstrakte Gegenstände. Semantik und Ontologie*, Frankfurt a.M.: Klostermann.

Laycock, H. (2014), "Object," in E. N. Zalta (ed.), *The Stanford Encyclopedia of Philosophy*. Available online: http://plato.stanford.edu/archives/win2014/entries/object/

Putnam, H. (1981), *Reason, Truth and History*, Cambridge: Cambridge University Press.

Reicher, M. E. (2013), "Wie aus Gedanken Dinge werden. Eine Philosophie der Artefakte," *Deutsche Zeitschrift für Philosophie* 61 (2): 219–32.

Sainsbury, R. M. (2009), *Fiction and Fictionalism*, London: Routledge.

Sainsbury, R. M. and M. Tye (2012), *Seven Puzzles of Thought: And How to Solve Them: An Originalist Theory of Concepts*, Oxford: Oxford University Press.

Thomasson, A. (1999), *Fiction and Metaphysics*, Cambridge: Cambridge University Press.

Tugendhat, E. (1982), *Traditional and Analytical Philosophy: Lectures on the Philosophy of Language*, Cambridge: Cambridge University Press.

6

Are Counterfeits Copies?

Massimiliano Carrara

1. Introduction

The aim of this paper is to analyze some possible answers to the question:

> (Q1) Which elements analytically compose the meaning of "counterfeit" (or "fake" or "forgery")?

I proceed in the following way. First, I observe that three elements analytically compose "counterfeit" (or "fake" or "forgery"[1]): (1) to be a copy of (2) an original object (3) falsely presented as the original. I argue that (1) "copy" is not analytic of "counterfeit," and (2) that "being original" should be taken distinct from "being authentic." Finally, I argue that if (3) "presented as the original" concerns—among the other things—*use conditions* of an artifact then something immediately goes wrong. Consequently, definitions of "counterfeit" using (1)–(3) run into difficulties. I consider, in particular, three of them:

> (D1) *x* is a counterfeit of *y* if and only if *x* is a supposed copy of *y* and *y* is an original object.
>
> Ryle

> (D2) x is a counterfeit of *y* if and only if *x* is an object falsely purporting to have the history of production required for the original *y*.
>
> Goodman

> (D3) An object *x* is a forged *XY*—where "*X*" is a term for a source of issue and "*Y*" a term for a kind of thing forged—if and only if it is not a genuine *XY*, but it is (re)presented as a genuine *XY* with the intention to deceive.
>
> Wreen

and I argue that all the three proposals, (D1)–(D3), are defective. In the last part of the paper I suggest two different definitions of "counterfeit", (D4) and (D5):

(D4) *x* is a counterfeit if and only if *x* has been intentionally produced to convince someone else that *x* has a *historical property* that it actually does not possess.

(D5) *x* is a counterfeit if and only if *x* is a *replica* produced either without an allowed procedure of replication or without an allowed network of commercialization or exchange.

I evaluate some pros and cons of (D4) and (D5).

2. Some linguistic data and (D1)

To begin our analysis, let us start with some dictionaries—for example, *Webster's English Dictionary*. Here, the entry for "counterfeit" is: "a copy that is presented as the original"; more in detail, in *Webster's Third New International Dictionary*, a counterfeit is "something that is made to look like an exact copy of something else in order to trick people." *Prima facie*, "counterfeit" is defined in terms of "copy." Moreover, observe that "counterfeit" and "copy" are usually related lexical entries. Take, for example, an Italian dictionary, the *Vocabolario della lingua italiana* of the Istituto dell'Enciclopedia Italiana, where "copia" is defined as "disegno, pittura, scultura che riproduce più o meno fedelmente, a scopo di *contraffazione* o anche per esercitazione, per la diffusione, un'opera d'arte originale."[2] Or, again, take a French dictionary—*Le grand Robert de la Langue Française* —stating that a "copie" is a "reproduction (d'une oeuvre d'art original)," and "copie" is linked to "contre-façon, imitation, reproduction." Counterfeits and copies share the property of being reproductions of an original object.

From the data above, one can observe that a counterfeit is a specific kind of copy, a copy falsely presented as the original, and that counterfeits and copies share the property of being reproductions of an original object.

Starting from language data, three elements compose—in the sense of being analytic of—"counterfeit":

(a) a copy of (b) an original object (c) falsely presented as (one of) the original(s).

Indeed, a counterfeit is (a) a copy of (b) an original object, and is (c) falsely presented as an original object. A forged Rockwell is a copy of an original Rockwell falsely presented as the original one at the Norman Rockwell Museum. On the basis of (a)–(c) a first characterization of "counterfeit" can be given in the following way:

(D1) *x* is a counterfeit of *y* (*x* is a fake *y*) if and only if *x* is a supposed copy of *y* and *y* is an original object.

From an ontological point of view—given the above characterization—a counterfeit *x* is ontologically dependent upon an original *y*:

> (OD) *x* is ontologically dependent upon *y* if and only if *x* cannot exist unless *y* does.

In terms of counterfeits and original objects (OD) can be rephrased in the following way:

> (OD′) A counterfeit *x* is ontologically dependent upon an original object *y* if and only if a counterfeit *x* cannot exist unless some original object *y* does.

In (OD′), then, a certain counterfeit banknote cannot exist if the *real* banknote does not. Following this train of thought, a counterfeit banknote, say, may appear to be a lowly object. There is a straightforward intuitive sense—based on the above notion of dependence (OD′)—in which a counterfeit banknote is a lesser thing than a banknote, professing to be something it is not.

(D1) (and (OD′)) comes from some remarks on counterfeits by Gilbert Ryle. In *Dilemmas* (1954) he observes that:

> A country which had no coinage would offer no scope to counterfeiters. There would be nothing for them to manufacture or pass counterfeits of. They could, if they wished, manufacture and give away decorated discs of brass or lead, which the public might be pleased to get. But these would not be false coins. *There can be false coins only where there are coins made of the proper materials by the proper authorities.*
>
> Ryle 1954: 94, my italics

Ryle's train of thought is the following one: a false coin (or a forged painting) is a copy of an original one. It could not be the case that all coins (or paintings) were counterfeit, for if there is no original coin (or painting), then there is nothing of which the counterfeit coins (or paintings) are copies or forgeries. So, there must be at least one coin (or painting) of which counterfeits should be copies: the original one. (D1) immediately follows.

Unfortunately, (D1)—and consequently (OD′) too—meets some difficulties. The most important one is that there can be counterfeits that *are not copies* (see Wreen 2002). Take, for example, the notorious case of the forged Vermeer made by van Meegeren. As laid out in most art history texts, Han van Meegeren was a Dutch painter considered one of the most ingenious art forgers of the twentieth century. He decided to prove his talent by forging paintings of some of the most famous artists, including Johannes Vermeer. He replicated so well the style and colors of the artist that the best critics and experts of the time regarded his paintings as genuine Vermeers. The forged Vermeers made by van Meegeren, however, *were not copies* of some original painting made by Veermer.

A counterexample to (D1): there are some *counterfeits* that are not *copies*. As a consequence, (OD′) does not hold; indeed a counterfeit *x* can exist even if there is not an original object *y*.

One can reply distinguishing two kinds of forgeries: *referential* and *inventive forgeries* (on this see Levinson 1980; different but similar distinctions can be found in Reicher 2011 and Schmücker 2011). A referential forgery is one in which some particular, original, pre-existing work has been copied. An inventive forgery, meanwhile, is a work attributed to the target artist, but which is not a copy of any pre-existing work by that artist. As Darren Hudson Hick observes: "Even in straightforward cases of inventive forgeries, however, there is usually copying taking place, though here it is typically an artist's style that is copied, and not any particular preexisting work" (Hick 2010: 1047). Certainly, van Meegeren's early forgeries copied Vermeer's style without copying any existing works by the master. However, van Meegeren's later forgeries in no way stylistically resemble *any* of Vermeer's paintings.[3] These later works are certainly counterfeits, but nevertheless not copies—neither of Vermeer's works, nor his style.

Consider the following thought experiment taken from Michael Wreen (2002: 148): Imagine a world without paintings. There are only sculptors. One day an artist, Ginus, announces to the world that the next day he would reveal a new form of art: painting. After a brief description of the nature of this new form of art, he isolates himself in his studio to produce the first painting but, during his solitude in the studio, he is kidnapped and a second artist, Minus, produces the first painting, making sure to attribute it to Ginus. The new painting exists and it is a counterfeit. If you accept this thought experiment, the thesis that it is possible for all paintings to be counterfeits turns out to be true.

But, observe that even if you do not accept Wreen's thought experiment, you could deny (D1) simply by admitting just a conceptual dependence of the notion of *counterfeit* on that of *original object. Conceptual dependence* does not per se entail *ontological dependence. Inventive forgeries* can be read as instances of conceptual dependence. But the fact that for a certain concept you need a second one does not entail that for the existence of a certain object (the counterfeit) you need the existence of a second one (the original object). And the van Meegeren example is a case of conceptual dependence that is not ontological dependence.

3. Counterfeits but not copies—on (D2)

Consider, then, a revision of "counterfeit" not involving in its definition that of "copy" (a). The following one, owed to Nelson Goodman, connects (b) *an original object* with something (c) *falsely presented as the original* without mentioning *copies*. A counterfeit is defined as:

> An object falsely purporting to have the history of production requisite for the (or an) original work of art.
>
> Goodman 1968: 122

With the expression "history of production," Goodman refers to any production element, giving *originality* or *authenticity*. The artist who produces a work, for example, is part of its history of production. How a certain object is produced—for example, the materials used to produce it or the techniques employed—are likewise parts of the history of production of the object.

According to Goodman's analysis, the new, alternative definition of "counterfeit" is:

> (D2) x is a counterfeit of y if and only if x is an object falsely purporting to have the history of production required for the original y,

where y is a case of *autographic art*. According to Goodman: "A work of art is autographic if and only if the distinction between original and forgery of it is significant; or better, if and only if even the most exact duplication of it does not thereby count as genuine" (Goodman 1968: 113). A painting, such as Rembrandt's *Self-Portrait*, is a specific item historically connected to the artist who produced it—in our example, Rembrandt. Following Goodman, it is a case of autographic art. Music, dance, theater, literature, and architecture are all instances of *allographic arts*. On Goodman's view, what makes something a genuine instance of a given poem, dance, or sonata is altogether independent of its history of production.[4]

What about (D2)? Is it a better definition of "counterfeit" than (D1)? In (D2) there is no *explicit* reference to *counterfeits* as *copies* of an original object and the expression "history of production" has been used to refer to any property relevant to its origin. One problem for (D2) is that it has not been specified *which* properties of an object's origin are relevant such that one can assign the *status* of *counterfeit* to the object falsely purporting to have the history of production required for the original. Observe that there are cases where it is perfectly correct to distinguish between an *original object* and a *counterfeit* without taking into account the historical properties of the object relevant to its origin. Consider, for example, Alexander the Great's armor: it will truly be Alexander's armor if it belonged to him or if it was used by him. But, it is not necessary that it had been beaten by a certain specific blacksmith with a particular alloy steel.

However, knowing the origin conditions of the armor—the properties relevant for its origin—may be of some help for assessing its *authenticity*: indeed, if we know that some armor, which someone argues was Alexander's armor, dates to a period later than Alexander's death, it is easy to infer that it is not the *original object*.

One first and general reply to this objection is that, in the above example, we have used an artifact, Alexander's armor, and not an artwork, say, a painting. And the defender of (D2) might contend that originality *via history of production* is here confined to artworks. Finally, following Goodman and taking for granted the distinction between *autographic* and *allographic* art, one can also observe that we talk of counterfeits or forgeries only in the *autographic* art case. And Alexander the Great's armor is not an autographic art case: it is not an artwork at all!

To this complex reply one can offer two, perhaps partial, rebuttals. First, take Duchamp's urinal called *Fountain*. Assume it is an artwork. Which of the historical properties relevant to its origin are also relevant to considering it *the Fountain*? In general, how does its *origin* guarantee its *authenticity*? How, for example, is the fact that it was produced with a specific, robust and durable material, with certain dimensions, etc., relevant to determining whether it is *the Fountain* or a counterfeit? In short: how, in this specific case, do the *original properties* of the urinal guarantee its *authenticity*?

Compare Duchamp's *Fountain* and Alexander's armor. We say that it will truly be Alexander's armor if it belonged to him or if it was used by him, so one can argue that in the Duchamp case it will be *the* true urinal called *Fountain* if it was the urinal that Duchamp called *Fountain*. Just as in the case of Alexander's armor it is unnecessary that the armor was beaten by a certain specific blacksmith with a particular alloy steel for its *authenticity*, so for Duchamp's urinal it is unnecessary that it was produced with a specific, robust, and durable material, with certain specific dimensions, etc., for *its authenticity*. In other words, the material or processes involved in bringing that material thing into being seem altogether irrelevant to its authenticity. As such, in these cases as least, it is perfectly correct to distinguish between an *original object* and a *counterfeit* without taking into account the *historical properties* of the object.

To the above rebuttal one can reply that Duchamp's *Fountain* is not a case of *autographic* art: Duchamp authorized a first reproduction of *Fountain* in 1950;

then, two more individual pieces followed in 1953 and 1963, and finally eight replicas in 1964. So there are different replicas (or copies) of the *same* artwork. I do not want here to delve deeply into the distinction between *autographic* and *allographic* art.[5] It is not the aim of the paper. Observe, however, that it is standard to say that in *allographic* art—different from *autographic* art—one exploits some notational system of symbols. On the basis of the following characterization, it has been argued that:

> An artwork is autographic *if and only if* the work is not notationally identifiable.

Instead, in *allographic* art, such as a poem, the expression of an artwork through a notational system gives *necessary and sufficient conditions for its identity*: a copy of a poem possessing all the aesthetically constitutive properties of the original one is nothing less than the original itself. On this characterization, it seems to me that there is room to argue that Duchamp's *Fountain* is a case of *autographic* art: indeed, *it is not* notationally identifiable.

A second, general rebuttal to the reply is the following one. One can simply wonder, why do we have to confine our analysis of counterfeits to artworks as in (D2) if artifacts in general are regularly forged: certainly, there are lots of counterfeit coins and counterfeit bags. Departing from Goodman's characterization of *counterfeits* or *forgeries*, it can be easily observed that, in order to define "counterfeit" or "forgery," one should consider also counterfeit coins and counterfeit bags as examples of counterfeits. There is no obvious or apparent *prima facie* reason to suggest some understanding of "counterfeit" peculiar to artworks. One might suggest, though (perhaps following Goodman), that this is where the notions of "counterfeit" and "forgery" begin to come apart: there are counterfeit bags, but would we call a fake bag a "forgery"?[6]

I would suggest that there are two morals to draw from the above rebuttals. First, we can distinguish between two properties: *being original* and *being authentic*. In order to devise a theory of counterfeits we need to take *authenticity* as the one that is truly complementary to *being counterfeit*. A counterfeit is such because it is not the authentic object someone claims it is. A second moral is that a general characterization of counterfeits should not be confined to artworks: as argued, artifacts in general can be forged. (D2) defines a notion of "counterfeit" just for artworks, but we need a definition for artifacts in general.

The second difficulty of (D2) is that it cannot be used to distinguish *counterfeits* from *simple errors of attribution* or *mistakes*: it can happen that a critic *mistakenly* attributes a Giotto fresco painting to Cimabue. It is commonsensical to suggest that the critic is *simply* making a mistake, and it seems wrong to suggest that she is creating a counterfeit or counterfeiting. However, following (D2), one can argue that the Cimabue's painting is an object *falsely purporting* (via our critic) *to have the history of production required for the original Giotto fresco painting*; so, following (D2) it is a counterfeit, and this seems wrong.

To conclude this section, if my criticisms are correct:

(a) (D2) fails to distinguish counterfeits and simple errors of attribution;

(b) (D2) does not specify which properties of the origin are relevant to the status of *being a counterfeit*; and

(c) (D2) defines the notion of counterfeit only for artworks; but artifacts in general can be forged.

4. Counterfeits as objects falsely presented as the original: (D3)

A *general* notion of counterfeits should not consider only artworks, but also artifacts more generally. On the basis of this notion, Wreen (1983, 2002) proposes the following characterization of "counterfeit":

> A forged work is a (supposed) work which is not genuine, but which is represented as genuine, with the intention to deceive; and genuineness or authenticity concerns provenance of issue, specifically, from whom (or, in some cases, what, when, or where) the work actually issued.
>
> Wreen 1983: 340

> A forgery has to be understood as a forged *XY* [...]. As I understand it, a forged *XY* is not a genuine *XY* but it is represented as a genuine *XY* and is so represented with the intention to deceive.
>
> Wreen 2002: 152

(Semi)formally:

> (D3) An object *x* is a forged/fake *XY*—where "*X*" is a term for a source of issue and "*Y*" a term for a kind of thing forged—if and only if it is not a genuine *XY*, but it is (re)presented as a genuine *XY* with the intention to deceive.
>
> Wreen 1983

Typically, the source of issue *X* is the artist who created the object, but it is also possible to forge objects created by groups. Also, *X* could be a designer or an artisan. Observe that, for Wreen, "since, by definition, every artifact has a source of issue—a human source of issue —and everything with a source of issue is, in the relevant sense, an artifact, it follows that every artifact is logically capable of forgery, and everything logically capable of forgery is an artifact" (Wreen 2002: 153). On the other hand, the name of a painting such as "La Gioconda," or of a particular artistic period such as "the blue period," or of a particular artistic movement such as "impressionism," or, finally, the name of a specific brand of artifacts—"Swatch" for example—can substitute the schematic letter "*Y*."

Observe that in (D3) Wreen introduces the expression "(re)presented": an object is a counterfeit only if it is *(re)presented* as an authentic *Y*. Further, to be such, the representation must be an *intentionally misleading representation* with the aim of deceiving. And this suggestion illuminates a third element usually regarded as analytic of "counterfeit"—that a counterfeit is:

(c) falsely presented as the original.

Following (D3) one can say that a counterfeit (a forgery or a fake) is a *mind-dependent (intentional)* object—someone (an artist or a designer for example) makes it—and *it is an action-dependent object involving a specific event,* an act of deceiving. The following (DA) is a typical case *of action-dependent object involving a specific event, an act of deceiving*:

(DA) Pino presents a certain object *O* to Pina. Pino falsely asserts that *O* is a Fontana masterpiece. For this reason he requests a certain adequate amount of money to sell it to Pina. Pina gives Pino the amount of money, buying the presumed Fontana masterpiece.

Notice that in (DA) there is an *historical dependence* of a specific counterfeit on a certain *event*, where with *historical dependence* we mean (following Amie Thomasson) that in order for the dependent entity to come into existence another entity must already exist: "One entity requires another in order to come into existence initially, although it may be able to exist independently of that entity once it has been created" (Thomasson 1999: 31). Observe that, if the historical dependence is between a certain object and the act of deceiving, then nothing requires that the deceiving agent be identical with the forging agent. (DAA) and (DAAA) exemplify, differently, the case just discussed:

(DAA) Pino makes a counterfeit of a Fontana and tries to sell it as a Fontana. Pina steals Pino's painting, and, unbeknown to Pino, sells it as an original Fontana.

(DAAA) Pino makes a copy of a Fontana for a study. Pina steals Pino's painting, and, unbeknown to Pino, sells it as an original Fontana.

In (DAA) there are two acts of deceiving: Pino's making a counterfeit and trying to sell it and Pina's selling it. In (DAAA) there is just one: Pina's selling the copy Pino has done. Moreover, notice that in (DAA) the two acts of deceiving have a different *status*. Pino is *representing* his counterfeit as an original Fontana, made with the intention to deceive. Pina is just *presenting* it: she did not make it. In (DAAA) there is just one act of deceiving: Pina's act of deceiving someone with Pino's *copy* of a Fontana.

Is there a difference between the first case of deceiving in (DAA) and the other two cases, i.e. the second case of deceiving in (DAA) and the case of deceiving in (DAAA)? If yes, what is it? In order to answer this question, consider some preliminary elements to a theory of artifacts.

Artifacts are usually characterized as "objects intentionally made for a certain purpose"[7] or function, i.e. they are functional objects and the function of an artifact determines (or plays a central role in the determination of) what kind of artifact it is.[8] In terms of kind identities: "for the most part it seems that what makes two artifacts members of the same kind is that they perform the same function" (Kornblith 1980: 112).

In the philosophical literature on the topic there are two main clusters of views on functions for artifacts: the *design view* and the *use view of function*.[9] In the first one, the *design view*, the functions of an artifact are the capacities or goals for which agents designed the artifact (on this position see, for example, Cummins 1975). In the *design view of function*, one holds that what defines an artifact *a* as an *F* is that *a* is a token of the designed artifact kind *F*. More precisely, an object *a* is judged to belong to the artifact kind *F* if *a* has the same function originally intended as that of *F*s. According to such a view, *a* will be classified as belonging to the kind *clock* if it was made to serve the same function that the inventor of the clock originally assigned to it, i.e. the function of measuring time. It is neither necessary nor sufficient to be an artifact that happens to function as a device for measuring time. By contrast, in the *use view*, the functions of an artifact are the capacities or goals for which agents *use* it. This view holds that what defines an artifact *a* as an *F* is that *a* is being, or could be, used as an *F*, irrespective of whether *a* was designed as an *F* in the first place. Its usability, or use, anchors it to a particular artifact kind. In the *use view* conception, an object *a* is judged to belong to kind *F* if its current function is that of *F*s. On this view, an object originally created as a bird house, but currently used as a doll house, will be categorized as belonging to the kind *doll house* (or toy, depending on the level of function which is taken to be relevant). This conception of function has been proposed, among others, by Neander (1991) and McLaughlin (2001).[10]

Note, *passim*, that if one takes the designer/creator of an artifact as one of its users, the use view may well subsume the designer/creator intentions account. It is a position that Dennett, for example, considers when he says that:

> The inventor is just another user, only circumstantially and defeasibly privileged in his knowledge of the functions and uses of his device. If others can find better uses for it, his intentions, clearheaded or muddled, are of mere historical interest.
>
> Dennett, 1990: 186

Take the difference between *design view* and *use view* on functions and consider again our deceiving acts exemplified in (DAA) and (DAAA). In (DAA) Pino makes a counterfeit of a Fontana: Pino's intention (the intention of the forger) is to produce a *counterfeit*. The Fontana counterfeit is not a genuine Fontana, but Pino *represented* it as a genuine Fontana with the intention to deceive. The function of the object is to deceive someone and this is the function that the designer of the object, in our case Pino, assigns to it by forging the Fontana painting. Pino's *representation* of the object concerns a certain *function* he himself has assigned to the object. Compare, now, (DAA) with (DAAA): in (DAAA), Pino's intention is to make a copy. The intention of the designer is not to deceive, so the function assigned to the object is to *be a copy for practice*. Pina, unbeknown to Pino, sells it as an original Fontana. She *presents* it as an original Fontana with the intention to deceive. In (DAAA), Pina's *presentation* concerns a certain *use* of the object. It was not designed to deceive, but it is *used* for that reason.

In the broadest sense, then, "(re)presented" in (D3) should be read in the following way:

> A counterfeit is an object that is misleadingly (re)presented, *designed or used* as an object originating in conditions different from the actual ones.

But, once we accept the disjunction "*designed or used*" in an expanded revision of (D3), we immediately encounter some unpleasant consequences.

First unpleasant consequence: as conditions of use can change, it immediately follows from this expanded revision of (D3) that a given object can be a counterfeit at a certain time t and not a counterfeit at a subsequent time t_1. But this seems false: if something is a counterfeit it is always a counterfeit.

Second unpleasant consequence: consider sentences (*) and (**):

> (*) The counterfeits Dino has done are better than the others that Pino has done.

> (**) The counterfeit Pino has done is the best counterfeit I have ever seen. It is indistinguishable from Giotto's painting.

(*) and (**) are sentences where one evaluates whether, for a certain object, a certain property holds. But, then, how do (*) and (**) fit with *use conditions*? Observe that if with "counterfeit" we mean *to be (re)presented, designed or used in a certain way*—as suggested by (D3)—then with "to be a better counterfeit of" we mean that Dino has designed or *used his counterfeit in a better way* than Pino. But this is not what we would like to say in (*). Paraphrase highlights that something goes wrong with (D3): in (*) and (**) we are evaluating how the object *is*—for example, its similarity with the original—and *not necessarily* how it fits its function or how it could be *used* for a certain function.

Finally, adopting *use conditions* would suggest that we should distinguish a *proper* and an *improper use* also for *counterfeits.* Indeed, we can discuss the improper use of a counterfeit banknote. Its proper use is to deceive the receiver, so if the bearer uses a counterfeit banknote to settle a debt with a receiver who knows that the slip of paper is a counterfeit banknote and attaches value to it *qua* collector of counterfeit banknotes, then the receiver is not being deceived and the counterfeit banknote is being *used* in violation of its *proper function.* That does not happen if we adopt a design view on functions where only *proper functions* are admitted. So, to conclude: in the *use view* we admit a proper and an improper use of counterfeits; in the *design view* there is not room for the two cases: if an object was designed as a *counterfeit*, an improper function of it is *not* an option.

5. Outline of a new characterization of "counterfeit": (D4)

Given the above analysis, I tentatively propose to define "counterfeit" in the following way:

> (D4) x is a counterfeit if and only if x has been intentionally produced to convince someone that x has a historical property that it actually does not possess,[11]

where a *historical property* is a property that something possesses merely in virtue of having been involved in some past event. For example, *to be born in 2008* is an example of a historical property of my son.

Observe that (D4) avoids the main problems of (D3) and (D2). Indeed:

> (a) It is formulated without making reference to the notion of *(re)presenting* as in (D3).

> (b) It specifies the relevant conditions of the origin as a certain kind of *historical*

properties of the original object faked by the producer of the counterfeit; in this way it avoids problems related to the origin conditions, as in (D2).

(c) There is not a problem of distinguishing between *counterfeit* and *misattribution*. (D4) explicitly places the dependence of counterfeits on the *intention* of the producer.

(d) The intention of the producer could be to fake either the historical properties related to the origin of the authentic object, or the historical properties related to its history. The only reference to conditions of origin is avoided.

Does (D4) satisfy all the deceiving events mentioned above? Consider the following examples (DAAA) and (DAAAA):

(DAAA) Pino makes a copy of a Fontana for a study. Pina steals Pino's painting, and, unbeknown to Pino, sells it as an original Fontana.

(DAAAA) Pino makes a copy of a Fontana for a study: *a*. He recognizes himself as a very talented painter. He decides to start a production of fake paintings, counterfeits, and to sell them. He produces a second copy *b* of another Fontana painting, and then he sells both *a* and *b* as authentic Fontanas.

About (DAAA): in the story, Pino does not produce a fake painting, thus the painting is not a counterfeit according to (D4). This much seems wrong, and is a gap in (D4).

About (DAAAA): if we take (D4) we cannot say that *a* is a counterfeit though we can say that *b* is one, and, of course, this is a problematic output for (D4). Observe that, in this scenario, it appears that "counterfeit" refers to a certain *use of an object*, i.e. the same fact that an object is passed off as an original means it can be considered a counterfeit. Moreover, if we follow the *use conditions* we get the additional problem of individuating *proper* and *improper use* of the counterfeit, as in the example of the counterfeit banknote above.

Difficulties for (D4) do not stop here. Notice that there is an important sense of "counterfeit" that (D4) (and also D1–D3) does not capture. It concerns mass-reproduced artifacts. Take, for example, a pirated DVD: the reason we consider a film copy to be a pirated copy, i.e. a counterfeit, is not necessarily related to the condition in which that particular copy has been produced. Indeed, it is possible that a specific copy has been produced according to the standard of the authorized copying process, but is nevertheless a counterfeit. And it may be that the pirated copy has *not* been intentionally produced to convince someone else that it is a standard copy of the DVD. Suppose that it was produced like the others, in the same factory, by the same workers, and that each DVD copy possesses the same brand, but that at a certain time one copy was sold through illegal distribution channels. Moreover, suppose the buyer and seller are both aware that it is a counterfeit: it is not presented as an object instantiating a historical property that it actually does not possess. But, then, following (D4), it is *not* a counterfeit.

(D4) does not work in this and similar cases, where we have (what I will call) *replicas* of the same artifact. At least for this kind of artifacts we require a different characterization of "counterfeit". In the next section, I first, briefly sketch a characterization of what replicas are. Then, I try to answer the question adopting a new definition of "counterfeit" (D5), apt to avoid the kind of difficulties mentioned above.

6. Replicas and counterfeits

Let *replicas* be mass-produced artifacts, perfectly alike, having the same causal-physical properties, and being *interchangeable*: If two objects are copies of the same original, they are replicas of one another (here I follow Tzouvaras 1993, 1995). This is the case for mass-produced objects that are all copies of some *prototype*; so, for example, CDs are all replicas of a master CD. The same will be true for musical scores, music mp3s, copies of a novel, but also chairs, tables, spoons, monitors, etc. Notice that I am here departing from the standard use in English of "replica" where such a term is usually taken to refer to an *inauthentic copy* of some original work, such as the replica of Michelangelo's *David* in Florence's Piazza della Signoria.

Are *replicas* simply *copies* of an artifact? In the following, I would like to give one element of distinction between *copies* and *replicas*.

First of all, observe that one can easily argue that the following principles are true for both *copies* and *replicas*:

(CR1) If x is a copy of y, x is the product of the human contrivance.

(CR2) If x is a copy of y, y is an original object, i.e. y is an *object taken as a model.*

(CR3) If x is a copy of y, x resembles y.[12]

I propose to distinguish *copies* from *replicas* on the basis of the meaning given to the expression "object taken as a model."

Consider copies: if we *characterize* a copy x of an original object y—in relational terms x is a copy of y ("x Copy y")—as an artifact produced with the *intention* of reproducing *some* of the (relevant) features of an object or *most* of the (relevant) features of an object *taken as a model* so that a copy *x* is *similar* to the original object *y*, and we take the expression "object taken as a model" in a quite strict way, we cannot always admit transitivity for the copy relation, i.e.

(CR4) $\forall x \forall y \forall z\ ((x \text{ Copy } y)\ \&\ (y \text{ Copy } z) \rightarrow (x \text{ Copy } z))$

does not (always) hold. Notice that here, with "the object taken as model," we refer, in the prototypical case, to the object *y observed* by someone during the process of copying *y*. If so, strictly speaking, if *x* is modeled on *y* and *y* is modeled on *z*, it is not true that *x* is modeled on *z* itself. This commitment on one side involves, or seems to involve, important restrictions with respect to the commonsensical notion of copy (think, for example, of copies done on the basis of a memory image of an original: strictly speaking these are not copies). On the other side it gives rise to a relevant feature concerning copies of an original object: that there is an *intentional aspect* that allows us to isolate the original object from its copies, i.e. that a copy is done with the *intention* of reproducing *some* of the (relevant) features of an object or *most* of the (relevant) features of an object *taken as a model.*

Moreover, observe that such a restriction on copies seems necessary in order to avoid a sort of sorites paradox for copies: if for being a copy of an original object *some* of the (relevant) features of an original object or *most* of the (relevant) features of an original object are reproduced so that (CR3) is satisfied and if we allow for transitivity, it would be possible to create chains of copies of an original object, which would be less and less *similar* to this first model, until we reach a final one which is far too different from the model to be considered a copy of it.

However, there is a large number of artifacts—computer programs or, in general, digital files, and most mass-produced artifacts—where copies and original(s) are perfectly alike, having the same causal-physical properties, and are *interchangeable*: transitivity (CR4) seems to be straightforward for them and *resemblance* is intended in terms of perfect likeness. In most of these cases there is—*at least in principle*—no difference between a copy and the original object: there is a designer who intentionally designed a template, a prototype, or a master, and some or many exemplars that are *replicated* from it. For these *copies*—I call them *replicas*—there is a *procedure of replication* that is eventually accounted for by the producer and that can be applied even without any explicit intention of producing a copy of something. If it is so, one can complete the above characterization of replicas claiming that:

(R) x is a replica of y if and only if there is a procedure accounted for by the producer of y allowing the production of objects bearing a certain *fixed standard* of similarity to one another and a certain *fixed standard* of similarity with an original object, if there is such an original object.

The producer knows the procedure and accepts this as a way of legitimately replicating objects.

Now, consider counterfeits in the replicas case. As said, it does not seem relevant, in order to have a counterfeit, to convince someone that a certain object possesses the historical properties that it does not have, as is suggested in (D4). It is easy to observe that authentic replicas themselves may have different historical and non-historical properties: take, for example, different film copies. They could be produced with different techniques and at different times. So, for example, there are replicas of Monty Python's *The Meaning of Life* on DVD, VHS, and streaming on the internet. Now, consider (D4):

(D4) x is a counterfeit if and only if x has been intentionally produced to convince someone else that x has a historical property that it actually does not possess.

and take, for example, a pirated copy of Monty Python's *The Meaning of Life*. The pirated copy is not produced to convince someone else that it has a historical property that it actually does not possess. So, following (D4), it is not a counterfeit. The reason seems to be that the notion of counterfeit used in cases of pirated replicas is just a *commercial* one, and it is grounded just in the distinction between replicas that are authorized and replicas that are not authorized. And (D4) does not say anything about this.

This being the case, a different notion of counterfeits is needed, one characterized by the distinction between allowed procedures of replication and networks of commercialization or exchange and disallowed ones. In general, there might be replicas of photos, movies, printing, music, chairs, tables, spoons, and watches that are allowed and others that are not allowed; but this fact has nothing to do with the ontological relation between the original object and its copies. Replicating one of the objects of these kinds does not threaten their intrinsic properties. If it is so, we should combine (D4) with another notion of counterfeit like the following:

(D5) x is a counterfeit if and only if x is a *replica* produced either without an allowed procedure of replication or without an allowed network of commercialization or exchange.

where (D5) is strictly confined to mass-produced *replicas*. Using (D5) we can distinguish a Swatch and a *fake* Swatch, a true copy of *The Lord of the Rings* and a pirated one, where the difference is merely a commercial matter: one is allowed and the other is not. (D5) gives us a distinction between authorized and unauthorized replicas.

7. Conclusions

How to conclude our analysis? First, "counterfeit" is not *strictly speaking* analyzable in terms of (1) a copy of (2) an original object (3) falsely presented as the original. Something goes wrong in definitions (D1)–(D3) that just consider (one of) (1)–(3) as an *essential* part of the definition. From this point of view, (D4) seems to be a better characterization of "counterfeit" than the others. But even (D4) is not without problems. (D5) offers a way to alleviate some of these problems, at least in cases of counterfeits of mass-produced *replicas*.[13]

Notes

1 Notably, I do not distinguish here between "counterfeit" and "forgery."

2 In English, "Drawing, painting, sculpture that more or less accurately reproduces an original artwork, with the aim of forging or for the sake of practice, or to spread (knowledge of it)."

3 Maria Elisabeth Reicher similarly suggests that, while it might be a foolhardy forger who attempts to create a new painting in the name of van Gogh while having a style utterly unlike that of van Gogh, the result, even if it is a bad fake, would be nevertheless a forgery. She suggests "to distinguish between *original forgeries* and *copy forgeries*. A forgery may be an original work. An unknown painter could pass off a work of his own as a work of a better-known colleague without copying an already existing work. This would be an original forgery. Usually, in such a case, the forger will at least attempt to imitate the style and workmanship of pre-existing paintings, in order to render the false history of production credible. But even this is not necessary. There could be a very bold or very stupid forger who tries to pass off a painting of his own as a van Gogh, although this painting does not show any significant similarity with already known paintings by van Gogh. Probably, this would be a bad forgery, but a forgery nevertheless" (Reicher 2011: 53; see also Bloch 1976).

4 For an extensive introduction to Goodman's distinction between *autographic* art

and *allographic* art and forgeries see Hick 2010. For a general introduction to Goodman's philosophy see Cohnitz and Rossberg 2006 (on the topic discussed above see esp. Ch. 7).

5 For criticisms to the distinction see Levinson 1980 and Pillow 2003.

6 I owe this observation to Darren Hick.

7 Baker 2007: 49. Alternative definitions of artifacts are in Dipert 1993 and Hilpinen 1992, 1993, 2008. Hilpinen writes that "Aristotle makes [...] a distinction between natural objects and artifacts ("artificial products," *Physica, Book II,* 192 b 28), and describes the latter as products of the art of making things. The art of making something involves intentional agency; thus an artifact may be defined as an object that has been intentionally made for some purpose" (Hilpinen 2008).

8 On artifact kinds see Franssen et al. 2014. On problems concerning the determination of artifact kinds *via* functions see Carrara, Gaio, and Soavi 2014.

9 For a more detailed characterization of artifact functions see Carrara and Vermaas 2009.

10 For an introduction to categorization of artifacts see Carrara and Mingardo 2013.

11 (D4) is first proposed in Carrara and Soavi 2010.

12 See Stroll 1998. I consider here some ideas on Carrara and Soavi 2008.

13 Parts of this paper have been read at *The Ethics of Copying* conference (Bielefeld, Germany, July 2014), and at the seminar of *The Ethics of Copying ZiF Research Group* (Bielefeld, Germany, November 2015). I am indebted to the participants in both talks for stimulating discussion. Thanks also to the editors of this volume, Darren Hudson Hick and Reinold Schmücker, for comments, suggestions, and stimulating discussions on early versions of this paper.

References

Baker, L. R. (2007), *The Metaphysics of Everyday Life: An Essay in Practical Realism,* Cambridge: Cambridge University Press.

Bloch, P. (1976), "Einleitung," in *Fälschung + Forschung,* 7–11, Essen and Berlin: Museum Folkwang and Skulpturengalerie Staatliche Museen Preußischer Kulturbesitz.

Carrara, M. and D. Mingardo (2013), "Artifact Categorization. Trends and Problems," *The Review of Philosophy and Psychology* 4: 351–73.

Carrara, M. and M. Soavi (2008), "Ontology for Information Systems. Artifacts as a Case Study," *Mind and Society* (7): 143–56.

Carrara, M. and M. Soavi (2010), "Copies, Replicas and Counterfeits of Artworks and Artifacts," *Monist* 93 (3): 417–35.

Carrara, M. and P. E. Vermaas (2009), "The Fine-grained Metaphysics of Artifactual and Biological Functional Kinds," *Synthese* 169: 125–43.

Carrara, M., S. Gaio, and M. Soavi (2014), "Artifact Kinds, Identity Criteria, and Logical Adequacy," in M. Franssen et al. (eds), *Artifact Kinds: Ontology and the Human-Made World*, 85–101, Berlin: Springer.

Cohnitz, D. and M. Rossberg (2006), *Nelson Goodman*, Chesham: Acumen.

Cummins, R. (1975), "Functional Analysis," *Journal of Philosophy* 72: 741–65.

Dennett, D. C. (1990), "The Interpretation of Texts, People and Other Artifacts," *Philosophy and Phenomenological Research* 50: 177–94.

Dipert, R. (1993), *Artifacts, Art Works and Agency*, Philadelphia: Temple University Press.

Franssen, M., P. Kroes, T. Reydon, and P. E. Vermaas (eds) (2014), *Artifact Kinds: Ontology and the Human-Made World*, Berlin: Springer.

Goodman, N. (1968), *The Languages of Art. An Approach to a Theory of Symbols*, Indianapolis, IN: Hackett.

Hick, D. H. (2010), "Forgery and Appropriation in Art," *Philosophy Compass* 5 (12): 1047–56.

Hilpinen, R. (1992), "On Artifacts and Works of Arts," *Theoria* 58: 58–82.

Hilpinen, R. (1993), "Authors and Artifacts," *Proceedings of the Aristotelian Society* 93: 155–78.

Hilpinen, R. (2008), "Artifact," *The Stanford Encyclopedia of Philosophy*, E. N. Zalta (ed.). Available online: http://plato.stanford.edu/archives/fall2008/entries/artifact/

Kornblith, H. (1980), "Referring to Artifacts," *The Philosophical Review* 89: 109–14.

Levinson, J. (1980), "Autographic and Allographic Art Revisited," *Philosophical Studies* 38 (4): 367–83.

McLaughlin, P. (2001), *What Functions Explain*, Cambridge: Cambridge University Press.

Neander, K. (1991), "The Teleological Notion of 'Function,'" *Australasian Journal of Philosophy* 69: 454–68.

Pillow, K. (2003), "Did Goodman's Distinction Survive LeWitt?" *Journal of Aesthetics and Art Criticism* 61: 365–80.

Reicher, M. E. (2011), "Vom wahren Wert des Echten und des Falschen," in J. Nida-Rümelin and J. Steinbrenner (eds), *Original und Fälschung*, 51–70, Ostfildern: Hatje Cantz.

Ryle, G. (1954), *Dilemmas*, Cambridge: Cambridge University Press.

Schmücker, R. (2011), "Lob der Fälschung," in J. Nida-Rümelin and J. Steinbrenner (eds), *Original und Fälschung*, 71–91, Ostfildern: Hatje Cantz.

Stroll, A. (1998), *Sketches of Landscapes*, Cambridge, MA: The MIT Press.

Thomasson, A. L. (1999), *Fiction and Metaphyics*, Cambridge: Cambridge University Press.

Tzouvaras, A. (1993), "Significant Parts and Identity of Artifacts," *Notre Dame Journal of Formal Logic* 34 (3): 445–52.

Tzouvaras, A. (1995), "A World of Homogeneous Artifacts," *Notre Dame Journal of Formal Logic* 36 (3): 454–74.

Wreen, M. (1983), "Goodman on Forgery," *Philosophical Quarterly* 33 (133): 340–53.

Wreen, M. (2002), "Forgery," *Canadian Journal of Philosophy* 32 (2): 143–66.

7

The Nature of Copying and the Singular Literary Work

Darren Hudson Hick

1. Ontology and copies

I want to try something new. I want to create a literary work—a novel, perhaps—that defies further instantiation. That is, I want to create a literary work that is, by its very nature, singular. What this will mean is that any reproduction—any further copy—of this work will not be a genuine instance of the novel.[1] Rather, it will be a *mere* reproduction, such that any attempt to sell the reproduction *as* the work itself would constitute an act of forgery. I hesitate to attempt this, however, not because of predictably low royalties for a work that only exists in one copy, but because I wonder whether it is even possible. Widely accepted wisdom in analytic aesthetics, after all, says this cannot be done.

In his seminal work, *Languages of Art*, Nelson Goodman suggests: "Any accurate copy of the text of a poem or novel is as much the original work as any other" (Goodman 1976: 114). Of course, the word "copy" can be cashed out in a number of different ways. We can use "copy" as a verb, referring to the intentional act of reproduction. Or, we can use "copy" as a noun, though here we face a further ambiguity. We can speak, first, of a copy in the sense of being a *mere* copy. The copy of Michelangelo's *David* that stands outside Florence's Palazzo Vecchio is a mere copy, an imitation: a replica. In this sense, if you have only seen the replica, you have not seen Michelangelo's *David*. In 2014, a painting attributed to Marc Chagall was discovered to be a "very bad copy" of a 1911 work by the modern master. The Chagall copy was a forgery, and the *David* replica is not, but both are *mere* copies. We can distinguish a copy in this sense from the sense in which my copy of Stephen King's *The Shining*, or my copy of David Hasselhoff's most recent album, is an authentic copy of the work:

a genuine instance of it. If I illegally downloaded these copies from the internet, then they are illicit copies, but genuine nevertheless.

On Goodman's theory, no act of copying could ever produce an *authentic* copy of Michelangelo's *David* or a Chagall painting—not an excellent act of copying, nor even one that produces an exact copy. At best, such an act will produce a mere replica, and at worst a forgery. Conversely, Goodman argues that, in the case of literary works, to be a copy in the sense of being a genuine instance requires only strict adherence to the linguistic structure of the work in question: those words and that punctuation in that formal arrangement. Goodman's distinction between allographic and autographic arts may provide some insight. Goodman writes:

> Let us speak of a work of art as *autographic* if and only if the distinction between the original and the forgery of it is significant; or better, if and only if even the most exact duplication of it does not thereby count as genuine. [...] Thus painting is autographic, music nonautographic, or *allographic*.
>
> Goodman 1976: 113

Literature, too, is allographic on this account. As Goodman goes on to suggest, it is centrally because they are built on notational systems—systems of characters with specifiable rules of use—that art kinds like literature and music are allographic. The syntax and semantics of natural language, for example, set out the rules for constructing works in that language, whether written or spoken, and so making a copy of such a work requires only following the rules. As well, the rules will tell us if the copy in front of us is genuine. But, as there is no notational system for paintings, there are no rules for creating another instance of a painted work, and so (in effect) *nothing* will count as a genuine copy except the original. There are, in this sense, no *authentic* copies of Michelangelo's *David* and no *mere* copies of *The Shining*: every copy is authentic. Assuming an *act* of copying, few philosophers would find fault here. However, on Goodman's view, to be an authentic copy of a literary work requires *no* act of copying—that is, no intentional reproduction. Rather, if, by sheer chance, someone happens to put the same words in the same order as did Stephen King, that person will have produced a genuine instance of his novel. As Goodman suggests, "To verify the spelling or to spell correctly is all that is required to identify an instance of the work or to produce a new instance" (Goodman 1976: 116). It is in this contention—that an authentic copy of a literary work could be produced without any intentional *act* of copying—that philosophers typically find fault.

Goodman is a textualist, and his view is widely opposed by *con*textualists—those who contend that there is more to a work than its formal features. On this view, Gregory Currie suggests that literary works are not reducible to their texts, but are "things which stand in certain relations to texts, are capable of being (multiply) interpreted, stand in certain other relations to acts of textual composition and to the cultural contexts in which those acts are embedded, etc." (Currie 1991: 337). Currie's central case in his article "Work and Text" is an imagined one in which gothic novelist Anne Radcliffe has penned a work word-for-word indistinguishable from Jane Austen's *Northanger Abbey*, but twenty years before Austen's writing. On a view like Goodman's, being textually indistinguishable, Radcliffe's and Austen's novels would be one and the same work (see Goodman and Elgin 1986). Currie argues otherwise, however, suggesting that what is a proper interpretation—and so, evaluation—of one may not be proper of the other. Austen's work, Currie suggests, is best read as a satirical work, while the same words written by Radcliffe could only reasonably be read as unironic. Further, Austen's *Abbey* makes thinly veiled references to works that Radcliffe's *Abbey* could not because the referenced works were written in the interim between the *Abbeys*. As the works differ in what readings could reasonably be made of them, the works differ in their properties, and as they differ in their properties, they differ in identity. On Currie's view, these differences arise because each act of authoring—Radcliffe's and Austen's—would have involved a distinct heuristic path on their respective authors' parts. That is, each author would be working under different conditions, responding to different factors in their literary traditions and wider cultural spheres, attempting to solve different artistic problems, and all of this is relevant to appreciating the respective products.[2]

Currie argues that artworks generally should be thought of as *action types*, distinguished one from another according to the heuristic paths taken by their respective authors in reaching their respective structures—in the case of literature, word-order structures. Another contextualist, Jerrold Levinson, argues that any given artwork should be thought of as an *initiated type* or *indicated structure*, being an abstract structure—a series of notes or words, for instance—as picked out by its author at some given time.[3] Both Levinson and Currie suggest that, where no act of copying has taken place, the writings of two authors—even if formally indistinguishable—should ordinarily be thought of as two distinct works. Even given textual indistinguishability, the identity conditions of works do not reduce to the identity conditions of textual strings. And so, Levinson and Currie (and contextualists generally) argue against the notion that two texts could amount to instances of the same work simply as a matter of textual coincidence. Rather, the instantiation of a second authentic copy of a work will typically require an act of accurate copying.

2. Getting inside *Getting Inside Jack Kerouac's Head*

As I have argued in "Ontology and the Challenge of Literary Appropriation," however, though an act of accurate copying seems necessary for the further authentic instantiation of a work, such an act may not prove sufficient. At the least, I suggest, neither Levinson nor Currie has shown that an act of accurate copying cannot be defeated (Hick 2013). My central case in the article is Simon Morris's work, *Getting Inside Jack Kerouac's Head*, a page-reversed but otherwise accurate word-for-word retyping of Kerouac's *On the Road: The Original Scroll*. Morris is open about his project and method, and although in one sense his goal is the same as Kerouac's—to put those words in that order—their projects are entirely distinct: Morris sets out to *copy* in much the same way that children playing follow-the-leader seek to copy. Although followers in both cases are, in one sense, *doing* the same thing as their leader, in another sense they are doing something entirely distinct: they are copying. This would seem to be, in Currie's terms, a distinct heuristic. And, on Currie's view, where two distinct heuristics arrive at the same structure (here, a structure made of words, punctuation, and formatting), we have distinct works. The complication is that the very same can be said about the typesetter for Kerouac's novel, who is likewise putting the same words in the same order as did Kerouac in an intentional act of copying. But, one presumes, we do not want to say that the typesetter is creating some work *distinct* from Kerouac's, but is instead bringing about an authentic instance of his novel. So, is there something about Morris's act (but not the typesetter's) that qualifies it as an *art-making* heuristic? Currie does not say, and so we are left in a sort of ontological superposition.[4]

If, as seems to be the case here, the accurate copying of a literary work is necessary but not sufficient for the bringing into being of an authentic instance of that work, then it seems we have room to allow for a literary work the copying of which can at most only bring about *mere* copies—replicas—and not genuine instances. In this case, *nothing* would be sufficient for the bringing into being of a second authentic copy of the work, so we needn't worry about what is necessary for doing so.[5]

One defense for the claim that Morris has created a work distinct from *On the Road* (and that the typesetter has not) is that *Getting Inside Jack Kerouac's*

Head is not a work of literature at all, but is rather a work of some distinct art kind. Morris himself refers to his works as "bookworks." Although Morris has, to my knowledge, never set out an ontology of his works, we might consider the possibility that a bookwork is a sort of conceptual art piece which happens to involve a copy—or the copy*ing*—of a pre-existing literary work, in much the same way that Robert Rauschenberg involved a drawing by Willem de Kooning in *Erased de Kooning Drawing*, or that Marcel Duchamp involved a postcard of the *Mona Lisa* in his *L.H.O.O.Q.* And so, it might be suggested, a copy of the bookwork *Getting Inside Jack Kerouac's Head* involves a copy of *On the Road*, but is not identical with that work.[6] Of course, this is the very danger that Arthur Danto warned us about in confusing the "is" of artistic identification with the "is" of identity *per se* (Danto 1964: 578). In purchasing a copy of *Getting Inside Jack Kerouac's Head*, on this suggestion, I will have *also*, in doing so, bought a copy of *On the Road*, and so will have purchased two works of distinct ontological kinds for the price of one, which is a good deal any way you look at it. And so we can, perhaps, help Currie out of his uncomfortable position by denying that *Getting Inside Jack Kerouac's Head* is a *literary* work at all.

There are complications for this suggestion,[7] though they do not impinge on my central case of the in-principle singular novel, because I specifically want to create a work of *literature*. In defying all authentic copying, this would admittedly be a rather *odd* work of literature, ontologically speaking, but the goal is that it be a work of literature nevertheless.

3. Creating novel kinds

Sherri Irvin argues that the ontology of a work of art will be centrally determined by what she calls "the artist's sanction"—essentially, the artist's publicly accessible actions and communications about the work. Irvin writes:

> The artist's sanction may serve to fix the boundaries of his or her work, to determine whether a particular feature is relevant to the work's interpretation, to establish in what genre the work belongs, and, in some cases, to determine whether it, *qua* artwork, has a particular feature or not [...] [T]hrough his or her sanction the artist can endow the work with certain features, just as he or she endows it with certain features by manipulating the physical materials that will ultimately be displayed to the viewer.
>
> Irvin 2005: 315–16

Irvin's view is that the artist's choices for her work—her *sanctions*—constrain the work's ontology.[8] However, Irvin's view suggests a two-layered schema for setting the ontology of a given work. Without some explicit, publicly accessible sanctioning, a work's ontology will be established by the traditional standards and conventions of its apparent kind (Irvin 2008: 5). So, as paintings are ordinarily treated as singular concrete objects either identical with or else tied in their persistence conditions to some physical painted surfaces, the same is likely to be true for the next painting produced by any given artist. Where an artist creates a work of a traditional kind, ontological conventions associated with that kind should be assumed to be in place. However, Irvin argues, this default ontology can be overridden by the artist's declarations to the contrary. When an artist seeks to "break the mold" and create a work of a *novel* ontological kind, some form of publicly accessible sanctioning is required: something that would make the artist's choices apparent to the public.

Amie Thomasson has suggested that Irvin's requirement that such a sanctioning be a public matter is not, in fact, necessary, and that an artist could create a novel kind as a matter of private intentional fiat (Thomasson 2010: 126). This may well be the case, but rather than considering that question here, I want instead to question whether such sanctioning is *sufficient* for determining the ontology of a work, especially when that work is intended to be of a novel kind. Curiously, Irvin herself provides the first opening by placing some limited restrictions on the efficacy of an artist's sanctions. She writes:

> [I]f the artist makes contradictory statements, or expresses preferences that would be dangerous or impossible to carry out within the framework of the institution, it may be necessary to rely on art world or institutional conventions to resolve the issue of what we should take to have been sanctioned.
>
> Irvin 2008: 56

If an artist's sanctions would require a work to be displayed in a space unavailable to a gallery, for instance, rather than saying that the work simply cannot be instantiated, Irvin suggests that this sanction may be overruled by the institution. Similarly, if a museum's conservators feel that following through on the instructions provided by the artist would put the museum's staff or visitors at undue risk, these sanctions may not be realized.[9] Put another way, at least in some cases, where a sanction lacks institutional uptake, that sanction may fail to dictate the nature of the work. And further, Irvin suggests, when institutional uptake fails, ontology defaults to conventional standards.[10]

Creating an artwork of a familiar ontological kind is unproblematic on this view. The ontology of paintings or music or literature is established by art-cultural practice. Here, Irvin follows a recent line of thought in aesthetic meta-ontology, according to which the ontology of art is largely determined by artistic practice—how we treat, refer to, and otherwise conceive of works.[11] Where an artist creates a work of a familiar sort—a painting, poem, or concerto, for instance—without anything apparent in the work itself or what the artist declares about the work suggesting otherwise, the work's ontology defaults to the conventional standards for that sort of work. It is only when the artist seeks to do something revolutionary that the artist's sanction truly comes into play.

Unsuccessful cases of ontological revolution are, perhaps predictably, difficult to research precisely because they were unsuccessful. It is easier, however, and perhaps more instructive, to look at cases of "near misses." By way of example, then, let us consider John Cage's most important work, *4′33″*. Originally consisting of 4 minutes and 33 seconds of a pianist not playing his piano (and later allowing for all manner of musicians not playing their instruments), Cage's piece is generally regarded today as a breakthrough in avant-garde music, and what has been called "inferential art" (Kostalanetz 1969). Consisting of no notes being played over three movements, the work reflects Cage's view that music is simply sound, and in *4′33″* the relevant sound issues not from the musicians, but from the audience and their environment. Understood not only institutionally, but also ontologically, Cage's work is widely considered revolutionary. The fame of the work today, however, belies its initial reception. The first performance of *4′33″* was in 1952 in Woodstock, NY, at a recital of contemporary piano music, with pianist David Tudor not playing the piano for the piece. Cage recalls: "People began whispering to one another, and some people began to walk about. They didn't laugh—they were irritated when they realized nothing was going to happen, and they haven't forgotten it 30 years later: they're still angry" (Kostelanetz 2003: 70). After the performance, Cage and Tudor (along with avant-garde composers Morton Feldman and Earle Brown) took the stage for questions from the audience. But discussion quickly gave way to uproar. At one point, an audience member stood and declared: "Good people of Woodstock, let's drive these people out of town!" (Revill 1992: 166) Things didn't end there. A *New York Times* review of a performance two years later carried the scare-quote-laden title:

> Look, No Hands! And It's "Music"
> "Work" by Cage, 4 Minutes, 33 Seconds of Silence Is "Played" by Tudor, Pianist
>
> "J. B." 1954: 34

Here, the reviewer's resistance to refer to *4′33″* as a work in general, or as a musical work in particular, suggests a lack of uptake echoing the 1952 audience's outrage. Indeed, it would be years before *4′33″* would come to be widely accepted as a musical work—and, importantly for our purposes, as a musical work consisting of no notes being played. And until it gained this sort of institutional uptake, I would suggest, the nature of the work was genuinely undetermined. That is, Cage had proposed an ontology for the work, but its realization was contingent upon buy-in from the artworld, and matters could easily have turned out otherwise.

It may be that minor deviations from the ontological norm are unlikely to raise much dust. Here, we might consider the case of poet Larry Eigner, who, critically palsied at birth, could only type his works using his right index finger and thumb. As a result of how he had to go about creating his works, Eigner became as interested in the typed layout of his poems as in their content. Working exclusively in the Courier typeface of his 1940 Royal manual typewriter, Eigner came to regard the exact physical arrangement of his poems, from the spacing between words to the poem's placement on the page, as critically ineliminable elements of his work. As Eigner suggests, "everything you do on the page matters" (Eigner 2010b: xxxvi; see also Eigner 1989: 154). And so, where a standard work of literature is taken to be variable over font and placement, editors have typically gone to great lengths to preserve these elements "as exactly as possible" in Eigner's work (Eigner 2010a: xv). Poet Steven Fama, for one, took great issue with the recent publication of Eigner's collected works, arguing that the entire edition should be recalled and pulped over the editors' choices about the spacing of margins (Fama 2010). Although a deviation from the ontological norm for poetry, Eigner's sanctions were nevertheless taken up without much difficulty by the literature artworld. And while there may be disagreement about precisely how much fidelity to the original must be maintained, there seems to be no question that the nature of Eigner's poems outstrips mere strings of words. Following in the wake of E. E. Cummings's typographical experiments, Eigner's sanctions were perhaps not too far afield of the ontological norm. Other authorial sanctions, however, may call for more than this—indeed, may call for ontological revolution.

Matters of copying—what makes something an authentic copy of a work, under what conditions copying is actually performed, and so on—are centrally ontological matters, tied up with the identity and persistence conditions of a work. Indeed, determining the copying conditions for a work determines much of its ontology. Although singularity is treated as standard for paintings, and the limiting of authentic instances by stipulation is conventional for printmaking, the creation of a novel that in principle would not allow for multiple instances would require overriding a *core* ontological conception for literature. Despite the differences in their views, the textualist and contextualist take it as given that works of literature allow for multiple genuine copies. The way that critics, laymen, and authors alike refer to their works reflects this notion. What institution there is for literature—primarily the publishing industry—depends upon this notion. That a literary work allows for multiple genuine copies is, I would argue, at the core of our widely shared ontological conception of literature, and so we should expect, I think, a great deal of push-back for a proposed literary work which in principle allowed for only a single instance—much more so than for a poem for which typeface was ineliminable. If the ontology of art depends upon practice (as I, Irvin, and many others believe it does), then an artist's revisionary declaration will only be the first, provisional step in such a practice.

On the view that the ontology of artworks depends upon cultural practice, it may be useful to consider an analogy (though an admittedly imperfect one) with language. In a famous case from Lewis Carroll's *Through the Looking Glass*, the character of Humpty Dumpty asserts that by "glory" he means "there's a nice knock-down argument for you!" Alice objects: "But 'glory' doesn't mean 'a nice knock-down argument.'" Humpty Dumpty replies that when *he* uses the word, "it means just what I choose it to mean—neither more nor less." An impressive amount of ink has been spilled over this little fictional conversation. Of course, there are innumerable cases—such as proper names and technical terminology—where a word *does* get its meaning through stipulation alone. So, it is not the mere fact that Humpty Dumpty has attempted to introduce some stipulative meaning that runs him into problems. Centrally, Humpty Dumpty runs into problems because he is attempting to stipulate some *new* meaning for an *already-familiar* word through intentional fiat. Hence Alice's push-back: "But 'glory' doesn't mean 'a nice knock-down argument.'" That is, it means something *else*. Now, this is not to say that "glory" *couldn't* come to mean, "there's a nice knock-down argument for you," but its doing so will depend on more than Humpty Dumpty's say-so: it will depend upon uptake by those using the language. Certainly, the meanings of words are extended all the time. Perhaps most commonly, the meaning of a word is extended when some new meaning is introduced that is relevantly similar to some accepted meaning, as when a noun like "host" or "bed" or "Google" gains use as a verb. However, the introduction of entirely novel meanings—as in Humpty Dumpty's case—will predictably be more difficult. I can intend the words I write or speak to mean all manner of things, but this is not enough to give them my intended meaning. Changing the meaning of, or adding new meaning to a word requires uptake to be efficacious, and cannot be done through stipulation alone. The same, I would suggest, is true of ontological revolution. Revolution is never a solitary activity.

Where an artist or author seeks to create a work in a category with an established ontology, she is unlikely to meet many challenges in this regard. She is, after all, working within an accepted cultural practice. Where she seeks to create a work within such a category but such that the work deviates from this standard, however, doing so is likely to depend upon public sanctioning, either explicitly through some declaration, or else implicitly through the apparent features of the work itself. Where an artist seeks to break the boundaries of tradition or convention by sanctioning ontological features that run counter to our deeply embedded concepts for a given category of art, success will require uptake by the artworld. In such cases of ontologically novel works, I would contend that an artist's declared choices (whether implicit or explicit) are *normative* in the sense that they prescribe a way of conceiving of (and so referring to and treating) the work, but where such sanctions prescribe a cultural practice, prescriptions can fail to actually *establish* such a practice, and it is ultimately practice that determines ontology.[12] At one point, Irvin compares the artist's sanction to the signing of a contract, i.e. to "making certain statements and/or performing certain acts under appropriate conditions" (Irvin 2005: 321). This comparison with contracts is an apt one, but Irvin overlooks the fact that a contract typically involves more than one signatory. People enter into contracts *with each other*, and one cannot pull another into a contractual agreement without the other's buy-in. In the case of the ontology contract, the "other" is the artworld.

4. Conclusion

So, what of my in-principle singular literary work? As we have noted, copying is centrally an ontological matter. However, with the ontology of art resting upon artistic practice, what counts as copying and what counts as a copy are themselves cultural issues. Even Goodman, the intransigent textualist, notes that authenticity conditions are grounded in cultural practice and so subject to change as practice changes (Goodman 1976: 121–2). My pronouncement that my novel simply does not admit of further authentic copies would amount to a prescription for practice, the realization of which would depend upon the uptake of the artworld. And in attempting this sanction, I am asking the public to override a core ontological conception for literature—no small thing. In large part, I would guess, the uptake of ontological revolution depends upon whether the audience has been suitably primed. Cage's *4′33″* was presented to the public in the midst of a wider avant-garde movement in music—indeed, it was presented to a public *prepared* to be challenged—but what Cage asked was almost too much. A decade earlier, it *would* have been too much to ask. Is the artworld, or the public at large, prepared to accept a literary work that simply cannot be authentically copied? I can't say. However, if anything, the general public seems, with the advent and widespread use of digital technology, to have embraced copying—accepting as authentic copies things that were previously taken to be mere replicas (see Marsh and Hick 2014). In large part, artistic practice changes as artists themselves test the boundaries of that practice, sometimes through minor deviations from the norm, and sometimes through leaps and bounds. As a first move towards the latter, then, copies of my novel will not be available for download on my website.

Notes

1 As such, my case differs from that of the Wu-Tang Clan's concept album, *Once Upon a Time in Shaolin*, released in a single copy in 2015, with opportunities to listen to the album being tightly controlled, taking place at individual museums and galleries, and only where the sole copy is present. The band was *not* suggesting, however, that a second copy would fail to be an *authentic* copy. Indeed, the album's producer suggests: "One leak [of the album] nullifies the entire concept" (Gorton 2014). For the sake of this thought experiment, I leave it as an open question whether a reading of my novel would qualify as a genuine *performance* of the work.

2 See, generally, Chapter 3 of Currie 1989. A more popular example from contextualists comes from Jorges Luis Borges' short story, "Pierre Menard, Author of the *Quixote*," in which the titular character sets about writing Cervantes' masterpiece from scratch, but without reference to the original.

3 A generalized version of Levinson's ontology of musical works, presented in Levinson 1980.

4 Similar problems arise for Levinson's account, which for space reasons I will not recount here. See Hick 2013: 156–9.

5 But, of course, this couldn't be the case for literary works generally, else every book in my home would be a unique work of its own.

6 This, apparently, was the case with appropriation artist Richard Prince's 2011

copy of J. D. Salinger's *Catcher in the Rye*, a word-for-word reproduction of the first edition, altered only by the replacement of Salinger's name on the cover with Prince's own, and the following disclaimer on the colophon page: "This is an artwork by Richard Prince. Any similarity to a book is coincidental and not intended by the artist" (Goldsmith 2012). The work was reproduced in multiple copies with a copyright notice in Prince's name.

7 Kendall Walton (1970) famously argues that a work's proper category—say, literature or conceptual art—depends upon four factors: (1) the category with regard to which the work in question has the most standard, and fewest contra-standard features; (2) the category in which the work comes off best; (3) the category in which the author intended the work to be perceived; and (4) the category in which the author's contemporaries perceived the work. In almost all cases, Walton suggests, the historical factors, (3) and (4), will trump the others. So, in our case, if Morris intended the work to be treated either as a literary work or as a work of conceptual art, then this would at least add considerable weight to the work's proper category and so ontology.

8 This is not to say the artist's *intentions*, and Irvin works to show that, while the artist's sanction is an "outgrowth" of the artist's intention (in the same way that most behavior grows out of intention), it is not identical with that intention.

9 See Irvin's case of *Time and Mrs. Tiber* (2005: 316–17).

10 Irvin's approach in her (2008) is much stronger, ontologically speaking, than her view as outlined in her (2006), in which she suggests that a museum should do its *best* to present a work in accord with the artist's sanctions, "in a way that provides the viewer with an experience that is as close as possible to that provided by the work as sanctioned by the artist; and where these experiences diverge, audience members should be made aware of this and provided, where possible, with the information required to imaginatively reconstruct the experience of the work as sanctioned by the artist" (Irvin 2006: 152).

11 Irvin cites David Davies' Pragmatic Constraint, such that "[a]rtworks must be entities that can bear the sorts of properties rightly ascribed to what are termed 'works' in our reflective critical and appreciative practice; that are individuated in the way such 'works' are or would be individuated[;] and that have the modal properties that are reasonably ascribed to 'works', in that practice" (Irvin 2008: 2, citing Davies 2004: 18). A similar view is presented by Thomasson (2004, 2005). The central difference between Davies' view and Thomasson's lies in the degree to which each will allow for variation in ontology from what is apparent in artistic practice.

12 Because she distinguishes an artist's sanction from her intentions, Irvin states that "there is no such thing as a failed sanction: sanctions are either successfully established or nonexistent" (Irvin 2005: 322).

References

Currie, G. (1989), *An Ontology of Art*, New York: St. Martin's Press.

Currie, G. (1991), "Work and Text," *Mind* 100 (3): 325–40.

Danto, A. C. (1964), "The Artworld," *Journal of Philosophy* 61 (19): 571–84.

Davies, D. (2004), *Art as Performance*, Oxford: Oxford University Press.

Eigner, L. (1989), *areas lights heights*, New York: Roof Books.

Eigner, L. (2010a), *The Collected Poems of Larry Eigner*, Vol. I, Stanford, CA: Stanford University Press.

Eigner, L. (2010b), *The Collected Poems of Larry Eigner*, Vol. IV, Stanford, CA: Stanford University Press.

Fama, S., "¿¿Fidelity to Eigner's Poem-Pages?? (no no oh no oh no no no)," *the glade of theoric ornithic hermetica*, March 7, 2010. Available online: http://stevenfama.blogspot.com/2010/03/collected-poems-of-larry-eigner.html

Goldsmith, K., "Richard Prince's Latest Act of Appropriation: A Catcher in the Rye," *Poetry Foundation*, April 19, 2012. Available online: http://www.poetryfoundation.org/harriet/2012/04/richard-princes-latest-act-of-appropriation-the-catcher-in-the-rye/

Goodman, N. (1976), *Languages of Art: An Approach to a Theory of Symbols*, 2nd edn, Indianapolis, IN: Hackett Publishing Company.

Goodman, N. and C. Z. Elgin (1986), "Interpretation and Identity: Can the Work Survive the World?" *Critical Inquiry* 12 (3): 564–75.

Gorton, T., "Only one copy of Wu-Tang Clan's new album will be made," *Dazed*, April 26, 2014. Available online: http://www.dazeddigital.com/music/article/19376/1/only-one-copy-wu-tang-clans-new-album-once-upon-time-in-shaolin-cost-millions

Hick, D. H. (2013), "Ontology and the Challenge of Literary Appropriation," *Journal of Aesthetics and Art Criticism* 71 (2): 155–65.

Irvin, S. (2005), "The Artist's Sanction in Contemporary Art," *Journal of Aesthetics and Art Criticism* 63 (4): 315–26.

Irvin, S. (2006), "Museums and the Shaping of Contemporary Artworks," *Museum Management and Curatorship* 21 (2): 143–56.

Irvin, S. (2008), "The Ontological Diversity of Visual Artworks," in K. Stock and K. Thomson-Jones (eds), *New Waves in Aesthetics*, 1–19, Basingstoke: Palgrave-Macmillan.

"J. B.", "Look, No Hands! And It's 'Music,'" *New York Times*, April 15, 1954, 34.

Kostalanetz, R. (1969), "Inferential Art," *Columbia University Forum* 12 (2): 19–26.

Kostelanetz, R. (2003), *Conversing with Cage*, 2nd edn, New York: Routledge.

Levinson, J. (1980), "What a Musical Work Is," *Journal of Philosophy* 77 (1): 5–28.

Marsh, J. K. and D. H. Hick (2014), "Beliefs About Experiencing and Destroying Art," *Proceedings of the 36th Annual Conference of the Cognitive Science Society*: 970–75.

Revill, D. (1992), *The Roaring Silence: John Cage: A Life*, New York: Arcade Publishing.

Thomasson, A. (2004), "The Ontology of Art," in P. Kivy (ed.), *The Blackwell Guide to Aesthetics*, 78–92, Oxford: Blackwell.

Thomasson, A. (2005), "The Ontology of Art and Knowledge in Aesthetics," *Journal of Aesthetics and Art Criticism* 63 (3): 221–9.

Thomasson, A. (2010), "Ontological Innovation in Art," *Journal of Aesthetics and Art Criticism* 68 (2): 119–30.

Walton, K. (1970), "Categories of Art," *Philosophical Review* 79 (3): 334–67.

Part Three

The Copying Artist: Aesthetic and Ethical Challenges

8

Illegitimate Legitimate Copies: A Grey Area in Dealing with Literary Works

Annette Gilbert

1. Authorization and actual copy authority

> I, doctor Abulensis of Lobera, his Imperial Majesty's personal physician / give authority to [the printer] Heynrich Steyner / that he may print this book / and also give him the authority that is bestowed upon me / by his Imperial Majesty for the whole empire.
> Doctor Abulensis[1]

It is the personal physician of Charles V, Holy Roman Emperor, who proudly pronounces the printing privilege of the emperor at the beginning of his health guide *Ein nutzlich Regiment der Gesundtheyt* (A Useful Health Regime) from 1531. Moreover, he, the author of the guide, also self-confidently authorizes his Augsburg printer Heinrich Steiner to print the work.

The printer's authorization by the author of a book has become an important sales-promotional advantage from the sixteenth century on. It complemented the printing privilege that the state could grant and provided the publisher with a "legal advantage" over his rivals. For a publisher to be the legitimate publisher of a work, the author had to agree on the publication and duplication of the work. The authorization "turns the publisher into the legal publisher" of the work. It was the precursor of the emerging copyright law (Bosse 2014: 27–30).[2]

The general authorization of the publisher by the author does not, however, mean that all copies produced under this mandate will always correspond to the author's expectations. The concrete manifestation of a work can in fact contradict the author's will—for instance because of deviations from the original text, changes that affect the meaning of the work, or disregard for the author's wishes concerning the design of the text or book. Therefore, authorized does not necessarily mean authentic. An authorization can also be a mere "apparent authorization" if an authorized text does not "comply with the author's will" (Polheim 2004: 65).

Cases of works that are authorized, but that violate the author's will or the integrity of the work, have hardly been investigated so far. Only very rarely have they become a matter of legal or public dispute. The reason is that, in most cases, the authors do not have the proper means of interfering with or sanctioning the publishing process that would give them the ultimate authority over the copy of their work. The author's work authority reaches its limits as soon as the general licence to duplicate is granted. The following discussion of literary examples is a plea for respecting the author's copy authority.

2. Double prints

One historical example of an illegitimate legitimate print—where the publisher's moral and legal transgression is obvious—is the phenomenon of double prints that was quite common in the eighteenth century. Double prints are the illegitimate production of additional exemplars by the authorized publisher that exceed the number of printed copies arranged with the author—without the author's knowledge, and without payment for the author.[3] These extra prints, also referred to as imitation prints, "copy the first prints as closely as possible"[4] so that nobody—including the author—would notice the deception.[5]

Since the difference is easy to overlook, the discovery or proof of a double print is not a trivial task. Authors who carefully proofread their texts, however, will notice these minimal differences. One victim of this dishonest process was, for instance, the renowned author of the epic poem *Messias* (*The Messiah*, vols 1–4, 1751–73), Friedrich Gottlieb Klopstock. By "comparing the exemplars" (Klopstock 1982: 110–11) he noticed that his publisher Carl Hermann Hemmerde, in Halle, had produced several editions by dating back double prints "without paying me the small sum determined in the contract" (Klopstock 1993: 71–2).[6]

3. Flawed copies

Klopstock, by the way, was not only unhappy about his publisher because of the double prints, but also because of the many printing errors. After each edition, and with each of his publishers, Klopstock had to fight for a "correct" edition. As a protest against the faultiness of the existing editions, among other reasons, in the end he even self-published his works, hoping that he would finally be able to publish his "holy" texts in an adequate typographical, orthographical, and aesthetic form (see Pape 1969).

Whereas double prints are a violation of the agreed-upon number of prints, faulty prints violate the integrity of the work. Given the frequent bad experiences that many authors have concerning their printed works, authors surprisingly seldom withdraw the authorization and demand the destruction of the whole edition. Paul Celan took this radical step in 1948 and demanded that his Vienna publisher, Sexl, should pulp his first work *Der Sand aus den Urnen* (*The Sand from the Urns*) and stop distributing it. The publication, which included the first German printing of his famous poem, "Todesfuge" ("Fugue of Death"), was supposed to be his ticket into the German-language literary scene. But:

> How great my horror was, when I received it! [...] The book was full of misprints, with the most tasteless cover that I had ever seen, and, on top of that, with two illustrations by a friend, who is a painter, and who could not stop himself from providing my book with two proofs of extreme tastelessness. The misprints were of the worst kind! I was forced to send a telegraph to ensure the book would be withdrawn.[7]

However, this took almost four years, and Celan only received the final report of the successful pulping of the 500 printed copies, of which nine exemplars had been sold and five delivered to libraries, in March 1952 (see Seng 2001). Today these copies are rarities, and on Abebooks they sell for up to 20,000 Euros. Strangely enough, even a primitive, self-made copy of the first edition is categorized as a rarity by the Philological Library of the Free University Berlin.

Celan's formulation that "the misprints were of the worst kind" suggests that this is not a purely quantitative matter. Whether misprints are relevant or not does not only depend on their number, but on their "quality," their placement and effect—and also on the author's subjective impression, since they might perceive every single error as an unbearable disfigurement of the meaning of the work and of their will.[8]

4. The fight for typesetting authority

Not every author would be able to, or would want to, take such drastic steps and have their book pulped or start their own publishing house. Another common strategy of securing text and work authority against printers, typesetters, and publishers is to make the lines of the conflict visible on the symbolic level of the book itself. The fight for text authority has, in several cases, become the subject of fiction. The best-known example might be E. T. A. Hoffmann's novel *Lebens-Ansichten des Katers Murr nebst fragmentarischer Biographie des Kapellmeisters Johannes Kreisler in zufälligen Makulaturblättern* [*The Life and Opinions of the Tomcat Murr together with a Fragmentary Biography of Kapellmeister Johannes Kreisler on Random Sheets of Waste Paper*] from 1819–21. The notes of the tomcat Murr are accidentally intermingled and merged with the biography of the composer Johannes Kreisler, because—as the editor explains in his (fictional) preface—the careless typesetter has also printed those passages that the tomcat only used as blotting paper or as a writing pad, but he accidentally left them in the manuscript.

A few years later, Karl Immermann addresses the misconduct of a bookbinder in his satirical novel *Münchhausen. Eine Geschichte in Arabesken* (Münchhausen. A story in arabesques) from 1838–9. The novel begins in medias res—with Chapter 11. After Chapter 15, a fictitious "correspondence between the editor and the bookbinder" is inserted that informs us that the editor has complained about the following:

> Today I received the first volume of my Münchhausen adventures, and I see that you have stuck the first ten chapters behind chapters eleven to fifteen. I send you the book back and ask you to rebind the book.
>
> Immermann 1838: 87

The bookbinder's answer, however, does not lack self-confidence:

> These days, when the author has muddled something, a good bookbinder has to assist the understanding of the work, by adding hints on the back cover, or wherever they might fit. [...] A bit of help is required then, as far as possible, and often the right perspective for a book can be determined just by adding or leaving out a full stop or comma, just to clear things up. [...] I have, as far as I was able to, assisted you in this work about Münchhausen and created a bit of confusion, so that the required thrills should arise.
>
> Immermann 1838: 87, 88, 92

And those thrills are, allegedly, what the audience wants. In order to "help" the book a bit more, the bookbinder suggests further "household remedies," including printing this very correspondence, because

> Exchanges of letters are popular now, even if they only contain news about a cold or cough attacks of the correspondents. Let us also print our exchange of letters in the first book, this will help promote it.
>
> Immermann 1838: 95–6

Neither the negligence of the typesetter nor the impertinence of the bookbinder that Hoffmann and Immermann portray in literary form are exaggerated. This is the bitter reality that many authors, to this day, are facing. It was quite common for typesetters, printers, bookbinders, or publishers to interfere with the text without consulting with the author first or pointing out in the text that changes have been made. They literally had the last word (see Wieland forthcoming).

A prominent example is Christoph Martin Wieland's *Geschichte des Agathon* [*The History of Agathon*] from 1766–7, the first German *Bildungsroman* (education novel). In the second volume, the publisher "on his own initiative, added an annotation about the title of the sixth chapter, due to reasonable worries about censorship" (Wieland forthcoming).[9] All that the angry Wieland could do was to ensure his text authority by at least virtually deleting the footnote again in the corrigenda: "p. 57 *deleatur* the very superfluous annotation" (Wieland 1767: Corrigenda).[10]

This dispute is not a jest and not fiction, but very serious. In trying to maintain the authority over their own work and its individual manifestations, authors discover types of text such as the corrigenda or the preface and postscript as a means of raising an objection, at least in this "semi-public space," and, so to say, "from the para-textual threshold." As Magnus Wieland points out:

> Christoph Martin Wieland purposefully uses the corrigenda as an [additional] authorial space for communication in order to override the non-authorized decision by the publisher and to [regain] the autonomy over his own work. The typesetter can use the footnote as an instrument of power to unsolicitedly interfere with the text, the corrigenda is the author's space for articulating revisions and replies—it is his battle ground for control over the work.
>
> Wieland forthcoming[11]

5. Excursus: Academic publishing

Work authority can still be undermined today, as can be seen in the recently published new edition of Heinrich Bosse's *Autorschaft ist Werkherrschaft* (Authorship means Work Authority), originally published in 1981. Its topic is work authority, and, in Germany, this is the standard work on the emergence of copyright law. The new edition from 2014 shows, involuntarily, the problems of work authority when it comes to the integrity of the prints. Very reasonably, the reviewers were disappointed that this

> new edition is very carelessly designed. The print image and countless errors

> suggest that someone has simply scanned the first edition with optical character recognition software and then mechanically inserted it into the new format—unbelievable paginations, footnote numbers that have wandered into the main text and absurd misprints spoil the delight over the new edition. The careless treatment of the work is rather ironic, since the book has become a digitally born descendant of those analogue quality failures that we know from earlier centuries.
>
> Schmidt 2015

Corrupted texts are not a new phenomenon and not at all uncommon even today, as can be seen, for instance, in the fact that the error-proneness of digitized texts has already become the subject of literary and artistic treatment. In her work *Phantoms (H__RT _F D_RKN_SS)* from 2011—the faulty title already indicates the problems of "mistranslations" (Syjuco n.d.) between different media—Stephanie Syjuco presents twelve different editions of Joseph Conrad's *Heart of Darkness* (1899). She took the digital text of the novella that is available on various internet platforms and retuned it into material form by offering it for sale on the print-on-demand platform Lulu. The typesetting of these "re-editioned texts" is unbearable: there are countless scanning and tagging mistakes, the text is entirely unformatted, typographically amateurish, and full of adverts and links. This shows the danger that digitized and abandoned texts face when wandering through the internet.[12]

The example of Heinrich Bosse's book shows that not only literary, but also academic authors may require a higher level of work authority. The reputation of the academic is easily at stake here. Even minor alterations can have significant consequences: if, for instance, a publisher inserts blank spaces into a quote, this might comply with the principles of good typesetting. But in an article that bemoans the careless use of quotes in literary studies and then uses this falsely edited quote to argue for the importance of exact quoting, the alteration is quite counterproductive. The same applies if, in a text about Marcel Proust's *In Search of Lost Time,* the name "Marcel" is always changed to "Marcel Proust," thus ignoring the difference between the narrator (Marcel) and the author (Marcel Proust). Each of these real-life examples has unwanted consequences: they disfigure texts, discredit the authors, and can damage their reputation.

6. Imprimatur

It is true that publishers are committed to faithfulness to the original work by publishing and copyright law and must not alter the work. Nevertheless, the author's means of opposing such alterations are, in practice, rather limited. The prevailing minimal alterations will hardly count as violations of the work's *substance* nor as *intense* alterations.[13] Despite their fatal consequences, alterations can therefore count as "legitimate," and, according to the German *Urheberrechtsgesetz* (Copyright Act), "the author cannot bona fide deny to agree" with them (§39, 2 UrhG).[14] Even denying the imprimatur, that is, the final printing approval by the author, is not an option, because neither copyright nor publishing law recognize a "denial of imprimatur": when signing a contract with a publisher, the author agrees to the publication of the work. An imprimatur that goes beyond this agreement is not necessary for publishing the work.

In cases of conflict such as the ones described above, there are hardly any means of enforcing the work authority of the author or objecting to the duplication of the work in the intended form. The only legally actionable factor is that there must not be any technical errors in the print and that it must comply with "commercial practice" and be "appropriate," meaning that it complies with other works of the same kind and does not damage the reputation of the author (see Wegner et al. 2011: marginal no. 75). These formulations allow for wide interpretation, though, which is why, in fact, there is hardly any actual authorization of the publication by the author at work here.

7. Design authority

Not only the correctness of the copies, but also the design authority and freedom are often a cause for conflict. Representative of the self-confident position of the publisher is Kurt Wolff, the important publisher of German expressionism, who claimed in 1917:

> I think that the publisher, a modest man, who deals with the minds and the productions of others and ideally mediates other people's values, should at least be—and in fact is—allowed to create the design that he is bringing onto the public stage by himself.
>
> Wolff 1999: 208

Of course, many authors disagree. One example of their uncompromising attitude would be Paul Valéry:

> Every reproduction or publication that does not correspond to the physical aspect that the author wanted should be treated as null and void.[15]

At least in Germany, the legal situation for this conflict of interests is clear: according to §14 of the German *Verlagsgesetz* (VerlG) (publishing law) from

1901, it is the right of the publisher to decide about the form and the features of the work:

> The publisher is obliged to duplicate and disseminate the work in an appropriate and established way. The form and features of the copies are determined by the publisher, acknowledging the common practice of the book market and the purpose and content of the work.

This routine division of labor has, however, become increasingly conflict-laden, since the authors' sensitivity concerning the design of their works has grown over the past decades.

The most recent example of a public conflict between an author and the publishing house concerning the typesetting is the novel *Alix, Anton und die anderen* (Alix, Anton, and the Others, 2009) by Katharina Hacker. Hacker is a successful contemporary German author, and winner of the German Book Award, so we are not merely concerned with a fringe phenomenon here.

The publishing house's behavior forced Hacker to go public via a press release on her homepage, saying that the novel "was not only [published] against the author's wishes—but also in a form that contradicts her aesthetic intentions" (Lovenberg 2009). Without consulting with Hacker first, Suhrkamp—her publisher back then—had changed the "manuscript that Hacker had delivered and that a designer had specifically layouted for her" (Lovenberg 2009). The changes distorted the meaning of the work, Hacker claimed. Her text featured two columns, whose relationship to each other was rather unclear. Suhrkamp had set the narrow column like a margins column, that is, in smaller letters and always at the edge. This created the impression that the column was not an equally valuable parallel narrative, but rather an annotation or commentary to the broader column: "the layout chosen by the publishing house changes the character of how the novel is narrated" (Lovenberg 2009) was the overall opinion of the arts sections of the newspapers.

Hacker's unusual step to go public is probably also related to the insecure legal situation that regularly puts authors at a disadvantage. An author can, in principle, decide if, when, and where, "and especially in which form he wants to reveal his work and thereby himself to the public" (Dreier et al. 2015: marginal no. 1; cf. §12 UrhG). But the law grants such a high degree of interpretive freedom to the publisher that, in particular, disputes between author and publisher that solely concern matters of taste will usually not amount to a breach of contract. Dissent about aesthetic questions concerning the layout will, if in doubt, not justify withdrawing from the contract.[16]

The outrage in the newspapers about Katharina Hacker's conflict—which, as most people thought, "by far exceeded the quarrels that are common in the book trade" (Lovenberg 2009)—showed that the legally established imbalance in favor of the publishing house is, now, considered to be unfair and even objectionable—because it violates the autonomy of art. At the end of her review, the literary critic Felicitas von Lovenberg demands: "In central artistic questions, the author has to have the last word" (Lovenberg 2009).

This is a remarkable statement. The fact that the *typesetting* of a novel can now be counted as one of the "central artistic questions" shows that fundamental transitions are happening here: not only the traditional conception of a literary work that reduces the work to its text—in the sense of an abstract, linguistic structure—needs to be revised, but also the responsibilities, rights, and obligations of everyone involved in the production and duplication of the work.

8. Books, not texts: The author as a sovereign

This revision is rather urgent. Nowadays, when texts are written on a computer and the writer therefore necessarily has to make certain initial design decisions, every writer automatically also effectively becomes a typesetter. Consequently, as the example of Katharina Hacker shows, an increasing number of authors no longer regard the design of text and book as contingent aspects of the instantiation of their works, but rather as properties that are constitutive of the work and are subject to their own authorship, and they want to be responsible for it.[17]

Authors such as Judith Schalansky, who explicitly says "I'm typesetting while writing," are no longer an exception, because, as Schalansky argues:

> It is impossible that an author does not care about the form in which his text meets with his readers. After all, the form is the place where they meet. [...] There is no such thing as a pure, immaterial text. [...] By typesetting my texts, I am at my own service, so to say. While writing, I am already thinking about the right font, about the pictorial concept, about the format, paper and proportions, invisible lines and optical axes that hold everything together—these are all calculations that have to be realized in the printed work.
>
> Schalansky 2011

This comment is based on the idea of a book as a *Gesamtkunstwerk*, in which "text, image and design are unified" and "form and content cannot be distinguished from each other" (Schalansky 2011).

Currently, there is a strong movement, both in mainstream as well as in avant-garde experimental literature, that is following the slogan "books, not texts." On the one hand, there is an increasing number of books that feature a very sophisticated design in material, visual, and typographical terms, such as Mark Z. Danielewski's *The House of Leaves* (2000), Jonathan Safran Foer's *Tree of Codes* (2010), and J. J. Abrams' and Doug Dorst's *S* (2013), where the narration and the medium of the book are fused into each other. Alexander Starre talks about the authorial practices of these millennial generation of writer-designers as "literary bibliographers," who "draw [...] book design into the signifying territory of the work" (Starre 2015: 168).

On the other hand, independent publishers like the British publisher Information as Material want to enable their authors "to write books rather than just texts" (Thurston 2013: 151). The Polish artist Zenon Fajfer and the literary scholar Katarzyna Bazarnik have created the neologism "liberature" in order to describe this "literature in the form of a book." It shifts the emphasis from "litera" (lat.: letter) to "liber" (lat.: book): "the material book, which can be of any shape and structure, ceases to be a neutral container for a text, but becomes an integral component of the literary work" (Bazarnik 2010: 7).[18]

What is envisioned here is the "sovereign author, who is responsible not only for the decision about the language and content, but also the material dimension of his text" (Falk 2006: 27) and its manifestations.[19] The notion of the author "taking over the responsibility" for the duplicated text is symptomatic for the debate about "holistic" conceptions of works of literature. The book artist, author, and publisher Ulises Carrión already defined the "new art of making books" in 1975 as follows:

> In the old art the writer judges himself as being not responsible for the real book. He writes the text. The rest is done by the servants, the artisans, the workers, the others.
>
> [...] In the new art the writer assumes the responsibility for the whole process.
>
> Carrión 1980: 8

For Nick Thurston, one of the three publishers of Information as Material, there is also no doubt that the author is not only responsible for the text these days, but also for the materialized and reproduced form that the text has taken on by publication: "the 'author' take[s] responsibility for the full object-status of the reproduced cultural object" (Thurston 2014: 424).

This, of course, contradicts both the traditional conception of literary works and the traditional, but still powerful paradigm of the labor division in the book trade which Roger Chartier has formulated in the well-known slogan: "authors do not write books; they write texts that become material objects" (Chartier and Cavillo 1995: 5). There is a good reason to believe that this slogan will not apply for much longer. Ulises Carrión already objected to it in 1975:

> In the old art the writer writes texts.
> In the new art the writer makes books.
>
> Carrión 1980

9. Reproduction as production

Nick Thurston has described this long-established "literary industry's model" of literary production by the formula "production-then-reproduction" (Thurston 2014: 425). When talking about literary production, until now this usually referred to the author who writes a text and hence creates an original creative product. When the text is finished by the author, this creative-productive stage also counts as finished. What follows is the stage of duplication and publication, where, usually, other people take over and "nothing essential," according to the still common conception, is added to the text or work.[20]

The alternative model that is currently being tested enthusiastically in the young literary scene can be described by Thurston's formula "reproduction-as-production" (Thurston 2014: 423; see also Gilbert 2016). It is the attempt to break up the logic of production and reproduction outlined above—even to reverse it. The aim is to increase the value of reproduction and to "re-conceptualize [it] as a form of production" for it to lose its subsequent, secondary character. "To write books rather than just texts"—the maxim of Information as Material—then means a literary practice in which the authors "implicate the processes of reproduction in the conscious processes of artistic production" (Thurston and Kivland 2013: 151). With his formula "reproduction-as-production," Thurston argues for an enormous broadening of the artistic scope within the field of literature.

This new self-conception of authors needs to be taken into account if authorship is indeed supposed to mean work authority and if—to borrow from Heinrich Bosse—"the master of the product [is also supposed to be] the master of the reproduction" (Bosse 2014: 36). The typesetting, layout, format—in short: any factors related to the reproduction of the literary work—gain importance and become an essential part of the creative, literary-artistic activity that is as valuable as writing.

10. From producer to reproducer

The responses to this concept and formula within the literature and art scene are overwhelmingly positive. Everywhere, people are talking about "creative modes of reproduction."[21] Reproduction is the order of the day.

But one should not forget that there is a certain ambiguity to the formula—which certainly contributed to its success and dissemination. It is not only a means of propagating reproduction in the sense of duplicating and producing tokens of a work as an aspect of literary-artistic production. The formula also comprises the reproductive, that is, quoting, copying, and appropriating ways of writing that are hugely popular in contemporary literature, but are often criticized, because they allegedly only use what already exists and do not create any "original," "new" content. For these unorthodox ways of writing, Kenneth Goldsmith and Marjorie Perloff have already provided the theoretical background and also, by now, well-established labels in their works on *Uncreative Writing* and *Unoriginal Genius* (Goldsmith 2011; Perloff 2010).

One of many examples of this literary trend is Simon Morris's *Getting Inside Jack Kerouac's Head* from 2010. It contains the almost unmodified text of Jack Kerouac's *On the Road*, which Morris had typed out word for word and posted on his blog over the course of one year, one page per day. Then he published it as a book that looked like the Penguin edition of *On the Road*, under his own name.[22] The book was by no means a one-hit-wonder; it was even followed by a successor, Joe Hale's *Getting Inside Simon Morris' Head* from 2014 (the text of which will be familiar to the readers of Morris's book). Morris's and Hale's books are part of a global movement which has been documented under the label of *appropriation literature* (see Gilbert 2014).

Both Morris's and Hale's books were published by Information as Material, following its agenda to support authors who "write books rather than just texts." In seeking to ennoble reproduction—by promoting it as a mode of literary production equal to writing—Information as Material stands with a growing number of authors in the vanguard of a movement celebrating "copy" in both its meanings: as the product of copying and as the copy of a token, as an exemplar. In this movement, work authority that does not entail authority over copy and reproduction is unthinkable.

Notes

1 Avila 1531: A ii verso. All translations in this chapter are by Michael Weh unless otherwise indicated.

2 The example of Lobera de Avila is also taken from Bosse 2014.

3 For the history of the concept see Boghardt 2008a.

4 Bogeng 1911, quoted in Boghardt 2008a: 137.

5 "The principle of the typographical cycle entailed the fact that, when all exemplars of an edition were sold, the printers had to create a new edition based on a new typesetting, because the old one would have dismantled during the printing process" (Boghardt 2008b: 186). This means that, in the age of hot metal typesetting, the first and the new typesetting cannot be 100 percent identical. There are always new printing mistakes and other errors, and the spaces between the letters are also always slightly different.

6 Klopstock took the fact that Hemmerde first told a bookseller that the book was sold out, and then delivered several copies to him, as further proof that the publisher had produced double prints. See Klopstock 1982.

7 Paul Celan, letter to Max Rychner from October 24, 1948, quoted in Seng 2001: 100. However, Celan had also tasked friends with correcting the printing mistakes. The illustrator was his friend the surrealist artist Edgar Jené.

8 Calculations such as the following are therefore not very significant: "After all, it contained at least seventeen printing mistakes—around 25 percent, that is, 13 out of the 48 poems of the volume, were flawed" (Seng 2001: 107).

9 I would like to thank Magnus Wieland for pointing this out to me.

10 The annotation in question was made in vol. 1, 57. See also Wieland 1975: 341.

11 A different strategy for self-assertion is to include the (in the end, unavoidable) printing and typesetting mistakes in the conception of the work. For instance, the Russian futurist Velimir Khlebnikov welcomed the contingent aspect of printing mistakes as a means of liberating the work from the solidification of language. In the context of his Zaum′ language, he developed a "poetics of the printing mistake." Another example would be Dieter Roth, who, in 1966, deliberately let his students in Providence who did not speak German handle the typesetting and printing of his volume *Scheisse. Neue Gedichte* (Shit. New Poems). This kind of deliberate conceptual inclusion of typesetting and printing mistakes could already be found in Hans Arp's and Raoul Hausmann's works.

12 The installation also includes printouts of low-resolution jpgs of CD covers found on Amazon of all the digital music files Syjuco has illegally downloaded, and a three-minute found-footage video that strings together numerous warnings at the beginning of YouTube films: "This film has been modified from its original version. It has been formatted to fit this screen." This refers to the loss-entailing

phenomenon of the historical changeability of media formats that is similar to the digitization of texts (see Syjuco, n.d.).

13 These are the general criteria employed in a corresponding balancing of interests (see Dreier et al. 2015: §39, marginal nos 5 and 16).

14 In the literature on publishing law, "correcting misprints," "correcting orthographic and punctuation errors," and "correcting obvious typos" are frequently counted as legitimate alterations that the author usually has to accept (see Dreier et al. 2015: §13 VerlG, marginal no. 8; Schricker 2001: §13 VerlG/§39 UrhG, marginal no. 11).

15 Paul Valéry, quoted in Christin 2007: 197.

16 In a review for the British Society of Authors—which was founded in 1884—S. Squire Sprigge already noted that, in the publishing contracts of his time, "the author is placed in an unfair position—that is, a position where he can be cheated with impunity" (Sprigge 1890: 108). Ever since there have been writers' organizations, they have been fighting for the contractual relationship between authors and publishers to be "based upon [...] fair and equitable principles" (ibid.: vii). There is still no study about the historical changes in the relationship between author and publisher as manifested in concrete contracts. I thank Kathy Bowrey for pointing this out to me.

17 This conforms with what Roland Reuß has observed: "If we look at the heritage of modernity from here, the tendency can easily be noted that writers increasingly try to influence questions of typographical design" (Reuß 2006: 69–71).

18 This is not an exclusively contemporary phenomenon. There have always been authors who pursued a "bibliographical" or a "liberatic approach," such as Laurence Sterne, Rétif de la Bretonne, William Blake, James Joyce, Raymond Queneau, William Gass, B. S. Johnson, Raymond Federman.

19 See also Bosse 2014: 7, who calls the author the "sovereign of his work."

20 Carl Denina, *Bibliopoeie, oder: Anweisung für Schriftsteller* (1783), quoted in Bosse 2014: 18.

21 See, for example, The Piracy Project by Andrea Francke and Eva Weinmayr (since 2010): "The Piracy Project is an international publishing and exhibition project exploring the philosophical, legal and practical implications of book piracy and creative modes of reproduction [...] The Piracy Project is not about stealing or forgery. It is about creating a platform to innovatively explore the spectrum of copying, re-editing, translating, paraphrasing, imitating, re-organising, manipulating of already existing works. Here creativity and originality sit not in the borrowed material itself, but in the way it is handled." http://www.andpublishing.org/projects/and-the-piracy-project/.

22 Since the latest entries are at the top of a blog, Morris's edition of *On the Road* is printed in reverse order with reverse pages numbers. Morris's work features

several interesting details concerning the textual basis, layout, and the paratexts that cannot be described in detail here. An extensive description can be found in Ramtke 2012 and Hick 2013.

References

Avila, L. L. de (1531), *Ein nutzlich Regiment der gesundtheyt/ Genant das Vanquete/ oder Gastmal der Edlen diener von der Complexion/ Eigenschafft/ Schad/ vnd nutz allerley Speyß/ Trancks/ vn[d] von allem/ darmit sich der mensch in ge=sundtheyt enthelt/ Mit sampt einem kurtzen Regiment/ Wye man sich in der Pestilentz/ Pestilentzischen fieber vnnd Schweyß halten soll*, Augsburg: Heinrich Steiner.

Bazarnik, K. (2010), "Time for Liberature," in Z. Fajfer, *Liberature or Total Literature. Collected Essays 1999–2009*, 7–8, Kraków: Ha!art.

Bogeng, G. A. E. (1911), *Umriß einer Fachkunde für Büchersammler*, Nikolassee: M. Harwitz.

Boghardt, M. (2008a), "Der Begriff des Doppeldrucks," in P. Needham (ed.), *Archäologie des gedruckten Buches*, 131–44, Wiesbaden: Harrassowitz.

Boghardt, M. (2008b), "'Meiner Freundin gewidmet.' Buchdruck, Raubdruck, Nachdruck, dargestellt am Beispiel von Klopstocks *Messias*," in P. Needham (ed.), *Archäologie des gedruckten Buches*, 175–92, Wiesbaden: Harrassowitz.

Bosse, H. (2014), *Autorschaft ist Werkherrschaft. Über die Entstehung des Urheberrechts aus dem Geist der Goethezeit* [1981], Paderborn: Fink.

Carrión, U. (1980), "The New Art of Making Books" [1975], reprinted in *Second Thoughts*, 5–22, Amsterdam: VOID Distributors.

Chartier, R. and G. Cavallo (eds) (1995), *A History of Reading in the West*, London: Polity Press.

Christin, A. (2007), "Ecriture et iconicité," *Europe*, 934/935: 196–207.

Dreier, T., G. Schulze, and L. Specht (2015), *Urheberrechtsgesetz, Urheberrechts-wahrnehmungsgesetz, Kunsturhebergesetz. Kommentar*, Munich: Beck.

Falk, R. (2006), "Literatur aus dem Winkelhaken. Zur literatur- und editionswissen-schaftlichen Bedeutung der Typographie," *Text. Kritische Beiträge*, 11: 27–47.

Gilbert, A. (2014), *Reprint. Appropriation (&) Literature*, Wiesbaden: Luxbooks.

Gilbert, A. (ed.) (2016), *Publishing as Artistic Practice*, Berlin: Sternberg.

Goldsmith, K. (2011), *Uncreative Writing: Managing Language in the Digital Age*, New York: Columbia University Press.

Hick, D. H. (2013), "Ontology and the Challenge of Literary Appropriation," *Journal of Aesthetics and Art Criticism* 71(2): 155–65.

Immermann, K. (1838), *Münchhausen. Eine Geschichte in Arabesken*, vol. 1, Düsseldorf: Schaub.

Klopstock, F. G. (1982), "Letter to Karl Hermann Hemmerde from October 16, 1778," in H. Riege (ed.), *Werke und Briefe*, section *Briefe*, vol. VII-I, 110–11, Berlin: de Gruyter.

Klopstock, F. G. (1993), "Letter to Georg Joachim Göschen from June 4, 1796," in H. Riege (ed.), *Werke und Briefe*, section *Briefe*, vol. IX-I, 71–2, Berlin: de Gruyter.

Lovenberg, F. von (2009), "Katharina Hacker und Suhrkamp. Chronik einer Zerrüttung," *Frankfurter Allgemeine Zeitung*, November 14, 2009. Available online: http://www.faz.net/aktuell/feuilleton/themen/katharina-hacker-und-suhrkamp-chronik-einer-zerruettung-1883557.html

Pape, H. (1969), "Klopstocks Autorenhonorare und Selbstverlagsgewinne," *Archiv für Geschichte des Buchwesens* 10: cols 1–272.

Perloff, M. (2010), *Unoriginal Genius. Poetry by Other Means in the New Century*, Chicago: University of Chicago Press.

Polheim, K. K. (2004), "Die scheinbare Autorisation oder Der Schutz des Autors vor sich selbst," in T. Bein, R. Nutt-Kofoth, and B. Plachta (eds), *Autor—Autorisation—Authentizität*, 65–72, Tübingen: Niemeyer.

Ramtke, N. (2012), "Ohne Begleitschutz—Texte auf der Schwelle. Überlegungen zu Textappropriationen und Paratext," in A. Gilbert (ed.), *Wiederaufgelegt. Zur Appropriation von Texten und Büchern in Büchern*, 103–19, Bielefeld: transcript.

Reuß, R. (2006), "Spielräume des Zufälligen. Zum Verhältnis von Edition und Typographie," *Text. Kritische Beiträge* 11: 55–100.

Schalansky, J. (2011), "Wie ich Bücher mache," *Bella triste* 30: n.p.

Schmidt, J. (2015), "Urheberrecht, analog. Heinrich Bosses Klassiker 'Autorschaft ist Werkherrschaft' ist neu erschienen," *literaturkritik.de* 3. Available online: http://www.literaturkritik.de/public/rezension.php?rez_id=20290

Schricker, G. (2001), *Verlagsrecht. Kommentar*, Munich: Beck.

Seng, J. (2001), "'Und ist die Poesie mein Schicksal …' Paul Celans Gedichtband 'Der Sand aus den Urnen'," in P. Goßens, and M. G. Patka (eds), *"Displaced." Paul Celan in Wien 1947–1948*, 99–108, Frankfurt/M.: Suhrkamp.

Sprigge, S. S. (1890), *The Methods of Publishing*, London: Henry Glaisher.

Starre, A. (2015), *Metamedia: American Book Fictions and Literary Print Culture after Digitization*, Iowa City: University of Iowa Press.

Syjuco, S. (n.d.), "Phantoms (H__RT _F D_RKN_SS) and related works". Available online: http://www.stephaniesyjuco.com/p_phantoms.html

Thurston, N. (2014), "Publishing as a Praxis of Conceptualist Reading Performances," *Journal of Writing in Creative Practice* 6 (3): 421–9.

Thurston, N. and S. Kivland (2013), "Reading. Some Positions," in R. Sawdon-Smith, and E. Waeckerle (eds), *The Book is a-live!*, 150–9, Sheffield: RGAP.

Ulmer-Eilfort, C. and E. I. Obergfell (2013), *Verlagsrecht. Kommentar*, Munich: Beck.

Wegner, K., D. Wallenfels, D. Kaboth, and S. Haupt (2011), *Recht im Verlag*, Munich: Beck.

Wieland, C. M. (1975), "Letter to Orell, Geßner and Cie from January 18, 1765," in *Briefwechsel*, vol. 3, 339–42, Berlin: Akademie Verlag.

Wieland, C. M. (1767), *Geschichte des Agathon*, vol. 2, Frankfurt/M. and Leipzig: [s. n.].

Wieland, M. (forthcoming), "Der Satz der Sätze. Praxis und Poesis des Schriftsetzers," in C. Ortlieb, and T. Fuchs (eds), *Büchermachen. Zur Materialität des Publizierens in der europäischen Literatur um 1800*, Hanover: Wehrhahn.

Wolff, K. (1999), "Letter to Mechtild Lichowsky from June 18, 1917," quoted in *Marbacher Magazin: Vom Schreiben 6. Aus der Hand oder Was mit den Büchern geschieht*, 88: 208.

9

Appropriating Fictional Characters

James O. Young

1. Introduction

Today there is increasing awareness that many intellectual property regimes are placing restrictions on artistic creativity. In particular, intellectual property laws protecting fictional characters are limiting the opportunities of other artists to produce works with high aesthetic value and limiting the public's access to such works. Consequently, there is an aesthetic case against current intellectual property regimes as they apply to fictional characters. This aesthetic case against intellectual property laws is part of a moral case against these laws: they enable individuals and corporations to steal from the public domain. Corporations are taking full advantage of the existing laws and are appropriating fictional characters to which they have no legitimate claim. Intellectual property laws are thus (at least in some cases) failing to achieve their intended goal of encouraging artistic creativity, and are instead wrongfully transferring wealth to those who already have far more than they deserve.

Artists who copy the characters of other artists are not difficult to find. Indeed, they are common throughout the history of the arts. Ancient poets mined the works of Homer for characters. Sophocles copied the characters of Agamemnon, Iphigenia, Clytemnestra, and others. Virgil appropriated Aeneas from Homer's *Iliad*. Modern poets like Tennyson continued to tell stories about Ulysses, and any number of painters have depicted characters from Homer, Virgil, and the other ancient poets. In the contemporary world, Sherlock Holmes and his companion John Watson have been frequently appropriated. I have in mind, for example, Michael Dibdin's *The Sherlock Holmes Story* (1978), and Laurie King's novels—beginning with *The Beekeeper's Apprentice* (1994)—featuring her own character of Mary Russell alongside Doyle's Holmes. Mark Gatiss, Steven Moffat, and Stephen Thompson have appropriated Holmes in their series *Sherlock*, as have directors Guy Ritchie (in his Sherlock Holmes movies featuring Robert Downey, Jr. and Jude Law) and Bill Condon (in *Mr. Holmes* [2015]). Just as many, if not more, reuses have been made of characters from the novels of Jane Austen.

The reuse of fictional characters is aesthetically valuable because a good character is a powerful tool for exploring human experience. One legal scholar, displaying some aesthetic nous, has written that "the best known characters, such as Mickey Mouse and Sherlock Holmes, become cultural artifacts and are of great value in creating new works. It is the power of these characters to evoke, to encapsulate, that makes them so important to the public domain" (Kurtz 1994: 452). A good character captures the imagination and becomes a lens through which we see our society and ourselves. A good character has associations and resonances that artists can draw upon. No single artist can conceivably explore all of the possibilities that good fictional characters open up.

Fictional characters can be reused in ways that comment on the original use to which they were put. Pia Pera's novel *Lo's Diary* (1999) tells the story of Nabokov's *Lolita* from the point of view of the title character. This sort of book functions as a critique of the original work, drawing attention to limitations of the point of view presented by the original author. An important sort of work that reuses characters in this way retells a well-known story from the perspective of minor characters. Perhaps the best-known example of this genre is Tom Stoppard's play *Rosencrantz and Guildenstern are Dead* (1966). Another example would be *Mary Reilly* (1990) by Valerie Martin, which retells *Dr. Jekyll and Mr. Hyde* from the perspective of a housemaid. This successful novel was nominated for a Nubula Award (1990) and World Fantasy Award (1991) and made into a movie starring Julia Roberts (1996). Judith Terry's novel *Miss Abigail's Part or Version and Diversion* (1986) similarly retells Jane Austen's *Mansfield Park* from a servant's point of view. Jo Baker retells another Austen novel, *Pride and Prejudice*, from a servant's perspective in *Longbourn* (2014). Alice Randall's novel *The Wind Done Gone* (2001) appropriates characters from Margaret Mitchell's *Gone with the Wind*. Randall's novel explores the experience of the African American characters during the events described in Mitchell's book, functioning as a critique of the racial assumptions of the original.

It is noteworthy that, of the cases just mentioned, the two that are covered by current intellectual property laws both faced legal challenges. Mitchell's trustees sought an injunction to stop publication of Randall's novel.[1] In the end, publication in the U.S. went ahead after Randall agreed to make a donation to Morehouse College. *Lo's Diary* also faced a legal challenge. Dmitri Nabokov,

Vladimir Nabokov's son, alleged copyright infringement. The publication of the book was halted in France and the U.K. The case in the U.S. was settled out of court when Pera agreed to donate half of her royalties to PEN, the writers' organization, and to allow Dmitri Nabokov to include a rather mean-spirited preface in the book.[2]

In general, despite the fact that the appropriation of characters can be so aesthetically successful, many jurisdictions place restrictions on the reuse of characters. Characters are deemed protectable by copyright and other intellectual property laws. Consequently, fictional characters cannot (without permission of the copyright holder or the holder of other legal rights) be appropriated by other artists. Restrictions on copying last (at a minimum) for the term of copyright: life of the artist who creates them plus seventy years in many jurisdictions, including the United States and Europe.[3] Some fictional characters enjoy other forms of protection, including protection under trademark and unfair competition laws that can extend restrictions beyond the term of copyright.

Given these many examples of aesthetically valuable works of art that involve the reuse of fictional characters, one can speculate for a moment about the works of art that we do not have because of current laws restricting the copying of fictional characters. What could have been done, for instance, with Lisbeth Salander (*Girl with the Dragon Tattoo* [2015] and its sequels), one of the most intriguing characters to be created in recent years, after Stieg Larsson's death, had the law not prevented other inspiring authors from making good use of the character? Under current law, Larsson's family owns the rights to the character and can decide who may use it. They have authorized David Lagercrantz (a writer best known for his biographies of footballers) to write the fourth volume in the series, *The Girl in the Spider's Web* (2015). In contrast, Eva Gabrielsson, Larsson's longtime companion, who may have access to partially completed novels by Larsson, cannot publish any work featuring Salander. Nor can anyone else. The public interest would be best served if anyone who wanted could appropriate the character and use her in new works. The public could then judge which of these works is best. Certainly, some rubbish would be produced, but some masterpieces would likely emerge.

Current intellectual property laws, as they apply to fictional characters, however, do not serve the public interest. Artists are discouraged or prevented from copying fictional characters and this denies the public the opportunity to experience works of high aesthetic value. For this reason, fictional characters ought not to be protected by copyright, trademark or unfair competition laws.

(I will, however, argue that authors ought to have a different sort of short-term right over their characters.)

It could be objected that the public interest is irrelevant here. While granting that the public interest would be served if anyone could copy fictional characters, one could nevertheless argue that the public interest would be served only at the cost of sacrificing property rights. People who believe that property rights are inviolable will conclude that the public interest must be allowed to suffer. So let us turn to the questions of whether artists have some sort of proprietary right to fictional characters, and, if so, what form this right takes, and how long it lasts.

2. Copyright and fictional characters

It is a little surprising that courts have found that fictional characters are copyrightable, but they have. Copyright laws typically do not mention fictional characters. Rather, they speak of the protection of works. For example, the copyright law of the European Union states that "Member States shall provide for the exclusive right to authorise or prohibit direct or indirect, temporary or permanent reproduction by any means and in any form, in whole or in part [...] of [...] works."[4] No mention is made of fictional characters. The Copyright Law of the United States similarly states that "original works of authorship fixed in any tangible medium of expression" may be copyrighted. It adds that "In no case does copyright protection for an original work of authorship extend to any idea, procedure, process, system, method of operation, concept, principle, or discovery, regardless of the form in which it is described, explained, illustrated, or embodied in such work."[5]

Despite the fact that fictional characters are not mentioned in copyright laws, courts recognized that characters could be copyrighted as early as the beginning of the twentieth century. *Mutt and Jeff* was a comic strip written and drawn by Bud Fisher, beginning in 1907. The strip was syndicated and immensely popular throughout the U.S. by 1908. In 1914, a court in the Southern District of New York found that the characters Nutt and Giff in a stage review entitled *In Cartoonland* violated the copyright on Mutt and Jeff, which had been licensed to Gus Hill, the producer of a rival review. The court ruled that Nutt and Giff "gave many direct quotations from the cartoons, and [...] were intended to be understood, and were understood, to be the same characters" as Mutt and Jeff, and that this amounted to violation of copyright.[5] The view that characters are copyrightable was reaffirmed by Judge Learned Hand: characters may enjoy copyright protection, he wrote, "quite independently of the 'plot' proper," so long as the characters are sufficiently developed.[6] In Hand's view, stock characters are not protected by copyright.

Some courts have taken a different view and suggested that no characters are protected by copyright. Dashiell Hammett sold the film rights to *The Maltese Falcon* to Warner Bros., but went on to write more stories featuring the fictional hardboiled detective, Sam Spade. Warner Bros. alleged copyright violation in Warner Bros. v. Columbia Broadcasting. The court found against Warner Bros. and went on to suggest that no character was copyrightable unless "the character really constitutes the story being told" and is not merely a "chessman in the game of telling the story."[7] On this view, stories are copyrightable while the "chessmen" used to tell the story are not.

Subsequent U.S. courts have rejected this view. The Disney v. Air Pirates case is particularly important. In the 1970s, the Air Pirates was a collective of cartoonists who produced counterculture comics in which Disney characters, including Mickey Mouse, engaged in sexual activities and drug use. Referring to the Hammett case, the Air Pirates court wrote that "while many literary characters may embody little more than an unprotected idea [...] a comic book character, which has physical as well as conceptual qualities, is more likely to contain some unique elements of expression. Because comic book characters therefore are distinguishable from literary characters, the Warner Brothers language does not preclude protection of Disney's characters."[8] Summing up the legal opinions, Melville Nimmer writes that "Although there has been some conflict in the cases, it is clearly the prevailing view that characters *per se* are entitled to copyright protection" (Nimmer 1963: §2.12). At any rate, well-delineated characters are widely treated as enjoying copyright protection.

This is problematic, and to make my point, I want to return to consider the Sam Spade case. Whether or not one thinks that fictional characters should be copyrightable, the court was right on one point: the court quite rightly found that ownership of copyright to a story does not necessarily carry with it any rights to control the character in the story. The court held that a "character is only the chessman in the game of telling the story." Since the characters "were vehicles for the story told" and not the story itself, the court concluded that "the vehicles did not go with the sale of the story."[9]

The decision of the court was exactly right. If the sale of the copyright had included the characters, then Hammett would have been legally prevented from using Sam Spade in a future work of fiction. The consequences for the production of future artworks would be potentially serious. Fortunately, the court found that ownership of the copyright on a work does not confer ownership of the characters in that work. Hammett was still free to write more Sam Spade stories, and he could sell the movie rights to those stories to someone other than Warner Bros.

Silverman v. CBS Inc.[10] leads to the same conclusion, namely that ownership of a story does not necessarily confer any rights to the characters who populate that story. Stephen M. Silverman, a playwright, applied for a declaration that the characters from the *Amos 'n' Andy* radio sitcom were in the public domain. CBS failed to renew the copyright on episodes aired prior to 1948 with the result that these episodes entered the public domain. CBS nevertheless maintained that, in virtue of holding copyright on post-1948 episodes of *Amos 'n' Andy*, it owned the rights to the characters themselves. The Second Circuit found that the characters in the series "were sufficiently delineated in the pre-1948 radio scripts to have been placed in the public domain when the scripts entered the public domain."[11] Even though CBS owned the copyright on post-1948 scripts, it did not own any rights in the characters. Consequently, Silverman could use the characters, but not any post-1948 additions to them.

This means that if characters are protected by copyright, it is not because the works in which they appear are protected by copyright. Rather, if characters are protected by copyright, it is because someone has, in addition to the copyright on a work, some copyright on the characters. However, this is possible if and only if a character is a work, since copyrights apply only to works. The trouble is that a character is *not* a work.

In order to see this, we need to reflect on what a fictional character is. Once we understand what a character is, we are in a position to note an important difference between a certain sort of work and characters. For present purposes, however, it is not necessary to enter the ontological debate about fictional characters, since one can ask what fictional characters are without addressing the question of the fundamental ontological category to which they belong. This is because we can understand what fictional characters are when we understand their function in works of fiction, such as novels, movies, plays, and comic strips. The fictional characters in a work determine what stories can be told in much the same way that the characters of real people determine their lives. Suppose a real person, call her Anna, has a certain sort of character: she is bold, courageous, principled, and compassionate. She will lead, in virtue of having such a character, an adventurous life and be concerned about justice. Suppose that Bruno is another real person. He is withdrawn, selfish, and small-minded. He will lead a life very different from Anna's. Just as real characters determine how a person lives, fictional characters determine how fictional lives and fictional stories unfold.

Consider an example that illustrates this point. The choice of Sherlock Holmes as a character for a story determines what sort of story can be told. Sherlock Holmes is an eccentric, rather tortured soul, with outstanding intelligence and curiosity. He is interested in solving mysteries, committed to justice, and lives in Baker Street in London. Once an artist has chosen Holmes as the protagonist of a work, only certain stories are possible. The artist cannot use Holmes in fashioning a comedy of manners in the style of Jane Austen. Whatever happens in a story about Sherlock Holmes, he will not be a feckless boulevardier who becomes involved in some romantic entanglements. The story will involve solving a mystery, likely in cooperation with his friend Dr. Watson. He will be brash, inconsiderate, and analytical. He will live, act, and dress in certain ways. He will have a brother named Mycroft. Of course, one of the features of the story is that the name of the protagonist will be Sherlock Holmes.

Another way to make this point is to say that fictional characters have certain sorts of moves. They are in this respect like pieces in a game. And this is precisely how fictional characters were described in one of the landmark court cases that has influenced legal thinking about them. As we have seen, a fictional character (the court was specifically thinking about Hammett's Sam Spade) is a "chessman in the game of telling the story." Chessmen can only move in certain ways. A king can only move one square in any direction (except, of course, when castling). Similarly, a fictional character can only move in certain ways. Sherlock Holmes must be analytical and unemotional. Bugs Bunny must be a brash smart aleck who outsmarts his opponents. A fictional character is, then, not a work. Rather, it is a device or tool used *in the production of* works such as novels and movies. When an artist chooses certain characters, certain stories can be generated while others cannot.

This conclusion is supported by an ontological consideration. Works of the sort in which characters appear have instances. I use the word "instance" here as a neutral term that applies to a variety of metaphysical categories. Some philosophers believe that novels, for example, are types, and individual copies of a novel are tokens of that type. So, for example, *Pride and Prejudice* is a novel type and my copy of the book is a token of the type. Other philosophers could adopt a different ontology of novels. They could hold that a novel is a set of copies of some original manuscript. On this view, *Pride and Prejudice* is the set of all of the copies of Austen's original manuscript and a particular copy is part of the work. Various other ontologies are possible. It seems, however, than any ontology of novels will distinguish between the work and the instance of the work (which is the token of a type, on the first ontology, or a part of the set, on the second ontology). A similar point can be made about movies, plays, comic strips, and other works in which characters appear. Regardless of the ontology one adopts, there are works and instances of works.

This distinction between works and instances is important for present purposes because characters do not have instances. There is something in the world that is an instance of *Pride and Prejudice*. I have one at home in my library. I do not, however, have an instance of Elizabeth Bennet at home in my library. I can buy a copy of *Pride and Prejudice*. I cannot buy a copy of Elizabeth Bennet. There is only one Elizabeth Bennet. Any work must have at least one instance, and Elizabeth Bennet is some sort of abstract entity that does not have instances. (She is, perhaps, an uninstantiated person type.) In this respect, she differs from works. Consequently, she is not a work.

Someone might object that characters are parts of works. Moreover, the objection continues, when one owns a copyright on a work, one owns a copyright on the parts of the work. After all, copyright prohibits reproduction of a work in whole or in part. Consequently, the objection concludes, ownership of a copyright on work does carry with it ownership of a copyright on the characters which are parts of the work.

The rejoinder to this objection is that characters are not parts of works. This is easily proven. Where there is an instance of a work, there are instances of the parts of the work. If a character is part of a work, then where there is an instance of the work there will be an instance of the character. But—as we have seen—characters do not have instances. Therefore, a character is not part of a work. Rather, the parts of works are items such as sentences, acts, scenes, and so on. Notice that it is possible for there to be instances of sentences, acts, scenes, and so on in my library. There is an instance of Scene I from *The Rivals* in my library in virtue of there being an instance of *The Rivals*. (If a scene is ripped from a book, it is possible to have an instance of the scene without having an instance of the work.)

These ontological reflections on works and characters have practical implications. Copyright laws (including European and U.S. copyright laws) explicitly state that only works may be copyrighted. Since fictional characters are not works, they do not belong to the sort of thing that may be protected by copyright. Some one might object to this conclusion by saying that "work" does not have the same meaning in law that it has in philosophy of art. While in philosophy of art, a fictional character is not a work, one might reason, it is a work within the meaning of copyright laws. This objection is undermined by the fact that copyright laws, such as the U.S. Copyright Act, provide no definition for "work." The U.S. Copyright Act does, however, provide in Section 102 a list of categories, including "literary works," "musical works," "pictorial, graphic, and sculptural works," and other sorts of work-creation all falling within our standard artistic understanding of the term. Nothing in the Act says that a character is a work. Courts have erred when they have extended copyright protection to fictional characters.

Moreover, these laws are right to extend copyright protection only to works. Some authors, recognizing that current legislation does *not* provide characters with copyright protection, have advocated changing laws with a view to making characters explicitly copyrightable.[12] However, such legislation would be a mistake since it would unduly limit artistic freedom. Moreover, such legislation would give to an individual (or, more likely, a corporation) rights that ought to be in the public domain. This is a point to which I will return.

3. Characters, trademarks, and unfair competition

Many fictional characters currently enjoy trademark protection in addition to the protection of copyright law. Trademarks are designed to indicate the origin of some product or service. The public, seeing a trademark, can be assured that a good or service will be of a certain quality, and so trademark laws serve the interests of the public. The owner of a trademark is, as such, protected against unfair competition: no competitor may represent a good or service as originating with the owner of the trademark. Some legal scholars have argued that fictional characters are appropriately protected by trademark laws. Indeed, some have held that trademark protection is the only protection fictional characters need (see e.g. Nevins 1991–2). I disagree. The trademarking of the names and likenesses of fictional characters is completely unjustifiable.

Nevertheless, corporations have turned to trademark law to protect themselves against what they hold to be unfair competition. For example, in an effort to protect their valuable fictional characters, DC Comics, Disney, Warner Bros., and other corporations have successfully argued that their characters enjoy trademark protection. A name or mark can indicate the origin of some product or service, and this can serve the interests of the public. You might think here of Apple, Coca-Cola or Band-Aid. This way of thinking has been extended to fictional characters. Leslie A. Kurtz suggests: "For example, if Smith creates and publishes a book of Donald Duck cartoons, using the name and likeness of the well-known Disney character, buyers are likely to be confused into believing that Disney created the book." Consequently, in a widely held view, "When a well-known fictional character appears in identifiable form in another work of fiction, the law of trademarks and unfair competition will usually provide protection" (Kurtz 1986: 489).

There is no doubt that the use of trademarks to restrict the use of fictional characters limits the possibilities for artistic creation. An example will illustrate the deleterious influence of trademarks on innovation. The permanence of trademark protection explains why no new Tarzan stories are appearing. The first Tarzan stories appeared in 1916 and are now out of copyright and one might expect that someone would appropriate the character. The trouble is that the heirs of Edgar Rice Burroughs, who wrote the Tarzan stories, trademarked the name "Tarzan."[13] Edgar Rice Burroughs, Inc. has successfully used its trademark to prevent the distribution of works using the name Tarzan.[14] In contrast, Peter Pan, no longer protected by any intellectual property laws, is beginning to appear in a variety of new works. At the time of writing, a new movie (produced by Warner Bros., not Disney, it is worth noting) is about to appear. I think that there is no question but that the trademarking of fictional characters is restricting the production of potentially aesthetically valuable works of art. Perhaps, however, the trademarking of the names and likenesses of fictional characters protects legitimate property rights.

I am sceptical about this claim since I am doubtful that characters are always appropriated in ways that deceive the public about the origin of a work. If I buy a bar of soap marked "Christian Dior Soap" I will reasonably assume that Christian Dior manufactured it. If the bar is a counterfeit, the name on the label is an attempt to mislead me. But if I write a book in which James Bond appears, and it has my name on the cover, and perhaps a disclaimer saying that the book is not by Ian Fleming, the situation is substantially different. There is no attempt to mislead the buying public about the source of the book. My action, in writing a novel featuring James Bond, is analogous to using one of the ingredients in Christian Dior's soap in a product that I label with my own name. As long as the ingredient is not protected by a patent, I have not done anything wrong. Simply put, courts have been too restrictive in allowing trademark and unfair competition laws to restrict the reuse of characters and in disregarding disclaimers.

Consider this example. In 1998 the publisher William Morrow issued a book called *Godzilla!* just as a new (licensed) Godzilla movie was released by Columbia/Tristar. (This was a non-fiction book about the Godzilla character, and not a story in which Godzilla appeared as a character. Still, the example illustrates the extent to which courts are prepared to enforce trademark protection.) The front cover was marked, "UNAUTHORIZED" and the rear cover contained the disclaimer that, "THIS BOOK WAS NOT PREPARED, APPROVED, LICENSED OR ENDORSED BY ANY ENTITY INVOLVED IN CREATING OR PRODUCING ANY GODZILLA MOVIE, INCLUDING COLUMBIA/TRISTAR AND TOHO CO. LTD."[15] The holder of the trademark on the fictional character of Godzilla, the Toho Corporation, sued, alleging trademark infringement.

The court sided with the Toho Corporation, citing academic literature that indicates that disclaimers of this sort are ineffective. The court added that "Perhaps if the information contained on the back cover were placed on the front cover, consumer confusion could be negated. The disclaimer is also not placed on the spine of the Morrow Book, a place where many consumers are likely to view before seeing the cover." The court also worried that people buying the book online would be deceived.[16] The court ruled in favour of Toho in large part because of the supposed ineffectiveness of the disclaimer.

While *caveat emptor* is scarcely a general principle, here it is fully applicable. If a buyer fails to examine the cover (which can be viewed online, though it could not be in 1998), and fails to notice a prominent and explicit disclaimer, they have no one to blame but themselves. If it is important to readers that they buy a book about Godzilla that is authorized by the Toho Corporation, then they should exercise due diligence and ensure that they are buying an authorized work. I doubt that many readers will care whether or not a book about Godzilla is authorized by the Toho Corporation, but doubtlessly, in some cases, the public will want to know that they are buying a book (or watching a movie) in which characters are wielded by the artist who created them. In these cases, protection is owed to the artist who created the character. An artist may not represent his work as the work of another. But reusing a character (under conditions that I will expound below) in a work whose authorship is clearly indicated is not misrepresentation. Characters can be copied without misrepresenting the origin of a work. Since the role of trademarks is to prevent misrepresentation about the origins of products (including works of art), trademarks are the wrong legal instrument for restricting the use of fictional characters.

Another compelling argument demonstrates that fictional characters ought not to be protected by trademark. The objection to the use of trademark legislation to protect fictional character is that it becomes a form of permanent copyright. If the promotion of innovation in the arts is our goal, protecting characters with trademarks is even worse than protecting them with long copyright terms. The effect of allowing the trademarking of the names and likenesses of fictional characters is that artistic creativity is restricted for an indefinite term.

One could, again, argue that artistic innovation must give way in the face of rights to private property. That is, one could grant that the trademarking of fictional character names and likenesses stifles artistic innovation, but contend that property rights to characters must nevertheless be respected. The trouble with this argument is that fictional characters are composites of elements that have been appropriated from the public domain. Artists who introduce new fictional characters have done something innovative and made possible the creation of new artworks that potentially have a high aesthetic value. They are plausibly held to deserve some exclusive use of the characters. But, given that fictional characters are not created *ex nihilo* but from elements of former authors' works and other sources which often are in the public domain, this exclusive use ought to be limited in a way balancing the legitimate interests of the contemporary authors with the legitimate interests of former creators and the society. As Jessica Litman notes:

> The elements that Walt Disney drew from the public domain belong to us, the public. The Disney Company has been hanging on to a particular combination of them for a time, but it has them *on loan* from us. Unless Disney is to pull up the bridge after itself, those elements, and their combination in the unique character of Mickey Mouse, need to be returned to the public domain so that the Walt Disneys of tomorrow will have raw materials that they can use to draw new characters.
>
> Litman 1994: 434

This is a thought that has guided intellectual property laws from their inception.

A few examples will illustrate how fictional characters are created from elements in the public domain but they can be created from elements created by other authors, too, and even by elements of copyrighted works. Sometimes appropriation from the public domain is easy to identify. For example, DC's character Wonder Woman draws freely on Greek myths about the Amazons. These myths have always been in the public domain. Despite the fact that this character was produced from elements appropriated from the public domain, DC owns a comprehensive trademark on the name and likeness of Wonder Woman. Marvel's characters of Thor and Loki are drawn from Norse mythology, and yet Marvel owns a trademark on the name and likeness of the Mighty Thor. Or consider, for example, Snow White. This character originated in the familiar German fairy tale. The story was already old when it was published in the first edition of *Grimm's Fairy Tales* (1812). Despite this, in 2013, the U.S. Patent and Trademark Office granted Disney a trademark on the name Snow White. Other characters, among them James Bond, are based on real persons. (Bond was based on several commandos known to Ian Fleming.)

Given that characters involve appropriation from the public domain and other sources, they ought to enjoy only temporary protection. Copyright legislation protects works for a limited time precisely because it is recognized that creative artists always appropriate something from the public domain. I believe that fictional characters also deserve some protection, but it ought not to take the form of trademark protection. The trademarking of fictional characters gives the owner of the trademark a perpetual right to characters. This perpetual right to fictional characters involves illegitimate appropriation from the public domain. At the least, the trademarking of the names of fictional characters is a morally indefensible circumvention of copyright law, which (in many jurisdictions) explicitly states that names may not be copyrighted.

One objection to my view remains to be considered. Someone might argue that the appropriation of a character could lead to dilution by tarnishment. Tarnishment of a trademark occurs when a competing mark portrays the infringed trademark in a negative way. For example, a U.S. court has ruled that two models riding a Viagra-branded missile at an adult entertainment exhibition and distributing condoms tarnished Pfizer's Viagra trademark.[17] Similarly, one might argue, certain uses of a fictional character might tarnish the character. Although the Air Pirates case was treated as a case of copyright infringement, it could have been regarded as an instance of tarnishment. That is, the value of Disney's trademark on Mickey Mouse was potentially reduced by Air Pirates having him engage in drug use and sexual activities.

The problem with this objection is that it is only successful if fictional characters are the sorts of things appropriately protected by trademarks. Suppose, as I have argued, that fictional characters ought not to be protected by trademarks. In this case, no legitimate trademarks are tarnished when fictional characters are appropriated. Still, there is something to this objection. When artists appropriate a character they could distort the public's perception of the character. Artists who create original fictional characters ought to have an opportunity to establish in the public's mind their own conception of a character. In the next section I will propose a way in which this can be accomplished without interference from artists who appropriate the character.

I conclude from the reflections in this section that trademark laws are the wrong instruments to use in defense of an artist's rights. Nevertheless, fictional characters deserve some proprietary protection. In the next section I will indicate what form this protection should take.

4. Patents and fictional characters

My proposal is that fictional characters be protected by something like patent law. This proposal strikes exactly the right balance. Artists have the exclusive opportunity to develop a fictional character for a limited period of time. Patents generally expire after about twenty years. This is a sufficient period of time for an artist to develop a character. After that time, a character ought to enter the public domain where it may be legitimately appropriated by other artists. On my proposal, artists would be given some protection, but artistic creativity would not be unreasonably restricted, and the public domain would be respected.

Before explaining why I think that patents are the best model for artists' rights to fictional characters, I will say a few words about why I think that protection is appropriate at all. Most defenses of intellectual property laws focus on the need to insure that artists are appropriately rewarded for their creations. This is an important consideration. By allowing patents on fictional characters, artists would be protected against market competition from other artists who would otherwise use the same characters. In my mind, however, there is a more important consideration. Artists deserve the opportunity to develop a character in the way they would like to see it develop. Artists deserve the opportunity to see their fictional characters realized in ways they want them to be realized.

Characters evolve over time. Once other artists start using a fictional character, it evolves in ways that are beyond the control of the artist who created it. Consider, for example, Sherlock Holmes. Everyone thinks that Sherlock Holmes wears a deerstalker but Conan Doyle never says that he does. This is an addition to the Holmes character made by an early illustrator of the Holmes stories. And, of course, the character has continued to evolve. Robert Downey, Jr.'s Sherlock Holmes, for example, differs from the Sherlock Holmes of Conan Doyle. There is an action hero aspect to Downey's Holmes that is not found in Conan Doyle's stories and a certain lack of gravitas that would have been anathema to the original denizen of 221b Baker Street. The James Bond of Sean Connery differs from the James Bond of Daniel Craig. This is fine, but the original artist deserves an opportunity to establish the character.

Let us turn now to my proposal that something like patents be used to protect fictional characters. Let us begin by reminding ourselves about what, in current law, may be patented. The European Patent Convention states that "European patents shall be granted for any inventions, in all fields of technology, provided that they are new, involve an inventive step and are susceptible of industrial application."[18] The Convention explicitly states that "aesthetic creations" shall not be regarded as inventions within the meaning of the Convention.[19] In the U.S., patent law provides that "Whoever invents or discovers any new and useful process, machine, manufacture, or composition of matter, or any new and useful improvement thereof may obtain a patent therefor."[20] Neither the European nor the U.S. law seems to have any applicability to fictional characters. It seems that patents only protect tangible ("compositions of matter") inventions that have an "industrial application."

Patents do, however, have a broader application than they would at first seem. Although the European Patent Convention explicitly states that patents are not granted for "schemes, rules [or] methods for performing mental acts, playing games or doing business, [or] programs for computers,"[21] many jurisdictions grant patents on intangible inventions. These intangible inventions include business methods and algorithms. As early as 1792, France issued a patent on a tontine, a method of raising capital (Christian 1828: 544–5). Jurisdictions such as Canada and Japan continue to grant patents on business methods.[22] Certainly, in principle, there is no reason why patents cannot be issued for something intangible, such as a business method or algorithm.

However, even if intangible inventions are allowed to be patentable, we are a long way from establishing that a patent is the proper instrument for the protection of fictional characters. Part of the case for thinking that patents are the appropriate instruments is found in the negative arguments of the previous sections: copyright law and trademark law are *not* the appropriate instruments. There is, however, a positive case. Patents are used to protect inventions and, in particular, inventions that can be used to produce a useful product. Fictional characters are inventions. This is just to say that they are artifacts that are brought into existence by the actions of artists. John Searle, for instance, makes this point, taking as his example Iris Murdoch's character of Andrew Chase-White in *The Red and the Green*. When Iris Murdoch writes about Andrew Chase-White, Searle suggests, she *pretends* to refer to him. Searle writes that:

> by pretending to refer she pretends that here is an object to be referred to. To the extent that we share in the pretense, we will also pretend that here is a lieutenant named Andrew Chase-White living in Dublin in 1916. It is the pretended reference which creates the fictional character and the shared pretense which

> enables us to talk about the character […] By pretending to refer to (and recount the adventures of) a person, Miss Murdoch creates a fictional character.
>
> Searle 1975: 302

For present purposes, the crucial part of this passage is that fictional characters are created. That is, they are inventions. Amie Thomasson adopts a similar view, describing fictional characters as "abstract artifacts." Moreover, as far as their ontological status is concerned, Thomasson compares fictional characters to inventions, such as the telephone (Thomasson 1999: 35, 153).

The status of fictional characters as inventions is not the only feature that they have in common with patentable items. Like many patentable items, fictional characters can be used to produce useful products. As noted above, fictional characters are devices for generating products. These products are stories such as novels, plays, motion pictures, and so on. I propose that this is all that is intended by the European Patent Convention's reference to an invention being susceptible of industrial application. We speak of the entertainment industry and cultural industries and these are the industries in which fictional characters are employed. This supports the claim that fictional characters ought to be protected by patents.

Someone might still object that fictional characters are aesthetic creations within the meaning of the European Patent Convention, and so not patentable. One might wonder whether the European Patent Convention's exclusion of aesthetic creations is defensible. Even if it is, however, it should not exclude the patenting of fictional characters since fictional characters are not aesthetic creations or aesthetic objects. The works in which they appear are aesthetic objects. That is, novels, plays, movies, and so on are objects of aesthetic appreciation. It is true that one might admire, from an aesthetic perspective, a well-crafted fictional character, but a clever process or an ingenious piece of machinery can also be an object of aesthetic appreciation; it does not follow from this that the process or the piece of machinery is not patentable. Similarly, the fact that a fictional character is an object of aesthetic appreciation does not entail that the character is not patentable. Only if something is designed primarily as an object of aesthetic appreciation is it not patentable. And, again, a fictional character is primarily created as a device to be used in the creation of aesthetic objects.

I have yet to give the most compelling reason for thinking that patents are the appropriate way to protect fictional characters. The short-term protection afforded by patents is appropriate given the values of fictional characters relative to the values of other inventions protected by patents. Patents have short terms because it is important that innovations in, say, engineering or medicine be placed in the public domain so that more valuable innovations may occur. Innovations in the fine arts have comparable value and consequently they too ought to enter the public domain within a short term. Long-term protection of fictional characters potentially denies the public great works of art just as long patent terms deny the public innovation in the sciences.

Long-term restrictions on the use of fictional characters are contrary to the aesthetic interests of the public. I have already mentioned the case of Lisbeth Salander. Given current intellectual property regimes, only an uninspired writer is in a position to use this inspired character. It is short-sighted and wasteful to forbid other writers from seeing what they can do with her. Some artists continue to use a fictional character long past the point when they make good use of it. Consider, for example, Bernard Cornwell's Richard Sharpe, who first appeared in *Sharpe's Eagle* (1981). Initially, Cornwell's use of the character was entertaining and engaging. However, it could be argued that the novels in which Cornwell employs Sharpe have become increasingly unimaginative and formulaic. The interests of the public might be best served if other writers had the opportunity to exploit the character.

All of this said, my proposal requires the amendment of intellectual property laws in all jurisdictions. As intellectual property laws are currently written, fictional characters do not fit comfortably into any category. I have argued that they do not belong to the sort of thing that may be copyrighted or trademarked. Fictional characters do not, despite what I have said, fit perfectly under patent laws. My claim is only that fictional characters are, in important respects, like the items protected by patents and that the sort of protection that they receive ought to be analogous in important ways to that provided by patents.

In particular, fictional characters should be protected for a term similar to that extended to other inventions. The term of patents on fictional characters should be in the range of ordinary patents. In both Europe and the U.S. the term is twenty years from the date of application for a patent.[23] Twenty years is a sufficient amount of time for an artist to develop a character. While an artist often continues to use a character for more than twenty years, the character is usually fully developed by that point. I also propose that patents on fictional characters expire upon the death of the artists who create them, even if this death occurs before the end of the usual term.

Whether or not the intellectual property restrictions extended to fictional characters are called patents, it is clear that we need to distinguish (for reasons enumerated above) between the rights to fictional characters and rights to the works in which they appear. Consequently, even when a patent on a fictional character has expired, an artist may continue to hold a copyright on the works in which the character appears.

Distinguishing between a copyright on works and patents on fictional characters has a major benefit yet to be mentioned. When this distinction is drawn, the deleterious effects of long copyright terms is, to some extent, mitigated. As we have seen, copyright terms in most jurisdictions are absurdly long (the life of an artist plus seventy years). If rights to fictional characters expire before the term of a copyright is reached, a compromise can be struck. Artists (and their estates and corporations who buy copyrights) can continue to collect royalties on works, but artists can appropriate fictional characters to create new works. Long copyright terms are still obstacles to artistic creativity, but would no longer be such serious obstacles.

5. Conclusion

Artists who create fictional characters appropriate from the public domain, and so the characters ought to enter the public domain. They ought not, however, to enter the public domain immediately. Artists are owed the opportunity to develop a character in the way they see fit. After the character has been developed (and a term of twenty years seems reasonable for the development of a character), other artists ought to be allowed to see what they can do with the character. A short term of protection, such as that provided by patents, would give artists the opportunities that they deserve and the public the aesthetic creations that they value.

Notes

1 SunTrust Bank v. Houghton Mifflin Co., 252 F.3d 1165 (11th Cir. 2001); Suntrust Bank v. Houghton Mifflin Company, 268 F.3d 1257 (11th Cir. 2001). For details of the litigation and the settlement, see: https://www.nytimes.com/books/99/09/26/bookend/bookend.html

2 *Lo's Diary* was originally published in Italian in 1995. Dmitri Nabokov only objected once the English translation appeared; see Garbus 1999.

3 Council Directive 93/98/EEC of October 29, 1993 harmonizing the term of protection of copyright and certain related rights, Article 1.

4 17 U.S.C. §102.
5 Hill v. Whalen & Martell Inc., 220 F. 359, 359 (S.D.N.Y. 1914).
6 Nichols v. Universal Pictures Corp., 45 F.2d 119, 121 (2d Cir. 1930).
7 Warner Bros. Pictures, Inc. v. Columbia Broadcasting System, Inc. 216 F.2d 945, 950 (9th Cir. 1954).
8 Walt Disney Productions v. Air Pirates 581 F.2d 751, 755 (9th Cir. 1978).
9 Warner Bros. Pictures, Inc. v. Columbia Broadcasting System, Inc., at 950.
10 Silverman v. CBS Inc., 870 F.2d 40 (2d. Cir. 1989).
11 Silverman v. CBS Inc., at 43.
12 This is the position advocated in Feldman 1999.
13 Tarzan was trademarked (0799908) in the U.S. in 1965.
14 See, for example, Edgar Rice Burroughs, Inc. v. Manns Theaters, 195 USPQ 159 (Central District of California 1976).
15 Toho Co., Ltd. v. William Morrow and Co., Inc., 33 F. Supp. 2d 1206 (C.D. Cal. 1998).
16 Toho Co., Ltd. v. William Morrow and Co., Inc.
17 Pfizer Inc. v. Sachs, 652 F. Supp. 2d 512 (S.D.N.Y. 2009).
18 European Patent Convention, Part II, Chapter 1, Article 52 (1).
19 European Patent Convention, Part II, Chapter 1, Article 52 (2).
20 35 U.S.C. 101.
21 European Patent Convention, Part II, Chapter 1, Article 52 (2). Computer programs are, however, copyrightable in Europe. See Directive 2009/24/EC of the European Parliament and of the Council of April 23, 2009 on the legal protection of computer programs. http://eur-lex.europa.eu/LexUriServ/LexUriServ.do?uri=OJ:L:2009:111:0016:0022:EN:PDF
22 Canada (Attorney General) v. Amazon.com, Inc., Federal Court of Appeals (2011 FCA 328). The Commissioner of Patents refused to issue a patent on Amazon's one-click method of online shopping. The Court directed the Commissioner to reconsider; http://www.ondatechno.com/English/ip/patent/faq_business.html.
23 European Patent Convention, Article 63(1); 35 U.S.C. 154.

References

Christian, M. (1828), *Description des machines et procédés spécifiés dans les brevets d'invention, de perfectionnement et d'importation*, vol. 1, Paris: Madame Huzard.

Feldman, D. B. (1990), "Finding a Home for Fictional Characters: A Proposal for Change in Copyright Protection," *California Law Review* 78 (3): 687–720.

Garbus, M. "Lolita and the Lawyers," *New York Times*, September 26, 1999. Available online: https://www.nytimes.com/books/99/09/26/bookend/bookend.html

Kurtz, L. A. (1986), "The Independent Legal Lives of Fictional Characters," *Wisconsin Law Review* 1986 (3): 429–525.

Kurtz, L. A. (1994), "The Methuselah Factor: When Characters Outlive Their Copyrights," *University of Miami Entertainment & Sports Law Review* 11 (2): 437–52.

Litman, J. (1994), "Mickey Mouse Emeritus: Character Protection and the Public Domain," *University of Miami Entertainment & Sports Law Journal* 11 (2): 429–35.

Nevins, F. M. (1991/92), "Copyright + Character = Catastrophe," *Journal of the Copyright Society of the USA* 39: 303–44.

Nimmer, M. B. and D. Nimmer (1963), *Nimmer on Copyright*, vol. 1, New York: Matthew Bender.

Searle, J. R. (1975), "The Logical Status of Fictional Discourse," *New Literary History* 6 (2): 319–32.

Thomasson, A. L. (1999), *Fiction and Metaphysics*, Cambridge: Cambridge University Press.

10

Plagiarizing Nonfiction: Legal Cases, Aesthetic Questions, and the Rules of Copying

David Oels

In 2013, I attended a conference on plagiarism in St. Gallen, Switzerland. The conference focused on literature, and the two legal scholars in attendance (one Swiss, one German) contended that there could be no copyright protection for nonfiction books, since the compiling of facts is not a creative achievement. There can only be copyright protection for the *creative editing* of these facts, they claimed. Now, as it happens, nonfiction books and their form make up one of my central areas of research, and I expressed my puzzlement at this claim. The legal scholars suggested: if I were to set an essay question for a history class, and two students were to hand in equally excellent answers, this would mean, in effect, getting the same essay twice. Nonfiction, on the legal scholars' view, does not constitute individual creation. Without individual creation there is no copyright, and without copyright there is no infringement in a copy. "Plagiarism" is not a legal term, and can certainly be separated from issues of copyright law. The cases of plagiarized scientific works that have recently aroused controversy in Germany are usually violations of examination regulations, or of academic honesty (see Horstkotte and Gerstlauer 2015). In the worst cases, they may constitute fraud. But, from the perspective of copyright law, these are usually legally unproblematic cases of "free editing." The question of the creative achievement of nonfiction—and anything owed that author—is centrally an ethical issue, and only by association a legal one. So, we should ask, what account can be given of the *ethical* rules of copying works of nonfiction? How should such works be honored by those who use them?

As an example, at the St. Gallen conference, blogger Kathrin Passig introduced the notion of a "discovery achievement" to describe blogging practices.[1] In essence, the idea is that *discovering* a text, picture, or video on the internet and embedding it into a blog constitutes an *achievement* that should be acknowledged, say, by others who piggy-back on the discovery. The acknowledgment needn't involve any sort of financial remuneration, but perhaps (depending on the case) requires only some reference to the original discoverer, say, when the find is forwarded.

Although plagiarism and copyright are conceptually distinct matters, where there *is* a legal dispute, plagiarism is often treated by the public as an ethical (or aesthetic, or cultural) wrong that may justify legal intervention. However, unlike the vague and sometimes ineffective public discussions, courtrooms are places where decisions—and sometimes sanctions—are made. And certainly, if the copying of a nonfiction book were found to be perfectly legitimate in terms of copyright law, we might expect this to have extralegal normative consequences, and perhaps effects on how we view and value that work.

In what follows, I will present some recent cases where nonfiction literature authors have lodged claims against fiction writers and publishers. I am not a lawyer, and I am not centrally concerned with legal questions per se, but rather with their aesthetic and cultural implications and effects. Throughout this chapter, I will expose a number of theoretical problems arising from these cases, and suggest a pragmatic solution.

1. *The Da Vinci Code*

Proceeding chronologically, our first case concerns Dan Brown's 2003 blockbuster novel, *The Da Vinci Code*. Brown's novel has been accused of plagiarism several times, and was the subject of more than one legal dispute. The case I am particularly interested in was tried in London in 2005. The claimants in the case, Michael Baigent and Richard Leigh—two of the three authors of the nonfiction book, *Holy Blood, Holy Grail*—argued that Brown had taken important motifs and plotlines from their book: in particular, first, the idea that Jesus and Mary Magdalene were married and produced a daughter, and that their shared bloodline extended through the Merovingians and Knights Templar to the present time; and second, the thesis that the "Holy Grail" is a metaphor for Mary Magdalene herself, her womb, or her shared bloodline with Jesus.

The case was not about literal congruence—the word-for-word replication of written material—but rather about so-called "non-textual infringements," resting on the plot and structure of the respective works as well as the claims advanced by each book. Although the court recognized the nonfiction book as an "original literary work," and found that Brown made *some* use of *Holy Blood,*

Holy Grail in his writing, the court concluded that there was not sufficient evidence that he had in fact drawn directly from the nonfiction book in plotting his novel. Rather, the judge suggests, it is more likely that the purported facts at issue were drawn from a *number* of nonfiction sources, themselves the products of original research. Independent of this, the court found that the *idea* that there is a bloodline from Jesus to the Merovingians and the present is not protectable. Justice Peter Smith writes:

> [W]here a book is intended to be read as a factual historical event and that the Defendant accepts it as fact and did no more than repeat certain of those facts the Plaintiff cannot claim a monopoly in those historical facts. It is accordingly perfectly legitimate for another person to contrive a novel based on those facts as otherwise a Claimant would have a monopoly of the facts.[2]

In this case, the in-principle worthiness of protection for nonfiction books was negated *ex post* regarding the plot and structure of the work in question. The structure of *Holy Blood, Holy Grail* was chronological, and since the structure was based solely on claims of fact (even false ones), such a structure is not a creative artifact, is not sufficiently original to merit copyright protection. Smith suggests:

> It is not significant in my view that a series of stated factual events or asserted factual events is listed in a chronological order. What other order could there be? It is itself too general and a low level of extraction itself to justify protection against copying.[3]

Indeed, Smith refers to the structure of *Holy Blood, Holy Grail* as a "lame chronological order."[4] As such, it seems, even had it been shown that Brown *had* significantly and directly drawn from *Holy Blood, Holy Grail*, it is doubtful whether the court would have come to a different overall assessment of the case. The complaint of infringement was dismissed, though it did damage Dan Brown's reputation. Doubts about his creativity remained, not only concerning the literary quality of his works, but also the integrity of his research (see Freund and Wiegelmann 2013).[5]

The nonfiction authors in this case were ordered to cover the defendants' legal expenses to the sum of £1.3 million (*Guardian* 2007). And, while the case increased sales for *Holy Blood, Holy Grail* (the German translation is emblazoned with a sticker: "A must for readers of Dan Brown's 'The Da Vinci Code'"), it is doubtful whether those increased sales would cover these legal costs.[6] After the verdict, some spoke of a victory for literature—quite surprising, given the usual contempt in literary circles for Dan Brown. But, we might ask: against whom did literature prevail?

2. *The Swarm*

Our next case concerns another very successful title: Frank Schätzing's *Der Schwarm* (2004), published in English as *The Swarm* in 2006. The apocalyptic science-fiction novel focuses on the rise of a hive-mind marine species set on eliminating humanity, but relies on actual, scientific research. In early 2005, science journalist Thomas Orthmann lodged a complaint, because (he argued) Schätzing took information from his website, ozeane.de, without acknowledgment, and further modeled one of the novel's central characters on information gleaned from the site. The case concerned both textual and non-textual infringements.

Orthmann documented nineteen passages from the novel—whole sentences or fragments thereof—taken from his website. In most cases, the passages are only slightly edited. For instance, page 222 of *Der Schwarm* contains the passage:

> Wie überlebte man als Robbe oder Fisch in den dunklen und kalten Gewässern der Antarktis? Wie erhielt man Einblick in ein Biotop, das von einer geschlossenen Eisdecke überzogen war?

Orthmann's website contains the nearly identical passage:

> Wie überlebt man als Robbe oder Fisch in den dunklen und kalten Gewässern der Antarktis? [...] Wie erhält man Einblick in einen Lebensraum, der [...] von einer geschlossenen Eisdecke bedeckt ist?

Beyond a change in tense, there are only slight changes in diction—for example, Orthmann refers to "einen Lebensraum" ("a living space") while Schätzing uses "ein Biotop" ("a biotope"—a habitat). Translated, Orthmann's passage asks (with Schätzing's alterations in parentheses):

> How to survive as a seal or fish in the dark and cold waters of Antarctica? How (was it) to get (give) insight into a living space (biotope) that is covered (coated) by a closed ice sheet?

Consider another example. Schätzing writes (here, in translation):

> Danny picked up the crossbow, squinted an eye, his hand on the cold metal. Slowly his finger tightened. With full concentration and impassively, Danny squeezed the trigger. At this moment, only he heard well the faint hiss as the arrow left the gun close to his ear, at over 250 kilometers per hour.
>
> Schätzing 2004: 272–3[7]

Orthmann's original text (again, in translation) reads:

> The finger at the trigger of the crossbow slowly bends. One eye is squinted, the

> hand rests calmly at the cold metal. With full concentration and a straight face, Stefan Ludwig pulls the trigger. A quiet hiss, and the arrow leaves the menacing looking weapon at over 250 kilometres per hour.[8]

Although more reworked than in the previous example, it is clear that Schätzing is taking (and Orthmann is offering) more than mere facts. Neither the "full concentration" nor the "quiet hiss" can be understood as purely factual descriptions of an external reality.

Despite the clear congruencies, the Cologne prosecution dropped the case, suggesting there were "no indications of a commercial, illicit use of works protected by copyright." The reason: "The elements of a crime of commercial trade require that the offender has repeatedly violated copyright law in order to make a non-temporary profit of a certain extent" (*Spiegel* 2005). Schätzing, apparently, did not qualify. Orthmann further abstained from possible civil action; the risk of having to cover both sides' legal costs was presumably too high.

The explanations and justifications offered by Schätzing—and their public discussion—however, are perhaps more interesting than the lawsuit itself. Schätzing did not deny copying the passages from Orthmann, but claimed that what he copied were mere facts (Pioch 2005). This information could not have been protected by copyright, he argued, since one could have researched these same facts elsewhere. Further, he claimed, the style of writing had been his before he lifted the passages from Orthmann; any stylistic parallels were only a coincidence (ibid.).

In the German newspaper *Frankfurter Allgemeine Zeitung*, Malte Herwig compares Schätzing to Thomas Mann, who had used several pages of scientific texts, mostly unaltered, in his works *The Magic Mountain* and *Dr. Faustus*. Of one passage about deep-sea diving that Mann took from *National Geographic*, Herwig writes:

> This example shows that a montage of quotes is not immediately plagiarism, but can be an artistic device that combines scientific realism with literary composition by stylistically exaggerating formulations and presenting facts, such as the bioluminescence of deep sea organisms, in the context of a pact with the devil and sinful temptation.
>
> Herwig 2005: 44

Schätzing, Herwig suggests, is but the "apt pupil" of Mann, in effect elevating Schätzing's novel to Nobel-Prize-winning material. In the media, the problem of plagiarism becomes effectively one of assessment—a matter of the *value* of the borrowing work. In legal discourse, in contrast, the main question concerns the threshold for originality in the nonfiction source material: whether the work was composed in such a manner as to merit protection.

3. *The Murder Farm*

Andrea Schenkel's crime novel *Tannöd* was published in 2006, and in English two years later as *The Murder Farm*. *Tannöd* was a surprise hit, selling 300,000 copies in its first year, and awarded several literary prizes. The novel, though fictionalized, is based on an unsolved murder case from 1922, known as the Hinterkaifeck massacre, in which six members of the Gruber household were brutally murdered on an isolated Bavarian farm. Peter Leuschner had previously written two books about the historical case and, in 2007, sued Schenkel and her publisher, claiming that *Tannöd* was a close adaptation of his second book. Leuschner's claim was that his book did not simply present the historical facts of the case, but combined these with dialogue and plot elements of his own invention. According to the foreword, Leuschner's book was "written under the theory: this is how it could have been."

In the first trial of the case, the focus was on individual aspects of the plot, bits of dialogue, and motifs. The following example was perhaps the most striking: it is the evening before the crime. A new maid has come to work at the house, and meets the youngest child. Leuschner writes:

> Little Josef is not at all timid because of the new maid. He boisterously pulls at her skirt. She has to extend her right foot. The boy laughs and sits down on it. "Hoppe hoppe Reiter" [a German nursery rhyme, usually sung while the child bounces on the singer's knee] … As she returns to the kitchen, Maria Baumgartner is already about to leave. "I don't want to oversleep on my first day," she says, apologizing. "Good night to all of you. I still have to unpack my things."[9]

The scene also plays out in Schenkel's novel, here being told from the maid's perspective. Yet the verdict in the case disregarded the matter: "The fact that the maid played 'Hoppe-hoppe-Reiter' with little Josef can hardly count as worthy of protection, since this is a child's game that has been played a million times."[10] Simply put, the scene was too common for Leuschner to lay claim to it.

In the 2009 appeal, Leuschner shifted his argument from individual passages to the

> overall picture of single elements that are perhaps not protectable in themselves, but as a whole could constitute a work of the claimant that is protectable by copyright. The claimant has pointed out in this context that he has created a texture that the defendant has adopted in her novel, *Tannöd*.[11]

This move, however, also proved futile. The court decided that Schenkel did *not* adopt this texture—if it existed at all. In general, it found, the "selection and arrangement and division of the material itself" was not worthy of protection:

> Overall, due to his work's aim to present facts, the claimant has not made a selection that can be protected by copyright law, and given the chronological presentation of the events, the arrangement of the material is also unworthy of protection.[12]

In the end, the court found that Leuschner's nonfiction book is not a creative achievement, and that *Tannöd* is a legitimate free adaptation. Again, the verdict was welcomed in newspapers' culture sections, one comparing *Tannöd* to Truman Capote's *In Cold Blood*, Droste-Hülshoff's *Judenbuche*, and Goethe's *Faust*—each of which transformed a real act of violence into literature.

4. Fiction and nonfiction

In the ethics of copying, we can note that, in general, the assessment of a copy depends not only on *how* something is copied, and how that copy is handled, but also *what* is copied. One could, however, call this legal practice into question. This would not depend on an argument to the effect that any factual insight is colored by the observer, or a postmodern move suggesting that the world of facts is ultimately itself fictional. There is no need to question the nature of facts themselves.

Perhaps most associated with historian Hayden White (see e.g. White 1973), but with tendrils stretching back to the nineteenth century, is the understanding among historians that historical writing does not only represent what has happened, but involves a creative move as well.

Recall the St. Gallen conference, from the beginning of this chapter, and the legal scholars' claim that two equally good answers to a history essay would be, in effect, the same essay. We might grant that our two students use exactly the same sources, and that both work brilliantly. However, as soon as their work goes beyond mere documentation to involve evaluation and choices in presentation, there will necessarily be differences in their essays implying individual creative achievement.

We might approach the issue from the side of literature, and note that both narratology and the theory of fiction have always had great difficulty in identifying text-internal criteria for distinguishing between fact-based and fictional texts—there seems nothing in the text per se that gives away the writing's nature as fictional or nonfictional. One suggestion to the contrary from German literary critic Käte Hamburger is that certain forms of statement—such as the "epic past tense" (say, "tomorrow was Christmas")—while workable in fiction, could not be intelligibly uttered by persons in a real, historical context (Hamburger 1994: 65). Franz K. Stanzel (1964) suggests that a sure sign that one is reading a fiction is that the narrator knows what is going on in the minds of the story's protagonists. Accepting this, however, would mean accepting that many historical nonfiction works qualify as works of fiction. And, of course, there are legions of fictional texts that feature no internal signs of fictionality. So, on what basis should we distinguish between creative fiction—where copying is impermissible—and facts that can be copied freely?

Similar problems arise in the field of narratology. Analysis of a narrative requires first distinguishing the plot from the underlying story. If one is analyzing a fact-based text and looking to reconstruct the story, then one might draw on documents, common knowledge, and other outside texts on the same topic in the reconstruction. But if one is analyzing a text without already knowing whether it is fictional or factual literature, then only the text itself—the structure of the plot—is accessible for such reconstruction. Determining *whether* one is dealing with a fictional or factual text usually depends on paratextual elements—forewords, publishers' announcements, blurbs, etc.—though there may be hints, at least, internal to the text.

Things become even more complicated when we dip a little deeper into the nonfiction category. In German, a nonfiction book of the sort you might pick up on the "new releases" shelf at your local bookstore is called a "*Sachbuch*." A *Sachbuch* is distinguished from a "*Fachbuch*": a technical book for specialists in a field. Where a *Fachbuch* offers pure research results or technical instructions, a *Sachbuch* is targeted at a lay audience, with facts chosen, edited, interpreted, and enriched, say, with entertaining elements. This process used to be called "popularization," and a *Sachbuch* may contain the very same facts as a *Fachbuch*, but in a simpler or more accessible form. While the *Fachbuch* appears to have a paradigm form—"just the facts," as they say—in the *Sachbuch* we see any formal distinction between fiction and nonfiction begin to dissolve away.

Certainly, it would be possible to use the epic past tense in nonfiction, though this happens only rarely. A narrator's description of another's psychological process, however, is quite common. We see this in Leuschner's book, for instance, and in the description of the whaler on Orthmann's website. Individual creative achievement can certainly be seen in the interpretations by the authors in *Holy Blood, Holy Grail*. The court in this case recognized the authors' understanding of their own book as "historical conjecture," allowing that, in their research, they:

> used techniques which had been criticised by orthodox historians such as giving weight to folklore legends and using literary work to help strengthen the plausibility of the argument. It is therefore suggested [...] that HBHG is a book written "*for ordinary people*" and [...] used techniques usually seen in novels.[13]

Orthmann's website, too, is not a neutral presentation of the facts, but involves literary techniques. Indeed, in his accusation against Schätzing, Orthmann did not refer to the facts at all, but to his *style*. Given his invention of dialogue and plot points in telling the story of the Hinterkaifeck massacre, Leuschner claims that his work "is not a nonfiction book (*Sachbuch*), but—just like the work of Schenkel—popular literature" (Schirg 2005).[14]

On the other side, curiously, the "literary" writers often referred to the factual basis of their works. For Dan Brown, this is part of the game: in the introduction of *The Da Vinci Code*, under the heading "Fact," he points to the real existence of Opus Dei and the Priory of Sion, two organizations playing key roles in the novel. An illustrated edition of Brown's book shows the buildings and artworks discussed, as well as maps of Paris and London, as proof of how closely the novel tracks reality. In the afterword to his novel, Frank Schätzing similarly describes the work as "full of science," expressing his gratitude to several scientists. Even Andrea Schenkel—who has stated in interviews that she had read no historical records (see Sippel 2007)—claimed after the accusations that most of what she describes follows from such records and general reason (see Schenkel 2007).

Now, one could attest (contrary, at least, to Brown's and Schätzing's claims) that these writers do *not* base their work on science or primary sources, but rather on popularized forms of these, but the matter is not so straightforward. It seems more important, rather, to see how the categorial differences between nonfiction books and literature, between facts and fiction, begin to dissolve, with various overlappings and gradations appearing.

In both the Schenkel and Brown cases, the courts considered points of congruency between the novels and their nonfiction sources. The *Tannöd* decision includes several pages reviewing congruencies between Schenkel's novel and Leuschner's work, detailing each point's worthiness of protection. In the Brown case, the court reviewed a list of "central themes," though these were considered too general or abstract to justify an accusation of plagiarism. Now, as the argument tends to go, even if those points of congruency between works *were* treated as protectable elements in the original, these congruencies would not themselves be sufficient for a finding of wrongdoing—there is nothing blameworthy when all that one takes are facts. However, this points at something odd in the practice of novel writing. On the one hand, authors normally include the relevant acknowledgments in their books; on the other hand (as we have seen in these cases), the novelists claim that their works are autonomous things. What's happening here?

One possibility is that the verdicts in our cases (and as echoed by the general public) reflect a belief that the charge of plagiarism is too severe, and that the financial claims of the nonfiction writers are simply too high. In the Dan Brown case, some €15 million and the abandonment of the film version—at that point finished but not yet released—were at stake (*Spiegel* 2006). Leuschner demanded that the sale of *Tannöd* should be halted, all remaining copies pulped, and that all profits should go to him as compensation (*Süddeutsche Zeitung* 2010). The rejection of the nonfiction authors' complaints in each of these cases, and the complaints themselves, reflect, I think, belief in an all-or-nothing dichotomy enshrined in the law: that either the fiction authors have plagiarized the nonfiction writers (in which case millions of euros are owed), or they have not (in which case nothing is owed). But this overly restrictive dichotomy needn't rule the day, and there is hope that more nuanced reasoning might prevail.

5. New Hope

Let's briefly consider a final case that was regulated more leniently, and which acknowledges the sort of "discovery achievement" highlighted by Katrin Passig. The case concerns a 2009 made-for-television movie starring Heike Makatsch, and an accompanying novel, about Hope Bridges Adams Lehmann, Germany's first female physician. Both the film and the novel are based on a scholarly biography for which the author, Marita Krauss, had gathered a great amount of material at her own cost (some €20,000, by her own account). The publication of the biography cost Krauss an additional €5,000 out of pocket. The film company tried to win Krauss over as a consultant, for which she would have received €9,500, but requiring that she forfeit her rights. Krauss declined the offer, instead publicly (and repeatedly) claiming that the scriptwriters "have used my book. My Hope biography is the central basis for the film and the novel" (Mäckler 2010). The German newspaper *Münchner Merkur* translated this into an accusation of plagiarism, and the film company, angered by the accusation, sued for an injunction (*Münchner Merkur* 2010). An amicable settlement was ultimately reached in 2010, with Krauss receiving €15,000 as "compensation for the scientific-journalistic work that consists of finding and presenting the material that was used for the film" (ibid.). This is exemplary. Although this is a modest sum given the size of the film project, it covered a sizeable amount of her costs, and, in the meantime, Krauss was able to publish a popular biography based on her research. She did not demand that the film be destroyed or that she be compensated by a six-figure sum. And, as a result, her discovery and research achievements were available for the public to appreciate. As Krauss suggests: "I think the force that we have all put into this conflict, we should now turn to other creative things again" (ibid.).

Such an approach would have benefited not only the nonfiction authors discussed in the cases above—Baigent, Leigh, Orthmann, and Leuschner—who asked for everything and got nothing (or worse), but also the novelists Brown, Schätzing, and Schenkel. However, the way forward suggested by this happy result requires a general calming of the current overexcitement about copies, plagiarism, and copyright. I believe this overexcitement has a number of interrelated causes. Certainly, I think, it relates to the disputes involving publishing, film, and music industries, where enormous sums are circulating that give rise to authors' desires to have their fair share of the cake. *The Da Vinci Code*, *Der Schwarm*, and *Tannöd* were all enormous financial successes, their nonfiction sources largely unknown by the public. Another likely cause is the insecurity arising from the unlimited digital means of copying, and, at the same time, the ensuing difficulties in tracking down illegitimate copies. A final cause—and one especially pertinent to our fiction/nonfiction cases, but perhaps beyond these—is the presumed border between fiction and nonfiction: between art that is considered worthy of protection and a presentation of facts that is not. The law, the literary public, and even literary theorists seem to assume the existence of clearly distinguishable categories of fiction and nonfiction, such that one of the former may be declared an autonomous original, even if it is copied from one of the latter, reasoning that further seems to suggest that a work of fiction's status as art would be questionable if it depended on source literature. On closer inspection, however, in most actual cases, there is no clean line to be found between the categories of fiction and nonfiction, but only gradations. As such, it seems, where there is a wrong to be had in copying, this will likewise come in degrees, as should any restrictions and sanctions. Perhaps the use of a *mere* fact requires recognition of something like Passig's "discovery achievement," even where the source is a *Fachbuch*. Certainly, popular nonfiction owes as much to its form as to its content, and perhaps Leuschner is correct in claiming that his books, with their hypothesized plot points and dialogue, have passed from *Sachbuch* to popular literature, but even this assumes there *is* such a line. Still, the borrowing of a nonfiction author's turn of phrase or imaginative construction seems a step beyond the use of another's mere facts. Whether or not it matters, at this point, that the source is a work of fiction or nonfiction seems an open question.

The task of the law would require developing a concrete measure for restrictions and sanctions in these sorts of cases. And while the task of an *ethics* of copying would require further analysis of these questions, the first necessary step lies in showing that restrictions and sanctions in the borrowing of nonfiction material should be treated as graded rather than absolute.

Notes

1 Visit Passig's blog (in German) at http://kathrin.passig.de
2 Baigent & Anor v. The Random House Group Ltd (The Da Vinci Code) [2006] EWHC 719 (Ch), par. 174.
3 Ibid., par. 261.
4 Ibid.
5 The American cousin of this case is *Hoehling v. Universal City Studios, Inc.* 618 F.2d 972 (2d Cir. 1980), in which the defendant's film borrowed from the plaintiff's "nonfictional" novelized account of the Hindenburg disaster, advancing a theory that the dirigible's destruction was the result of sabotage—a theory with no documented evidence. The Court of Appeals held that such a hypothesis, advanced as "fact," is no more protected than any documented fact.
6 During the trial, sales of *Holy Blood, Holy Grail* increased six-fold in the U.S. and twenty-six-fold in the U.K. (Murphy 2006).
7 English translations throughout this chapter are by Michael Weh and Darren Hick.

8 Thomas Orthmann's website has been taken down. Quotes are from Hahnemann 2006.

9 Cf. Regional Court (Landgericht, LG) of Munich I, May 21, 2008 - 21 O 15192/07. In: 2008 Zeitschrift für Urheber- und Medienrecht (ZUM) 709, at 712.

10 Ibid. In the American case of *Hoehling v. Universal City Studios*, discussed above, the court similarly denied copyright to certain scenes in the source work, referred to as *scènes à faire*—scenes that are, as a matter of practicality, indispensible in the telling of certain stories.

11 Court of Appeal (Oberlandesgericht, OLG) of Munich, November 12, 2009 - 6 U 3595/08. In: 2010 Neue Juristische Online-Zeitschrift (NJOZ), 2112, at 2113.

12 Ibid.

13 Baigent & Anor v. The Random House Group Ltd (The Da Vinci Code) [2006] EWHC 719 (Ch), par. 11.

14 Regional Court (Landgericht, LG) of Munich I, May 21, 2008 - 21 O 15192/07. In: 2008 Zeitschrift für Urheber- und Medienrecht (ZUM) 712, at 714. Jörg Sundermeier (2007) agrees, suggesting that the inclusion of such invented elements makes Leuschner suspicious as a "nonfiction" author.

References

Freund, W. and L. Wiegelmann, "Die sieben Siegel des Dan Brown," *Die Welt*, May 13, 2013. Available online: http://www.welt.de/kultur/literarischewelt/article116121475/Die-sieben-Siegel-des-Dan-Brown.html

Guardian, "Authors loses appeal over Da Vinci Code plagiarism," March 28, 2007. Available online: http://www.theguardian.com/uk/2007/mar/28/danbrown.books

Hahnemann, A. (2006), "Footnotes are Real. Populäre Literatur als Medium der Wissensvermittlung," in D. Oels (ed.), *DokuFiktion*, 142–54, Berlin: Weidler.

Hamburger, K. (1994), *Die Logik der Dichtung*, 4th edn, Stuttgart: Klett-Cotta.

Herwig, M., "Wer einen Roman schreibt, muss ein Meer austrinken. Wie Fakten zu Literatur werden: Frank Schätzing, Thomas Mann und das höhere Abschreiben der Meeresbiologie," *Frankfurter Allgemeine Zeitung*, April 13, 2005: 44.

Horstkotte, H. and A. Gerstlauer, "Kein Fall wie Guttenberg," *Die Zeit*, September 28, 2015. Available online: http://www.zeit.de/studium/hochschule/2015-09/plagiat-von-der-leyen.

Mäckler, A., "Vergleich vor Gericht zu 'Dr. Hope': Filmproduktion muss 15.000 Euro an Prof. Marita Krauss zahlen," *meine-biographie.com*, March 15, 2010. Available online: http://www.meine-biographie.com/vergleich-vor-landgericht-zu-„dr-hope"-filmproduktion-muss-15000-euro-an-prof-marita-krauss-zahlen/

Münchner Merkur, "Plagiatsvorwürfe gegen 'Dr. Hope'-Autorenteam," February 17,

2010. Available online: http://www.merkur.de/tv/plagiatsvorwuerfe-gegen-dr-hope-autorenteam-634554.html

Murphy, M., "'Da Vinci Code' Lawsuit Lifts Sales Before Judgment," *Bloomberg*, April 6, 2006. Available online: http://www.bloomberg.com/apps/news?pid=newsarchive&sid=aQVP7b.oSjXQ

Pioch, Y., "Frank Schätzing: Kann denn Recherche Sünde sein?" *Frankfurter Allgemeine Zeitung*, April 7, 2005. Available online: http://www.faz.net/aktuell/feuilleton/buecher/frank-schaetzing-kann-denn-recherche-suende-sein-1234088.html

Schätzing, F. (2004), *Der Schwarm*, Köln: Kiepenheuer & Witsch.

Schenkel, A. M., "Es geht nur ums Geld," *Frankfurter Allgemeine Zeitung*, April 13, 2007. Available online: http://www.faz.net/aktuell/feuilleton/buecher/plagiatsvorwurf-gegen-tannoed-andrea-m-schenkel-es-geht-nur-ums-geld-1435332.html

Schirg, O., "Eins zu Eins übernommen," *Die Welt*, April 6, 2005. Available online: http://www.welt.de/print-welt/article572848/Eins-zu-eins-uebernommen.html

Sippel, S., "Eine wirkliche Schauergeschichte," *Die Zeit*, April 19, 2007. Available online: http://www.zeit.de/2007/17/KA-Plagiat

Spiegel, "'Der Schwarm': Staatsanwaltschaft entkräftet Plagiatsvorwurf," November 25, 2005. Available online: http://www.spiegel.de/kultur/literatur/bestseller-der-schwarm-staatsanwaltschaft-entkraeftet-plagiatsvorwurf-a-386817.html

Spiegel, "'Sakrileg': Dan Brown gewinnt Plagiatsprozess," April 7, 2006. Available online: http://www.spiegel.de/kultur/gesellschaft/bestseller-sakrileg-dan-brown-gewinnt-plagiatsprozess-a-410318.html

Stanzel, F. K. (1964), *Typische Formen des Romans*. Göttingen: Vandenhoeck & Ruprecht.

Süddeutsche Zeitung, "'Mordfall Hinterkaifeck' contra 'Tannödmord'," May 17, 2010. Available online: http://www.sueddeutsche.de/muenchen/rechtsstreit-um-bestseller-mordfall-hinterkaifeck-contra-tannoedmord-1.241800

Sundermeier, J., "Kleinmut der Neider," *taz.de*, August 15, 2007. Available online: http://www.taz.de/!5196592/

White, H. (1973), *Metahistory: The Historical Imagination in Nineteenth-Century Europe*. Baltimore: Johns Hopkins University Press.

11

Appropriation and Derogation: When Is it Wrong to Appropriate?

Lisa Jones

1.

Artworks have always been copied. Why they are copied—to what purpose and with what intentions—makes all the difference as to whether we judge the copying of them to be legitimate or illegitimate. When the budding art student copies paintings by the grand masters in order to practice her technique, this is a legitimate form of copying; indeed, it is a mainstay of traditional visual arts training. The student does nothing that is morally, or aesthetically, wrong. On the other hand, when a forger copies a work or copies the style of a grand master in order to pass off the copies for her own gain, this is illegitimate copying—made so morally by the act of deceit involved, but also aesthetically by the lack of proper art-intentions on the part of the forger.[1] That these two kinds of cases exist at opposite ends of a spectrum seems clear-cut; however, between them lies a whole swathe of activity falling under the broad sense of "copying" whose legitimacy, or otherwise, is harder to judge.

The activity I have in mind is what we have come to call *appropriation*, which involves the use of an existing artwork, or image, or artifact in the creation of a new work or artifact. In some of its forms, appropriation has received a good deal of critical attention, insofar as a number of instances of appropriation art have led to complex copyright infringement court battles. But beyond the world of these legal disputes, appropriation has not received the further attention from philosophers and aestheticians that it perhaps demands.[2] In this chapter I wish to focus on whether, if at all, it might be *aesthetically* wrong to appropriate artworks, and my approach will be to consider whether some appropriations can be *aesthetically destructive*. This is not a concern that has been much at the forefront of contemporary discussions of appropriation, which to date have taken place mostly in the law literature. Those discussions, focused on the copyright infringement cases provoked by appropriation art, mostly tend to reflect the idea that appropriation art is sometimes akin to theft, since it involves the taking of another's expression of ideas. This, of course, is a moral concern. Yet theft and ownership are not the only kinds of worries we might have about appropriations, and there may well be much more to say about appropriation that is either not reflected in the legal discussions, or is not usually drawn out from them. I will aim to show that, outside of the legal arena and its concerns of copyright infringement, outside of moral concerns about ownership and theft, we should also consider that appropriation can occasionally be aesthetically destructive, and this can count towards it being aesthetically illegitimate.

One obvious sense in which acts of appropriation might be judged aesthetically destructive is if they involve the literal, physical destruction of an existing work. Since destroying artworks is something of a taboo, to put it mildly, we might think it an unlikely scenario that an appropriation artist would carry out such an act—except, of course, that one already did, famously, in 1953. In this year, Robert Rauschenberg made use of a Willem de Kooning sketch in order to create the work *Erased de Kooning*. The source work was a mixed-media drawing by de Kooning, which was then—as the title of Rauschenberg's piece suggests—completely erased by Rauschenberg in an "act of art," though not without de Kooning's permission. No photographs exist to show us what the erased drawing was like, nor was the process of erasure—the "act of art" itself—recorded. De Kooning's piece, being the kind of thing whose continued existence depended upon the continued existence of particular marks on a particular surface, has ceased to exist: it has gone forever.[3] Here, then, is an act of appropriation in which the source work was actually, physically, and quite literally, destroyed.

One might wonder whether this fact should lead us to make a severe judgment when it comes to aesthetically evaluating the work that was brought into being by the appropriative act. We might think that outright destruction of a source work is something that goes too far, that can never be counterbalanced by any value that the newly created work may have. But in this case it seems the artworld did not think so. Rauschenberg's "act of art," his act of erasing the de Kooning sketch, is widely understood to be of enormous significance, culturally and aesthetically. Although it scandalized many who saw it as an act of vandalism, it has also been hailed as a landmark of postmodern art in its subversion of our ideas of "art" and "artwork." It can be read both as a gesture of protest—against abstract expressionism, or the entire tradition of painting—and as an act of homage. It is also a major work of conceptual art, its main conceptual point lying precisely in the fact that it was a de Kooning that was erased—a work by the reigning master of the time, who himself habitually erased and revised the drawn elements of his paintings. In sum, the aesthetic value of Rauschenberg's "act of erasure" is significant.

When we try to balance this against the fact that bringing *Erased de Kooning* into being cost the world a de Kooning drawing, we could say that this cost detracts from that value, at least to some degree. But we must also bear in mind that de Kooning agreed to the process, even if reluctantly at first. And we also need to recognize that, in destroying one de Kooning sketch, Rauschenberg helped to elevate de Kooning's reputation and body of work even further. All things considered, in this case we might allow that the aesthetic derogation of the source—here, a literal destruction—was a price worth paying for a significant work to be brought into being, and a key moment marked in the narrative of art's history.

Erased de Kooning is a highly unusual case, however, and most other instances of appropriation do not involve the literal destruction of the source work that is copied or otherwise made use of. In the main, appropriations involve the use in a new context of a copy (in part or in whole) of an existing work, and as such they leave the source intact, physically speaking. But this is not the same thing as saying the source works are always left aesthetically intact. In exploring how appropriations might be aesthetically destructive, I will be looking at some cases where the aesthetic derogation that occurs is of a much subtler kind, involving, as I see it, the despoiling of the artwork experience rather than the art object itself. And in such cases, the question remains to be considered whether the appropriative act is worth the price paid.

2.

Before going any further, we should clarify the objects of our discussion. It is useful to mark a distinction between appropriation per se, and appropriation art. The term "appropriation art," as the name for a genre of—primarily, visual and plastic—contemporary art, came into currency in the latter half of the twentieth century, particularly with reference to the work of 1980s American artists like Sherrie Levine and Jeff Koons.[4] Levine, for instance, regularly appropriated works of art by others and remade them as her own, from paintings by Monet to photographs by Walker Evans, in the latter case simply rephotographing from a catalogue Evans's Depression-era photographic images of migrant workers, and presenting them as new artworks, without having manipulated them in any way. Meanwhile, Koons has regularly taken images from popular culture—from postcards, advertisements, and promotional materials—and created artworks that present these images either relatively unchanged (as in his piece *Moses*, an advertisement poster for the Nike sportswear brand which Koons simply framed and presented as a Koons work) or in different media (as in his *String of Puppies*, a sculpture version of a photographic postcard image by another artist). In contemporary art, appropriation is now a well-established genre, largely understood to have begun emerging in the 1960s. But as an art-genre its roots reach further back in time, to the first decades of the twentieth century, to the collages of Picasso and Braques, and the readymade works of Duchamp, which were already forecasting appropriation as a new way of creating artworks. The appropriations of Picasso, Braques, and Duchamp involved often simply incorporating non-art objects into their artworks, such as the use of newspaper in the collages or the presentation of an ordinary urinal as a sculpture; but later—for Duchamp at least—this began to develop into the taking and repurposing of existing artworks, or copies of such artworks, as illustrated by his well-known appropriation of the *Mona Lisa*, *L.H.O.O.Q*. The mid-twentieth century saw this practice of appropriating images and art objects increasingly adopted by post-modern, post-expressionist artists such as the aforementioned Robert Rauschenberg as well as Jasper Johns and Andy Warhol—all of whose work, in turn, was later reproduced by others, in a seemingly continuous spiral of appropriation.

While the term "appropriation art" is usually restricted to refer to the body of work of a certain group of artists working in visual and plastic media, it is worth remembering that appropriation occurs outwith this narrow genre of art too; the term can also be applied to a variety of activities that take from existing objects or artworks and issue in new objects and artworks—not merely collage and rephotography in the visual arts, but also samplings and mashups in music, and "found poetry" in the literary arena, for instance. What these activities all have in common is that they involve the use, either in part or in full, of existing artworks, images, texts, or artifacts, for some further purpose. Some of these appropriations, such as music mashups, may not merit the status of *appropriation art* due to their not being visual art forms, or due to the fact that they are "mass-art" phenomena rather than "high art," but they are nonetheless recognized as pop-culture appropriations. There are also appropriations that are not carried out for the purpose of creating new art, but rather for more utilitarian or practical ends, such as advertising and marketing.[5] In what follows, I will primarily be considering art-purposed appropriations, though not only those recognized as belonging under the art-historical category of appropriation art. I will also take into account some non-art-purposed appropriations where these bear on the main discussion.

3.

As already noted, acts of appropriation have often led to copyright infringement cases being brought against appropriation artists, notably against U.S. contemporary artists Jeff Koons and Richard Prince, each of whom has experienced both defeat and victory in the courtrooms (sometimes with respect to one and the same artwork).[6] It is doubtless unsurprising that appropriation artists, who seek to make "new" works precisely by self-consciously and openly taking from prior works, should often find themselves in legal trouble given the natural tensions arising between the aims and practices of their art form and the aims and practices of copyright law. It is similarly unsurprising, as a result of these legal skirmishes, that most of the critical discussion there is of appropriation art has taken place within the law literature. The legal discussions—while primarily concerned with the limits of the law, and the evolving construal of key legal concepts—provide an illuminating backdrop for the aesthetician, and it is instructive to take an overview of the main trajectory traceable from copyright infringement cases, to see what they reveal about the perceived value and legitimacy of artistic acts of appropriation.

Copyright law, in both the U.S. and the U.K., exists on the face of it to establish and protect the rights of those deemed copyright holders—authors, publishers, producers—with respect to the particular expressions of ideas in their works or products. Copyright holders have the right to control distribution of their works, a right that extends to copies and further derivative works, preventing the production of copies by others, including copies with changes. Therefore, when an appropriation artist takes an existing work—either in whole or in part—and uses it to create a new work, this act may fall foul of copyright law, resulting in the appropriator's creation being judged as an infringing copying, or derivation, of the source work—with the attendant moral undertone that the appropriation artist has stolen the source artist's expression of ideas. The issue here is not, as with forgery, one of deception. Often, appropriation artists make quite plain the sources of their appropriations, or at least have no intentions to deceive anyone as to these sources.[7] Rather, the concern is that the appropriation artist has benefited from something she has no right to; she has profited without having put in the hard artistic labor. The appropriation artist is taking, and profiting from, the property of another, and this is plausibly viewed as a moral, as well as a legal, transgression.

But copyright law's aim of protecting creators of works is often in tension with its primary avowed purpose of promoting creativity and progress. This purpose is written into the very fabric of copyright law, as can be read off from the titles of the U.S. Copyright Clause (in Article 1, Section 8 of the United States Constitution) and its precursor, the U.K. Statute of Anne, with their explicit references to the "encouragement of learning" and "progress of Science and useful Arts."[8] These goals, along with the protection afforded by copyright law to creators of works, are construed as incentivizing the creation of art, music, and literature for the good of civilization and culture, yet these creative aims would at times appear to be thwarted by the restrictions copyright law itself places on the uses that may be made of existing expressions of ideas, and the changes to these that may be permitted. This inherent incongruity at the heart of copyright law is brought under the spotlight by appropriation art, with its creative aims and extensive "borrowing" practices. Where court judgments have ruled against appropriation artists, this has often been regarded as a death toll for artistic freedom and creativity, and for this particular contemporary art form—that is, until the next, contrary, judgment comes along.[9]

There is, however, an area of copyright law that provides some elbow room for the fostering of creativity, and thus some space for alleviating the inherent tension in the aims of the law: namely, the doctrine of fair use, which permits uses of copyrighted works "for purposes such as criticism, comment, news reporting, teaching, scholarship, or research."[10] Many of the most recent defenses against copyright infringement in the U.S. have invoked this doctrine, arguing that the allegedly infringing appropriation counts as a "fair use" of the source material in accordance with one of the permitted purposes, and thus does not constitute unlawful infringement. Such "fair use defenses" have sometimes succeeded, resulting in findings of no infringement of copyright despite the fact that explicit and avowed appropriation of another artist's work has taken place. But fair use defenses do not always succeed. The doctrine has proven difficult to apply consistently across infringement cases, and judicial applications of it have been deemed difficult to understand, as well as inconsistent to the point of misuse. As a result, the fair use doctrine has been deemed to provide little guidance for either courts or artists.[11]

The "fair use test" requires courts to consider four factors in the relation between the appropriative work and the source, copyrighted, work. These are: (i) the purpose and character of the use; (ii) the nature of the copyrighted work; (iii) the amount and substantiality of the portion used in relation to the copyrighted work as a whole; and (iv) the effect of the use upon the potential market for or value of the copyrighted work. These four factors are not ordered hierarchically, nor is there any clear intention that they should be evenly weighted; the intention is rather that courts consider each of these four factors when trying to determine whether use of a prior work counts as fair use under copyright law, and this is done on a case-by-case basis. As might be anticipated, consideration of these very different factors can lead to complex permutations in how a single case might be considered, hence the lack of clarity in the application of fair use doctrine.

While each of the factors draws attention to important features of appropriation, the first factor—regarding the purpose and character of the use—is the one that has been relied on most for delivering a non-infringement verdict. As already noted, where use is made of an existing work for the purpose of criticism or comment, this may be considered legitimate (non-infringing); thus the key question becomes that of determining whether a given appropriation of a prior artifact counts as comment or criticism. Judgment on such issues would naturally seem to require a good deal of aesthetic interpretation and evaluation, yet these are activities in which the judiciary are expressly supposed to avoid engaging, and so the difficulties for the legal profession of deciding fair use are compounded.[12] Nevertheless, the law does find itself making such aesthetic judgments, and in fair use decisions these judgments now most often hinge on the notion of *transformativeness*. That is, uses that can be seen as "transformative" are favored under the first of the fair use factors, and this will often tip the balance against considerations weighing under the other factors. Two key sagas in copyright infringement law history highlight the centrality of this notion of transformative use, and its evolution.

First, transformativeness became increasingly central to fair use determinations ever since the 1994 landmark case of pop music appropriation *Campbell v. Acuff-Rose Music, Inc.*, in which the allegedly infringing work—a rap song by 2 Live Crew that appropriated elements of Roy Orbison's "Oh, Pretty Woman"—was defended on the basis that it constituted a parody of the source work.[13] While the District Court initially granted summary judgment for 2 Live Crew, endorsing the view that the song was a parody, this ruling was later reversed by the Court of Appeals, which held that the obvious commercial nature of the parody weighed too heavily against the transformative (parodic) element for the song to possibly be considered a fair use of its source. The commercial nature was thus taken as presumptive of unfair use, and the transformative element was clearly considered insufficient to negate this presumption. The Supreme Court, however, in turn later reversed the Court of Appeal's judgment, holding that even commercial parodies may constitute fair use. In determining this, the Supreme Court explicitly placed the focus on "whether the new work merely supersedes the objects of the original creation, or whether and to what extent it is 'transformative', altering the original with new expression, meaning, or message," and stipulated that "[t]he more transformative the new work, the less will be the significance of other factors, like commercialism, that may weigh against a finding of fair use."[14]

Following *Campbell v. Acuff-Rose*, fair use defenses have increasingly been expected to show the presence of new meaning or new material in order to ground a claim of transformative use, and thus fair use. While the centrality of transformativeness has been criticized by some,[15] to all intents and purposes it is now the case that fair use determinations in the realm of appropriation art are inextricably linked with an emphasis on transformativeness, understood as alteration with new expression, meaning, or message. This, however, does not mean that it has become a more simple matter for courts to find fair use; rather, it has simply shifted the problem to a slightly different level. Courts are still faced with the "dangerous undertaking" of making predominantly aesthetic judgments in determining whether a given appropriation of an existing work does or does not display new meaning or expression.

To avoid stepping too far into the judicial danger zone, courts have often sought to relieve themselves of the burden of aesthetic interpretation and judgment by one of two methods: either by appealing to the artist's own testimony of their intentions, or by invoking the idea of a "reasonable observer standard," that is, appealing to how an artwork might reasonably be perceived by an ordinary audience. Each of these strategies were involved at different stages in the saga of *Cariou v. Prince*, a long-running case in which the appropriation artist Richard Prince was sued by photographer Patrick Cariou over the use of Cariou's series of photographs of Jamaican Rastafarians, which Prince partially transformed with the addition of collage-like elements, before exhibiting the manipulated images as fresh works in a series entitled *Canal Zone*. The District Court initially found against Prince, after hearing his artist's testimony that he had not intended to aim any commentary or criticism at the source works in his appropriation of them. The court relied on this declared lack of intention with respect to criticism in making its decision that no transformative use had been made of Cariou's works; thus, the court concluded the issue of transformativeness wholly by considering Prince's statements of authorial intent. Since Prince had not intended to criticize or aim comment at Cariou's works in his appropriation of them, then there was no transformative use. This court was therefore holding fast to the view that fair (transformative) use requires comment on the source work.[16]

When the case came up for appeal to the Second Circuit court, however, this strategy of relying wholly on statements of authorial intent was criticized by that court, which deemed it preferable to determine transformativeness by asking how Prince's works appear to the reasonable observer.[17] The judiciary, presumably in the guise of a "reasonable observer," undertook an aesthetic interpretation of Prince's appropriation works and deemed them to be fundamentally different and new, in terms of appearance and expression, when compared with Cariou's photographs. What was striking about this reversal by the Second Circuit was that it set a new standard—a finding of transformative use was no longer limited to works that could be shown to comment on their source works. Indeed, there was no longer any requirement that a work make any comment at all, in order to be transformative. Moreover, the court also focused on the work itself, through the eyes of a reasonable observer, in order to try to establish whether there was a different aesthetic between Prince's appropriated images and Cariou's original photographs. These strategies, arguably, have brought the law into closer touch with the practices of the artworld and in particular this art form, insofar as it now accepts that the mere act of placing images in a new context can change the way observers see and think about them.

4.

What are we to learn, then, from this legal backdrop, that can usefully be applied when it comes to the aesthetic evaluation of works involving appropriation? A few lessons seem clear: transformative use of an existing work—where it can be identified—is considered a "good thing," given that it is sufficient to overcome a claim of infringement. Transformative uses of prior, established works are largely assumed to add value in some way to our existing cultural landscape, usually through providing parody or critical comment directed either at the source work in and of itself, or at the source-as-signifier for some broader cultural attitude or outlook. Yet they may even be valuable where they do not provide direct comment on or criticism of existing culture—they might bear value just by showing us something in a different context. Thus, transformative uses can provide valuable opportunities for broadening or deepening our understanding, giving us ways of seeing things anew, bringing us to question what we have become used to, or simply by playfully placing old things in a new context.

Moreover, under a broad construal of the notion of aesthetic value—that is, one that is not narrowly formalist, or does not appeal only to the perceptible properties of an object—it can be admitted that such transformative uses of existing works can be aesthetically valuable, since the socio-cultural and cognitive goods referred to above can be just as much part of an artwork's overall aesthetic value as can the visible, audible or tactile properties it has. Many appropriative artworks, then, will have aesthetic value partly by virtue of the transformative use they make of their prior source material.

So we have learned from the legal skirmishes that transformation equals newness, that such newness is itself often aesthetically a good thing, and that these days newness or originality does not have to mean that a work cannot share many features with previously existing works. Copying is embraced, where it becomes appropriation, quotation, reference, parody, or just repositioning, whether or not it offers direct commentary on its source. And it can be aesthetically valuable, thus aesthetically legitimate. But a note of caution must be sounded here. While transformative use may constitute newness, this is not in itself a guarantee of worthwhileness. Transformation is not always for the better, and there are two main ways that it can fail to be so.

First, a work of appropriation could be an instance of transformative use without bringing anything of added value to the table. While a legal judgment of such a work might hold it to be legitimate, since the transformative use would guarantee that there was no copyright infringement, the new work might nonetheless be pointless, banal, or otherwise unnecessary from a social, cognitive, or aesthetic point of view, notwithstanding its status as transformative. Secondly, a work might count as transformative use in a valuable sense, but in some cases this value could come at too high a price—the worry raised, but then dismissed, earlier with respect to Rauschenberg's *Erased de Kooning*—that is, a transformative use that results in a valuable work might be too costly if it requires or necessitates the destruction or derogation of the source work. In such a scenario, even an interesting, enlightening transformative use might, all things considered, not be worthwhile. In what follows below, I will consider cases of appropriation that would appear to be concrete examples embodying one or both of these possibilities.

In the first sort of case, where we have a transformative appropriation that is banal, it might still be thought there is nothing particularly wrong with this. It makes little difference, one might think, whether a banal appropriation comes into being—while it might not contribute anything of value to our culture, it does no real harm either; it is perhaps just morally, socially, and cognitively neutral, while possibly being entertaining for a brief burst of time. However, we would be mistaken to assume that appropriations never do any harm. Thus far, in looking to how the law sees appropriations, we have been assessing the positives of such works by focusing on the result of the appropriative act—the new work that is brought into being by the transformative use of a source work or artifact. Thus far, it has mostly mattered what this new work brings to the table, as it were—whether it brings something new, something that is worthwhile. Yet we also need to consider what is left behind when an act of appropriation occurs. In assessing the value of appropriative art and appropriative activity, we should look not only at the new object that is brought into being by the act of appropriation, but also at what remains of the source work in the wake of the appropriative act.[18]

When we turn our attention this way, we can observe that appropriative works may occasionally despoil or devalue the very source from which they appropriate. They may do this not by literally physically harming the source work (as in the Rauschenberg case), but rather by spoiling our subsequent appreciation of the source work, in interfering with our ability to appreciate that work the way we did previously. Where this occurs, this negative effect on the source work is an aesthetic derogation; when combined with the fact that the new work brings nothing of value to the table, this adds up to a pointless aesthetic derogation, and this, I would argue, would make the act of appropriation wrong.

Do appropriations sometimes aesthetically despoil or devalue the source works from which they appropriate? I would argue that some do, and there are many examples we can appeal to, to affirm this point. We might think first of the easiest cases of banal appropriations—those carried out not for art-purposes, but for purely commercial purposes. In the world of advertising, artworks of all kinds are routinely pressed into the service of selling, and in being used in this way they arguably lose something of their value. Some empirical study has been carried out in this area—looking at how the use of visual art in advertising negatively affects people's future aesthetic appraisals of the relevant artworks—and it appears to be a proven phenomenon.[19] Musical examples can also be found. For a certain generation of British people, for instance, the cor anglais melody from the slow movement of Dvorak's *New World Symphony* cannot be heard without a nostalgia-tinged moving image coming to mind of a small boy pushing a bicycle up a steep hill, delivering loaves of bread (see Scott 2007). This piece of film is from an advertisement for Hovis, a bread company which ran this bucolic, wholesome advert for a number of years during the austere British 1970s. Directed by Ridley Scott before he hit the Hollywood big time, its influence was widespread among an entire generation of television-watching Britons, who eventually voted it their favorite advertisement of all time (see Byrne 2006). The effect this has on those exposed to the advertisement is that they simply cannot hear the music without associating it with the product, or at least with the romanticized vision promoted by the advert. Dvorak's symphony is now "so closely associated with the brand that [radio station] Classic FM regularly receives requests for the 'Hovis music'" (ibid.).

For those exposed to the advert, it is fair to say their experience of the source artwork is now and forever tainted quite forcefully by the close association forged through the music's appropriation by Hovis, insofar as they cannot hear the work without elements of the advert coming to mind—elements that should not legitimately be part of one's experience of the symphony as an artwork. It is not far-fetched, then, to talk here of a despoiling of the work, by the appropriative use made of it. Of course, it is not that Dvorak's symphony is *literally harmed*, since it remains the same object it always was—its identity is not altered, and its existence is intact. But we can talk of it being despoiled insofar as certain future experiences of it have, for certain listeners, been compromised. That the advertisement has despoiled the musical work in this way is a mark against it, as a cultural object.

So much for the advertising case, admittedly a somewhat different phenomenon from the art-purposed appropriations we have hitherto been considering. If we return our attention to appropriation for the purposes of creating new art, is there reason to think that "despoiling" occurs here too? I believe so. Once more, examples can be drawn from music. Consider the 1989 hip-hop song by American rapper Vanilla Ice, "Ice Ice Baby." Released on Vanilla Ice's debut album, and initially also as a single B-side, it became his best-known song, and was the first hip-hop single to top the Billboard charts in the U.S. Notably, it interpolates the striking bassline of another pop single, the Queen/David Bowie collaboration "Under Pressure" (1981). Ice's sampling of the bassline from "Under Pressure" was not without controversy, since he initially gave no credit to Queen or Bowie, though he later did concede credit and royalties to both for all remixes and versions he produced of "Ice Ice Baby."[20] But aside from the legal controversy, this is a case of appropriation where the appropriative work could be considered to have aesthetically despoiled the source.[21]

Ice's hip-hop song, while initially acclaimed and popular—and heard far and wide in Western pop culture—did not manage to attain critical longevity, and was later deemed to be among the worst of the "most awesomely bad songs ever."[22] By comparison, the original Queen/Bowie single it sampled is widely considered to have stood the test of time, and is as critically acclaimed today as it was after its release when it reached number one in the U.K. pop charts. Recorded by Queen and Bowie at the height of their respective careers, "Under Pressure" is a remarkable collaboration in which the vocal skills of Bowie and Freddie Mercury trade off one another, shifting from moving harmonies to melodic scatting, to powerful crescendo, all the while underpinned by that striking bassline. *Stylus* magazine's music critic, Anthony Miccio described it as "the best song of all time" (Miccio 2004). It is fair to conclude, then, that Vanilla Ice's single was significantly inferior to the Queen/Bowie single, aesthetically speaking.

This inferiority is not the main point, however. It is one thing if, as a result of this marked difference in aesthetic quality, Ice's appropriation counts as a fairly banal work appropriating from a more aesthetically interesting work while adding very little of interest; the more important point concerns what effect it has on its source. As with the use of Dvorak's symphony discussed above, the use made by Ice of Queen/Bowie's work unfortunately has a negative afterlife—once heard, it renders it impossible for us to experience the superior "Under Pressure" without aspects of "Ice Ice Baby" being brought to mind. Our aesthetic engagement with "Under Pressure" comes to be infected with a—largely involuntary—remembered awareness of the inferior hip-hop song.

Now, to some, these claims may sound melodramatic. It might be thought that if I really want to enjoy an unencumbered experience of "Under Pressure," then I simply have to focus on the song itself, paying proper attention to it and not allowing my awareness to be affected by memories of other works experienced. In short, I should adopt the proper attitude towards my listening, and not allow myself to be distracted by extraneous phenomena. If I'm unable to do so, then that is my fault, not the fault of the appropriative act carried out by Vanilla Ice. This is a reasonable comment—but only up to a point. It is true that our engagement with artworks, even mass artworks like pop songs, demands a certain kind of deliberate attention on our part, and that if we are to do them justice we must make an effort to attend to them fully and with concentration. But, as suggested above, sometimes there can be an involuntariness to the connections we find ourselves making when dwelling on artworks, depending on what other things we might have been exposed to; we cannot always control what comes to mind when we let the experience of an artwork wash over us and, given how interconnected and intertextual artworks tend to be, it is unsurprising if certain connections with other works or artifacts are made during that experience.

This is not a matter of idiosyncratic inattention, but of objective similarities and relations between cultural objects that cause them to be juxtaposed in our experience and that cannot easily be put aside in our engagement with them. This is particularly true of music, perhaps, given the "earworm" effect—the capacity of tunes or parts of tunes to become stuck in our heads. Not much is understood about what causes this phenomenon and why it happens to some people more than others, but plausibly it plays a role in, or shares a common root with, the "infection" phenomenon described above.[23]

It is reasonable then to hold that, in the case of the "Ice Ice Baby"/"Under Pressure" pairing, exposure to the former can negatively effect one's future experience of the latter, even if one is attempting to pay full attention to the latter and experience it in its "pure," original state; the hip-hop song's repetitive banal refrains, once heard, will tend to surface, earworm-like, during a listening of "Under Pressure" even if one wills otherwise. Moreover, this is not an isolated case. Other cases certainly exist within hip-hop music especially, given that genre's nature of sampling and appropriation: think of MC Hammer's "U Can't Touch This," whose refrain comes inevitably to mind when one listens to the Rick James funk-R&B single, "Super Freak," from which it appropriated its most notable riff; or the track "I'll Be Missing You" by Puff Daddy and various artists, in tribute to the Notorious B.I.G., which extensively samples The Police's signature pop/rock song, "Every Breath You Take"; or "Ghetto Supastar" by Pras, which interpolates the chorus of well-loved Country-and-Western classic "Islands in the Stream." Each of these appropriations, whether or not they are as banal as "Ice Ice Baby," have the same unfortunate negative afterlife as that song does, in terms of their elements infiltrating or infecting subsequent experiences of the source work.[24]

This infection phenomenon amounts, in my view, to an aesthetic derogation or despoilment of the source work by the appropriating work, whether intentional or not. Where an act of appropriation leads to this kind of aesthetic derogation of the source, I suggest that this should bear on the aesthetic judgment we make of that appropriation work. The act of despoiling its source is a mark that can count against it in our overall, all-things-considered judgment of the appropriation work. While such a work might, in addition to the despoiling effect, bear positive aesthetic properties sufficient to outweigh the harm it does in derogating its source, it nonetheless remains that the despoiling effect is always a bad-making feature of a work. In cases where we might also think that the appropriation work has little aesthetic value as a form in itself, and that it adds little to the cultural landscape (as with "Ice Ice Baby") we may for these reasons judge the appropriation work to be, overall, aesthetically illegitimate, or—to put it another way—to instantiate an aesthetic wrong. Moreover, the higher the aesthetic stock of the source work that is despoiled, the greater an aesthetic crime the derogation is. Thus, for example, we might judge the derogation of "Under Pressure" by "Ice Ice Baby" as being a worse aesthetic crime than is the derogation of "Super Freak" by "U Can't Touch This."

While this kind of "infection derogation" occurs fairly commonly within music, it can also occur with other art forms too. As noted earlier, experiences of visual artworks can be also devalued by the appropriation of those works when their images are used commercially in advertisements, and made too ubiquitous. But aesthetic derogation of visual artworks can also occur, I believe, when they are used in art-purposed appropriative acts, where the effect of the appropriation is not so much that the image of the source becomes too ubiquitous but rather that the experience of it is despoiled, as in the musical cases.

Take Jake and Dinos Chapman's 2003 work *Insult to Injury*. This work, which appropriated Goya's *Disasters of War* etchings (1810–20), could actually be viewed either as a "literal destruction" similar to the Rauschenberg case, or as another instance of "denigration through despoiling of future experiences," as in the musical examples discussed above. For their work, the Chapman brothers bought up eighty prints of Goya's etchings and quite literally defaced them, altering their visual features by adding montages of clown and puppy faces. The work was shown in a 2003 exhibition entitled—with typical Chapman impertinence—"The Rape of Creativity," and caused quite a stir. Many viewers and critics were shocked by the use the artists had made of these historic prints, and cries of "vandalism" were heard. The brothers themselves insisted they were improving, rather than vandalizing, Goya's original work, with Dinos Chapman claiming "you can't vandalise something by making it more expensive."[25]

Vandalism or not, the artworld seemingly accepted that the Chapman brothers' *Insult to Injury* is a work that bears considerable aesthetic value. It has been described as brilliant and profound (Jones 2003). Conceptually, it claims Rauschenberg's *Erased de Kooning* as its antecedent, and like that work can be read as both a gesture of violence and an act of love, or homage, towards the source artist. The alterations the Chapmans have made to Goya's prints arguably serve to amplify their power, an effect that may seem surprising given that the alterations involve something so kitsch as clown and puppy faces. But while kitsch, they are also nasty and disturbing, and as a result these defacings seem to be at home in the prints, adding a further, psychotic, layer to Goya's terrible images of violence.

Here, then, we have an appropriation case where the newly created work is of recognizable aesthetic value, so the transformative use it makes of the source work is not trivial. But is the value of the new work worth the price of what it has done to the source? Reflecting on this question is not a simple matter, since in this case there are two ways we can think about what the source work is, and depending on which way we think about it, we will either think the Chapmans physically ruined their source, or that they didn't. It all depends very much on whether we think we are dealing here with singular or with non-singular artworks, ontologically speaking, and it is far from obvious how prints and etchings should be construed, ontologically. The prints the brothers had bought were a mint-condition full set produced in 1937, and it is only these prints that were defaced/montaged, not the etching plates themselves. But there is no clear consensus in the philosophy of art literature about whether, in the case of etchings, we are dealing with a multiply realizable abstract work which is encoded in the etching plates, and whose prints are construed as instances of that work (that is, similar ontologically to photographs, and their relations to their negatives or digital code), or whether we should rather think of the prints themselves as singular, unique works (each of them like a painting or drawing, say).[26]

If we hold the latter view, seeing prints as unique works in themselves, this implies that the Chapman brothers did literally, physically alter the work that is Goya's *Disasters of War*. This was perhaps the view of those commentators who referred to the Chapmans' actions as vandalism, destruction, and the breaking of art's ultimate taboo (Jones 2003). On this view, one may well consider that the Chapmans' new work—even if of considerable value itself—cannot make up for what has been lost. Even if Rauschenberg's appropriation and destruction of the de Kooning sketch is not considered too high a cost for the sake of what it brought to us, this does not mean the Chapmans' use of Goya's work should be judged similarly: there are important differences between Chapman/Goya and Rauschenberg/de Kooning, not least that de Kooning offered up his work to Rauschenberg, thus implicitly endorsing the project. Goya, of course, got no say in the matter of his work's appropriation.

But if we hold the other view, that is, if we think of Goya's prints not as singular objects, but rather as instances of a multiply realizable entity, then we will not be considering the same question. We will instead be considering whether the Chapmans' transformative use of the Goya could be thought of as destructive, given that it was only *one instance* of Goya's series of prints that was defaced, not *the work itself.* There are two responses to be made in this scenario. The first is that, even if we assume that the prints themselves are *not* singular unique artworks, there may still be good reason to be dismayed at what the brothers have done to *that set* of prints, given that the 1937 set they used was itself a historically significant edition. It may be devastating to those who value such prints from an art-historical standpoint, over and above an aesthetic standpoint. Such appreciators may indeed feel that the price paid for the new work to be brought into being was too high, and thus that the Chapmans' appropriation is illegitimate. Note, however, that this does not amount to the claim that the appropriation is *aesthetically* illegitimate—just that it is illegitimate for reasons of preservation.

The second observation is that even if we reject the idea that the Chapman appropriation did any literal physical harm to any existing artwork, we may still want to claim that it did harm in the other sense proposed here, that of despoiling any subsequent experience we may have of the source work. For the "infection derogation" discussed in relation to music sampling could also be a possibility in this case too. A thorough aesthetic experience of *Insult to Injury* is one in which we come to see the defacings as an amplification of Goya's original unflinching images of horror and suffering; as noted above, we see them as *belonging* to those terrible images. This aptness of intervention is what makes *Insult to Injury* such a success. But it also makes it destructive in the "infection" sense, for once we have appreciated this work, we can hardly un-see the defacings when we return to Goya's untouched prints. A subsequent experience of Goya's untransformed prints is inevitably infiltrated by the memory of the grinning clown heads and kitsch puppy faces, against one's best viewing intentions. And this counts as a negative effect of the Chapmans' appropriation work. Even if we are impressed by *Insult to Injury*, even if we find it aesthetically valuable to a high degree in its interplay with *Disasters of*

War, we will nonetheless find its negative after-effect unfortunate, and should consider this a matter of aesthetic derogation of our experience of Goya's work. Accordingly, this effect should count as a mark against *Insult to Injury* in our overall aesthetic evaluation of that work. How much this tips the balance in our overall evaluation may be negligible, given the positive features of the work, but it ought to be taken into account as one bad-making feature among the many features that contribute to an overall aesthetic judgment. Those viewers who cried "vandalism" may not just have intended to point out physical changes to a particular set of objects—they may well have intended the cry to capture a loss of aesthetic experience, in the impossibility of ever seeing Goya's prints again without involuntarily seeing clown faces. There may yet then be aesthetic reasons for deeming the Chapmans' work too costly.

5.

Once we begin to recognize the kind of aesthetic derogation I have been describing here in these few cases, we might start noting how it occurs elsewhere, to a stronger or weaker degree. For instance, it is likely that a proper engagement with Richard Prince's *Canal Zone* series will make it very difficult for us to view Patrick Cariou's original *Yes, Rasta* photographs without imagining, involuntarily, the collaged additions and scribblings that Prince added to those images in his work. This effect is a cause for complaint, not only on Cariou's part but also on the part of viewers who may well have enjoyed Cariou's work but later find their ability to enjoy it compromised by their exposure to Prince's work.[27] And there are surely many more visual and musical examples of this derogation effect that can be summoned.

Taking this effect seriously, we can hold that the recognition of transformative use—which provides a powerful defense against copyright infringement and helps secure copyright's and art's aims of progress and creativity—is not to be considered in isolation when it comes to our evaluative judgments about appropriations, and certainly not without balancing alongside the cost of what the transformative use might do to the source. Where an appropriation transforms an existing source work, this may be enough to count as a new work and avoid a legal judgment of infringement, it may even be enough to create a new work of substantial aesthetic value, but this does not mean that all is entirely positive. The transformation may bring about negative effects, creating something valuable but whose value is reduced or even negated by a corresponding loss of value on the other side of the ledger.[28]

It is important for this to be acknowledged, and taken into account in our overall aesthetic judgments of appropriative works. In making all-things-considered judgments of works of appropriation, we should look to what they leave in their wake as well as what they bring into being, otherwise our judgments will be deficient. This matters because we live in a culture of increasing appropriation, and must be discerning about the appropriations that surround us. We need to be able to make evaluative judgments that separate good works of appropriation from bad, so that by recognizing and encouraging the good, and by ignoring or discouraging the aesthetically banal or overly destructive, we stand a better chance of nurturing a creative culture in which valuable and worthwhile appropriations enrich our aesthetic environment, while resisting a tide of ever-repeated, but aesthetically depleted, imagery and music.

Notes

1 For discussion of what is aesthetically wrong with forgeries, see Dutton 1965; Irvin 2005; Kulka 2005; Hick 2010.

2 Philosophers of art who have addressed issues raised by appropriation art include Irvin 2005; Young 2006; Hick 2010, 2013.

3 Notwithstanding the fact that the San Francisco Museum of Modern Art, which owns the Rauschenberg work, brought to light the remaining traces of de Kooning's drawing using digital capture and other technologies, http://www.sfmoma.org/explore/collection/artwork/25846

4 One of the first artists to whom the label of "appropriation artist" was applied was Elaine Sturtevant, who was actively appropriating artworks during the 1960s, some years before Levine and Koons. Sturtevant reproduced existing works by other artists, variously repainting other artists' paintings, reproducing Warhol screenprints, and rebuilding Claes Oldenburg's *Store*. For a useful summary of the emergence of appropriation art and artists, see Hick 2013 and also Jasiewicz 2014.

5 One way to mark a distinction between appropriation art as an art genre, and acts of appropriation more generally, is to note that appropriation art is self-consciously and self-reflexively *about* appropriation. See Hick 2013: 1178.

6 Koons has been sued numerous times, including a case brought against him by Art Rogers, the creator of the *Puppies* postcard whose image Koons recreated as a kitsch sculpture, *String of Puppies*; see Rogers v. Koons 751 F. Supp. 474 (SDNY 1990), *aff'd*, 960 F. 2d 301 (2d Cir.), *cert. denied*, 113 S. Ct. 365 (1992). Koons lost that case, as he did several others in the wake of it, but he later successfully defended against another infringement case, Blanch v. Koons, 467 F. 3d 244 (2d

Cir. 2006). Prince, too, famously lost a case against photographer Patrick Cariou whose works he had reproduced, in Cariou v. Prince, 784 F. Supp. 2d 337 (2011), but this District Court outcome was later spectacularly overturned by the Second Circuit in a landmark ruling, Cariou v. Prince, 714 F. 3d 694 (2d Cir. 2013). To be discussed below.

7 See, for instance, Sherrie Levine's appropriation work entitled "After Walker Evans," which explicitly acknowledges the appropriation of photographic works from Walker Evans.

8 See: U.S. Copyright Office, "Copyright Law of the United States of America" http://copyright.gov/title17/92preface.html and "The Avalon Project: The Statue of Anne; April 10, 1710" http://avalon.law.yale.edu/18th_century/anne_1710.asp

9 The aforementioned Cariou v. Prince lawsuit is a good example of reversals of judgment.

10 The doctrine of fair use is explicitly given in U.S. copyright law, in section 107: "[T]he fair use of a copyright work [...] for purposes such as criticism, comment, news reporting, teaching [...] scholarship, or research, is not an infringement of copyright" 17 USC §107 2006, http://www.copyright.gov/title17/92chap1.html#107. In U.K. law, a more restricted "fair dealing" provision is set out in Section 30 of the U.K. Copyright, Designs and Patents Act 1988, http://www.legislation.gov.uk/ukpga/1988/48/contents which has potential to be developed into a broader "fair use" exception. For present purpose, U.S. copyright law will be the main focus.

11 For discussions of the problems of application of the fair use doctrine, see e.g. Leval 1990; Carroll 2007; Butt 2010; Gorman 2011.

12 See Jasiewicz 2014: 157–9. The very title of Jasiewicz's article—"A Dangerous Undertaking"—references the famous admonishment from Justice Oliver Wendell Holmes in 1903 that "it would be a dangerous undertaking for persons trained only in the law to constitute themselves the final judges of the worth of pictorial illustrations, outside of the narrowest and most obvious limits," in Bleistein v. Donaldson Lithographing Co., 188 US 239, at 251 (1903).

13 Campbell v. Acuff-Rose Music, Inc., 510 US 569 (1994).

14 Campbell v. Acuff-Rose Music, Inc., 510 US at 579.

15 See Tushnet 2004 (arguing that there are negative consequences of equating fair use and transformativeness, since it leads to non-transformative copying being penalized).

16 Cariou v. Prince, 784 F. Supp. 2d 337, 348-49 (SDNY 2011).

17 Cariou v. Prince, 714 F. 3d 694, 706-07 (2d Cir. 2013).

18 It should be noted here that the fair use doctrine within U.S. copyright law does make reference to the fate of the source, copyrighted work, under the fourth of its four factors: this requires courts to consider "the effect of the use upon the

potential market for or value of the copyrighted work." However, this requirement is mostly concerned with (and taken to be about) the financial status and market value of those source works, and so does not refer explicitly to their aesthetic value—though presumably, if the financial value of a work were to be lessened by an act of appropriation this would likely sometimes be due to the fact that the appropriation of it renders it less aesthetically valuable. This possibility is the only one I am interested in exploring here.

19 Dinu 2004 discusses an empirical test of the contention, suggested by earlier qualitative studies, that appropriating art in the service of advertising results in both (a) the advertisement gaining some aesthetic value, and (b) the artwork losing some of its original aesthetic value. Dinu's study found that, overall, art images placed in an advertising context are indeed evaluated by subjects as less aesthetically and financially valuable than when the same images are evaluated in a non-advertising context.

20 The case never actually went to court; Vanilla Ice (real name Robert Van Winkle) settled out of court, since it was so obvious that the bassline was copied. Had he gone to court and attempted a fair use defense, who knows what might have transpired.

21 I owe this example to Darren Hudson Hick (in conversation).

22 It was accorded fifth place in VH1's 2004 list of "50 most awesomely bad songs ever," compiled by VH1 music channel and *Blender* magazine. See PR Newswire 2004.

23 See the "Earworm Project" at Goldsmiths, University of London: http://www.gold.ac.uk/music-mind-brain/earworm-project/ (last modified March 11, 2014).

24 Note this is not to be confused with the more widespread phenomenon of pointless or banal cover versions. A cover version—where an existing song is performed and recorded by another artist or band—is a kind of copying that could perhaps be considered a form of appropriation, although the aim of cover versions is simply to produce a new *version* of a given work, rather than produce a *new work*. Bad cover versions may be pointless, or annoying, but they seldom involve the "infection" phenomenon I am here ascribing to certain samplings, since they don't usually introduce anything new in the cover of the existing song that could then "'infect" a subsequent experience of that source work.

25 Dinos Chapman's comment was allegedly made in response to criticism of the next stage of their Goya appropriation work, when they reworked Goya's *Los Caprichos* prints, in their show *Like a Dog Returns to its Vomit*, at Frieze 2005 (O'Keefe 2005). The brothers had previously interacted with Goya's prints in their 1994 work, *Great Deeds Against the Dead*, a three-dimensional working of a scene of dismembered corpses from the *Disasters* print series.

26 It may be tempting to view printmaking as a singular art form, and see prints as

singular artworks, due to the fact that individual prints are often treated as objects of value in a way that mere copies of visual artworks are not; prints are usually limited and numbered, and command higher prices than mere copies on the market. But these features need not be decisive in determining that printmaking falls into the "singular" ontological category. Nelson Goodman has argued instead for seeing printmaking as multiple, though autographic rather than allographic—autographic works being those of which not even the most faithful duplication counts as genuine. See Goodman (1976: 113–21). For a related view of prints as "restrictedly multiple artworks," see Weh 2010.

27 In its consideration of Cariou v. Prince, the Second Circuit court did consider how Prince's appropriation affected Cariou's work under the fourth factor of the fair use doctrine, i.e. the effect of the secondary use upon the value of the source work, but the court's reflections here were limited to the potential market for, and financial value of, the works; they were not considerate of the effect of Prince's appropriations on the aesthetic value of Cariou's works. Cariou v. Prince, 714 F. 3d 694, 707 (2d Cir. 2013).

28 The question may be raised at this point of whether there could be an inverse case of what I am describing as "aesthetic derogation": could there be a case where an appropriative work results in an infiltration of one's experience of the source work in a way that enriches, rather than derogates? This may well be possible. An example that comes to mind is Cornelia Parker's 2003 work, *The Distance (A Kiss with String Attached)*. For this temporary work, Parker wrapped one of the marble versions of Rodin's *The Kiss* in a mile of string. The work was intended—among other things—to be suggestive of the constriction, and even claustrophobia, of relationships, making explicit how a kiss binds and holds lovers together. This intervention in Rodin's well-known work received mixed responses, and from my own experience of it I would argue that Parker's work does indeed "infiltrate" subsequent engagement with the string-free source work—visual memories of the string come forcefully into that experience, just as the Chapman Brothers' cartoon faces infiltrate the subsequent engagement with Goya's work. Yet in the Parker/Rodin case, the memory of the wrapped string arguably enriches one's viewing of the stringless marble work, prompting one to think of the new layers of meaning revealed by the wrapped version; it does not disturb, but rather deepens, our experience of the Rodin. But fuller discussion of this phenomenon is beyond the scope of the present chapter, and ultimately the question whether "positive infection" by an appropriation work is or is not possible does not affect the argument here as to whether "negative infection" occurs and should be considered a bad-making feature.

References

Butt, R. I. (2010), "Appropriation Art and Fair Use," *Ohio State Journal on Dispute Resolution* 25 (4): 1055–93.

Byrne, C., "Ridley Scott's Hovis Advert is Voted All Time Favourite," *The Independent*, May 2, 2006. Available online; http://www.independent.co.uk/news/media/ridley-scotts-hovis-advert-is-voted-alltime-favourite-476424.html

Carroll, M. W. (2007), "Fixing Fair Use," *North Carolina Law Review* 85 (4): 1087–154.

Dinu, L., "Do Ads Degrade Art? Advertising and Art Appropriation," (paper presented at the annual meeting of the International Communication Association, New Orleans Sheraton, New Orleans, Louisiana, May 27, 2004). Available online: http://citation.allacademic.com/meta/p_mla_apa_research_citation/1/1/3/2/4/p113248_index.html

Dutton, D. (1965), "Artistic Crimes," *British Journal of Aesthetics* 19 (4): 333–45.

Goodman, N. (1976), *Languages of Art: An Approach to a Theory of Symbols*, 2nd edn, Indianapolis, IN: Hackett Publishing Company.

Gorman, E. D. (2011), "Appropriate Testing and Resolution: How to Determine Whether Appropriation Art is Transformative 'Fair Use' or Merely an Unauthorized Derivative?" *St Mary's Law Journal* 43 (2): 289–332.

Hick, D. H. (2010), "Forgery and Appropriation in Art," *Philosophy Compass* 5 (12): 1047–56.

Hick, D. H. (2013), "Appropriation and Transformation," *Fordham Intellectual Property, Media & Entertainment Law Journal*, 23: 1155–95.

Irvin, S. (2005), "Appropriation and Authorship in Contemporary Art," *British Journal of Aesthetics* 45 (2): 123–37.

Jasiewicz, M. I. (2014), "'A Dangerous Undertaking': The Problem of Intentionalism and Promise of Expert Testimony in Appropriation Art Infringement Cases," *Yale Journal of Law & the Humanities* 26 (1): 147–51.

Jones, J., "Jones on Art: Jake and Dinos Chapman," *Guardian*, March 31, 2003. Available online: http://www.theguardian.com/culture/2003/mar/31/artsfeatures.turnerprize2003

Kulka, T. (2005), "Forgeries and Art Evaluation: An Argument for Dualism in Aesthetics," *Journal of Aesthetic Education* 39 (3): 58–70.

Leval, P. N. (1990), "Toward a Fair Use Standard," *Harvard Law Review* 103 (5): 1105–36.

Miccio, A., "On Second Thought: Queen—Hot Space," *Stylus Magazine*, November 23, 2004. Available online: http://www.stylusmagazine.com/articles/on_second_thought/queen-hot-space.htm

O'Keefe, A., "Frieze Show Puts the 'Art' into Party," *Observer*, October 23, 2005. Available online: http://www.theguardian.com/uk/2005/oct/23/arts.friezeartfair2005

PR Newswire, "VH1 & Blender Magazine Present: 50 Most Awesomely Bad Songs …

Ever," *PR Newswire*, April 23, 2004. Available online: http://www.prnewswire.com/news-releases/vh1--blender-magazine-present-50-most-awesomely-bad-songs--ever-premiering-wednesday-may-12-900-pm-72640707.html

Scott, R., "Hovis Bike Advert 1973 (Britain's Favourite TV Ad)," YouTube, uploaded June 30, 2007. Available online: https://www.youtube.com/watch?v=6Mq59ykPnAE

Tushnet, R. (2004), "Copy This Essay: How Fair Use Doctrine Harms Free Speech and How Copying Serves It," *Yale Law Journal* 114 (3): 535–90.

Weh, M. (2010), "Production Determines Category: An Ontology of Art," *Journal of Aesthetic Education* 44 (1): 84–99.

Young, J. O. (2006), "Art, Authenticity and Appropriation," *Frontiers of Philosophy in China* 1 (3): 455–76.

12

The Paradox of Style as a Concept of Art

Jan Bäcklund

I have walked past this sculptural structure several times and without giving it much thought or any contemplation I have just assumed—subconsciously—that it was the one of many brickworks by Per Kirkeby. For some reason that I don't remember, I came to talk to an artist friend and colleague of mine in the vicinity of the brickwork. He informed me that the sculpture was not a sculpture by Kirkeby, but one created by a professor in architecture. My artist friend was quite upset by the sculpture and told me that he and other artists for a long time without success had tried to convince the schools of architecture to remove the structure, with the argument that it parasitized on Kirkeby's brick sculptures. At a later occasion I recounted this to two theoreticians of architecture, who knew of the maker of the "Kirkeby-like" structure. Not unsurprisingly, they saw nothing in the line of Kirkeby in it, but just, as intended, a piece of architectural research in brick structures of high interest, but unrelated to art. I believe they are right, underlining that the question of stylistic copy or plagiarism is first and foremost related to the developments of the concept of art, that is, the institutions, markets, history and discourses of visual art.

I got the name of the author, but I don't remember it. I could, of course, find it out, but as a crucial part of my argument is that this namelessness—seen from the perspective of visual art—is intrinsically linked with a positive assessment of plagiarism, I will let the author remain anonymous and authorless; had my focus been theory of architecture, I would have looked upon an authored structure, and the subject of my discourse would be fundamentally different.

Of course there exist a great number of "stylistic copies" within the field of visual art. We have all seen them, but we don't remember them, as they linger in the periphery, at inconsequential and local exhibitions, and they never "get a name," precisely because they are so blatantly embarrassing in their crime against art, in not understanding the first rule of artistic production that you should develop your own *uniquely identifiable style*. Now, "artist" is not a protected title, and art is not a static discourse. One of the most dramatic changes in the art world during the last decade has undoubtedly been the inclusion of practices never intended to be seen as art, but in the light of different recent developments suddenly makes perfect sense within the institutions, markets and history of art. Some cases in point would be the inclusion of projects like those of Erkki Kurenniemi, Anton Zeilinger or Korbinian Aigner in the Documenta 13 (2012) or the even more extra-artistically inclusive Biennale di Venezia of 2013, but can be observed in the vast majority of any major trend-mapping exhibition of the twenty-first century.

Thus the indignation of my colleague is not only understandable, but furthermore orthodox to our views of art and artistic integrity. *As an artist*, you may very well copy other artists' works, as appropriation art has demonstrated. This is because appropriation art is another *style*, however contradictory it may sound. Appropriation is a double signing—"a Walker Evans by Sherrie Levine" or "a Warhol by Sturtevant"—and articulates a different artistic enunciation than the work appropriated, even if the works in question are aesthetically or physically indiscernible. *As a non-artist*, on the other hand, the first rule of artistic creation does not apply and you may—of course—use whatever style you might find appropriate in your extra-artistic project, as for instance our Danish architect. But as soon as a work makes a claim (intentional or non-intentional) towards art, or can be confused with art, the reaction of the art world will show that style has in reality become an unregistered trademark.

Technically, we call this unacceptable and non-discursive (as opposed to the acceptance and discursiveness of appropriation art) form of artistic parasitism *plagiarism*, that is, issuing another's work as your own, in opposition to forgery, which is issuing your own work as another's. My argument here will be to assess on the one hand why plagiarism of an artistic style must necessarily be the most embarrassing thing an artist can do, and on the other hand why plagiarism is artistically necessary as well. As the argument is not an ontological one, but a historical one, the paradox proposed here is a question to the future of art.

1. Image and style

An artistic style that can be plagiarized is one that can be the subject of copying. As we know from the studies of Hans Belting (1991) and others, style, as we understand it, was if not invisible, then at least unobservable during the late

Middle Ages. This invisibility can be tested with the help of an example, taken from Alexander Nagel (2004: 104–5), of a painting brought home to Cambrai from Rome by a Flemish prelate in 1440. This was a *Madonna and Child* attributed to St. Luke—not necessarily because it was believed that St. Luke himself had conducted the brush, but because it was believed that it was a true and authentic copy, that is, an original image of Our Lady and the Christ Child. When it was painted was irrelevant: the image was authentic. Today we know that the image was painted in the mid-fourteenth century, probably in Siena, in a Byzantine style, and even a copy of this type, *Virgo Eleousa*, was regarded as an original image by St. Luke as well. The Cambrai Madonna, in its turn, was copied at least fifteen times, among others, by Petrus Christus, Hayne from Brussels, and Rogier van der Weyden. The image was, of course, never signed, as its authority was self-evident, St. Luke being the only one who had ever painted Our Lady. Thus, the copies were as authentic images as their prototype because, as we now know from digital images, there was no such thing as "an original" and "a copy"—the copyability being an intrinsic property of the image, which the legend of the Mandylion clearly illustrates (see Lenain 2007; Lenain 2011: 74–6, 123–33; Belting 1991: 349–82). On the other hand, it is not at all improbable that no one could see the—for us—obvious stylistic differences between the copies, as there were no observation apparatus to detect any such differences. The question of attribution, the author function, concerned the image, not the style. The authenticity was first and foremost related to the image, not to the indexical traces in matter. Correspondingly, when Alexander Sforza had an image of Madonna and Child copied with the inscription: "These had Saint Luke painted in the living (*in vivo*). The painting is the authentic portrait (*propria effigies*). Alexander Sforza gave the commission, Melozzo has painted it. Luke would say it would be his own work (*diceret esse suam*)" (Belting 1991: 382, my translation). The authenticity or originality of the painting is altogether related to the image (Lucas Painting Our Lady) and the authority of issuing (Alexander Sforza), not at all in the painting of it or any painterly style, as Luke still would recognize it as his own work.

During the early modern period, style became a predominantly normative or qualitative concept like Vasari's distinction between disegno and color, or like the later distinction between antique and modern, or between the beautiful and the sublime. This qualitative and normative concept of style was also the reason why the practice of copying became paramount in any artistic training. The concept of *imitatio* was not so much related to the motive, as to the normative style of the fine arts. This concept is especially obvious with the *Musée des*

Études, a collection of copies established 1834 within the École des Beaux-Arts with the purpose of instructing students in the work of the classical masters. It was this museum that inspired Charles Blanc for his *Musée des Copies*, a project which, however, failed immediately after its realization in 1873. The art historian Albert Boime laconically notes, in an article from 1964 on *La Musée des Copies*, "that the favorable attitude towards the copies produced for the *Musée des Études* was expressed a year before the Revolution of 1848; by 1871 it will have been completely reversed. The loss of the École's grip over the national art and the undermining of academic training discredited the essential value of copies" (Boime 1964: 237, my translation).

The revolutions of Manet and Courbet, together with the advent of art history as an academic discipline, have been two important factors in this reversal of values, and I will return to them, but I believe that the effects of one incident especially have been underestimated in relation to this reversal of values. I am thinking about the Bastianini affair, which emerged with the Louvre's spectacular acquisition of a Renaissance portrait bust (the so-called "Benivieni bust") in January 1866 for the enormous sum of 14,000 French Francs. In comparison the French state had paid 6,000 French Francs for *Venus de Milo* in 1820. The sculpture had been exhibited in Paris a year before and there caused a lot of excitement as a masterpiece of Renaissance art. After a heated debate it finally turned out that the sculpture was not by Donatello, Mino da Fiesole, Desiderio Settignato or by any other early Renaissance artist, but a modern product by the Florentine sculptor Giovanni Bastianini. In the aftermath of the passionate debates between Italian and French art historians, it turned up that Bastianini had produced a number of portrait busts in an Early Renaissance style (see Moskowitz 2004, 2006; Warren 2005).

Since then Bastianini is used as a case among other in the annals of art forgery, but it can be argued, as Anita F. Moskowitz does, that more than being a case among other, the Bastianini case marked a paradigmatic shift in our qualifications of images. During the 1850s and 1860s, Bastianini produced and exhibited such portrait busts under his own name, although they were not signed (Moskowitz 2004: 169). They are indeed made in an antique style and artificially aged. But this was requested by the buyers and a not uncommon practice by a number of Italian sculptors from the Renaissance all the way up to the twentieth century, as the later parallel case with Alceo Dossena demonstrates. Dossena was in 1928 exposed as the forger behind a number of antique, medieval, and early modern works and since archived in the shameful dossiers of art forgery (see Sox 1987), but his "legitimate" work operates with the same modus as those now considered fake, as a half-length marble bust of Minerva Tarquinio Maiullo (1889–1973) commissioned by her father illustrates. Not only does she pose "in a carefully articulated costume of square-necked dress and pendant necklace in the Italian Renaissance style" of Antonio Rosselino or Benedetto da Maiano (Darr et al. 2002: 120), mixed with a more contemporary and loose way of carving the hair, but the surface of the marble is artificially tinted to give the bust an antique appearance. Nevertheless it is signed "ROMA—ALCEO DOSSENA" on the front left part of the base.

Thus, rather than a forger, one could argue that Bastianini, Dossena and this tradition practiced a kind of stylistic remembrance, or a physical immanent linking, of different persons and subjects through a stylistic glue. It was rather the meeting of the Italian tradition of sculpture as a traditional *craft* with the emerging new paradigm of *art*, which in the 1860s caused the confusion on the Parisian art market where authenticity for the one became forgery for the other. For Bastianini, the image was a true portrait made in a customary, that is, impersonal and continuous, style.

For the emerging art world in Paris, operating with the new "art-historical hanging" at the Louvre, and a chronotopological plotting of the history of art, Bastianini's Benevieni bust was a modern fake in adopting a style not congruent with its chronotopological origin. The dispute whether Bastianini's or Dossena's productions are fakes is unfortunately blurring the question. The crux of the conflict is the question of the *identity of style*. To put it bluntly: the iconoclasm of modernism is the replacement of images with the avant-garde of individual styles. With Courbet, Manet, and the emergence of modernist art, the significance of art images made its final shift from a question of iconic veracity to a question of a discrete—that is, well-defined—stylistic identity. Arguably, Eduard Manet and Gustave Courbet were the first artists who copied *motives* (images) in an ostensibly different *style*—in Courbet's case, in the reference to Vélasquez in his *Artist's Studio*, and, in Manet's case, in references to Tizian/Giorgione with *La Déjeuner* and *Olympia*. In both cases the method is heavily dependent on the visibility—and hence discernability—of the originals in public museums, which thus disrupts the flow of historical styles as a continuous tradition with its variation of an invariance to an anachronistic re-enactment. This is especially obvious if one compares Manet's early copy of *Venus of Urbino*, which is perfectly in concordance with the pre-modern notions of artistic training through (stylistic) imitation, and Charles Blanc's motivation for a *Musée des Copies* with Olympia, where Manet uses a well-known motive to differentiate his *own uniquely identifiable style*. The stylistic discernability thus becomes an image of a second order. It is not the first order image (Cézanne's apples or Van Gogh's landscapes) that is recognized as such, but the work's being immediately recognizable as "a Cézanne" or "a Van Gogh."

Neither is there any coincidence that the Bastianini affair took place simultaneously with the emergence of art history as an academic discipline of which connoisseurship and attribution constituted the foundation and where the discernability of individual and chronotopological *style* became the values and arguments which made up the art-historical discourse. When style during the nineteenth century became an art-historical terminus it also lost its normative and qualitative implications. Now style was used to identify and attribute works to individuals in an art-historical, chronotopological grid. When an art work thus became (historically) defined as, for instance, "French seventeenth century," this identification was (art-historically speaking) more fundamental than a description of what was depicted on the canvas or carved in marble. Attribution is a certain type of observation, an apparatus specifically calibrated to disregard the image for instead to search for traces and indices of its historical origin.

The confusion caused by the Bastianini affair is a confusion between this aesthetic non-locality and non-identity on the one hand, and the new art historical attributionism, on the other, with its focus on discrete indexicalities—or the paradigm of trace, as Thierry Lenain calls it with reference to Carlo Ginzburg (Lenain 2011).

The consequences of this shift became even more apparent when the art world moved to New York. The painters of abstract expressionism were typically producing one and the same image over and over again, which can then be distributed to virtually every museum around the world in accordance with Alfred Barr Jr.'s principle of museological art collecting under the dictum of "one-of-each." Now, the iconic invisibility of modern iconoclasm is totally eclipsed under the veil of the individual trademarked style. This style is named. We are immediately aware of what a Pollock, a Morris Louis, a Jasper Johns looks like, and we know equally perfectly well what a Gerhard Richter, a Sigmar Polke, a Joseph Beuys, or a Gotthard Graubner looks like, even though most artists adopt different genres or styles. That is, one style is always linked to one and only one individual, but any individual can be linked to one or more styles. Again, appropriation art is the recognition of this trademarked style's function as an image and as structurally identical to a subject matter. The concept of "likeness" (*eikon*) became, during Modernism, transformed from the deep structure of a subject matter to the flat surface structure of stylistic signifiers.

The purpose of first order images, be it within or without an art context, has always been to make the absent present, hence images are intrinsically representational, and there is no such thing as a non-representational image. And if, as I believe, artworks since the late nineteenth century have been producing images of a second order—that is, traces and indices readable as an individual style—what, then, do they represent?

Here one could take a pessimistic stance and conclude that they represent the very close-circuit of the art world between a relic and a proper name, containing as much intrinsic value as a bank note, which a number of art critics have done during the last decades (see, e.g. Kuspit 2004; Clair 1988). But I believe there is something more fundamental going on here, and that we have witnessed a paradigmatic change in our representational device, best described by Lev Manovich in his essay "The Database as a Symbolic Form" (Manovich 2001), the title of course deliberately (and explicitly) playing on Erwin Panofsky's "Die Perspektive als symbolische Form." The argument is, to put it crudely, that paradigm takes precedence over syntagm, database takes precedence over narrative, and consequently algorithm takes the place as the representational device instead of linear perspective.

This makes immediate sense when we look on minimal or conceptual art. But it is precisely the algorithmic character of style as an image of the second order which makes it possible for the contemporary Chinese painter Zhang Hongtu to produce images of "a Cézanne" or "a Van Gogh" above one of the icons of Chinese ink painting, Fan Kuan's *Wanderers by Streams and Mountains* from the early eleventh century. In China, style has always been copied and subject for art theoretical discourse with a highly sophisticated conceptualization far beyond what has been the case in the West. On the other hand, Chinese ink painting consists of a very narrow spectrum of images (typically mountains, bamboos or plum blossoms) whereas the represented image was the parameter of originality in the West. The precise observation in Zhang Hongtu's many paintings of this type lies in the reversing of likeness and style between West and East. It would thus not have been possible to make Fan Kuan's *Wanderers* in the style of Poussin or Caspar David Friedrich (we wouldn't be able to observe the Poussin or Friedrich part of the superposition), nor would it be possible to make one of, for instance, Picasso's reclining nudes in the style of any Chinese painter, as we wouldn't be able to identify the image as Picasso's. By the same logic we note that making Cézanne's apples in the style of Van Gogh is as impossible as making a Pollock in the style of Mark Rothko.

Style, as an image of a second order, then, is the representation of a proper name where the proper name carries with it connotations of much the same type as earlier motives did when paintings and sculptures didn't need titles:

"Madonna and Child Enthroned," "Rest on the Flight to Egypt," "Portrait of an Old Man," "Venus and Amor," "View over Naples" or whatever was depicted on the painting. The shift happens when titles become necessary to explain what is no longer self-evident and when signatures disappear because they have become redundant as it is smeared out all over the picture plane, or, as Michel Foucault famously phrased it:

> It would seem that the author's name, unlike other proper names, does not pass from the interior of a discourse to the real and exterior individual who produced it; instead, the name seems always to be present, marking off the edges of the text, revealing, or at least characterizing, its mode of being. The author's name manifests the appearance of a certain discursive set and indicates the status of this discourse within a society and a culture. It has no legal status, nor is it located in the fiction of the work; rather, it is located in the break that founds a certain discursive construct and its very particular mode of being.
>
> Foucault 1984: 107–8

2. Style and code

The consequence of this shift, beginning already in the second half of the nineteenth century, has surprisingly enough remained largely unnoticed within the Western concept of art, but I believe the inherent paradox became sharply exposed in the aftermath of the controversial selling of Count Giuseppe Panza's collection of minimalist and conceptual art to the Guggenheim Foundation in 1990. This transaction raised a number of concerns in the art world on the role of the museum, including deaccessioning and the originality of the physical object.

For the conceptual and minimal artists of the 1960s and 1970s it had become clear that artistic style and identity was of an algorithmic character and concept art just took the consequence of this matter of fact. What produced "a Rothko," "a Pollock," or even "a Van Gogh" was a processural code of execution. In his "Paragraphs on Conceptual Art" from 1967, Sol LeWitt wrote: "In conceptual art the idea or concept is the most important aspect of the work. When an artist uses a conceptual form of art, it means that all of the planning and decisions are made beforehand and the execution is a perfunctory affair. The idea becomes a machine that makes the art" (LeWitt 1999: 12). This method is maybe most clearly illustrated in Lawrence Weiner's practice of stating the algorithm as the title of the work, as, for instance, "A SQUARE REMOVAL FROM A RUG IN USE" or

"THE RESIDUE OF A FLARE IGNITED UPON A BOUNDARY," all pieces followed by the statement of intent:

1. The artist may construct the piece.
2. The piece may be fabricated.
3. The piece need not be built.

Each being equal and consistent with the intent of the artist the decision as to condition rests with the receiver upon the occasion of receivership (Siegelaub 1969: folio 12 recto, f.12).

Many years later Alexander Galloway saw very clearly that conceptual art is nothing but a type of code for art making, an algorithmic process. "Code," he wrote in 2002, "draws a line between what is material and what is active, in essence saying that writing (hardware) cannot do anything, but must be transformed into code (software) to be affective" (Galloway 2002). Galloway continues discussing the difference between code and text in the following way:

> How can code be so different than mere writing? The answer to this lies in the unique nature of computer code. It lies not in the fact that code is sub-linguistic, but rather that it is hyper-linguistic. Code is a language, but a very special kind of language. Code is the only language that is executable. As Kittler has pointed out, "[t]here exists no word in any ordinary language which does what it says. No description of a machine sets the machine into motion."
>
> Ibid.

It is my hypothesis here that this relation between text and code can be transposed to the relation between image and style. So that style (and now I paraphrase the following paragraph in Galloway's text) is an image of a second order that actually does what it shows—it is a machine for converting meaning into action. Style has a visual meaning, but it is foremost an enactment of meaning. Thus, while images such as *Madonna and Child*, *Reclining Nude* or *Untitled* only have a visual state, style has both a visual state and an executable state. In this way, style is the summation of images plus an executable meta-layer that encapsulates that visuality.

Count Panza was an early mover in collecting conceptual and minimal art, and even if supportive of the above-mentioned critical potential of the artistic practices, he nevertheless wanted to defend his investment by having the artist sign a legal statement, saying: "I certify that the above work is my original and unique creation, and I undertake not to do, realize, sell, or authorize the same work" (Hapgood 1990: 116, quoting Knight 1987: 184, 219, 243). Now, in an artistic context where the work is not a production of an image in a certain style, but the execution of an identifiable style as the code of the author, the precision of this legal statement is not very high, as the phrase "the same work" turns out to be quite void of precision given the distributive character of the stylistic identity of the modern artist. Is the work an image or a style? An idea or the material? Would yet another drip painting qualify as "the same work"? Would an execution of one of Lawrence Weiner's pieces qualify as "the same work" as another execution of the piece? This is because there is no such thing as "originality" or "uniqueness" in the execution of a style as in the execution of code. Style and code only exist when executed, that is, when copied and actualized, re-enacted and iterated.

Count Panza's legal approach to his acquisitions did backfire when he wanted to sell his collection. Donald Judd and Carl André both denounced exhibited refabrications of their works by Count Panza as "fakes," insisting on the supervision of the artist in any refabrication of a piece or relocation of any site-specific work (Hapgood 1990: 120). Although both Judd's and André's works share this obvious "algorithmic" character with Lawrence Weiner's and others' works from the time, neither Judd nor André would under any circumstances approve of Weiner's Statement of Intent that the piece may be fabricated by anyone, or that the piece need not be built. For them, only the artist may perform the piece as only the artist can guarantee the integrity of every aspect of the piece. In a letter to the editors of *Art in America*, Judd described one piece refabricated as: "its appearance was not mine: the galvanized surface was wrong and the details were wrong. I remember that three narrow panels ineptly made the left corner" (Judd 1990: 33). In a similar letter Carl André didn't specify what was wrong, just that it was wrong: "No such 'refabrication' of my work has been authorized by me and any such 'refabrication' is a gross falsification of my work" (André 1990: 31).

Judd and André thus state that their works are not algorithms or scores, which can be performed or refabricated, but "classical" sculptural originals carrying with them the unique sensibility of the artist in material and handling. This is obviously not the case aesthetically speaking. I believe Judd and André here, at best, are fooling themselves. Nothing but legal actions hinders anyone from making "a Judd" or "an André"—as little as anyone performing a piece by John Cage. Not even skill is needed. Judd and André are here confusing themselves as individuals with an author function.

Most other artists have taken another stance on the question of copying and refabrication. Even though paying lip service to the idea of originality and authenticity of the work so as to protect the collector's investment, Sol LeWitt did not consider any unauthorized use of his instructions for a wall drawing to be unethical. Instead, he would consider it a compliment. Robert Morris has taken a similar position as LeWitt and doesn't seem to care much about the issues of originals or unique works (Hapgood 1990: 120–1). The argument for both is that you can't own ideas, only physical objects, and correspondingly that you can't own a style, only a physical embodiment as an example of a style.

When style was a historical subconscious or a normative concept, style was that which *should be* copied. The symbolical value of art was primarily measured in the attribution to a remembered name, "a Rafael," "a Rembrandt," "a Corot," with correspondingly lesser values linked to attributions like "a copy of Rafael," "in the style of Rembrandt," or "circle of Corot"—denominations that wouldn't make any sense at all if we should apply them to modern or contemporary art. What would an attribution like "in the style of Pollock" or "circle of Polke" mean? When style starts to be a symbolical value, intrinsically linked to an author function through a sort of performative signature code, a software (the algorithmic performative act of the artist) producing a hardware, which can't be referenced through any concept of subject matter, skill, or quality, then what is copied is nothing but the author function as such, that is: the algorithmic performative act. And this has been the great taboo in art since the late nineteenth century. It *must not* be copied. On the other hand, as a concept of style as code, it must (as any style or code) be copied, else it would cease to exist—style or code being entities whose existence is defined by their continuous executions and re-enactments, images which primarily exist in an executable state.

The image of a second order is thus a superposition of a series of antinomic concepts. It is the superposition of representation with code or algorithm, the superposition of the chronotopological index with the transhistorical image, and the superposition of an author function with the anonymity of style.

Compared to the negotiations of appropriation art or the more-or-less established artists' remakings and paraphrases of modern classics, like Marcel Duchamp's *Fountain* or Robert Morris's *Mirrored Cube*, all of which are well-known strategies during the past decades, but which rather strengthen the author function of art works than challenge it, works like the "anonymous plagiarism" of Kirkeby's brick code, confusing the logic of art from an adjacent discourse, are a more potent and threatening challenge to the authority of art, as they make our complex system of art unstable and collapse the antinomical superpositions the system of fine art is constructed on—antinomical structures which were first recognized with the emergence of the production logic of minimal art and becoming even more insistent with the "inclusive" concept of art of recent years.

References

André, C. (1990), "Artist Disowns 'Refabricated' Work," *Art in America* 78 (3): 31.

Belting, H. (1991), *Bild und Kult. Eine Geschichte des Bildes vor dem Zeitalter der Kunst*, München: Beck.

Boime, A. (1964), "La Musée des Copies," *Gazette des beaux-arts* 64: 237–47.

Clair, J. (1988), *Paradoxe sur le conservateur* précédé de *De la modernité conçue comme une religion*, Paris: L'Échoppe.

Darr, A., P. Barnet, and A. Boström (eds) (2002), *Catalogue of Italian Sculpture in the Detroit Institute of Arts*, Detroit: The Detroit Institute of Arts and Harvey Miller Publishers.

Foucault, M. (1984), "What Is an Author?," in P. Rabinow (ed.), *The Foucault Reader*, 101–20, New York: Pantheon Books.

Galloway, A., "How We Made Our Own 'Carnivore'," *rhizome.org*, June 20, 2002. Available online: http://rhizome.org/discuss/view/2654/

Hapgood, S. (1990), "Remaking Art History," *Art in America* 78 (3): 115–23.

Judd, D. (1990), "Artist Disowns 'Copied' Sculpture," *Art in America* 78 (4): 33.

Knight, C. (1987), *Art of the Sixties and Seventies: The Panza Collection*, New York: Rizzoli.

Kuspit, D. (2004), *The End of Art*, Cambridge: Cambridge University Press.

Lenain, T. (2007), "Perfect Fakes and the Modern Religion of Authenticity," in V. I. Stoichita (ed.), *Das Double*, 47–58, Wolfenbüttel: Harrassowitz.

Lenain, T. (2011), *Art Forgery. The History of a Modern Obsession*, London: Reaktion Books.

LeWitt, S. (1999), "Paragraphs on Conceptual Art," in A. Alberro and B. Stimson (eds), *Conceptual Art: A Critical Anthology*, 12–16, Cambridge, MA: The MIT Press.

Manovich, L. (2001), "The Database," in *The Language of New Media*, 218–43, Cambridge, MA: The MIT Press. [Originally published online in 1999 as "Database as a Symbolic Form." Available online: http://manovich.net/index.php/projects/database-as-a-symbolic-form]

Moskowitz, A. F. (2004), "The Case of Giovanni Bastianini: A Fair and Balanced View," *Artibus et historiae* 25 (50): 157–85.

Moskowitz, A. F. (2006), "The Case of Giovanni Bastianini. II. A Hung Jury?" *Artibus et historiae* 27 (54): 201–17.

Nagel, A. (2004), "The Copy and Its Evil Twin: Thirteen Notes on Forgery," *Cabinet* 14: 102–5.

Siegelaub, S. (1969), *January 5–31, 1969*, New York.

Sox, D. (1987), *Unmasking the Forger. The Dossena Deception*, London: Unwin Hyman.

Warren, J. (2005), "Forgery in Risorgimento Florence. Bastianini's 'Giovanni delle Bande Nere' in the Wallace Collection," *Burlington Magazine* 147 (1232): 729–41.

13

Blurred Lines: A Case Study on the Ethics and Aesthetics of Copying

Eberhard Ortland

On March 10, 2015, a U.S. federal jury found that Pharrell Williams and Robin Thicke had, with their tremendously successful 2013 song, "Blurred Lines," infringed the copyright on Marvin Gaye's 1977 hit, "Got to Give It Up."[1] The court declared:

> that any past and ongoing reproduction, preparation of derivative works, distribution, sale or other transfer of ownership, rental, lease, lending or public performance of "Blurred Lines", or any authorization of these activities, by any of the Counter-Defendants, individually or in combination, infringes the Gaye Parties' copyright in "Got to Give It Up".[2]

Thicke and Williams owe the Gayes damages and a share of their profits amounting to more than $5.3 million, plus 50 percent of any future songwriter and publishing revenues they might receive for the song. The judgment has been appealed and it will be some time before an appeals decision will be issued.[3] The case was widely reported, due to the attention focused on the controversial piece, the celebrity status of the litigants, and the huge amount of damages awarded. It is an instructive case for a discussion about the ethics and aesthetics of copying or, more precisely, about the interdependencies and interferences of moral, juridical, and aesthetic judgments, and empirical assessments of matters of fact concerning alleged acts of copying.

1. A dubious hit

"Blurred Lines," the song, is about the ambiguities of an erotic attraction between a man (represented by the lead singer's voice) and a desired—maybe also interested, but apparently hesitating—woman who is in a relationship with another man. She might want to leave this man in favor of the crooner who addresses her in the song, bluntly asserting his ability to give her more exciting sexual experiences than her "last guy." According to Thicke, the title refers to "the good-girl/bad-girl thing and what's appropriate" (Payne 2013). The singer's voice repeatedly cries: "I hate these blurred lines!" With everything he says to her, he seems to try to overcome the woman's ambiguity and to encourage a move on her part, a decision hopefully in favor of his own desire. Like any work of art, the song is open to other readings, too. Instead of being interpreted as the singer actually addressing the desired "bitch," it might even more plausibly be read as something going on only in his own head. Or it might be read as a reflection on certain gender stereotypes. Feminist critics objected that "the very title of the song draws from the rhetoric of rape apologists who believe that date rape isn't *real* rape and that sexual assault is often a 'gray area'" (Brinkley 2013; Romano 2013).

The enormous attention focused on the song, and hence its commercial success (which only made it an attractive goal for copyright infringement claims in the first place), was largely due to the video, directed by Diane Martel and featuring Thicke, Williams, and rapper T.I. in stage suits playing strange games with three young women in underwear.[4] The video was produced in two versions, one with more underwear,[5] the other one with less. The version advertised as "uncensored," "unrated," or simply as the "nude version,"[6] was removed from YouTube for its alleged obscenity[7] just one week after it was released in March 2013, while remaining accessible on other sites. This was perfect PR. Everybody wanted to see the scandalous work. The thing went viral. Both versions of the video have been viewed hundreds of millions of times on various platforms.

Countless parodies and adaptations of the video quickly popped up (Golden 2013). Such derivative works are an important measure of a song's cultural impact and contribute to its power to attract public attention (Jurgensen 2013). Those who prefer to watch, for example, fully dressed women playing strange games with men in underwear while the same catchy rhythm is played behind variously improved lyrics, can choose from several versions.[8] The most successful adaptation was an English grammar lesson dubbed over the "Blurred Lines" tune.[9] Musically, each of these works would infringe the copyright of Marvin Gaye's estate if the current verdict should stand (more about this in Section 4), since they all feature essentially unaltered copies of the very music deemed infringing in the Thicke song. So far, none of them seems to have been commercially interesting enough or sufficiently annoying for the Gayes to file suit. And there is a good chance that such cases would be regarded as fair use on the parody defense, even though they are parodies not of "Got to Give It Up" but of "Blurred Lines." As long as "the quoted matter is used as raw material, transformed in the creation of new information, new aesthetics, new insights and understandings," it should be regarded as fair use (Leval 1990: 1112; cf. Samuelson 2009: 2549–51).

On video platforms, news channels, and blogs, hundreds of thousands of people have published their opinions on the video, the song, the singer, and the copyright lawsuit, expressing their admiration or disapproval. The video and some of the song's lyrics were blamed for promoting "rape culture"[10] or, more generally, for what critics perceived as a demeaning attitude towards women.[11] Many enthusiastic listeners and critics, perhaps concerned more about free speech than the song itself, defended the piece as a legitimate expression of sexual attraction among adults, as "satirical," "playful," "tongue-in-cheek," or "just fun" for everybody involved.[12]

The video's director, Diane Martel, did her best to explain that her video ought to be seen as basically "goofy and innocent." She found the lyrics "misogynist," too, but also quite funny, and decided to deal with the song "in a way where the girls were going to overpower the men" (Ducker 2013). Emily Ratajkowski, whose career as a model and actress was boosted with her appearance in the "Blurred Lines" video, supported this view, arguing that the video makes fun of pervasive stereotypes in contemporary pop music, "the attitude of guys being super-gangster": "The way we are annoying them, being playful and having a good time with our body—it's something very important for young women today to have that confidence" (Ayers 2013). Singer Robin Thicke, on the other hand, did not do much to help his case when he reacted to objections that the video might appear degrading to women in a grossly sarcastic way: "Of course it is. What a pleasure it is to degrade a woman. I've never gotten to do that before" (Phili 2013). Not surprisingly, this ignited even more outrage. Thicke later admitted that he was intoxicated when he gave that interview, as well as during the recording session (Brown 2014), which did not make things much better.

2. A moral controversy

Quite a lot of the anonymous or pseudonymous online comments on the moral and aesthetic defects or merits of the "Blurred Lines" video, lyrics, and music, on its lead singer, or on the opinions of other commentators, gush with insults and stupidity. Nevertheless, these debates deserve attention. They produce arguments worthy of consideration for a better understanding of the ethics and aesthetics of copying, which is not only about copyright issues, but also about moral reasons for finding certain acts of copying objectionable, or for demanding that certain objects or representations ought not to be copied or distributed at all, or only under certain restrictions. Thus it also concerns questions of censorship: whether or not—or under which conditions—it should be permissible to distribute or make accessible copies of artifacts with certain aesthetic qualities or with meaning attributed to them that some find objectionable.

The spokeswoman of a U.K. charity striving to raise awareness of sexual violence criticized both the lyrics of "Blurred Lines" and the aesthetic choices made in the production of the video as "glamourising violence against women and reinforcing rape myths":

> Both the lyrics and the video seem to objectify and degrade women, using misogynistic language and imagery that many people would find not only distasteful or offensive but also really quite old fashioned. More disturbingly, certain lyrics are explicitly sexually violent and appear to reinforce victim-blaming rape myths, for example about women giving "mixed signals" through their dress or behaviour, saying "no" when they really mean "yes" and so on.[13]

For such and similar reasons, "Blurred Lines" was banned from more than twenty U.K. universities and university radio stations.[14] An advertisement for an audio device featuring a derivative version of the "Blurred Lines" video[15] was banned from daytime TV in the U.K. (Blake 2013).

The harm inflicted by these mostly symbolic acts of censorship may be considered negligible. Actually the piece may have received more attention due to these controversies; the record company may have sold even more copies than they would have otherwise. On the other hand, one might argue that the overwhelming popularity of the song was—to a certain extent successfully—exploited by those who took advantage of the occasion to gain attention for wider moral or political concerns. One of the organizers of the boycott against "Blurred Lines" at U.K. universities told the *Guardian*: "Blurred Lines was banned because it was unusually well known and widely discussed rather than because it was exceptionally offensive" (Lynskey 2013).

NPR's music editor, Frannie Kelley, describes feeling "more violated by people trying to tell me that that song and video is problematic than by that song and video" (Romano 2013). One commentator exclaimed: "The outrage here is itself outrageous."[16] Others welcomed the discussion. Ratajkowski pointed out how important it is to distinguish between images of nude women that are objectifying, sexist, and harmful, and others that are not, but which rather convey the models' self-confidence (Ayers 2013). This is certainly an important distinction, not only for professional models, but for anybody exposed to the various types of images in our media-saturated world. Yet the much-needed critical debates about the kinds of images or representations whose accessibility or circulation deserves to be deemed welcome, acceptable, problematic, or intolerable, must take further aspects into account.[17]

Apparently it never occurred to Ratajkowski that some might have reasons to feel ambivalent, not only about outright offensive, degrading, or humiliating images, but also about the kind of images that she herself prefers: pictures of strikingly beautiful, self-confident young women celebrating the privileges of superiority accrued from the desire, adoration, and envy their images arouse in others. One of the problems with highly idealized images of strikingly beautiful human bodies is that those who observe them cannot help but compare them against both their own self-images and their impressions of those around them, inevitably affecting their self-esteem as well as their attitudes towards their peers, and hence any relationships they might develop.[18]

Should we therefore generally refrain from producing such pictures, distributing copies of such pictures, or making them accessible? Maybe. But who is included in that "we"? And what are "we" going to do about those who do not share this concern and who do not want to refrain from producing, distributing or making accessible such pictures? Do we need (more) censorship? How should it be enforced? And what kinds of pictures are we actually talking about? How should we discriminate between acceptable images and others that we want to see suppressed? How can we know we want to see them suppressed, if we don't see them in the first place? Can there be general, objective criteria? How should they be established? To whom would we want to entrust the task of making such distinctions for us? Psychologists? Activists? Students' unions? International commissions? The Grand Imam of al-Azhar? Automatic surveillance software? Should it be possible to appeal take-down decisions? What kinds of arguments ought to be accepted as sufficient to justify making certain images available?

What about images deemed problematic by some, but benign by others? Should they be banned at the first complaint to avoid any suffering by those who might feel offended? Or should they be allowed so long as no serious harm has been demonstrated, since censorship not only stifles the freedom of expression and establishes unjustifiable inequalities, but also undermines any trust we might have that we have access to all of the information we need?[19]

Should it make a difference how many people complain, or what percentage of the population is believed to feel offended?

Does it make any difference, ethically, whether such potentially problematic pictures are broadcast on TV or printed on billboards, or whether they are rated and offered only to those who know exactly what they are looking for, perhaps with some kind of "adults-only" or other restriction?

These and further questions become more urgent with the growth of the internet and in particular with cross-cultural controversies about the moral evaluation of certain images equally accessible from virtually anywhere around the globe, while the criteria underlying our moral or aesthetic judgments are far from universally shared. Careful ethical reflection and ongoing critical debates are called for.

3. A catchy tune

Even listeners who found the lyrics and the video rather disgusting widely agreed that "Blurred Lines" is a very catchy song.[20] What makes it so catchy? The rhythm, the "groove," hummable melodic phrases on an easily remembered pentatonic scale. Critics pointed in particular to the bass line and the chorus (Howard 2013; Pasick 2013). In 2013, when the song was released and climbed to the top position of the charts (where it stayed all summer), this success was credited mainly to the voice and performance of Robin Thicke, who was at that time also believed to have written the song (Rosen 2013). During the trial the latter assumption was corrected: "Blurred Lines" was essentially written and composed by hit-maker Pharrell Williams.[21] That Pharrell had a decisive hand in it was obvious to anybody familiar with contemporary pop music (see Howard 2013; McKinley 2013; Caramanica 2013). But was it his own achievement, or did he draw on some previously existing model? What exactly might have been his template, if there was one? To what extent was it used and to what extent does "Blurred Lines" depend on it, if it does?

Bridgeport Music Inc., the owner of the copyrights in some of the musical works of the influential 1970s band Funkadelic, approached Thicke and Williams in the summer of 2013, when "Blurred Lines" topped the charts, with allegations that the song infringed on the Funkadelic song, "Sexy Ways" (1974).[22] This catalog company owned by a former music producer named Armen Boladian has been known for years as a "sample troll"—a company that makes its money mainly by threatening and suing musicians for allegedly using unauthorized snippets of music from its catalog (Wu 2006). George Clinton, the former lead singer of Funkadelic and writer of "Sexy Ways," publicly dismissed Boladian's allegations of infringement on his own song and supported the "Blurred Lines" musicians (Pasick 2013). Bridgeport soon withdrew from the litigation (Gardner 2014).

The complaints raised by the children of Marvin Gaye were more serious. Frankie and Nona Gaye alleged that:

> the Blurred writers intentionally and unlawfully copied and assembled a constellation of distinctive and important elements from the musical composition, "Got to Give It Up." "Blurred Lines" is so substantially similar to "Got to Give It Up" that ordinary observers all over the world would have remarked that the two songs sound the same, which they do.[23]

Their brother, Marvin Gaye III, accused the writers of "Blurred Lines" of:

> intentional and actionable copying of numerous significant compositional elements of "Got to Give It Up," without which blatant copying Thicke's "Blurred Lines" would never have come to exist in its present form or become a massive worldwide success beginning in or about 2013.[24]

Similar arguments were produced in the extensive debates about the prominent lawsuit:

> The public made this song a hit because of Marvin Gaye's genius in crafting the song [...] and its "feel." NOT because of Pharrell's feat of changing one note here and there on Protools to try and pre-empt a plagiarism charge, and certainly not for the spoiled brat in the vocal booth, nose-singing his lecherous, opiate-influenced rape fantasies.[25]

Over thirty-five years after its release, "Got to Give It Up" still has a remarkable number of ardent admirers, though it is certainly not familiar to everybody, in particular those of younger generations. The song never reached the pervasive popularity of a global mega-hit like "Blurred Lines," though it was a Number 1 hit in 1977 and a notable success at its time. The funky disco piece has influenced generations of pop musicians, including superstars like Michael Jackson,[26] and continues to move its audience.

Many people said on hearing "Blurred Lines" that they felt immediately reminded of Marvin Gaye's "Got to Give It Up." "Both share a R&B/funk flavor, with upbeat percussion, sparse instrumentation and similar vocal lines" (Ciotola and Pelletier 2015). But does that mean that "Blurred Lines" is a copy, or a derivative version, or maybe an interpolation, of "Got to Give It Up"? One commentator suggests:

> Of course it reminds you of 'Got to Give It Up'—that was the whole point. But reminding you of something and being the exact copy of something is not the same. You can't copyright a feel or a sound, only the composition, and in this case, the composition was not used.[27]

Others did not even find the songs particularly similar.[28] The audience was split.[29]

That Williams and Thicke deliberately wanted to appeal to the enthusiasm of the (predominantly black) audience of "Got to Give It Up" seems quite obvious, both from some aesthetic choices they made in creating "Blurred Lines" and from numerous public statements they uttered in promoting their song (Pasick 2013). Williams proclaimed himself a "huge fan of Marvin Gaye" (Associated Press 2013). In a deposition he stated that he remembered from his childhood how his aunt used to play "Got to Give It Up" all the time.[30] Thicke was also raised with Marvin Gaye records on the turntable[31] and he has been known for his "Marvin Gaye fixation" throughout his career (Rosen 2013). He seemed quite flattered when his music reminded critics of the Prince of Soul, and did his best to make sure Marvin Gaye was mentioned often enough with his own name that it should stick and people who liked Marvin Gaye might find out they liked Robin Thicke, too.[32] His 2009 song "Million Dolla Baby" was an outright remake of Gaye's "Trouble Man" (1972), and Gaye is rightly credited for an essential part of the songwriting.

In the spring of 2013 Thicke told several interviewers that Marvin Gaye inspired "half of his music," that "Got to Give It Up" in particular was one of his "all time favorite songs" (Phili 2013), and that he had actually suggested to Williams to "make something like that, something with that groove" (ibid.), which, according to that story, eventually resulted in the composition and recording of "Blurred Lines." In contrast to what he publicly said on many occasions, Thicke later played down the relevance of Marvin Gaye for his music, claiming instead that "Marvin is one of many of my idols [...] and no more than any of my others,"[33] while "90 percent" of his songs "sound nothing like or have any connection to him."[34] Despite his attempts to distance himself from his earlier statements which, he claimed, had been insincere and merely aimed at selling more records,[35] these interviews seem to have played a crucial part in convincing the jury that the Gayes' claims were indeed substantial and that Thicke deserved to lose his case.

Being convinced that Thicke and Williams deserved to lose their case is one thing. But to show that they—or either of them—actually infringed any copyrights of Marvin Gaye's estate is quite another thing. The jury found that they did, but the verdict did not explain why or how. Many critics and musicians were flabbergasted.[36] The judgment reads more like a letter to the court of appeals, arguing that none of the objections raised by the Thicke parties' legal team against the trial and the verdict are justified.

4. Legal matters

"Copyright," the jury was instructed, "is the exclusive right to copy. This right to copy includes the exclusive rights to (1) authorize, or make additional copies, or otherwise reproduce the copyrighted work in phonorecords; (2) to recast, transform, adapt the work, that is prepare derivative works based upon the copyrighted work; (3) to distribute sound recordings of the copyrighted work to the public by sale or other transfer of ownership; (4) or to perform publicly a copyrighted musical work."[37]

To infringe someone's copyright is to do any of the mentioned activities with a protected work—or with a substantial and original part of a protected work—without the necessary authorization by the copyright holder. The jury in the "Blurred Lines" case was instructed: "One who reproduces, prepares derivative works from, distributes, or performs a copyrighted work without authority from the copyright owner during the term of the copyright, infringes the copyright."[38] Whether or not authorization by the copyright holders of some earlier work is required for certain activities which somehow deal with, make use of, or relate to such earlier works, depends very much on what exactly is being done with or to the earlier works or the material taken from copyrighted works, and on further circumstances, since there are statutory conditions and limitations to the exclusive right to copy that may be applicable.[39]

In order to find out if Williams, Thicke, Clifford Harris (a.k.a. T.I.) and/or their record companies did or did not infringe the copyrights of Marvin Gaye's heirs with the creation, performance, and distribution of various instantiations of "Blurred Lines," the jury had to determine, first of all, what "the work covered by copyright" actually is. This is in many cases not an easy task. In this case it was particularly difficult because Marvin Gaye did not own a copyright in the sound recording, but only in the musical composition of his song, "Got to Give It Up (Part 1 and 2)," insofar as it had been fixed in musical notation on paper and submitted to the U.S. Copyright Office for registration.[40] The deposit copy[41] is a hand-written lead sheet representing the lyrics and only some of the melodic, harmonic, and rhythmic features that appear in the phonorecord.[42] It was controversial among the opponents (and also among the expert witnesses involved in the case) to what extent features and elements that for most listeners would seem to contribute decisively to the particular character and aesthetic appeal of the piece (as it was performed on several occasions by Marvin Gaye with his band and documented on various phonorecords),[43] but which are not explicitly marked in the score (like the bassline, percussive choices, backup vocals, electronics and sound engineering) were nevertheless "implied" by the notes and other marks that do appear in the deposit copy (Hutchens 2015; Siegal 2015).

Furthermore, do "implied notes" meet the basic requirement of copyright law that only expressions somehow fixed in a "tangible medium," but not ideas, however rich in implications, qualify for copyright protection?[44] And would the musical material supplied by the band or studio musicians who knew what they had to do when they saw the indicators for keys and chords as marked in the lead sheet qualify as "original parts" of an "original work of authorship" created by Marvin Gaye? Answering this question would require a much more detailed analysis of "Got to Give It Up" (and its relations to its sources and influences from the musical traditions of blues, jazz, soul, and funk, as well as from 1970s disco music[45]) than has been carried out by any of the musicologists involved in the case. Some of the contributions by the other musicians may well have been original contributions to a complex work of joint authorship, but they were not credited and not registered at the Copyright Office as was required by the law at that time; by consequence any claim to a copyright in such elements would be void.[46] Anyway, it is not clear how Marvin Gaye's children could have inherited a copyright in features of their father's works that were in fact not their father's work.

Only after having established an understanding of which elements of the piece known under the title "Got to Give It Up" are in fact the original parts or achievements that can be attributed to Marvin Gaye and subject to an exclusive copyright now controlled by his children, could one begin searching for any "substantial similarities" between these features and possibly similar features of "Blurred Lines."

The jury was instructed to look for "substantial similarities" between "Blurred Lines" and any alleged models or sources in Gaye's song only with regard to certain elements previously identified as "protected expression" in the Gaye song, and to distinguish these "original elements"[47] from "common ideas," "general concepts," "elements borrowed from another author or from the public domain," "expression that is so standard in the treatment of a given idea that it constitutes something that must be done in expressing that idea," and of course from "ideas" that may be taken up freely as long as the protected expression is not unduly appropriated.[48] The triers of fact were told: "The original parts of the Gaye Parties' works are the parts created (1) independently by the works' author, that is, the author did not copy it from another work; and (2) by use of at least some minimal creativity."[49] Luckily, the jury members were not asked to find out for themselves which parts of the musical compositions attributed to him might have been created independently by Marvin Gaye. They merely had to evaluate the evidence presented to them by the parties and witnesses and make up their minds regarding the evidence submitted to them in the strictly limited framework of the trial.

In accordance with the two-part test for "substantial similarity" used by the Ninth Circuit,[50] jury members were informed that in order to "show by a preponderance of the evidence that there is substantial similarity" between "Got to Give It Up" and "Blurred Lines," "the Gaye Parties must show that there is both substantial 'extrinsic similarity' and substantial 'intrinsic similarity.'"[51]

Unfortunately, the explanation of the relevant criteria for "extrinsic similarity" given to the jury tends to blur the idea-expression distinction that was previously introduced as essential for singling out the elements of "original expression" exclusively capable of copyright protection: "Extrinsic similarity is shown when two works have a similarity of ideas and expression as measured by external, objective criteria. To make this determination, you must consider the elements of each of the works and decide if they are substantially similar."[52]

The "analytical dissection of a work" required for the extrinsic test[53] is usually entrusted to expert witnesses. The jury must consider the elements and relationships described by the experts and decide about their relevance. One problem with forensic expert testimonies is that they often yield contradictory results. In fact, the disagreements between the musicologists were the main reason why this case was submitted to a jury for trial and not decided by summary judgment.[54] But how should the trier of fact be able to assess the credibility of the expert witnesses and the value of their contradictory statements?[55]

Jury members are not allowed to "do any research [...] make any investigation or in any other way try to learn about the case" themselves, apart from what is presented to them as relevant evidence in the court sessions.[56] This restriction might be necessary in order to ensure the impartiality and fairness of the trial. But it hampers the capacity of jury members to really understand and critically examine the often controversial claims and allegations made by the parties, lawyers, or witnesses. Under these conditions, jury verdicts are notoriously prone to errors.

A demonstration (by a preponderance of the evidence) of substantial similarity—or sufficient difference—with regard to the objective, extrinsic qualities of defendant's and plaintiff's works is an important step towards clarifying the question whether an alleged act of unauthorized copying has occurred or not. Yet the analysis of matters of fact and the evaluation of the similarities and differences observed will not suffice to establish "substantial similarity" and a presumption of copying. If the traces of substantial similarity found in the extrinsic test are not matched by an equally substantial impression of "intrinsic similarity," a jury may not find "substantial similarity," and so should find no infringement of copyright.[57] Likewise, when people do have a strong feeling that one work is "intrinsically similar" to another one, but substantial extrinsic similarities cannot be figured out,[58] the court will not have sufficient reasons to find substantial similarity.

"Intrinsic similarity" sounds odd (Sanders 2015). After all, similarity is a relation between two things (events, actions, persons …), not "intrinsic" to any one thing or anybody. What sense does it make to distinguish an "intrinsic similarity" from objectively demonstrable "extrinsic similarities"? Two things (phrases, images, melodies, whatever) may show a high degree of correspondence: similar or even identical parts in similar or perfectly analogue positions and relations to other, equally similar or identical parts of either object; but for all their extrinsic similarity they might still be "intrinsically" different. Intrinsic similarity is not altogether independent from extrinsic similarity, however. It does not make much sense to talk of an intrinsic similarity between two things that do not seem similar at all in any relevant aspect of their perceivable objective qualities. But intrinsic similarity does not automatically follow from extrinsic similarity, either.

Assessing intrinsic similarity between two things or works requires an act of judgment of a particular kind, different from the kind of classificatory subsumptions and distinctions used in keeping track of extrinsic similarities. In contrast to the assessment of "objective" qualities in the extrinsic test, the assessment of intrinsic similarity is dubbed "subjective." Copyright lawyers often feel ambivalent about this aspect of the substantial similarity test: "Intrinsic similarity is best described as the jury's gut instinct" (Sanders 2015).

What kind of judgment is required here? A judgment of reflection about the particular profile of a more or less complex bundle of aspects or qualities relevant for our inclination to distinguish certain occurrences of artifacts (material objects or sequences of events) from their surroundings and to identify them as instantiations of a particular type. Juries are asked to consider "the total concept and feel" of the defendants' and plaintiffs' works respectively and assess the predominance of similarity or difference between these holistic impressions.[59]

5. Aesthetic judgment

Insofar as "feel" of the respective works is regarded, the judgment that is asked for will be an aesthetic judgment about those qualities that make up the distinctive, overall identity of a work. This singular comparative judgment about the similarity or difference in feeling and overall impression between two objects must, of course, not be confused with an axiological judgment about the relative aesthetic merit of either or both, nor with a "pure aesthetic judgement of taste" about the beauty of a given object in the Kantian sense.[60]

It is perfectly possible to judge that "Blurred Lines," while not being the same song, nor a copy or a derivate of Marvin Gaye's "Got to Give It Up," but an independent, original work of authorship in its own right, displays some features more than coincidentally reminiscent to those familiar with late 1970s soul music of Marvin Gaye's "Got to Give It Up,"[61] and at the same time to pass a comparative judgment of aesthetic merit in favor of the Gaye song, or the other way round. Aesthetic preferences may lean in either direction, or may not be satisfied at all with any of the disputed works. They are not relevant and should not interfere[62] when a jury is asked to determine merely if the "total concept and feel" of the defendant's work is substantially similar to that of the plaintiff's work.

Comparative aesthetic judgments of the kind required here involve irreducibly subjective capacities of the persons asked to give their judgment, including their sensitivity and understanding as well as all kinds of background knowledge from their own experience. It may be difficult to state general criteria, since in each case, the triers of fact have to make up their own minds about which criteria would be adequate regarding the nature of defendant's and/or plaintiff's works, the nature of the audience to which the respective works typically appeal or are addressed, the relevant background (styles, genres, etc.), the reasons why people would want to engage with either or both works, and how to assess the relative weight of the relevant aspects. Questioning such judgments will be as difficult as justifying them. But they are certainly not immune to critical inquiry.

In order to curb the arbitrariness of their inevitably subjective aesthetic judgments, juries are asked to assess whether the "ordinary, reasonable person would find the total concept and feel" of the defendant's and plaintiff's works "substantially similar."[63] Yet who is this everyman, the "ordinary" or "average, reasonable person"? With the emergence of social media it becomes possible to observe (and impossible to ignore) the ruptures that divide our society even about such minute and esoteric topics as the question whether or not "Blurred Lines" is substantially similar to "Got to Give It Up." Not only do many people profoundly disagree about the moral and aesthetic value of both pieces of dance music, they actually seem to hear them differently and to get different impressions concerning the similarities or differences between them.

These differences in perception correlate to the background of our previous aesthetic experiences which contribute in various ways to structuring our sensitivity and inevitably selective attention to certain qualities in either of the disputed pieces. This background of previous aesthetic experiences which inform our sensitivity and selective patterns of attention is not idiosyncratic throughout, different for each individual. For everybody, it is to a significant degree interlinked with other people's experiences, since many of the relevant experiences are essentially shared ones—shared to a certain extent among peers of the same generation in the same culture, subculture, or social group.

Aesthetic experiences and aesthetic preferences are an important part of what we share with others. Sharing and further developing them together with others is an important part of what makes certain practices relating to the arts meaningful for those to whom these practices matter. Ultimately, this is why copies and acts of copying (Ortland 2015) are so important, why we care about the right to reproduce certain works and distribute copies, about the rights to perform or to make derivatives, and the right of access to copies of certain works: we need copies to share experiences, to engage in critical discussions, and to develop shared preferences. But we would not share everything with everybody indifferently. We want to distinguish ourselves, express (or even achieve) affiliations and disassociations, by making the distinctions we make, by developing a certain "taste" (Bourdieu 1979). Therefore, many people feel they cannot remain indifferent when confronted with the question of who should be allowed to copy, use, perform, or transform particular works that have attained some relevance for the group they themselves identify with.

Copyright opinions inevitably involve aesthetic choices. The only way to control the problem of aesthetic bias is to face it and to try to take into consideration alternate aesthetic sensibilities (Yen 1998: 250, 301). The "Blurred Lines" case demonstrates that aesthetic judgment not only affects the moral or legal evaluation of certain acts of copying as legitimate, appalling, or actionable, but also already the preceding question of fact—of whether an act of copying or of using another work as template for producing some kind of derivative has actually occurred, or not at all.

Notes

1 Williams v. Bridgeport Music Inc., Case No. CV13-06004-JAK (AGRx), Dkt. 320, 321 (C.D. Cal. Mar 10, 2015) (special verdict).

2 Ibid., Dkt. 450 (C.D. Cal. Dec 2, 2015) (judgement).

3 Ibid., Dkt. 458 (C.D. Cal. Dec 8, 2015) (notice of appeal).

4 See e.g. Ducker 2013; McKinley 2013.

5 Online: https://www.youtube.com/watch?v=yyDUC1LUXSU

6 Online: http://vevo.ly/W0OCcA

7 See Star Trak (2013), Ha (2013). The YouTube guidelines for admissible contents can be found at: http://www.youtube.com/yt/policyandsafety/communityguidelines.html#communityguidelines-line-crossing; https://support.google.com/youtube/answer/2802002?hl=en

8 See e.g. FullFrontalFreedom, "#WomensRights: A Pro-Choice Parody of Robin Thicke's 'Blurred Lines,'" https://www.youtube.com/watch?v=NNX9OT9Z7i8 (299,608 views as of January 3, 2016); Mod Carousel, "Sexy Boys," https://www.youtube.com/watch?v=tKfwCjgiodg (2013; 5,579,981 views as of January 3, 2016); Adelaide Dunn et al, "Defined Lines," https://www.youtube.com/watch?v=L4WM4d_mhGM (online since August. 31, 2013; 2,908,840 views as of January 3, 2016).

9 "Weird Al" Yankovic, "Word Crimes," https://www.youtube.com/watch?v=8Gv0H-vPoDc (online since July 15, 2014; 29,267,763 views as of January 10, 2016).

10 See e.g. Huynh 2013; Wyatt 2013; Brinkley 2013.

11 See e.g. Brandes 2013; Munn 2013.

12 "Feminist in LA" Blog from June–August, 2013, http://feministinla.blogspot.co.uk/2013/04/in-news-robin-thickes-rape-song.html or among the readers of the *XO Jane* platform in June–July 2013 (see Rasmus 2013).

13 Katie Russell, spokeswoman for Rape Crisis, as quoted in Wyatt 2013.

14 Young-Powell and Page 2013; Lynskey 2013.

15 https://www.youtube.com/watch?v=1HTou-VZvbw. One anonymous reader of the "Feminist in LA" blog wrote on August 3, 2013, 4:35 a.m., that she was particularly upset about this "TV advertisement for some Unidentified Phallic Object [...] inserted in the original video in the hands of the half-naked ladies, manipulating

them very suggestively. That ad was the last straw for me and I can't even hear the song on the radio anymore without feeling the urge to change frequencies." http://feministinla.blogspot.com/2013/04/in-news-robin-thickes-rape-song.html?showComment=1375529757649#c4195651340729550624

16 Anonymous, June 18, 2013, 2:06 pm, http://feministinla.blogspot.de/2013/04/in-news-robin-thickes-rape-song.html?showComment=1371589584937#c7667269358837626295

17 For an overview of (mainly American) debates on image ethics, see Gross et al. 1988 and 2003; and the more up-to-date approach of Ess (2013).

18 See e.g. Cattarin et al. 2000; Monro and Huon 2005; Crouch and Degelman 1998.

19 Hamamoto (2003) argues in this vein that "so-called hate speech, 'words that wound,' and 'pornography' are protected by the First Amendment to the U.S. Constitution. Intellectual inquiry, artistic expression, and political dissent are likewise protected" (264).

20 Huynh 2013; Romano 2013; Rasmus 2013; McKinley 2013; Rosen 2013.

21 Thicke 2014: 78–80, 86–8, 93, 145; Williams 2014: 68-95.

22 Williams v. Bridgeport Music Inc., CV13-06004-JAK (AGRx), Dkt. 1 at 4 (C.D. Cal. Aug 15, 2013) (complaint for declaratory relief): "Representatives of Bridgeport have recently notified plaintiffs that, if plaintiffs do not pay a monetary settlement of Bridgeport's claim, Bridgeport intends to initiate litigation for copyright infringement against plaintiffs and others."

23 *Ibid.*, Dkt. 14 at 16 (C.D. Cal. Oct 30, 2013) (counterclaims).

24 *Ibid.*, Dkt. 36 at 4 (C.D. Cal. Nov 19, 2013) (counterclaim).

25 "FirstTimeCaller," March 11, 2015, 2:53 am, http://www.theatlantic.com/entertainment/archive/2015/03/why-the-blurred-lines-verdict-could-be-bad-for-music/387433/#comment-1900341363

26 Most notably in his breakthrough hit "Don't Stop 'Til You Get Enough" (1979).

27 "sarah," August 16, 2013, 6:30 pm, http://www.hollywoodreporter.com/thr-esq/robin-thicke-sues-protect-blurred-607492#comment-1003857027

28 Some listeners felt reminded not of Marvin Gaye, but rather of other music—for example, of Prince. See e.g. readers "sambodia7" and "ibivipb" of the *New York* magazine's *Radio Vulture*, posting on July 21 and 22, 2013, http://www.vulture.com/2013/07/robin-thicke-is-the-dork-king-of-r-and-b.html#comments

29 See, for instance, the debates among readers of an article about the jury verdict in the *Guardian* on March 10, 2015, http://www.theguardian.com/music/2015/mar/10/blurred-lines-pharrell-robin-thicke-copied-marvin-gaye#comment-48698064; or of *USA Today* on the same day: http://www.usatoday.com/story/life/music/2015/03/10/blurred-lines-trial-verdict/24492431/

30 Confidential deposition of Pharrell Williams, taken April 21, 2014, at 60, 65, available at http://www.hollywoodreporter.com/sites/default/files/custom/Documents/ESQ/pharrellwilliamsdepo.pdf

31 McKinley 2013; Confidential deposition of Robin Thicke, taken April 23, 2014, at 72, available at http://www.hollywoodreporter.com/sites/default/files/custom/Documents/ESQ/robinthickedepo.pdf

32 Confidential deposition of Robin Thicke, taken April 23, 2014, at 74.

33 Ibid., at 73.

34 Ibid., at 75.

35 And that he had been high on drugs and alcohol while making those interviews—see ibid., at 103–4.

36 Sisario and Smith 2015; Pasick 2015; Kornhaber 2015; Mandell 2015; Caramanica 2015; Matos 2015; Wu 2015; Richards 2015; Ragusea 2015.

37 Williams v. Bridgeport Music Inc., CV13-06004-JAK (AGRx), Dkt. 322 at 25 (C.D. Cal. Mar 10, 2015) (jury instructions). 17 USC 106 further mentions (5) the exclusive right "to display the copyrighted work publicly" or authorize display. This right is also mentioned in the jury instructions, 36. The term to "perform" has a broad meaning in current American copyright law: "to recite, render, play, dance, or act it, either directly or by means of any device or process or, in the case of a motion picture or other audiovisual work, to show its images in any sequence or to make the sounds accompanying it audible" (17 USC 101). Thus it includes all kinds of broadcasting or distributing through cable networks as well as making works available online.

38 Williams v. Bridgeport Music Inc., CV13-06004-JAK (AGRx), Dkt. 322 at 38; cf. ibid., at 28: "Anyone who copies original elements of a copyrighted work during the term of the copyright without the owner's permission infringes the copyright." This phrasing was criticized as misleading: "it seems to say that all copying of original elements is unlawful—which, as a proposition of law, is simply false. Copying something original is often perfectly lawful, not to mention ethical [...] Copying an idea—even an idea that's original—is not merely within the law: it's encouraged by it" (Gordon 2015); see also Ciotola and Pelletier (2015).

39 See 17 USC 107–19.

40 Williams v. Bridgeport Music Inc., CV13-06004-JAK (AGRx), Dkt. 139 at 2, 7 (C.D. Cal. Oct 30, 2014) (order re plaintiffs' and counterdefendants' motion for summary judgement); Ibid., Dkt. 322 at 37.

41 U.S. Copyright Office, Reg. N° EP 366-530; renewed as RE 910-939.

42 Williams v. Bridgeport Music Inc., CV13-06004-JAK (AGRx), Dkt. 91, Ex. C (C.D. Cal. Jul 22, 2014).

43 Marvin Gaye, *Got to Give It Up*, Tamla, 1977 (single version: 4:12; EP version: 11:52); the longer version is also included on the album Marvin Gaye, *Live at the*

London Palladium, 1977. A different version was recorded at the 1980 Montreux Jazz Festival and later released by Eagle Records in 2003: Marvin Gaye, *Live in Montreux 1980*. Critically comparing these diverse recordings would corroborate the result that any similarities people may have heard between "Blurred Lines" and "Got to Give It Up" were mainly similarities to certain features in one particular recording and not to the composition as it was fixed on the lead sheet.

44 U.S. Copyright Act of 1976, as amended, 17 USC 101, 102. Cf. the Jury Instructions, Dkt. 322, at 26.

45 For example, a reader of an article on the "Blurred Lines" verdict in the *Guardian* of March 10, 2015 pointed to the Bee Gees' "You should be dancing" (1976) which also featured cowbells, falsetto singing, and many of the other elements mentioned in the "Blurred Lines" case as characteristic features of "Got to Give It Up"; JanfransZuidema, March 11, 2015 1:25, http://discussion.theguardian.com/comment-permalink/48703230

46 U.S. Copyright Act of 1909, as amended, §14.

47 Williams v. Bridgeport Music Inc., CV13-06004-JAK (AGRx), Dkt. 322 at 28, 29, 37, 40.

48 Ibid., at 31.

49 Ibid., at 40.

50 Pasillas v. McDonald's Corp., 927 F.2d 440, 442 (9th Cir. 1991); Swirsky v. Carey 376 F. 3d 841 (9th Cir. 2004).

51 Williams v. Bridgeport Music Inc., CV13-06004-JAK (AGRx), Dkt. 322 at 46.

52 Ibid. The wording of the instruction closely follows the relevant precedent decision, Swirsky v. Carey.

53 Three Boys Music Corporation v. Michael Bolton 212 F.3d 477 (9th Cir. 2000), at 485.

54 Williams v. Bridgeport Music Inc., CV13-06004-JAK (AGRx), Dkt. 139 at 6 (C.D. Cal. Oct 30, 2014) (order re plaintiffs' and counterdefendants' motion for summary judgement).

55 On the dubiousness of the testimonies presented in the "Blurred Lines" case for the extrinsic similarity test, see Weinstein 2015; Fink 2015.

56 Williams v. Bridgeport Music Inc., CV13-06004-JAK (AGRx), Dkt. 322 at 10 (C.D. Cal. Mar 10, 2015).

57 16 F. 3d 1042 – Kouf v. Walt Disney Pictures & Television, at 1045.

58 An independent analysis by the musicologist Joe Bennett (2014) found no substantial extrinsic similarities between "Got to Give It Up" and "Blurred Lines," except in the tempo (120 or 122 beats per minute, respectively) and instrumentation choices, which are not "original" features of either song: "The vocal melodies and lyrics of the songs are very obviously different from one another. The songs have different chord patterns from each other. The recordings

are in different keys [...] The basslines use different notes, rhythms and phrasing from each other; they're even taken from different musical scales. Thicke's bass notes are all taken from the mixolydian mode; the Gaye bassline is based around the pentatonic minor scale. [...] Thicke's cowbells (actually a cowbell and another percussion instrument that sounds to me more like an electronic clave) syncopate on the 16th notes (a semiquaver groove); Gaye's song is very clearly an 8 groove. The only similarity is that each riff plays the first three 8th notes (quavers) of the bar."

59 Roth Greeting Cards v. United Card Co., 429 F.2d 1106, 1110 (9th Cir. 1970); Sid & Marty Krofft TV v. McDonalds Corp. 562 F.2d 1157 (9th Cir. 1977). Cf. Williams v. Bridgeport Music Inc., CV13-06004-JAK (AGRx), Dkt. 322 at 46 (C.D. Cal. Mar. 10, 2015).

60 See Crawford 1980; Budd 1999; Zangwill 2014.

61 See Herman 2013. Similar arguments by "cruxer" and 'swift2" commenting on an article about the "Blurred Lines" verdict in the *Atlantic* on March 12, 2015: http://www.theatlantic.com/entertainment/archive/2015/03/why-the-blurred-lines-verdict-could-be-bad-for-music/387433/#comment-1903069277, and http://www.theatlantic.com/entertainment/archive/2015/03/why-the-blurred-lines-verdict-could-be-bad-for-music/387433/#comment-1903772591

62 Bleistein v Donaldson Lithographing Co., 188 U.S. 239, 251 (1903): "It would be a dangerous undertaking for persons trained only to the law to constitute themselves final judges of the worth of pictorial illustrations, outside of the narrowest and most obvious limits."

63 Three Boys Music v. Michael Bolton 212 F.3d 477 (9th Cir. 2000), at 485; cf. Litchfield v Spielberg, 736 F.2d 1352 (9th Cir. 1984).

References

Associated Press, "Pharrell Williams talks battle with Marvin Gaye's estate over Robin Thicke's 'Blurred Lines,'" *New York Daily News*, September 13, 2013. Available online:, http://www.nydailynews.com/entertainment/music-arts/pharrell-williams-talks-battle-robin-thicke-blurred-lines-article-1.1454895

Ayers, M., "Q&A: Emily Ratajkowski on 'Blurred Lines' and Her Song of the Summer," *Esquire*, July 22, 2013. Available online: http://www.esquire.com/entertainment/interviews/a23933/emily-ratajkowski-interview-blurred-lines/

Bennett, Joe (2014), "Did Robin Thicke steal 'Blurred Lines' from Marvin Gaye?" (February 1, 2014). Available online: http://joebennett.net/2014/02/01/did-robin-thicke-steal-a-song-from-marvin-gaye/

Blake, J., "Robin Thicke: I don't think people got 'Blurred Lines,'" *BBC Newsbeat*, October 10, 2013. Available online: http://www.bbc.co.uk/newsbeat/article/24471006/robin-thicke-i-dont-think-people-got-blurred-lines/

Bourdieu, P. (1979), *La distinction. Critique sociale du jugement*, Paris: Les éditions de minuit.

Brandes, B., "Robin Thicke's New Video Is Horrible, Misogynist Bullshit," *Vice*, June 5, 2013. Available online: http://www.vice.com/en_uk/read/robin-thickes-blurred-lines/

Brinkley, E., "Is 'Blurred Lines' a 'Rapey' Song?," *Wall Street Journal*, August 8, 2013, http://blogs.wsj.com/speakeasy/2013/08/08/is-blurred-lines-a-rapey-song/

Brown, A., "Robin Thicke on 'Blurred Lines': 'I was high on Vicodin and alcohol,'" *Los Angeles Times*, September 15, 2014. Available online: http://www.latimes.com/entertainment/music/posts/la-et-ms-robin-thicke-blurred-lines-deposition-high-vicodin-alcohol-20140915-story.html

Budd, M. (1999), "Aesthetic Judgements, Aesthetic Principles and Aesthetic Properties," *European Journal of Philosophy* 7 (3): 295–311.

Caramanica, J., "'Blurred Lines' Makes Robin Thicke White Soul's Leader," *New York Times*, August 2, 2013. Available online: http://www.nytimes.com/2013/08/03/arts/music/blurred-lines-makes-robin-thicke-white-souls-leader.html

Caramanica, J., "What's Wrong With the 'Blurred Lines' Copyright Ruling," *New York Times*, March 11, 2015. Available online: http://nyti.ms/1AgBs5v

Cattarin, J. A., J. K. Thompson, C. Thomas, and R. Williams (2000), "Body Image, Mood, and Televised Images of Attractiveness: The Role of Social Comparison," *Journal of Social and Clinical Psychology*, 19 (2): 220–39.

Ciotola, M. P. and G. A. Pelletier, "Fuzzy Jury Instructions Affected 'Blurred Lines' Case," *IPFrontline*, May 15, 2015. Available online: http://ipfrontline.com/2015/05/blurred-lines-fuzzy-jury-instructions-affected-blurred-lines-case/

Crawford, D. (1980), "Comparative Aesthetic Judgments and Kant's Aesthetic Theory," *Journal of Aesthetics and Art Criticism* 38 (3): 289–98.

Crouch, A. and D. Degelman (1998), "Influence of Female Body Images in Printed Advertising on Self-ratings of Physical Attractiveness by Adolescent Girls," *Perceptual and Motor Skills* 87 (2): 1–2.

Ducker, E., "Q&A: Veteran Music Video Director Diane Martel on Her Controversial Videos for Robin Thicke and Miley Cyrus," *Grantland*, June 26, 2013. Available online: http://grantland.com/hollywood-prospectus/qa-veteran-music-video-director-diane-martel-on-her-controversial-videos-for-robin-thicke-and-miley-cyrus/

Ess, C. (2013), *Digital Media Ethics*, 2nd edn, Cambridge: Polity Press.

Fink, R., "Blurred Lines, Ur-Lines, and Color Lines," *Musicology Now*, March 15, 2015. Available online: http://musicologynow.ams-net.org/2015/03/blurred-lines-ur-lines-and-color-line.html

Gardner, E., "'Blurred Lines' Lawsuit No Longer Involves Funkadelic's 'Sexy

Ways,'" *Hollywood Reporter*, March 27 2014. Available online: http://www.hollywoodreporter.com/thr-esq/blurred-lines-lawsuit-no-longer-691729/

Golden, G., "12 Parodies of Robin Thicke's 'Blurred Lines,'" *Crave*, July 26, 2013. Available online: http://www.craveonline.com/lifestyle/articles/542435-12-parodies-of-robin-thickes-blurred-lines

Gordon, W., "The jury in the 'Blurred Lines' case was misled," *Newsweek*, March 18, 2015. Available online: http://europe.newsweek.com/jury-blurred-lines-case-was-misled-314856/

Gross, L., J. S. Katz, and J. Ruby (eds) (1988), *Image Ethics: The Moral Rights of Subjects in Photographs, Film, and Television*, Oxford: Oxford University Press.

Gross, L., J. S. Katz, and J. Ruby (eds) (2003), *Image Ethics in the Digital Age*, Minneapolis, MN: University of Minnesota Press.

Ha, P., "Officially NSFW: YouTube's Naked Lady Problem (NSFW)," *Gizmodo*, April 1, 2013. Available online: http://gizmodo.com/5993196/officially-nsfw-youtubes-naked-lady-problem/

Hamamoto, D. Y. (2003), "White and Wong: Race, Porn, and the World Wide Web," in L. Gross, J. S. Katz, and J. Ruby (eds), *Image Ethics in the Digital Age*, 247–67, Minneapolis, MN: University of Minnesota Press.

Herman, Bill (2013), "Blurred Lines: Offensive, But Probably Not Copyright Infringement," *Shouting Loudly*, August 28, 2013. Available online: http://www.shoutingloudly.com/2013/08/28/blurred-lines-offensive-but-probably-not-copyright-infringement/

Howard, J., "Robin Thicke's 'Blurred Lines' successfully samples classic beats for layered product," *Michigan Daily*, April 4, 2013. Available online: https://www.michigandaily.com/arts/04single-review-robin-thickes-blurred-lines-successfully-samples-classic-beats-produce-layered-pr04/

Hutchens, B., "How Sweet It Is to be Sued by You (for copyright infringement)," *IP Watchdog.com*, February 19, 2015. Available online: http://www.ipwatchdog.com/2015/02/19/how-sweet-it-is-to-be-sued-by-you-for-copyright-infringement/

Huynh, L., "In the News: Robin Thicke's rape song, Tennessee legislation, and my continued obsession with Sheryl Sandberg," *Feminist in LA*, April 2, 2013. Available online: http://feministinla.blogspot.co.uk/2013/04/in-news-robin-thickes-rape-song.html

Jurgensen, J., "Staying Power of a Song Depends on the Imitations," *Wall Street Journal*, July 25, 2013. Available online: http://www.wsj.com/video/staying-power-of-a-song-depends-on-the-imitations/9CEDB756-8908-4123-891D-C8B083945D17.html

Kornhaber, S., "The 'Blurred Lines' Verdict Could Be Bad for Music," *Atlantic*, March 10, 2015. Available online: http://www.theatlantic.com/entertainment/archive/2015/03/why-the-blurred-lines-verdict-could-be-bad-for-music/387433/

Leval, P. (1990), "Towards a Fair Use Standard," *Harvard Law Review*, 103 (5): 1105–36.

Lynskey, D., "Blurred Lines: The most controversial song of the decade," *Guardian*,

November 13, 2013. Available online: www.theguardian.com/music/2013/nov/13/blurred-lines-most-controversial-song-decade/

Mandell, A., "'Blurred' Verdict is Bad News for Music Biz," *USA Today*, March 10, 2015. Available online: http://www.usatoday.com/story/life/music/2015/03/10/pharrell-responds-music-industry-reacts/24727763/

Matos, M., "The 'Blurred Lines' Verdict Is Bad News, Even If You Hate Robin Thicke," *Concourse*, March 11, 2015. Available online: http://theconcourse.deadspin.com/the-blurred-lines-verdict-is-bad-news-even-if-you-ha-1690817200/

McKinley, J. C., "Robin Thicke: A Romantic Has a Naughty Hit," *New York Times*, July 21, 2013. Available online: http://www.nytimes.com/2013/07/21/arts/music/robin-thicke-a-romantic-has-a-naughty-hit.html

Monro, F. and G. Huon (2005), "Media-portrayed Idealized Images, Body Shame, and Appearance Anxiety," *International Journal of Eating Disorders*, 38 (1): 85–90.

Munn, C. (2013), "Hip Hop's Misogyny Quotient," *Daily Beast*, June 23, 2013. Available online: www.thedailybeast.com/witw/articles/2013/06/23/robin-thicke-and-hip-hop-s-misogyny-quotient.html

Ortland, E. (2015), "Kopierhandlungen," in D. M. Feige and J. Siegmund (eds), *Kunst und Handlung. Ästhetische und handlungstheoretische Perspektiven*, 233–58, Bielefeld: transcript.

Pasick, A., "Summer Song Lawsuit Exposes the 'Blurred Lines' of the US Copyright System," *QUARTZ*, August 16, 2013. Available online: http://qz.com/115994/

Payne, C., "Robin Thicke Talks 'Happier' New Album, Calls 'Blurred Lines' Video 'Semi-Existential,'" *Billboard*, May 13, 2013. Available online: http://www.billboard.com/articles/columns/the-juice/1561343/robin-thicke-talks-happier-new-album-calls-blurred-lines-video

Phili, S., "Robin Thicke on that banned video, collaborating with 2 Chainz and Kendrick Lamar, and his new film," May 6, 2014. Available online: http://www.gq.com/story/robin-thicke-interview-blurred-lines-music-video-collaborating-with-2-chainz-and-kendrick-lamar-mercy/

Ragusea, A., "How 'Blurred Lines' Could Make Pharrell the New Bill Gates," *Time*, March 13, 2015. Available online: http://time.com/3744102/robin-thicke-pharrell-blurred-lines-verdict-appeal/

Rasmus, G., "Should We Be Concerned About Robin Thicke's 'Kind of Rapey' Single 'Blurred Lines'?" *XOJane*, June 21, 2013. Available online: http://www.xojane.com/entertainment/should-we-be-concerned-about-robin-thickes-kind-of-rapey-single-blurred-lines/

Richards, C., "It's okay if you hate Robin Thicke. But the 'Blurred Lines' verdict is bad for pop music," *Washington Post Style Blog*, March 11, 2015. Available online: http://www.washingtonpost.com/blogs/style-blog/wp/2015/03/11/the-blurred-lines-of-the-blurred-lines-verdict/

Romano, T., "'Blurred Lines,' Robin Thicke's Summer Anthem, Is Kind of Rapey," *Daily Beast*, June 17, 2013. Available online: http://www.thedailybeast.com/

articles/2013/06/17/blurred-lines-robin-thicke-s-summer-anthem-is-kind-of-rapey.html

Rosen, J., "How Robin Thicke Became the Dork King of R&B," *radio vulture*, July 19, 2013. Available online: http://www.vulture.com/2013/07/robin-thicke-is-the-dork-king-of-r-and-b.html

Samuelson, P., (2009), "Unbundling Fair Uses," *Fordham Law Review* 77 (5): 2537–621.

Sanders, R., "The Lines of Copyright Infringement Have Always Been Blurred," *IP Breakdown*, March 12, 2015. Available online: http://ipbreakdown.com/blog/the-lines-of-copyright-infringement-have-always-been-blurred/

Siegal, D., "Gayes' Expert Faces Absent Notes At 'Blurred Lines' Trial," *Law 360*, February 27, 2015. Available online: www.law360.com/articles/626345/gayes-expert-faces-absent-notes-at-blurred-lines-trial/

Sisario, B. and N. Smith, "'Blurred Lines' Infringed on Marvin Gaye Copyright, Jury Rules," *New York Times*, March 10, 2015. Available online: http://nyti.ms/1Boy78l/

Star Trak, "'Blurred Lines' Banned By YouTube As Robin Thicke's Video Features Nude Models," *Huffington Post*, April 1, 2013. Available online: http://www.huffingtonpost.com/2013/04/01/blurred-lines-banned-by-youtube-robin-thicke-nude-models_n_2994676.html

Weinstein, G., "The Blurred Lines of Musicological Expertise," *Two Strikes Blog*, March 11, 2015. Available online: http://twostrikes.gregoryweinstein.com/the-blurred-lines-of-musicological-expertise/

Wu, T., "Jay-Z Versus the Sample Troll. The shady one-man corporation that's destroying hip-hop," *Slate*, November 16, 2006. Available online: http://www.slate.com/articles/arts/culturebox/2006/11/jayz_versus_the_sample_troll.html

Wu, T., "Why the 'Blurred Lines' Copyright Verdict Should Be Thrown Out," *New Yorker*, March 11, 2015. Available online: http://www.newyorker.com/culture/culture-desk/why-the-blurred-lines-copyright-verdict-should-be-thrown-out

Wyatt, D., "Robin Thicke's Number One Single 'Blurred Lines' Accused of Reinforcing Rape Myths," *Independent*, June 21, 2013. Available online: http://www.independent.co.uk/arts-entertainment/music/news/robin-thickes-number-one-single-blurred-lines-accused-of-reinforcing-rape-myths-8667199.html

Yen, A. C. (1998), "Copyright Opinions and Aesthetic Theory," *Southern California Law Review* 71 (2): 247–302.

Young-Powell, A. and L. Page, "Universities Ban 'Blurred Lines' on Campuses Around UK," *Guardian*, September 20, 2013. Available online: http://www.theguardian.com/education/2013/sep/20/robin-thicke-blurred-lines-ban/

Zangwill, N. (2014), "Aesthetic Judgment," in E. N. Zalta (ed.), *Stanford Encyclopedia of Philosophy* (Fall 2014 edn). Available online: http://plato.stanford.edu/entries/aesthetic-judgment/

Part Four

Freedom for All? Towards an Ethics of Copying for the Digital Age

14

The Ethics of Copyright and *droit d'auteur*—An Outline

Thomas Dreier

1. Introduction

When discussing the ethics of copying, the legal instrument that first comes to mind is the set of legal rules commonly referred to as copyright, as it is called in the U.K. and the U.S., or *droit d'auteur* and its national equivalents (*diritto di autore, derecho de autor, Urheberrecht*), as it is called in continental Europe. After all, in spite of certain historically grown conceptual differences, copyright and *droit d'auteur* legislation deals with the question of whether, and if so, which acts of copying, reproducing, and adapting creations of the mind are reserved to individual authors and right holders. Modeled after the right of property in physical objects, copyright and *droit d'auteur* legislation grants to authors and other rights holders exclusive rights to authorize certain uses of their copyrighted works, among them most notably the reproduction right, i.e. the right to make copies.

Although it might be expected that the underlying ethical decisions are openly discussed, surprisingly, after copyright and *droit d'auteur* legislation had been established, ethical questions of copying or reproducing were for a long time no longer central to the legal discussions in the field of copyright and *droit d'auteur*. According to the thesis put forward in this chapter, once the dies were cast in favor of a legally guaranteed exclusivity to the benefit of publishers and authors in the form of a reproduction right—and, one might add, a right to authorize public performances to the benefit of composers of music—the ethical foundations of both copyright and *droit d'auteur* appeared no longer to be in need of ethical justification (see below, Section 2). Rather, the issues discussed focussed on details such as (a) the exact contours of what constitutes a "reproduction" within the sense of the law, (b) the reason for and the scope of exceptions to the exclusive rights, as well as (c) the legitimacy of limiting the freedom of media companies to contract with authors who are considered as the weaker parties to the negotiation process (see below, Section 3).

This relative absence of ethical discussion changed, however, with the advent of digital and networking technologies which sparked anew a fundamental discussion about the ethics of copying. This discussion invariably goes back to the roots of the fundamental rationales underlying the exclusive protection granted to authors. Interestingly, however, as regards academic writing, this debate originated and is mainly led in the U.S. In Europe, the debate took and still takes place to a great extent outside of the circle of legal scholars. Consequently, ethical lines of argumentation are inextricably intertwined with lines of argumentation that are interest-driven (see below, Section 4).

2. The decision to protect publishers and authors against unauthorized reprints of books

2.1 The *telos* of the exclusive reproduction right

Each legal statute—and, within each statute, each legal rule—has its *telos*, the aim the legislature intended to achieve when enacting a particular statute or rule. Law cannot itself change the outer world, but—apart from definitions and distinctions—has to rely on commands and prohibitions directed at the addressees of a particular norm, i.e. the persons acting in the area regulated by the norm in question. It is hoped that those to whom a particular norm is addressed will accept and follow this norm. The *telos* of a norm is to influence the behavior of a particular group of people—the addressees—in a certain intended way. The *telos* behind the formulation of legal rules determines, by way of interpretation, their contents as well as their boundaries. In addition, the *telos* tells something about the ethical considerations underlying the political decision to adopt and enact a particular law or legal rule. At the same time, the *telos* can itself be judged according to ethical standards.

Discussing the ethics of copying in copyright and *droit d'auteur* legislation, the first question is, therefore, what were the ethical considerations underlying the decision to create an exclusive reproduction right?

Historically, copyright and *droit d'auteur* legislation, and with it the prohibition to make copies of originals without prior authorization by the creator of the initial work, was a late arrival in the discourse on the ethics of copying. Firstly, it required that an understanding of a person as an individual had developed as well as an understanding of an individual being the author of a particular work ("*fecit*"). This had only occurred since the Renaissance and was subsequently supported by enlightenment theory. Second, the regulation of copying activities only became a major issue after the advent of reproduction technologies (the Gutenberg press) which allowed for the mass production of books and which, if used for reprinting books without authorization of the initial publisher, had the potential for severely undermining the first publisher's investment. It is not to be discussed here that, in addition, protection granted by way of aristocratic privileges was of course linked to the issue of censorship.

Irrespective of the differences of the historical development in different European States—restraint of competition in the U.K., replacing royal privileges in revolutionary France, and overcoming problems in trans-border dealings in territorially fragmented Germany—the main purpose of legislation against the unauthorized reprint of books was to regulate economic market activities and competition in the area of printing. The same was true, by the way, in the field of music where unauthorized and unpaid public performances of operas and musical compositions were to be repressed. Since reproduction and public performance were the acts that needed to be controlled, both the reproduction right and the public communication right served as the cornerstones of copyright and *droit d'auteur* regulation right from its start. In this respect, it mattered little that, influenced by idealistic philosophy and in line with the idea of natural law, a shift occurred in the late eighteenth and the beginning of the nineteenth century, in countries following the *droit d'auteur* tradition, from the publisher to the authors as the central actor of *droit d'auteur* legislation. In contrast, in the U.K. and the U.S., the law continued to be based on utilitarian considerations—"to promote the Progress of Science and the useful Arts," as it is formulated very clearly in the Constitution of the U.S. (art. I, §8, cl. 8)—which left room for justifying the exclusive rights with the needs of both authors and publishers alike.

Consequently, right from the start, the reproduction right was contained in all copyright and *droit d'auteur* legislations. That it was added to the Berne Convention for the Protection of Literary and Artistic works only at the revision conference in Stockholm 1967 was not because Member States of the Convention could not agree on the reproduction right as such. Rather, the Convention was mainly concerned with minimum rights of authors abroad, where works were usually circulated not in their original language but in translations. Hence, as far as the reproduction right was concerned, only the scope of exceptions was subject to debate. At the international level, this debate was put to an end with the formula of the famous three-step test, according to which it was considered as ethically fair "to limit exceptions in certain special cases, provided that such reproduction does not conflict with a normal exploitation of the work and does not unreasonably prejudice the legitimate interests of the author" (Berne Convention, art. 9(2)).

In other words, once the decision had been taken and universally accepted that authors of copyrighted works should enjoy an exclusive reproduction right in order to control the dissemination of copies of their works—and by exercising this control have the chance to obtain a fair and adequate remuneration—the need for further ethical discussion of the right to make copies had largely vanished. Instead, ethical considerations shifted mainly to the question of how exceptions and limitations to the exclusive reproduction right could be justified and how far such exceptions and limitations should reach (see below, 3.2).

2.2 "Copies" and "reproductions"

Before discussing the ethical issues linked to the questions just mentioned, a brief look at the differences between the notions of "copies" on the one hand and "reproductions" on the other hand is called for. Even if, for practical purposes, the result of a right to make "copies" is largely identical to the result of a right to make "reproductions," the intellectual construction of the two differs in at least one major respect. This difference has to do with the differences in the underlying rationales of copyright on the one hand, and *droit d'auteur* legislation on the other.

Somewhat simplified, it may be said that "copies" point back at originals which are themselves physical objects. It goes hand in hand with this understanding that the legislation in some copyright countries—such as in the U.S.—requires that a particular work needs to be fixed in tangible form in order to enjoy copyright protection, even if such an understanding appears to be based on the assumption that "work" and "fixation" are to be intellectually separated. Moreover, since the notion of "copy" is less abstract than the notion of "reproduction," and was, at least originally, primarily aimed at books, it can easily be defined by statutory language that certain duplications are not to be considered as "copies." This is the case, e.g. of phonorecords in the U.S., which are expressly exempt from the definition of copies in the U.S. Copyright Act, in order to provide for compulsory licensing only with regard to phonorecords.

In contrast, under the influence of idealistic theory, a work is generally understood as the immaterial object which is materialized for the first time in the original. Further copies thereof are then considered as reproductions, not of the original, but of the immaterial work as such. Strictly speaking, the original can be described as the work's first reproduction. According to this understanding, without further ado, any material object that embodies an immaterial copyrighted work falls under the definition of "reproduction," even if it is only a data set stored on some storage medium which cannot be perceived by the human senses without the aid of a technical device. Also, any three-dimensional rendering of a two-dimensional drawing appears to be a reproduction—again not of the drawing, but of the immaterial work made visible in the drawing, provided the three-dimensional rendering takes over the decisive creative features of the work as embodied in the two-dimensional drawing which qualify that work as copyrightable (and vice versa).

These questions vexed copyright scholars and the courts for a long time. In contrast, they were much less of a problem for countries in the *droit d'auteur* tradition, since their understanding of the work as an immaterial object enabled them to decide these questions by way of logical and rational deduction from principles that were initially underpinned by ethical concerns.

As has been said, the practical differences of these rather subtle distinctions are minimal for the simple fact that, with the notable exception of bootlegging of live performances of improvised music or spontaneous dance performances, it is hardly possible to make copies of a work which was not fixed before in a tangible medium.

3. Ethics of details

Once the reproduction right was adopted as the cornerstone of the exclusivity granted by copyright legislation to publishers and then to authors, ethical considerations were mainly limited to more detailed questions such as the definitions of what exactly constitutes a reproduction, and, most importantly, on what grounds and how far the exclusive reproduction right should be limited by way of so-called exceptions. Finally, another issue of great practical importance is to know whether the freedom of contract between authors and publishers should be regulated, and if so, on what ethical grounds.

3.1 The contours of the exclusive reproduction right

Independently from the differences between the concepts of "copies" and "reproductions" discussed above, after its inception, the notion of reproductions has undergone a few minor, yet noteworthy precisions.

One of the issues that arose in the early days in this respect was whether the recording of musical works by mechanical means (piano rolls, phonograms, etc.) and the subsequent duplication thereof, constituted a reproduction of the musical composition within the meaning of the law. As long as the respective technology was not widespread, in many countries as well as in the initial version of the Berne Convention of 1886, such duplications were not considered as copyright infringement. However, the issue became pressing once a large industry had developed specializing in these instruments. Holders of musical rights argued that they should benefit from this new spreading of their music, and they based their demand on the argument that mechanical reproductions of musical works were, after all, reproductions. The industry, in contrast, asserted that an extension of the reproduction right would ruin their businesses which were established in good faith assuming that they were not covered by copyright and that hence no royalties had to be paid. This way of arguing is a recurring argumentation to be found whenever later revisions of national or international copyright laws are under discussion. Although the matter has now since long been settled, even today many copyright acts still expressly state that a sound or visual recording shall be considered as a reproduction for the purposes of the respective copyright law.

As regards artistic works, the issue was whether "reproduction" also includes a change in dimensions of the original work. In other words, and as already indicated above, should it be considered an infringement on the basis of an unauthorized reproduction if a sculpture was represented in a painting or a photograph, or if a drawing was realized as a three-dimensional model? This question was answered quite differently in different countries' national legislations. Differences were also to be found in national legislations with regard to the issue of whether the exclusive reproduction right also covers the industrial application of artistic works. However, this was less a question of defining what constitutes a "reproduction" and what does not, and rather a limitation of the scope of the exclusive reproduction right granted to authors of artistic works.

Later on, the issue arose of what should be understood as "reproduction" in the digital environment. The problem is that for technical reasons the use of copyrighted works in a digital format necessitates not only one, but several technical acts of reproduction (storage on the hard drive, temporary acts of loading into the working memory, and arguably even the display on the screen). Should all these instances of reproduction be considered as "reproductions" within the meaning of copyright legislation? The question ultimately is about how far the legal control of the rights holders should extend regarding the use of copyrighted works. The issue was fiercely fought over when the Computer Programmes Directive of the E.U. was adopted in 1991, and the insecurity in this regard can still be perceived in the legislative text of this Directive which provides that "insofar as loading, displaying, running, transmission or storage of the computer program necessitate such reproduction, such acts shall be subject to authorization by the rightholder" (Council Directive 91/250 on the Legal Protection of Computer Programmes, art. 4(a)). The international convention in this area is more cautious in merely stating, in an agreed statement, that "the reproduction right [...] fully appl[ies] in the digital environment" and in only specifying that "the storage of a protected work in digital form in an electronic medium constitutes a reproduction" (WIPO Copyright Treaty, agreed statement to art. 1(4)). Ultimately, in Europe the term "reproduction" is now defined extremely widely in the Information Society Directive as the "direct or indirect, temporary or permanent reproduction by any means and in any form, in whole or in part" (Information Society Directive, art. 2), which even includes "transient and incidental" reproductions. This is a long way away from the initial copy of a book with which it all began.

Another battle regarding the definition of the contours of the exclusive reproduction right was fought over the appropriate reach of the translation right. Although from an ontological perspective it can be argued that a translation is a reproduction of the immaterial contents of the text translated, albeit presented in the form of another language, and although the translation right was central to the early bilateral treaties and the multilateral international convention in the area of copyright, the translation right was seen as not forming part of the reproduction right. The reason for this separation of the reproduction and the translation rights is simply that the states, while recognizing the reproduction right, wanted to retain the freedom to grant either no translation right at all, or have it run only for a term shorter than the one of the reproduction right, in order to incite the making and distribution of translations of foreign books for the benefit of their own nationals.

3.2 The reason for and the scope of exceptions to the exclusive reproduction right

In view of the extremely broad legal definition of the term "reproduction" and the general acceptance of the reproduction right, the emphasis of deciding the scope of legal protection conferred upon the author by the exclusive reproduction right rests on the limitations and exceptions to these exclusive rights. Already the early bilateral treaties and the multilateral international convention in the area of copyright had bestowed great care on the issue of defining the limits of the exceptions which other states were allowed to make. In this respect, two different issues were at stake and hence two different ethical questions. The first is to what extent foreign states were allowed to curtail the legal protection with regard to foreign authors, and the second is on what grounds the exceptions to the exclusive rights could themselves be justified.

The reasoning behind the answer to the first question is that states do want to see their own authors protected abroad against unauthorized translations and they do not want to see the reproduction right which is granted to their own authors abroad to be unduly curtailed. Whereas this expectancy is stabilized by the element of reciprocity enshrined in the bilateral treaties and the multilateral convention (State A grants protection to authors from State B because State B grants protection for authors from State A), the content of exceptions, i.e. what is to be exempted from the authorization requirement resulting from the exclusive reproduction right, required the consensus or common conviction shared by those living within a particular state or community of states.

The answer to the second question, i.e. the rationales and ethical reasons behind individual exceptions to the exclusive reproduction right, depends on a mix of national traditions, cultural predispositions, and economic needs as well as on the different purposes which are pursued by a particular exception. As regards the latter, one may distinguish uses with minimal economic significance, uses for the purposes of freedom of expression and information, and other uses facilitated by the exceptions in order to promote social, political, and cultural objectives as well as to enhance competition. Moreover, on the one hand, the higher the general interest served is valued, the stronger is the ethical argument that use acts should not only be exempt from the requirement of authorization, but that they should likewise not trigger the payment of remuneration. If, on the other hand, the main purpose of an exception is to overcome difficulties or impracticalities with regard to licensing, then there is no justification to likewise eliminate the authors' claim for remuneration. In addition, in the digital environment, exceptions which have been introduced for the sole reason of overcoming market failure—i.e. where individual licensing was impractical or difficult—lose some, if not much of their raison d'être to the extent to which digital technology can be used in order to facilitate the licensing process.

Needless to point out that the discussions and the development which ultimately lead to the adoption of an exception are not always of a purely ethical nature. Rather, the adoption of exceptions as well as their scope often serve the interests of a particular interest group which proves—on the basis more of its power than on the convincing force of its ethical perspective—to be successful in the law-making process. At the European level, the latest of such interest-driven fights in political debate in this respect is about the freedom to reproduce, distribute, and make available to the public works located permanently in public roads or public open spaces.

3.3 Dealings in the reproduction right

A third battlefield where ethical concerns are fought over—and which can only briefly be mentioned here for the sake of completeness—is the area of copyright contracts. As private law contracts, copyright contracts are subject to the general rule of private autonomy, i.e. both parties are legally free to contract with whom, when, on what conditions, and for what price they want to contract. If practice shows that publishers and media companies make authors transfer most if not all of their rights while at the same time retaining most of the profits generated by exploiting copyrighted works, the question may be asked whether legal intervention is justified or even called for in order to support the authors as the structurally weaker contracting party. Some countries, such as France and Germany, have answered this question in the affirmative, whereas other countries have not done so. The reason for an affirmative answer may ethically be well founded, especially in countries in which it is generally assumed that copyright not only protects the moral interests of the authors, but also "to ensure equitable remuneration for the exploitation of the work," as it is phrased, e.g. in the German Copyright Act (art. 16). The practical problem, however, remains: what is an "adequate" remuneration and who decides about the adequacy? Are the courts really in a position to make balanced calculations as regards the production and dissemination of products and services which make use of copyrighted materials? Of course, the legislative decision not to enact special protection for authors against far-reaching transfers of rights and low remunerations can likewise be justified on ethical grounds, e.g. insofar as it is hoped to strengthen national publishers and media companies in international competition which in turn indirectly may be believed to benefit individual authors. Finally, it should be noted that the open access movement provides some sort of self-defense for authors with regard to what is to be considered as "fair" with regard to reproduction activities in the field of scientific publishing.

4. The ethics of copyright and *droit d'auteur* revisited

Apart from these individual issues, in order to discuss the ethics of copying within copyright in general, one has to go back to analyze the ethics of the rationales that underlie the granting of exclusive copyright protection in general. However, to an increasing extent, discrepancies between the ethical underpinnings of copyright protection on the one hand and the actual behavior of both artists and users can be observed in particular in the digital and networking age. Finally, directing the view towards the future, the issue of the right balance between the traditional public policy perspective on the one hand and private ordering activities made possible by technological access and use-control mechanisms on the other hand will be of paramount importance to shape future relationships with regard to copying activities in an ethically justified way.

4.1 Back to the ethical roots

The main factor which triggered a new debate about the rationales underlying copyright protection as a whole were the advent of digital and networking technologies and the ensuing extension of the reproduction right into the realm of the private and other activities which used to be copyright-free in the analog world. If the initial ethically founded rationale was to secure investment and regulate market activities as well as investment, over time the interpretation approaches toward the rationales and functions of both copyright and *droit d'auteur* legislations have multiplied.

One of the main changes which may have brought about new explanations for the existence and justification of copyright may have to do with the fact that after it had all started with the protection of publishers and a pendulum swing towards the protection of authors mainly in the *droit d'auteur* countries, beginning in the 1980s, a backswing of the pendulum from authors to copyright "industries" as the main actor in the field regulated by copyright was to be observed. On the one hand, this backswing can be explained by the general crisis of natural law in legal philosophy, in spite of the fact that copyright is protected as individual property in many catalogues of human rights, including the Universal Declaration of Human Rights and the European Charter of Fundamental Rights. This backswing coincided—whether by historical accident or by way of an intrinsic connection is subject to debate—with a more economic explanation of the rationale underlying exclusive protection by copyright. Increasingly, intellectual property laws were regarded as incentives to innovate and create for industries which otherwise would not accumulate the investment necessary for the production of new, innovative, and creative products and services. Although this approach was mainly tailored to patents, it was also applied to copyrighted material, which was increasingly regarded as a commercial good rather than as a personal creation. As part of the bigger endeavor of an economic analysis of law, the property rights theory used the metaphor of the "tragedy of the commons" (under-investment and over-use of a limited resource) in order to justify the creation of contrafactual normative exclusivity which was thought necessary so that immaterial goods could be traded. Possible negative effects ("tragedy of the anti-commons," i.e. over-investment and under-use) were generally believed to be corrected by the market, since irrespective of how the rights were initially allocated, in a functioning and undistorted market the goods would invariably end up in the hands of those who were paying the optimal price. Of course, this line of argumentation almost completely discarded the idea of the author as the main actor around which the whole logic—certainly of *droit d'auteur*, but to an extent also of copyright protection—was initially built. Taken to its extreme, the individual author merely served as a placeholder to calculate the term of protection, the prolongation of which was mostly justified with the extended life expectation of the generation of the author's heirs.

Both lines of thinking—the traditional, author- or industry-centered approach which tends to lead to an ever-increasing protection and to reduce limitations and exceptions, as well as the economic optimization ideology which largely eliminated the human author from its equations—also met with criticism. This criticism is fueled from more than one source. For example, partly being in line with neo-liberal thinking, one such source takes the free market as the starting point. However, contrary to both the theory of property rights and a natural law based justification of exclusive rights granted to authors, it regards the absence of exclusive intellectual property rights as the rule and emphasizes the role of property rights as exceptions to that rule. In other words, intellectual property rights should not be granted, unless it has been demonstrated that free competition did not work in a particular area. Another source looks to the consumers' rather than to the producers' side and pleads for an opening up of access, in particular where the application of the existing reproduction right leads to an extension of copyright control in areas where this was not the case in the analog world before. At the same time, this line of argumentation pleads for a full exploitation of the possibilities which digital technology makes available for quicker information retrieval. From this perspective, wherever feasible, the exclusive rights should be reduced to a claim for remuneration or even be made free of any payment obligation altogether. This case is made in particular as regards reproductions for scientific education and research, since it is believed that these areas are more important for the innovative activities and the economic output than mere consumptive use, which if allowed free of charge diminishes the return both of investment and fair remuneration of authors. It seems worth noting that this approach is likewise ambiguous with regard to authors. While wishing to protect all authors mainly with regard to their personality rights (in particular the right of name attribution on reproductions), authors are told to step back with their financial interests in all cases where no incentive is needed to secure the creation of new works and where access by users is valued higher than proprietary and monetary interests of individual creators. It is interesting to note, however, that most authors placing their works under a Creative Commons (CC) license only make use of the option to allow non-commercial, but not commercial uses of their copyrighted works.

Finally, it is somewhat surprising that most of these theories criticizing traditional exclusive reproduction rights seem to turn a blind eye to the immense concentration of economic and even political power currently in the hands of big players (Google, Facebook, Apple, Amazon, and Microsoft, the "big five"). This is true for free market adepts who deprive authors of a good deal of their possibilities to control the reproduction of their works and generate income therefrom, in much the same way as it is true of the adepts of a broad unhindered access to the benefit of all or certain groups of users. After all, it appears to be an anomaly that traditional copyright doesn't even list or address internet service providers (ISPs) as actors in the field of copyright and reproductions. In cases in which their activities are to be regulated, the courts therefore have to resort to other means of redress such as secondary infringement, which, however, is limited in the E.U. under the E-Commerce Directive to injunctive relief and does not include damages, irrespective of the fact that ISPs receive by far the biggest share of the income generated on the basis of making reproductions and using other people's copyrighted material. Moreover, in the few cases where the activities of ISPs—such as in the case of thumbnails in picture search engines—are covered by the exclusive reproduction right, national courts tend to find other legal means in order not to subject the service to payment or even an obligation to cease and desist—such as by way of the assumption of an implied license as decided by the German Federal Supreme Court (in a country where the fair use exception is not available). So far, these issues have hardly been discussed in ethical terms. What is lacking in this respect is a legal theory which would incorporate the activities of internet service providers as direct infringers into copyright proper, not limiting their role to so-called secondary infringement.

4.2 Ethical theory v. factual behavior: Discrepancies

The general ethical debate about the legitimacy of the exclusive reproduction right has to be seen against the backdrop of increasing practices of using copyrighted material which follows its own ethical rules that to an increasing extent are not in line with the ethical rules underlying the normative granting of the exclusive reproduction right. This is true with regard to artists as well as with regard to users in general, albeit for different reasons.

4.2.1 Artists

As long as mastering the technique and studying the old masters was part of the training to become an artist, copying for the purpose of studying and learning was not only allowed, but required. Of course, it is yet another matter to what extent outright copies were passed on as originals. However, the ethical issues pertaining thereto are about the importance and foundation of attribution of ownership and on the fraud committed *vis-à-vis* buyers and possibly the community at large, but no longer about the ethics of reproduction in the strict sense.

No doubt, later on, the emphasis which modern art placed on innovation and creativity invariably led to a decrease of one-to-one copying activities by artists. But even then the old saying holds true that, like every maker or inventor, no artist creates *ex nihilo*. Artistic activities form part of a historical tradition, new artworks refer back to pre-existing artworks, individual parts of older works are being copied, adapted, or modified, and integrated into newer ones, ideas are taken over, developed further, refined, refuted, etc. Often, the link to the past is made visible by way of a partial takeover of a pre-existing work of art and its integration onto the new work. In general, copyright legislation has taken note of this. The freedom to develop pre-existing artistic concepts and ideas further is reflected in the non-copyrightability of general ideas. In addition, even outright copying is generally allowed as long as it stays within the limits of the classical citation right. Moreover, in countries with a strong constitutional control of statutory legislation, the constitutional guarantee of the freedom of the arts reserves to the artist a realm for creation without being hampered all too much by copyright. Of course, the line between what is permitted without authorization and what is not can only be drawn on a case-by-case basis by the courts. This creates a tricky dilemma for the courts, since the freedom of the arts mandates state authorities, including the courts, not to interfere with artistic activities. And yet, in order to apply the freedom of the arts, a definition of what constitutes art and what can thus benefit from the constitutional freedom of the arts and what cannot is necessary.

All of this can only be briefly touched upon here. More importantly, however, it should be noted that traditional copyright and its underlying ethical choices are difficult, if not impossible to reconcile with two art forms which have been prominent in the last decades. Both conceptual art and appropriation art are at odds with the ethics underlying the exclusive reproduction right, each of them for a different reason. In conceptual art, what counts is the idea which is located, so to speak, outside of the picture frame, i.e. of what's physically visible. But according to copyright logic, mere ideas are not protected. Conceptual art is then either not covered by copyright laws (which would run counter to copyright's fundamental ethical aim to protect the authors of artistic works), or the concept of "idea" would have to be redefined for purposes of copyright (which would result in a change of fundamental copyright ideas and its underlying ethical rules). Appropriation art has the opposite problem linked to it. It is not about ideas outside of the realm of copyright, but in copying already existing visual or textual copyrighted material it flatly falls under the prohibition to make reproductions without the consent given by the author of the work copied. What counts here is the strategy of attacking the very notion of authorship. Appropriation art not only attacks the idea of novelty and creativity, but the fictional character of the artistic, societal as well as legal construct of the individual "author" in general. The question raised in view of these dilemmata is in itself an ethical one. Should or should copyright not be altered—or at least be interpreted—so that it also covers and deals with these art forms in an appropriate way? In spite of their differences, the solution could indeed be similar in both cases, if one were to look not for similarities and differences in form, but for distances of the underlying artistic ideas.

The discrepancies between artistic activities on the one hand and copyright rules on the other hand do not, however, stop there. In digital art, pixels are either copied or they are not. In many cases, the production of digital artworks includes the copying of pixels and the use of outside data formatted in bits and bytes. Whenever a digital artwork takes some parts or elements from another digital artwork but not the prior work's underlying idea, or reuses the content of someone else's protected database, this artistic practice invariably involves the infringement of someone else's reproduction right. Once again, bringing the ethical rules which underlie copyright and, in particular, the reproduction right back in line with already established artistic practices in the digital era seems only possible if the focus is placed not on the outer, visible distance between original and copy (the factual reproduction), but rather on the inner distance which the resulting work takes from the prior work from which it has borrowed certain elements (i.e. the artistic gap that lies between old and new).

4.2.2 *Users*

If one is to believe the statistics, it seems that users are generally aware of the ethical foundations of copyright as an institution. However, the social practices that evolved on the basis of using smartphones and, in general, social media have led to a discrepancy between the ethical foundation underlying the normative reproduction right and the social practices of making reproductions without the consent of the copyright holders.

A first of these problem areas is what is commonly referred to as user-generated content, mostly video clips, selfies, and other photographs posted on platforms such as YouTube, Instagram, Flickr, and DeviantArt. In many cases this content incorporates and hence reproduces someone else's copyrighted work or part thereof—mainly music, but also pictorial material. The problem is similar to the one just described for artists, with the notable difference that users may not in all cases be able to invoke the freedom of the arts. The exceptions provided for under copyright laws as regards citations, parodies, the incidental inclusion of some else's copyrighted works, other copyright-free uses thereof and, in some jurisdictions, the requirement that substantial parts of the copyrighted work must be taken before infringement can be found, may not always be sufficient in order to justify this well-established practice. Since individual licensing proves to be totally impractical in view of the sheer mass of these cases, the only solution from the copyright perspective appears to be to collect at least some remuneration from the platform providers via collecting societies.

A second problem from the copyright perspective is the reproductions which take place whenever pictures are shared by social media such as Facebook, WhatsApp, and the like. According to traditional copyright analysis, such reproductions are only exempt from the application of the exclusive reproduction right to a limited extent as fair use, fair dealing, or private copying. At the center of the problem lie the different angles from which the factual situation is seen and judged. Whereas copyright focuses on the technical acts involved in the transmission from the sender to the recipient of the data set incorporating the particular picture, a description of the social practice of sharing the picture focuses on the communicative act. Indeed, this communicative act of sharing a picture has more in common with the gesture of showing, of attracting the recipient's attention to the picture or the object depicted, than passing on a reproduction, i.e. a duplicate of a copyrighted work which satisfies part of an existing market demand. In ethical terms it hardly seems appropriate to subject the act of pointing towards an object to the permission of the person who holds the copyright in this particular object. The discrepancy between these two different attitudes, descriptions, and ethical perspectives would have become even bigger had a recent proposal to subject the commercial use of street photography to the requirement of consent by the holders of the exclusive reproduction rights been enacted by the legal committee of the European Parliament.

In all these cases the discussion is not only about which private interests shall ultimately prevail. The discussion also has to be seen against the backdrop of the ethical question of which strategy shall be followed in order to best reconcile the legitimate protection of authors and rights holders on the one hand, and interests of users to access copyrighted works on the other hand. The strategy which takes copyright as its starting point does not want to see the already beleaguered exclusive reproduction right further weakened. The strategy which takes the issue of access as its starting point wants to see copyright protection opened up to make full use of the digital access and communication technologies. Perhaps it might be ethically appropriate to make the changes to the system as it presently exists which are necessary to create an adequate legal framework also for these new social practices, with the aim of saving the copyright and *droit d'auteur* system as a whole.

4.3 Public policy v. private ordering?

However, another clash of ethical dimensions lies ahead. In the analog as well as in the first decades of digital communication, the situation was characterized by a loss of control over copyrighted material which, in turn, caused the legislature to increase the level of legal protection against unauthorized reproduction, as well as against unauthorized publicly making available of copyrighted works. This resulted in far-reaching legal protection which was still coupled with under-enforcement. In contrast, digitized networking technology increasingly allows for waterproof enforcement by both end-user license agreements (EULA) and technical access control devices (commonly referred to as technical protection measures, TPM) which, if used together, risk leading to a disruption of the balance between rights holders' and users' legally protected interests. The problem is that by applying TPM, copyright holders may limit accessibility to copyrighted—and, moreover, even to non-copyrighted—works only to those users who have agreed to the conditions contained in the EULA. The danger is that both the technical and contractual conditions as designed by private parties (private ordering) can be less favorable to the users than what the legislature deemed appropriate and just (public policy).

Under these circumstances, from a systematic as well as from a pragmatic point of view, the question is which of the two—private ordering or public policy—shall ultimately prevail. According to which ethical standards shall this question be decided? In a liberal market society, traditional contract law works on the basis of the general rule of private autonomy. If this is taken as the starting point, any deviation from this rule can only be justified if it satisfies the burden of proof that the general rule should be corrected. This burden can be met by demonstrating that there is an imbalance in the level of information of both sides (such as, for example, in the case of consumer online contracts), or that the parties are structurally not at arm's length (such as, for example, in the case of the authors regarding the conclusion of copyright contracts discussed above, or as regards standard terms and conditions). According to this logic, in case of doubt the market is the ultimate "arbiter." Provided there is undistorted competition and no abuse of a dominant market position and, moreover, that substitutes are available, consumers can choose whether they prefer an offer that is less restrictive in its EULA and/or TPM. However, in the presence of currently existing oligopolistic market structures, it can be questioned to what extent consumers do in fact still have the option of choice.

As regards copyright and the reproduction rights, the legislature seems to be rather unsure which way to follow. As regards TPM, the option taken in the E.U. is to provide for a right of access to copyrighted works as long as the use to be made of the copyrighted work by the person wishing to get access is covered by an exception to the exclusive reproduction right. It should be noted, however, that this right of access by a third party does not exist with regard to all exceptions. Most notably it is left to each E.U. Member State's discretion whether or not to grant such a right with regard to the private copying exception. Moreover, no access right exists if copyrighted works that are protected by TPM are offered online (article 6 (4) of the Information Society Directive 2001/29/EG). The insecurity of the legislature is even greater as regards the relationship between public policy exceptions to the exclusive reproduction rights and the freedom to contract these exceptions away. Apart from a limited number of outright prohibitions to have contractual terms override statutory exceptions, the E.U. has created several new hybrid exceptions to the exclusive reproduction and performance rights. Under these hybrid exceptions the statutory exception only applies if the protected work in question is not subject to purchase or licensing terms. Of course, this entails a dilemma. Why should a person or institution benefiting from the statutory exception conclude a contract which takes away some of the freedoms granted by the statutory exception? If, however, a mere offer of a contract made by the right holder has the legal power to override the statutory exception, what is left of the statutory exception? Without going into too much detail, it should be noted that with the possible exception of the European Court of Justice (ECJ), the national courts still seem to turn a blind eye to these fundamental questions, the answers to which will undoubtedly shape our future society.

5. Outlook

The preceding remarks are hardly more than a brief outline of a whole field of ethical as well as legal issues to be further explored in more detail. It has been shown that the ethics of copyright in general, and of the exclusive reproduction right in particular, are by no means questions that have a simple answer. True, the relative absence of an ethical debate concerning the reproduction right as such can be explained by the fact that once it was generally accepted that publishers and authors should be protected by legal means against the unauthorized reprint of books, the exclusive reproduction right was no longer in need of fundamental ethical justification.

However, with the advent of digital technology, both the general rationales and ethical foundations for granting exclusive copyright protection as such and an increasing number of individual issues concerning the definition of reproduction are raised concerning the exact contours of exceptions of the exclusive reproduction right, as well as issues of contracting and technological protection measures. Even if copyright law seems to be the prime candidate to look at when discussing ethical issues of copying, it has become clear that the question of both a descriptive and a normative ethics of copying reaches far beyond copyright legislation. Rather, it touches upon numerous issues of law, and has to do with social practices triggered by technological development, unfolding themselves in an economic environment. In a multilayered legal system of national, European, and international levels, the current normative framework is, last but not least, set by the fundamental decision for the market economy, triggering the everlasting question to what extent the reliance on the free market leads to adequate and ethically justifiable results.

Even if no eternal ethical values and rules may be ascertained, it is still possible to describe, explain, and test the ethical rules followed and the ethical decisions taken at a particular time and under particular historical, sociological, and economic circumstances as regards their effects and capacity to solve the particular problems to which the regulation regarding the activities of copying and making reproductions was accepted, in its time, as the appropriate answer. And this also holds true for the future.

15

Self-Copying and Copyright

Lionel Bently

The topic of "self-plagiarism" has recently attracted the attention of ethicists, most prominently with respect to self-copying in academic journals in the fields of science and medicine (see Bruton 2014; Bruton and Rachal 2015). The chief concern has been to identify whether, and if so in what circumstances, self-copying is ethically wrong, and to apply their conclusions in formulating the policies and practices of such journals (see Bruton 2014; Garfinkel 2014; Scanlon 2007). Although the commentary is not uniform, and "self-plagiarism" is said to raise a number of different ethical problems (including that of "misrepresenting" previously presented ideas or data "as new"—see Committee on Publication Ethics 2014; Bruton 2014), one common claim is that instances falling within the sub-category of "copyright infringement" are evidently unethical self-plagiarism.[1]

This paper suggests that resting the ethics of self-copying on notions of copyright violation is problematic for two distinct reasons. First, while there is an increasing degree of copyright harmonization at an international level, the question of self-copying has never prompted sufficient levels of concern to be placed on the inter-governmental agenda. There is therefore no single response by "copyright law" to self-copying, but rather a diverse range of responses in national copyright laws (in particular, jurisprudence), sometimes with different rules for different types of work. In such circumstances, resting the ethics of self-copying on "copyright law" seems both practically problematic (which law to apply?) and theoretically unsound. Second, even if the positive law of different countries were relatively uniform on this topic, there are reasons to doubt that this is a sound guide to when self-copying is "ethical." A better way to understand if, and if so when, self-copying is unethical would be by reference to the normative arguments that justify protection. However, this approach would suggest that significant amounts of self-copying might be justifiable (and thus that corresponding copyright laws *should permit* such recycling).

1. The diversity of copyright law's treatment of "self-copying"

Basing the ethics of self-copying on copyright law is problematic for the simple reason that while the desire of commentators appears to be to develop a single internationally applicable "ethics" (that could inform international publishing practice), copyright laws are not harmonized internationally. Despite the existence of three international agreements (Berne [1886–1971], TRIPs [1994] and the WIPO Copyright Treaty [1996]) which establish standards of copyright protection that are to be granted in most countries of the world, only some aspects of copyright are standardized (most obviously what works should be protected, what rights conferred and for how long) and even those that are standardized are done so only in terms of a baseline (thus permitting more restrictive national laws). The issue of self-copying is not addressed, and thus when self-copying counts as infringement is left (more or less) to individual nation states.[2]

The responses of different jurisdictions to self-copying largely focus on two distinct issues. The first relates to a fundamental feature of all copyright laws, namely that they only prevent copying or use of material that has been copied, and do not impede "independent creation." In the situation where one person, (B), is alleged to have infringed the copyright in a work created by a third party, (C), the idea of copying seems rather intuitive. Applied to the situation where one person, (A), is copying a pre-existing work that was itself created by (A), the notion of whether there was copying is less easily answered. The second question that arises is whether a particular national copyright law offers greater freedom to a person such as (A) who copies their own work (even though they no longer own the copyright in that work) than it would to the situation where (B) copies the work of (C).

1.1 Establishing copying in the case of works produced by the same author

In most, if not all, countries, in order to determine whether there has been an infringement of copyright one needs to answer three questions. First, as a matter of law, is the defendant's action within the scope of exclusive rights conferred on the copyright holder? Second, if there has been a relevant act, was the act done with material derived from the copyright-protected work? There must be derivation, or a causal connection, as opposed to "independent creation." The claimant's work must be the (or at least a) source, direct or indirect, of the expressive material used by the defendant. Third, was the material that the defendant has used (in a way which falls within the exclusive rights of the copyright owner), and which has been derived from the copyright holder, extensive enough to count as infringement?

It is the second stage of the analysis—that of derivation or causation question—that raises the clearest problems for cases of self-plagiarism. In regular cases, where (B) is alleged to have copied work created by (C), courts look for direct and indirect evidence of copying—understood as utilizing (C)'s work as a source of the expression used by (B). Direct evidence may be provided, for example, by persons who were present when (B) created the work in question—for example co-workers. Occasionally, (B) will admit to having used (C)'s work. But even if such evidence is not available, courts are willing to infer derivation from the presence of similarities between the works of (B) and (C), and the possibility that (B) had access to the work of (C). Such similarities might come from the overall appearance of the works, or from individual components. These similarities give rise to presumptions of derivation which it falls for the defendant/alleged infringer to rebut.[3] The more peculiar and the more numerous the components of the earlier work by (C) that are replicated in the later work by (B), the stronger the presumption of copying. (B) may be able to rebut the presumption, by demonstrating that the features that are similar in the works of (B) and (C) in fact derive from a third (public domain) source—the works of (D), (E), (F)—or from functional or other constraints on their "creative freedom." Or (B) may be able to argue that the similar features are truly co-incidental, for example, by providing the court with clear evidence of how (B) came to create the work in the form it took (see Bently and Sherman 2014: 190–5).

In the case of self-plagiarism, where (A) is alleged to have infringed copyright in a work that he or she created, there may be direct evidence of copying—as where an artist is asked to make a copy of a painting for a second buyer and the artist creates the duplicate working from the original painting.[4] Moreover there are many cases where copying will be established indirectly—for example, where the work is copied wholesale, as would be the case where whole paragraphs of one literary work appear in identical form in another.

While demonstrating copying through indirect evidence is in one respect easier in the case of self-copying, because there can be no doubt that the author had access to and, moreover, was familiar with the earlier work, establishing copying through indirect evidence is much more problematic in the case of self-copying. This is for the simple reason that the assumptions which underpin the inference of copying by (B) of a work created by (C), are highly unreliable in relation to a situation where (A) is said to have copied from a work created by (A).[5] In particular, while it might be highly improbable that two distinct people, (B) and (C), would independently use the same combination of features, or the same highly idiosyncratic phrase or even make the same grammatical or syntactical mistake, it seems quite conceivable, indeed probable, that the same person (A) might well do so. The features from which copying by (B) from (C) can be inferred have sometimes been referred to as the "fingerprints" that a particular author (C) leaves in the work. The analogy is useful because we would not infer from the fact that the creator's fingerprints could be found on a painting or pot that had been stolen from its owner that the creator was the thief. The existence of (A)'s fingerprints are as consistent with independent creation as with derivation.[6]

The point is illustrated by a U.S. decision, *Esquire, Inc. v. Varga Enterprises.*[7] Alberto Vargas (1896–1982), a painter of saucy, scantily dressed "pin-up girls" (known as "Varga girls"), had for many years provided artwork to the claimant

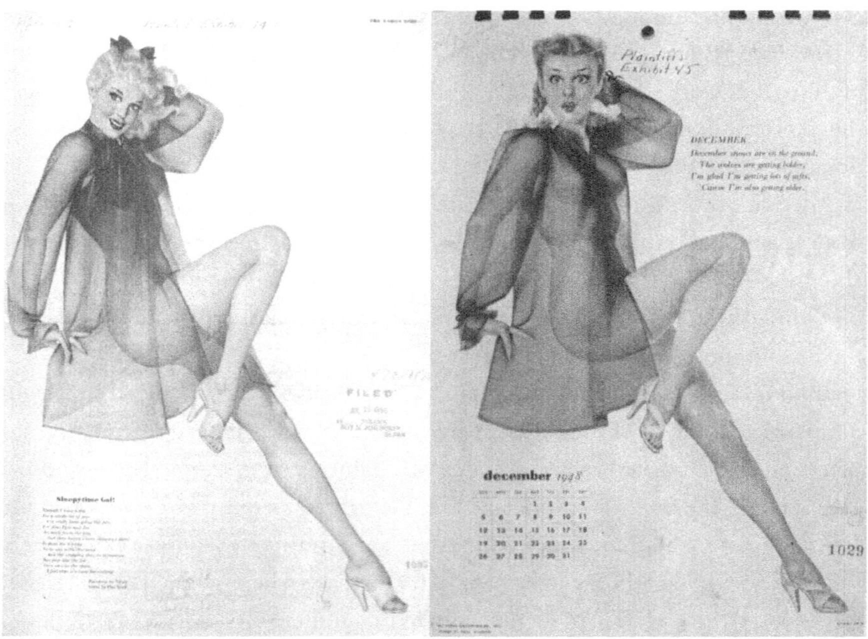

Figure 15.1 *Exhibits in Esquire, Inc. v. Varga Enterprises, "Original" (left) and "Accused" (right)*

for use in *Esquire* magazine and in its calendars. Having begun to work independently, the claimant brought an action alleging four copyright infringements. District Judge Campbell identified the following (referenced as Exhibits 14B and 14A in the trial document) as the closest example.[8]

The judge identified these differences:

> The remaining two drawings, i.e., Exhibits 14A (Accused) and 14B (Original), reveal a closer similarity than the foregoing sets, but they do, nevertheless, possess a sufficient number of distinguishing elements. (a) Hair—Accused's hair is red, is parted in the middle and drawn back over the ears, whence it falls in braids; Original's hair is blonde, apparently unparted and, from its tousled appearance, is designed to produce the effect of "studied carelessness"; (b) Head—Original's is tilted slightly downward and to the left; Accused's is in a perfectly upright position, which causes a distension of the vertical muscles on the left side of the neck, a condition which is not evident in the Original; (c) Face—there is virtually a total variance between both the features and expressions of the two subjects, as can be seen from a comparison of the eyebrows, eyes, mouths and chins; (d) Left arm—Accused's upper arm is extended in an almost horizontal plane from the shoulder, whereas Original's is inclined upward from the shoulder at an angle of approximately 30 degrees; (e) Right hand—only two fingers are inclined directly downward in Original, whereas three fingers are so inclined in Accused with the middle finger hidden by the ring finger; (f) Body position—Original is tilted back somewhat from the hips, whereas Accused is in a more nearly vertical position.

Dismissing the action, the court emphasized the general stylistic similarities between the many paintings by Vargas explained the similarities between these two specific works, and that there were sufficient differences in the paintings in issue to rebut a claim of copying.[9] The judge had viewed over one hundred Vargas paintings, all of which portrayed half-naked women with "exaggerated torso and the subtly curved but unduly long leg[s]." The judge recognized that "all [Vargas's] future drawings will bear some similarity to his previous work, whether or not his past creations are before him at the time he is painting. He has a certain type of art in his mind and consequently, that is all he is able to express on the drawing board."[10] On appeal, *Esquire* contended that the judge had erred in that he had not determined whether there had been copying at all. The Court of Appeals for the Seventh Circuit found the argument unsustainable, Circuit Judge Lindley explaining that by describing the alleged infringing drawings as new artworks, the lower court had "impliedly, if not expressly" found that the accused drawings were not copies.

The case highlights clearly the difficulty with proving copying in cases where the work that has said to have been copied is by the very same author. Even if the later work has the same sort of subject matter, the same themes, and is created in the same style, it is not possible to draw any inference that there has been copying (Vaver 2011: 110 n.243). This forces the court to appraise copying by looking at differences rather than similarities. In cases of alleged copying by (B) from a work by (C), the changes made by (B) are irrelevant; the key question is the degree to which (C)'s work is used by (B) (not what (B) adds—though in the United States at least, that would be relevant to a defense of "fair use"). However, in cases of self-copying, such as *Esquire v. Varga*, the court focuses on differences as establishing that there has not been any copying.

1.2 Exceptions to copyright that preserve author freedom

Where an author can be shown to have reproduced material from their own works, the relevant national regime may permit such reuse. The legal provisions fall into two types: those which are specifically formulated as limitations on copyright for the benefit of "authors"; and those which are framed as open-textured standards, but appear to be applied with greater liberality to authors as regards reuse of their own material.

1.2.1 Specific author-protective rules

The most obvious example of a specific provision giving authors freedom to "self-copy" is provided by U.K. law. Section 64 of the U.K.'s Copyright, Designs and Patents Act 1988 (CDPA) declares that

> Where the author of an artistic work is not the copyright owner, he does not infringe the copyright by copying the work in making another artistic work, provided he does not repeat or imitate the main design of the earlier work.[11]

A similar exception has been adopted in many former British colonies,[12] as well as under the Netherlands Copyright Act 1912.[13] It is notable that this exception is limited to painting and is subject to the possible agreement to the contrary. During the passage of what became the CDPA through Parliament, the Government spokesman in the Lords, Lord Beaverbrook, explained that the purpose of section 64 "is to allow an artist to repeat parts of the design of his earlier works without infringing copyright."[14]

The predecessor of section 64 of the U.K. Act has been considered and applied in only one case, *Preston v. Raphael Tuck*.[15] Here Chloe Preston (1887–1969), an artist and illustrator of children's books (most famously the "peek-a-boo" series) objected that Raphael Tuck had been selling a calendar featuring a picture by Preston which had been modified by the manufacturer, and Tuck counter-claimed that Preston herself had infringed copyright in another work that had been assigned to Tuck. That work was called "Floreat Etona," created in 1922, a scene at Lord's cricket ground, on the day of the match between the two most well-known English public schools, Eton and Harrow. The picture featured three Eton boys and one from Harrow. Tuck alleged that Preston herself had infringed copyright by reproducing the image of the Harrow boy in another later work where the boy was presented as of "undetermined school origin."

Preston argued both that "all that [she] did was to reproduce a type invented by her," and that section 2 of the Copyright Act 1911 applied. Justice Tomlin, himself a Harrow boy, rejected the claim to copyright infringement on both grounds. With respect to section 2, he acknowledged that in cases of "partial copying" it was necessary to examine the relation between the part reproduced and the totality. In doing so, he emphasized the absence of insignia or indications as to which school the boy who was featured in the later picture attended.[16] Implicitly, it seems, Tomlin equated reproducing the "main design" with reproducing features that would be of greatest significance to purchasers of the earlier work, and he knew the likely market for the "Floreat Etona" image was former pupils of Eton. In the absence of such insignia, the later image would not jeopardize the market or intended audience of the earlier image.

1.2.2 More generous application of general defenses

In the United States, authors might benefit from the specific application of the flexibility embodied in the famous "fair use" exception. Indeed, given the emphasis placed on "transformative use" by the Supreme Court of the United States in *Campbell v. Acuff Rose* as lying "at the heart of the fair use doctrine's guarantee of breathing space within the confines of copyright,"[17] most uses which fall within the U.K.'s "artist's defence" would probably count as fair use. But this would be so, whether or not the transformation was by the artist him or herself. Is there any reason to think that U.S. courts would offer the artist more freedom to reuse their own work than that offered by section 107 of the U.S. Copyright Act to all?

Justin Hughes is firmly of the view that U.S. copyright law gives "creators more leeway to reuse elements of their creations than we give non-creators to *use* elements of those creations" (Hughes 1998: 134). Likewise, Pamela Samuelson argues that the fair use defense would be applied with greater liberality to the original author (Samuelson 1994: 23–4). Although these views carry considerable weight, it is worth noting that the very limited case-law that exists casts doubt over whether U.S. law offers any special freedom to authors. In *Gross v. Seligman*,[18] the creator of a photograph was held liable for copyright infringement therein when, having assigned the copyright to a third party, he restaged and photographed anew a very similar scene. The photograph in issue, entitled *The Grace of Youth*, featured a nude model. The assignee of copyright took exception when, two years later, the photographer created a similar scene, this time entitled *Cherry Ripe*, using the same model, though on this occasion she held a cherry stem between her teeth. Sitting in the District Court of New York, Judge Learned Hand granted the injunction, and the Court of Appeals affirmed (*New York Times* 1914). He concluded that "the identity of the artist and the many close identities of pose, light, and shade, etc., indicate very strongly that the first picture was used to produce the second."[19] The judge stated that it did not matter whether the photographer had the original picture before him, or merely relied on his memory of it, if the effect of his actions were to reproduce the earlier picture.

German law has allowed a certain degree of authorial self-copying via its notion of "free use" (*freie Benutzung*) in Article 24 of the Copyright Law. This concept, narrower than the U.S. notion of fair use and targeted at re-creation, allows that "an independent work created in the free use of the work of another person may be published or exploited without the consent of the author of the work used." In one notable decision, the statutory precursor of Article 24 was used to justify reuse of material by the same author.[20] An Austrian painter, *Hans Zatzka* (1859–1945),[21] had granted the claimant, an art printer/publisher house (*Adolf May*), rights to make and sell copies of a painting called "*Elfenreigen*," a depiction of a ring of nine dancers. Subsequently, the painter created a somewhat similar painting in the same size called "*Blumenreigen*" and authorized the second defendant *Felix Freund* permission to reprint and sell it. Applying Article 16 of the 1907 KUG,[22] which stated that the "free use" of work was permissible if it resulted in a specific individual creation, the Court of Appeal reversed the finding of infringement by the Landgericht (Regional Court) Dresden on the basis that "*Blumenreigen*" was not a copy of "*Elfenreigen*," but a work of personal artistic character. It explained that every individual work was protected separately and that the protection given to each work did not include "those things that, according to the recognised conventions of art, constitute the available building blocks and tools of artistic endeavour," such as the subject matter, the concerns or goals of an artist or the style he or she uses.[23] Applying these principles, the court found no infringement of the artistic copyright in "*Elfenreigen*": the use was a "free use." Whether such a reuse would be permitted under the existing law is not clear: in 1965 the new Copyright Act "codified" the former rules in Article 24, but did so in textually distinct terms.

Some countries also recognize a right of quotation that could justify some instances of self-copying. The quotation right, though recognized in international law, has not been implemented consistently, with many countries adding additional conditions.[24] Under Article 10(1) of the Berne Convention it appears to be mandatory for members of the Berne Union to allow the making of quotations from a work.[25] The defense is limited to "quotation" from works that have been made available to the public, is subject to a requirement that the source and original author be attributed, only applies to the extent to which the quotation is "justified" by the purpose for which it is being used, and even then must be in accordance with "fair practice." Clearly, such an exception will justify the author's reusing of short passages of text in quotation marks and with full citation. Although the concept of "fair practice" might facilitate broader application to authorial self-quotation than would be offered to third party use of material, it is much less clear that the concept of "quotation" could comfortably be applied to many of the sorts of "self-copying" which we have been considering here.

1.3 Diversity of legal approaches

This discussion highlights a diversity of responses to the question of whether, and if so, in what circumstances, self-copying is unlawful. Under British law, it might be that, outside the particular exceptions of fair quotation, textual recycling (as opposed to artistic reuse) is never permissible (without authorization); whereas in Germany and the United States, textual reuse might be regarded as fair. In the face of divergent approaches, which law should apply to a determination of whether self-copying is ethical? Some commentators have referred to U.S. law; others have claimed to develop standards from specific rules in other national jurisdictions.[26] Insofar as what is being sought is an international ethical standard for publishers, it is not at all obvious why one particular regime or approach should be preferred over any other.

2. Copyright's ethics and the question of self-copying

The second reason one might doubt whether copyright law is a good basis on which to ground the ethics of self-copying is that copyright law itself has been the subject of a great deal of criticism.[27] One such criticism is that copyright law has become "bloated": the subject matter covered and rights conferred have been expanded beyond their justifiable extent, primarily as a result of failings endemic to contemporary political processes—a combination of rent seeking by existing holders of intellectual property rights and an inability of the legislative branches of government to scrutinize effectively the arguments used by such lobbyists (or willingness to confront them) (see Bently 2008: 3–16, 26–41, 57–62). These criticisms raise serious doubts as to whether the current scope of copyright law is itself justified, and in turn suggest that the positive rules of contemporary copyright law are not a suitable benchmark for an ethics of self-copying.[28]

A better starting point for an ethics of self-copying might be to consider how the normative arguments commonly deployed to justify copyright protection might be applied to the question of self-copying. The three most common types of argument are autonomy-based arguments, natural rights ("moral rights") arguments and utilitarian arguments. Without appearing to subscribe to any of the theories (or the conceptions of authorship that they appear to endorse), I want to suggest that all three arguments would justify only relatively narrow limits on self-copying (much narrower than most current copyright laws). More specifically, the autonomy arguments result in so limited a conception of copyright that it would seldom impede authorial self-copying; the personality-based natural rights arguments imply a limited but inalienable moral freedom for authors; and the utilitarian conceptions might well imply an even broader reuse exception in favor of authors.

2.1 Autonomy-based (Kantian) arguments

Drawing on the work of Immanuel Kant, this justification for copyright frames it as a set of rules that are designed to protect an author's "expressive autonomy" (see Treiger-Bar-Am 2007, 2008; Borghi 2011; Biron 2012; Barron 2012). The wrong that copyright infringement seeks to prohibit is "compelled speech," the forcing of the author to speak when he or she does not want to do so. Abraham Drassinower, perhaps the leading exponent of this theory, playfully explains that "copyright infringement is a ventriloquism practised on an unwilling subject. The infringing speaker speaks not from his mouth but from his belly, making it seem that it is another who speaks. This seeming is the wrong to the other, whose mouth is being moved, so to speak, behind her back" (2012: 204–5 n.212; 2015: Ch. 4). For Drassinower, speech is an "interpersonal relationship," more specifically an invitation to dialogue, and such freedom to respond is, in turn, guaranteed by the non-protection ideas and the immunity from liability for fair use, particularly in cases of transformative use (2012: 206–7 n.219; 2015: 7, 8, 55). The unauthorized use of another's expression is to be regarded as lawful "where reasonably necessary" to the author's own engagement (2015: 12, 74, 78). Thus "neither appropriation art nor fan fiction is actionable to the extent that it is an instance of authorial engagement in its own right" (2015: 8). Copyright targets the "parrot" not the "parodist" (2015: 79).

On one reading of Drassinower's account, a prohibition on self-copying is not justified at all (rather than needing to be accommodated within an exception). After all, there is no violation of the author's autonomy when the author himself speaks again in the same words.[29] Indeed such reiteration may be an affirmation that the author continues to subscribe to their previously stated views. If the nature and role of copyright reflected this approach, the law would offer an extremely wide reuse freedom. However, such a reading fails to take account of the limitations inherent in Drassinower's project. Drassinower does not claim to be offering an account of *all* features of copyright law, and thus does not address the issue of assignments. In fact, Kantian norms would generally support the principle of enforcement of contractual promises and respect for property. Thus, if an author has assigned the exclusive right (seen as a "prerogative" rather than as "property") to "repeat or reproduce an act of authorship" to a publisher, they are not entitled to reprint the work even though such reprinting would not involve *someone else* speaking in the voice of the author. Although Drassinower does not purport to be repeating Kant,[30] the German philosopher in fact said as much when he addressed the issue of the lawfulness of reprinting books in 1785 (Kant 1785).

What about reworking of a work in which copyright has been assigned? The better view appears to be that Kantian principles do not afford better protection to authors than to third parties, but that the freedom that Kantian interpretations of copyright offer would legitimate much "self-copying." According to Drassinower, "independent creation" is one of the fundamental principles of copyright, insofar as it acknowledges a place for all authors; while copyright should not operate to prevent *any* person from speaking *in their own voice*, so that insofar as an author is continuing to develop and express ideas or themes, copyright law should not prevent this. In contrast, there would be no basis in such a theory for allowing an author to (for example) re-communicate significant amounts of works in which they have assigned rights to publishers (for example, by publishing a "complete works of…").

2.2 Natural rights arguments

A second set of arguments commonly used to justify copyright draw on natural rights precepts. The typical premise for such arguments in relation to copyright regulation is that "works are not regular commodities, but rather expressions of the author's inner self" (Rigamonti 2007: 73), the "extension" of the author into the world. According to natural rights theories (of this type), the author has a natural right not just to the economic benefits from exploitation of the work, but also certain "moral interests." These moral interests are the ones closest to the "inner self," and are normally regarded as including the right to decide whether, when and how the work is disclosed to the public (divulgation), the right to be attributed when the work is exploited, and the right to prevent distortion or mutilation of the work (the so-called "right of integrity"). Importantly, the moral rights are regarded as inalienable.

Such arguments seem also to point towards legal rules that recognize authorial immunities from legal liability. In particular, while any single discrete work might be protected by copyright, an author's personality underpins not simply each particular work, but his or her complete "oeuvre." Authorship might involve the elaboration of stories and events in the life of a particular character through *a series* of short stories or novels. Authorship might involve the process of developing ideas or theories progressively through *a series* of articles, each building on the arguments or conclusions of the earlier articles. Authorship may involve a sustained playing with themes or motifs.[31] In all these cases the activities of a particular author will produce a body of works that are themselves connected. Although the "idea-expression" distinction may offer some freedom to the author, the overlaps between works might relate to material that counts as expression.[32] Insofar as these connections involve expressive material, any particular work might reproduce an original part of an earlier work. Indeed, there may be some parts of the work that are more intimately linked to the author than others.

At the very least, even after assigning copyright in a single "work," an author needs to retain the ability to continue to explore themes and characters, to use motifs and stylistic devices. Even if these form part of the property in the work assigned, the authors must retain the right or freedom to use these raw materials in subsequent works. Under a personalist conception of creativity, it seems that copyright should in no circumstances operate to limit the creative freedom of individuals insofar as they are continuing to pursue and develop ideas, themes, or subjects with which they have previously engaged.

Relatedly, authorship can be conceived as an expressive practice in which outputs, even on different subjects, have similarities that we would call "style." Sometimes the term "style" is used to describe the broad style of a movement associated with a number of artists (cubism, for example), but "style" might comprise characteristics that are individual to a particular writer.[33] The continued use of such style might be inevitable (insofar as that is the only way in which the artist or author is able, willing or happy to work) or even necessary for them to achieve what they are seeking to achieve.

It is notable that the moral rights literature does not generally include such an immunity when articulating the legal protection of an author's moral interests.[34] This may be because authors moral and economic interests have been generally articulated as "rights." However, historically, at least in France, many of the early interventions in favor of authors and artists occurred in the context of contractual disputes between authors and their assignees/publishers.[35] In the context of contracting, moral "rights" often operate as mandatory rules of contractual practice (allowing the author certain powers to control how an authorized exploiter carries out acts of exploitation) (see Rigamonti 2007: 72). "Authorial immunities" can be conceived in a similar manner, as overriding terms of contracts between authors and assignees of copyright, so as to reserve to the author the freedom to continue to exploit the work him or herself (Hughes 1998: 131–2, 138). For this reason, such immunities should not be capable of being overridden by contract.[36]

2.3 The utilitarian incentive analysis

The third type of justification for copyright, dominant in the literature from the United States, views the purpose of copyright in utilitarian terms: copyright constitutes an exception to general freedom to copy, to express oneself and to compete, that is justified only insofar as it is a necessary mechanism to promote investment in the production of works. As copyright serves a public interest of incentivizing the production of works, it becomes especially problematic where rights conferred by copyright impede further production of works.[37] In such cases, the optimal solution exists if the copyright vested in the earlier creator can be limited without damaging the *ex ante* incentive effect, and in such a way that there is no disincentive or impediment to the production of subsequent works.

Special rules protecting authors against liability for self-copying have been readily fitted into this analysis. For example, Pamela Samuelson observes that "[a]ny society committed to promoting an abundance of authors and works of authorship must provide breathing room for iterative copying that is a necessary part of authorial work" (Samuelson 2009: 2577).[38] On the assumption that authors will be more productive if they are allowed to reuse material from their earlier works, a utilitarian conception of copyright ought to allow for reuse of material (even where rights have been assigned) if to do so does not significantly undermine the incentives to produce in the first place. Such an approach would likely exempt, in most cases, situations where an author could not help but develop ideas or themes or continue to utilize their own style. It might, however, go further than the immunity conceived under a "natural rights" conception of copyright, and allow reuse where it was merely desirable to maintain a continued flow of creative output (for example, insofar as an artist has developed a market or group of fans that expects the artist to continue to produce in the same style, as might be the case with singer-songwriters) (see Hughes 1998: 131). Seeking to explain the practices of self-borrowing by some of the greatest composers, Winston Dean listed a variety of motives: "to save time or trouble, to preserve what seems too good to waste, to gratify the public or the performer with the same titbit over again, to develop material that offers a further creative stimulus—all have played a part. So have less conscious processes, such as the apparently accidental discovery of the perfect context for an idea born in quite different circumstances" (Dean 1960: 238). The utilitarian conception of the immunity might also justify reuse of material simply where it is convenient. An author might wish to draw on their own work because the earlier work says precisely what they wanted to say in the way they wanted to say it. In particular in circumstances where the description is technical or primarily informative,[39] there would be no social benefit in requiring them to rewrite it. (Indeed, it might be argued that forcing an author to adopt a new form of expression necessarily introduces ambiguities, in the same way that concurring judges often prefer to signify accordance with the terms of another judgment, rather than to pen their own).[40] Insofar as they deploy the material in building something that is, of itself, original and valuable, then it is simply efficient to permit replication of earlier works.

Why should a utilitarian conception distinguish between authorial reuses and uses by third parties? If it is permissible for the author to reproduce a section from an existing work (in which they no longer hold copyright) and incorporate it into a later work because it is convenient, efficient, and facilitates the production of that new work, should that not also be the case for third parties? The answer might possibly be "yes," because maximizing utility is an empirical exercise. But there are at least two good reasons to expect that the "incentives–access" trade-off at the heart of the utilitarian calculus as to the scope of copyright might differ in the case of the original author compared with third parties. The first reason is that the connection between an author and their own earlier work means it is likely to be *especially* convenient for them to reuse material therefrom—as part of a continuing project, or a further elaboration. The second is that the impact on the publisher (and thus on the copyright "incentive") is likely to be less if the broad immunity in relation to reuse is limited to the author's reuse in their own work. Publishers frequently allow authors freedoms that they would not offer the public.

The utilitarian calculus would, however, suggest at least two significant limitations on any immunity. First, it must not be such as to undermine the ability of the copyright to fulfill its role as an incentive to produce the initial work. This suggests that the immunity provided to an author to reuse material must not interfere with the expected or normal exploitation of the earlier work by the assignee. Quite when this would occur might vary from work to work. Take the example of a painting; it might be that for the same artist to produce another version would significantly diminish the value of the original. This could explain why so many of the statutory immunities which relate to artistic works prohibit the making of any version which repeats the main design of the earlier work. However in other fields, such as musical composition, the value may lie in the cumulation of detail, and the general shape and feel of the song might be regarded as standardized or part of the artist's style. Limiting the freedom of some composers so that they must not copy "main design" of the music of a particular song might be unduly restrictive of the composer, and ineffective to protect what is really of value to both society and to the copyright holder. For this reason, a utilitarian version of authorial immunities might best be achieved in open-textured terms that can be concretized in specific instances in the light of the particular practices of the cultural sector in question.

It is not obvious that under the utilitarian approach the immunity would need to be conditioned on attributing the original source, though this might again depend on the specific situation in hand. In the case of a journalist, for example, who wishes to create a collection of his earlier works, it seems likely that the publishers of the journals would value their attribution (as confirming the quality or prescience of their editorial decision making), while recognizing that such republication would not interfere with their primary market. Where a motif is reused by an artist over and over again, as with Matisse's bilboquets, such attribution would be more problematic, and less obviously useful in minimizing the effect of the authorial reuse exception on initial incentives.

A second difference between the utilitarian and natural rights conception of an "authorial immunity" concerns the interaction with contract law (and practice). As we have observed, the natural rights conception of "moral immunities" is linked to an author's personality right, as part of the human right or freedom to create, and is consequently inalienable. In contrast, the utilitarian conception is built on social benefit, which turns on convenience and efficiency in modes of creative production (and development). Whether the utilitarian immunity should give way to contractual agreement to the contrary ought, in principle, to turn on whether permitting variation of the utilitarian calculus of rights and immunities will increase or decrease overall utility. Contracting away the exception might be 'welfare-enhancing' if, for example, the author gains a higher price, is not prevented from doing any further work he may wish to do, and the assignee is able to exploit the work to greater effect. However, it is conceivable that permitting contractual variation of the optimal position might reduce the utility-enhancing effect: if authors readily limited their freedom, only to find in due course that they were not permitted to utilize the same style, themes, etc. There might be intermediate positions that are more utility enhancing: for example, permitting waiver only where the author has received legal advice or is given significant compensation.[41] The important point is that it seems conceivable under a utilitarian conception of authorial immunities that contracting the freedom away might be possible.

2.4 Copyright's ethics and self-copying

The three dominant justificatory theories of copyright thus would appear to imply that significant limitations on the scope of such laws are appropriate in cases of "self-copying." While few positive laws offer this level of flexibility to authors, it seems likely that this is because the applicable legal provisions have been formulated without "self-copying" in mind. Only occasionally has the legislator explicitly considered the question of authorial self-copying. As a consequence, the theories, rather than the laws, offer a better starting point for the development of an ethics of self-copying.

In codifying such an ethics, one possibility would be to select between the theories. However, there is no consensus as to which theory is the "best" or most readily defensible (and it would not seem appropriate for a particular journal or group of journals to make such a selection). Moreover, if one is looking for an internationally applicable ethical standard, it needs to be acknowledged that certain theories have more support in some places than others. The development of an internationally applicable rule then might best be achieved by locating a standard that is compatible with all three theories. More specifically, it would be defensible to propose a rule that self-copying is unethical where it would be regarded as falling within the justifiable scope of protection under all three theories or approaches. In the context of periodical publishing, the effect of so doing is likely to be that only cases of replication (text recycling as opposed to rewriting) of substantially the whole of a research paper would be regarded as unethical. Less extensive practices of self-copying, which might be regarded as the continued exercise of an author's autonomy, their right to create, or simply to facilitate their productivity (without undermining substantially returns to the copyright-holder)—and thus ethical under any of the three theories—would not fall within the scope of the prohibition.[42]

Notes

1 Bruton 2014: 181 ("violating others' copyrights is certainly unethical"); 182 ("duplicate publication may violate a publisher's copyright and is for that reason both illegal and unethical. This is hardly a mere technicality, since the economic viability of much academic publishing depends on copyrights"). The American Psychological Association's guidance, for example, directly links permissible self-copying with copyright norms when it permits "text-recycling" that complies with "fair use" standards: see Callahan 2014: 5, 9. Perhaps the discussion of self-plagiarism that deals most extensively with copyright infringement is Andreescu 2013: 786–8.

2 Insofar as limitations that benefit authors are understood as exceptions, Article 9(2) of Berne, Article 13 of TRIPs and Article 10 of the WIPO Copyright Treaty constrain national action. However, no limits exist in international copyright law to national rules formulated in terms of contractual regulation.

3 For British law, see *Designers Guild v. Russell Williams* [2000] 1 *WLR* 2416, 2425 (Lord Millett); *Mitchell v. BBC* [2011] EWPCC 42, [25].

4 Or where a self-copyist is involved in replicating their own work, and indirectly reusing the contributions of others: *Lucasfilm v Ainsworth* [2009] *FSR* (2) 103.

5 *Schiller & Schmidt v. Nordisco Corp.*, 969 F.2d 410, 414 (7th Cir. 1992) ("one is also more likely to duplicate one's own work without copying than another person would be likely to do. If Cézanne painted two pictures of Mont St. Victoire, we should expect them to look more alike than if Matisse had painted the second, even if Cézanne painted the second painting from life rather than from the first painting.")

6 MacDonald 1965–6: 27 ("At the smaller end of the scale, self-borrowing merges with the normal stylistic fingerprints to be found in the work of any composer"); Sadler 1989: 260.

7 81 F. Supp. 306 (N.D. Il. 1948), *affirmed in part, reversed in part,* 185 F.2d 14 (7th Cir. 1950), 307–8. See also: *Franklin Mint Corp. v. National Wildlife Art Exchange Inc.,* 195 U.S.P.Q. 31, 34–35 (E.D.Pa. 1977), 575 F.2d 62 (3d Cir. 1978); *Freefall Trading 211 (Pty) Ltd. v. Proplink Publishing (Pty) Ltd.* [2005] ZAWCHC 87 at [18]–[24] (S. Afr. H.C.)

8 I am grateful to Professor Stephen Goddard and Andrea Pitt of the Spencer Museum of Art at the University of Kansas who tracked down these images for me.

9 81 F. Supp. 306, 309.

10 Ibid.

11 This repealed and replaced section 9(9) of the 1956 Act which was significantly more elaborate, which, in turn, derived from section 2(1)(ii) of the 1911 Act and proposals that can be traced back over the previous half-century to a Bill which Lord Westbury presented to Parliament in 1869. *Royal Commissioners' Report*, London (1878), in L. Bently and M. Kretschmer, *Primary Sources on Copyright (1450–1900)*, www.copyrighthistory.org: xxi [123–4].

12 Copyright and Related Rights Act 2000 (Ireland), section 95; Copyright Act (Canada) section 32(2); Copyright Act 1968 (Australia), section 72; Copyright Act (cap 63) (Singapore), section 71; Copyright Act (1962 No 33) (New Zealand), section 20(9).

13 Article 24 (in English at http://www.wipo.int/wipolex/en/text.jsp?file_id=128942) states that: "Unless otherwise agreed, the author of a painting continues, notwithstanding the assignment of his copyright, to be entitled to make similar paintings." Unless they can be shoe-horned into Article 5(3)(d) of the EU Information Society Directive, 2001/29/EC, (the quotation exception), Section 64 of the CDPA and Article 24 of the Dutch law appear justified only under Article 5(3)(o), and thus only insofar they are limited to analog uses.

14 Hansard, HL Deb 12 November 1987, vol. 489, col. 1539.

15 [1926] Ch 667. Lord Williams of Elvel, Hansard, HL Deb 8 December 1987, vol.

491, col. 190 (Committee stage) (stating that Section 9(9) of the 1956 Act "had never, in the experience of our advisers, been brought into play at all").

16 [1926] Ch 667, 675–6.

17 501 US 569 (1994).

18 212 F.930 (2d Cir. 1914).

19 Many commentators have puzzled over the *Gross v. Seligman* decision. A later case suggests that the court had wrongly relied on the English House of Lords' decision in *Hanfstaengl v. Baines & Co.* [1895] A.C. 20 which the Second Circuit misunderstood as finding infringement, when the opposite was the case; see Seidel 2001 (describing Judge Cahn's research in *Franklin Mint Corp. v. National Wildlife Art Exchange Inc.*, 195 U.S.P.Q. 31, 34–5 (E.D.Pa. 1977)); Hughes 1998: 127 (arguing that the "*Gross* opinion is probably wrong on a factual analysis: it appears that Seligman's new photograph was visibly different from *Grace of Youth*"); Callmann 1940: 658–9 (in reprint, 897) (suggesting that the case was inappropriately presented as a copyright case and that the "real cause of action" was passing off—the public would not realize that *Cherry Ripe* was different from *Grace of Youth*—and interference with contractual relations (presumably the interference by Seligman in the contract between Rochlitz and Gross)).

20 Note also the Italian Supreme Court decision, Court of Cassation, January 12, 2007, No. 581, *Diritto di Autore*, 2007, 510, described by Musso (2015), to the effect that two computer programs created by the same firm with the same functions, but different in structure and organization, were both original, so that the later program did not infringe rights transferred to the purchaser of copyright in the earlier one.

21 Reichsgericht, Judgment from 14 January 1928—I 60/27. My thanks to Professor Alexander Peukert for drawing my attention to the case, and to Janine Discher (Cambridge LLM 2014-5) for assistance with translation.

22 Gesetz betreffend das Urheberrecht an Werken der bildenden Künste und der Photographie, 1907.

23 409 (citations omitted). The court went on to consider the possibility of liability based on contract, rejecting the claim.

24 Such a defense was recognized unconditionally in the U.K. only from October 1, 2014, prior to which time there had been a requirement that the quotation be for purposes of "criticism or review."

25 Berne Convention, Art 10(1).

26 Bretag and Mahmud 2009: 197 (defining self-plagiarism as "10% or more textual re-use of any one previous publication by the author without attribution" by reference to the Australian Copyright Act 1968, section 40, which permits reproduction of works for research or study, and indicates that an article in a periodical or 10 percent of a published work will be regarded as a "reasonable

portion," and thus a fair dealing). It is not obvious to me that section 40 has any bearing on the question of what an author may reproduce in later published work from earlier work in which they no longer own copyright.

27 None of the commentaries that advocate use of copyright rules as a mechanism for defining the ethics of self-copying explicitly endorses a position on the existence of a moral obligation to obey the law. Although just about everyone agrees that such a moral obligation could not oblige subjects to carry out obviously immoral acts, the question of whether and why such an obligation exists, and, if so, its nature and extent, has generated a voluminous debate. This is not the place to attempt to survey it, except to say that according to some such accounts, there might be an ethical obligation not to engage in self-copying *because* there is a legal obligation not to do so.

28 One might say (in Razian terms) that in such circumstances, the legal rules no longer carry moral force (i.e. there is no longer a moral obligation to obey the law) because the rules are not meant to reflect the "balance of reasons" which would apply when each individual decided upon the "rightness" of particular acts.

29 Drassinower 2015: 116 ("copyright infringement impinges on the author's autonomy as a speaker").

30 Drassinower discusses Kant explicitly in (2015): 112–13, explaining "[w]hile Kantian, the argument I offer is not Kant's."

31 During the passage of the 1988 Act, Lord Hutchinson argued that "surely […] no artist can be restrained from creating numerous versions of the same theme. All through the ages artists have created versions of the same theme. Indeed, *artists almost always become obsessed with one particular subject.*" Hansard, HL Deb 12 November 1987, vol. 489, col. 1500 (emphasis added).

32 For example, the composer Iannis Xenakis, admitting to reusing, stated in 1981, "Therefore, a whole vocabulary, at the highest level, forms itself and constitutes an artist's style as in Brahms, Beethoven, Debussy or Messiæn. There are strata of objects, or architectures, or entire sequences taken and used, reused, reemployed until others come to replace them"; cited in Gibson 2011: xix.

33 In art criticism it is said that "style" helps define from whom, when, and where a work originated; see e.g. Goodman 1975.

34 See Roeder 1940: 558 (describing positive right to create); Strauss 1955: 507 ("the right to safeguard his artistic reputation"); Katz 1951a; Katz 1951b: 102 ("The moral right is *the right of the author to create*, or not to create, to present the creation to the public in a form of his choice, or to withhold it, to dispose of this form as he alone desires, and to demand that his personality be respected in so far as it relates to his status as an author" [emphasis added]). Cf. Simon 1981: 74.

35 A number of contemporary commentators have noted this link too: see e.g. Netanel 1992–3: 350 n.383.

36 Seen in this way, authorial immunities and moral rights are analogs to the common law prohibition on unreasonable restraints of trade, a doctrine which prohibits employers from restricting any activity of an ex-employee that goes beyond what is necessary to protect the ex-employer's legitimate proprietary interests.

37 Additional incentives might be problematic even if they did not impede further creation, simply because they might cause resources to be diverted from other productive activities without significant social benefits.

38 See also Melville 1994: 427 ("since every author is only a finite source of ideas and expressions, copyright law may undermine its Constitutional purpose by chilling authorship. In addition, variations on a theme are often used to push the frontiers of an art. The spirit of experimentation may be stifled if copyright law is too restrictive").

39 In contrast, in some fields, the social benefit lies in the particular expressive form, so that such an immunity might be regarded as undesirable. In many cases, of course, authors' ideas alter so that they will no longer be happy with describing the same phenomenon in the same way.

40 It is for this reason that in scientific publication it is often regarded as acceptable to reproduce the "methodology" section even if it has already been published: Bruton 2014: 184 (giving the example of *Anesthesia & Analgesia's* "Guide for Authors"); Committee on Publication Ethics 2014 ("large amounts of text recycled in the methods might be more acceptable than a similar amount recycled in the discussion"); Callahan 2014: 4 (citing authors who argue that "scholars can, do, and even should reuse their written words and ideas, within reason"); Cronin 2013 (offering a range of circumstances where reuse might be justifiable).

41 Compare the legal responses to agreements by employees that restrict their ability to operate in certain fields in the post-employment period. In some countries, such restrictions are permissible as long as the ex-employee is remunerated; in other jurisdictions, they are prohibited irrespective of the level of remuneration the employee has received. See Aplin et al. 2012: Ch. 12.

42 My thanks go to those who commented on earlier drafts of this paper at the 'Fair copyright' conference, Tel Aviv University in January 2014 and in Bielefeld in July 2014, in particular to Professors Abraham Drassinower, Darren Hick, Marc Perlman, Alexander Peukert, Pamela Samuelson, Dr. Richard Danbury. Ms. Janine Discher (Cambridge LLM 2014–15) gave valuable research assistance.

References

Andreescu, L. (2013), "Self-Plagiarism in Academic Publishing: The Anatomy of a Misnomer," *Science and Engineering Ethics* 19 (3): 775–97.

Aplin, T., L. Bently, P. Johnson, and S. Malynicz (2012), *Gurry on Breach of Confidence: The Protection of Confidential Information*, 2nd edn, Oxford: Oxford University Press.

Barron, A. (2012), "Kant, Copyright and Communicative Freedom," *Law and Philosophy* 31 (1): 1–48.

Bently, L. (2008), "*R. v. The Author*: From Death Penalty to Community Service," *Columbia Journal of Law and the Arts* 32 (1): 1–109.

Bently, L. and B. Sherman (2014), *Intellectual Property Law*, 4th edn, Oxford: Oxford University Press.

Biron, L. (2012), "Public Reason, Communication and Intellectual Property," in A. Lever (ed.), *New Frontiers in the Philosophy of Intellectual Property*, 225–60, Cambridge: Cambridge University Press.

Borghi, M. (2011), "Copyright and Truth," *Theoretical Inquiries in Law* 12 (1): 1–27.

Bretag, T. and S. Mahmud (2009), "Self-Plagiarism or Appropriate Textual Re-use?" *Journal of Academic Ethics* 7 (3): 193–205.

Bruton, S. V. (2014), "Self-Plagiarism and Textual Recycling: Legitimate Forms of Research Misconduct," *Accountability in Research*, 21 (3): 176–97.

Bruton, S. V. and J. R. Rachal (2015), "Education Journal Editors' Perspectives on Self-Plagiarism," *Journal of Academic Ethics* 13 (1): 13–25.

Callahan, J. (2014), "Creation of a Moral Panic? Self-Plagiarism in the Academy," *Human Resources Development Review* 13 (1): 3–10.

Callmann, R. (1940), "Copyright and Unfair Competition," *Louisiana Law Review*, 2 (4): 648–68 (reprinted as "Copyright and Unfair Competition," *JPOS* 22 (12): 885–908).

Committee on Publication Ethics (2014), "How To Deal with Text Recycling," *BioMed Central*. Available online: http://publicationethics.org/files/BioMed%20Central_text_recycling_editorial_guidelines_1.pdf

Cronin, B. (2013), "Self-plagiarism: An Odious Oxymoron," *Journal of the American Society for Information Science and Technology* 64 (5): 873.

Dean, W. (1960), "Bizet's Self-Borrowings," *Music and Letters* 41 (3): 238–44.

Drassinower, A. (2012), "Copyright Infringement as Compelled Speech," in A. Lever (ed.), *New Frontiers in The Philosophy of Intellectual Property*, 203–24, Cambridge: Cambridge University Press.

Drassinower, A. (2015), *What's Wrong with Copying?*, Cambridge, MA: Harvard University Press.

Garfinkel, M. (2014), "A Fresh Look at Self-Plagiarism," *Professional Ethics Report* 27 (4): 1–3.

Gibson, B. (2011), *The Instrumental Music of Iannis Xenakis: Theory, Practice, Self-Borrowing*, Hillsdale, NY: Pendragon Press, 2011.

Goodman, N. (1975), "The Status of Style," *Critical Inquiry* 1 (4): 799–811.
Hughes, J. (1998), "The Personality Interest of Artists and Inventors in Intellectual Property," *Cardozo Arts & Entertainment Law Journal* 16 (1): 81–181.
Kant, I. (1785), "Von der Unrechtmäßigkeit des Büchernachdrucks," trans. F. Kawohl, in L. Bently and M. Kretschmer, *Primary Sources on Copyright (1450–1900)*. Available online: www.copyrighthistory.org.
Katz, A. (1951a), "The Doctrine of Moral Right and American Copyright Law," *Southern California Law Review* 24 (2): 375–427.
Katz, A. (1951b), "The Doctrine of Moral Right and American Copyright Law: A Proposal," *Copyright Law Symposium* 4: 78–156.
MacDonald, H. (1965–6), "Berlioz's Self-Borrowings," *Proceedings of the Royal Musical Association*, 92nd Sess.: 27–44.
Melville, D. W. (1994), "An Author's Right to Return to a Theme: Protecting Artistic Freedom in Visual, Musical and Literary Works," *Loyola Los Angeles Entertainment Law Journal* 14 (3): 427–64.
Musso, A. (2015), "Italy," in L. Bently (ed.), *International Copyright Law and Practice*, New York: Lexis-Nexis.
Netanel, N. (1992–3), "Copyright Alienability Restrictions and the Enhancement of Author Autonomy: A Normative Evaluation," *Rutgers Law Journal* 24: 347–442.
New York Times, "Art Picture of Girl in Copyright Suit," June 29, 1914: 9.
Rigamonti, C. P. (2007), "The Conceptual Transformation of Moral Rights," *American Journal of Comparative Law* 55 (1): 67–122.
Roeder, M. A. (1940), "The Doctrine of Moral Right: A Study in the Law of Artists, Authors and Creators," *Harvard Law Review* 53 (4): 554–78.
Sadler, G. (1989), "A Re-examination of Rameau's Self-Borrowings," in J. H. Heyer (ed.), *Jean-Baptiste Lully and the French Baroque: Essays in Honor of James R. Anthony*, 259–89, Cambridge: Cambridge University Press.
Samuelson, P. (1994), "Self-plagiarism or Fair Use," *Communications of the ACM* 37 (8): 21–5.
Samuelson, P. (2009), "Unbundling Fair Uses," *Fordham Law Review* 77 (5): 2537–621.
Scanlon, P. M. (2007), "Song from Myself: An Anatomy of Self-Plagiarism," *Plagiary*, 2 (17): 1–10.
Seidel, A. (2001), "A Case of Variations on a Theme," *The Philadelphia Lawyer* 64 (1). Available online: http://www.philadelphiabar.org/page/TPLSpring01Variations.
Simon, J. (1981), *Das allgemeine Persönlichkeitsrecht und seine gewerblichen Erscheinungsformen*, Berlin: Duncker & Humblot.
Strauss, W. (1955), "The Moral Right of the Author," *American Journal of Comparative Law* 4 (4): 506–38.
Treiger-Bar-Am, L. K. (2007), "Authors' Rights as a Limit to Copyright Control," in F. Macmillan (ed.), *New Directions in Copyright*, vol. 6, 359–76, Cheltenham: Edward Elgar.

Treiger-Bar-Am, L. K. (2008), "Kant on Copyright: Rights of Transformative Authorship," *Cardozo Arts and Entertainment Law Journal* 25 (3): 1059–103.

Vaver, D. (2011), *Intellectual Property Law*, 2nd edn, Toronto: Irwin Law.

16

Ethical Approaches for Copying Digital Artifacts: What Would the Exemplary Person [*junzi*]/a Good Person [*phronimos*] Say?

Charles Melvin Ess

1. Introduction

In this chapter I approach questions of copying first by way of a cross-cultural comparison between classic "Western" and "Eastern" understandings of copyright and property. This approach simultaneously introduces three main ethical frameworks: (Western) deontology, utilitarianism, and then *virtue ethics*. I take up virtue ethics here initially as it undergirds strongly positive attitudes towards copying, in contrast with typical arguments from deontology and utilitarianism. Virtue ethics further forces us to consider the most basic philosophical notions of selfhood: briefly, virtue ethics rests upon a strongly *relational* sense of self, in contrast with strongly individualistic understandings of selfhood that background deontology and utilitarianism. These conceptual connections will help establish a basic framework correlating our conceptions of selfhood with foundational notions of property and privacy. Most simply: more individualistic conceptions of selfhood correlate with more exclusive notions of property, such that copying without requisite permission is usually sanctioned, while more relational conceptions of selfhood correlate with more inclusive notions of property, whereby copying is often a positive *virtue*. In parallel, more individual selfhood requires *privacy* as a positive good, *vis-à-vis* privacy as morally suspect for relational selves.

I then explore shifting attitudes towards and practices of privacy and property as indexing a shifting emphasis in Western societies from more individual towards more relational selfhood. This shift in selfhood thus helps explain and to some degree justify movements away from classic (high modern) notions of copyright as protecting individual, *exclusive* property, towards more *inclusive* attitudes and practices, as exemplified and formalized under Free/Libre Open Source Software (FLOSS) and Creative Commons licensing.

Contra the temptation to view individual/relational selfhood and exclusive/inclusive property as exclusive binaries, I then explore more carefully recent developments in social science and philosophy that rather foreground hybrid notions—most importantly, contemporary understandings of *relational autonomy*, especially as these correlate with Helen Nissenbaum's increasingly important understanding of privacy as "contextual integrity" (2010). I seek to show that these developments are not solely theoretical, but in fact can be seen to operate in practice in important ways, taking Norway as my example.

All of this suggests that we will see a continuing hybridization of what might initially seem to be opposite understandings of selfhood and thereby property, with increasing emphasis on property, especially in digital contexts, as more of an inclusive rather than exclusive right. To see how this is so, I conclude with three brief explorations of copyright questions from the standpoint of deontology, utilitarianism, and finally virtue ethics.

2. Copyright: Initial cross-cultural considerations

On the one hand, there are clear and important distinctions between European and American understandings and traditions of copyright and copyright law. To begin with, European approaches emphasize first of all the moral rights of the author. In this way, copyright is justified as an intrinsic *right of the author*, as conjoined with a foundational recognition of the author's identity or personhood. In this tradition, a creative work is seen "as an artifact that has been invested with some measure of the author's personality or that reflects the author's *individuality* [so that out] of respect for the *autonomy* and humanity of the author, that artifact deserves legal recognition" (Burk 2007: 96, emphasis added). Such an approach is consistent with strongly deontological ethics, as affiliated first of all with Kant. Indeed, the German Federal Constitution (*Grundgesetz für die Bundesrepublik Deutschland*) articulates *Urheberrechte* (rights of the author) in ways closely connected with "personality rights" (*Persönlichkeitsrechte*) that ultimately rest on the idea of a human being as an autonomous self, the dignity (*Würde*) of which must be acknowledged and protected.[1] Kant would be pleased.

Indeed, as the German Federal Constitution further exemplifies, this Kantian conception of the human being as an autonomous being grounds still more broadly the liberal-democratic state, whose primary role is just to protect the rights that unfold from and are required by human autonomy. Especially in the case of author's rights, these rights are defined along the lines of property understood as *exclusive* rather than *inclusive* property. That is, where "property" entails a right to have access to or use a given entity, such a right can be construed as either inclusive or exclusive. An *inclusive* property right recognizes a particular person or entity as a primary owner, but his or her rights do not automatically exclude others from accessing or using a property. In Norway and the Baltic countries more broadly, for example, a (premodern) conception of inclusive property still holds in the *allmennsretten* (all people's rights—more colloquially translated as "rights of access"). This includes rights to go on foot (or on skis) wherever one likes in uncultivated country; pick berries, mushrooms, and flowers; and pitch a tent for two nights, before needing to ask permission of the landowner ([Norwegian] Outdoor Recreation Act, 1957). By contrast, following the Enclosure movement of the seventeenth and eighteenth centuries in England, property rights become increasingly defined in *exclusive* terms—i.e. by default only the owner enjoys access rights (cf. Tavani 2012: 256f.; cf. Peukert 2014).

Copyright as an exclusive right is further established on *utilitarian* grounds. That is, copyright and other forms of intellectual property protection are justified as these contribute to the larger public good over the long run:

> authors, artists, software designers, and other creative agents will take the trouble to innovate and develop new products and services that will benefit the larger public only if those agents can themselves be assured of a significant personal reward—primarily in terms of money or other economic goods.
>
> Burk 2007: 96

However different these two modes of justification may be, for our purposes it suffices to note that both justify copyright as an individual and exclusive property right.

By contrast—and as intimated in the example of the *allmennsretten*—in premodern societies both Eastern and Western property notions were frequently more *inclusive* than *exclusive*. As a particular and well-known example: within Confucian tradition, the production of a book—as the most well-known example, *The Analects* or sayings of Confucius—is understood primarily as a beneficent act of sharing for the benefit of others; by the same token, copying is understood as an act of respect for the master, and as a way of appropriating these essential lessons. As further exemplified by medieval scribes in the West, copying manifests the highest respect for the work, and so constitutes a religious act of devotion and piety (Burk 2007: 101). Both examples, more foundationally, rest on strongly *relational* understandings of selfhood. Very briefly, selfhood and identity are constituted through the multiple relationships that a given person may have with others—beginning with familial relationships, and extending from there through the larger society and (super)natural orders. One *is* one's relationships—and to remove any one of the relationships defining the self is thereby to alter and diminish the self. As should be apparent, for such relational selves, property is by default *inclusive*: most sharply, there *is* no atomistic individual as conceptualized Western modernity who could justify or lay claim to *individual* property in the inclusive sense.

Finally, as we will soon see more carefully, such relational selves are primarily oriented towards virtue ethics. Virtue ethics foregrounds the acquisition and practice of specific habits and abilities ("virtues") that are seen to contribute to both individual contentment (*eudaimonia*) and larger social and (super) natural harmonies. In this light, as we will see by way of conclusion, copying an important text entails the acquisition and practice of important *virtues*—manifestly, the practice of respect, as well as care and patience. In particular, as the Western example of the commonplace book (to be discussed below) suggests, copying as a way of appropriating important examples and lessons from a master text thereby contributes to reflection upon and *cultivation* of one's own ethical judgment (*phronesis*) and thereby one's character as a human being. Broadly stated, then, what is for relational selves and inclusive understandings of property the *virtues* of copying become for individual selves and exclusive property concepts the vice of copyright violation.

Still more broadly, we can now see a strong correlation between selfhood, privacy, and property. For the relational self, the default understanding of property as an inclusive one suggests that there is something excessively selfish and greedy about some form of exclusive property—of attempting to keep something exclusively for oneself. By the same token, "privacy" for the relational self can only be understood as a moral negative—as an effort to hide something shameful or dirty (Lü 2005). In contrast, as we emphasize especially strongly atomistic versions of a more individual self in Western modernity, so we justify both exclusive property and strong notions of individual privacy as a positive good (see Ess 2013: 58–61).

3. Changing notions of selfhood, privacy, and property

While these contrasts are sharp and, I hope, clear, at the same time they should not be misread. That is, especially with regard to the foundational notions of selfhood, the distinction between individual and relational selfhood is not a simple exclusive binary; rather, as Charles Taylor (1989: 112–13) points out, even the most relational self is in important ways individual, while the most atomistic self is relational (e.g. insofar as such a self employs a shared language).

Similarly, while these contrasts were fairly reliable markers of the differences between Western and Eastern societies in the previous century, for a host of complex reasons these contrasts are blurring (Ess 2013: 62–8). In particular, Western conceptions of selfhood, precisely as indexed by changing attitudes towards and practices of both privacy and copying, are shifting towards more relational emphases.

3.1 Relational selfhood and privacy (and virtue ethics)

With regard to privacy, to begin with, especially in conjunction with the rise of social media and social networking sites (SNSs) such as Facebook, a wealth of evidence—ranging from parental "moral panics" over what their children post online through an array of studies and discussion—documents strong shifts away from more individual conceptions of privacy towards what Patricia Lange (2007), for example, demarcated as two different forms of "group privacy": the "publicly private" and the "privately public." These forms of privacy—as hybrids conjoining both individual and shared notions—are further characterized by Stine Lomborg (2012) as "public personal" spaces within which individual privacy is negotiated alongside a shared or group privacy (cf. boyd and Marwick 2011).

At the same time, these empirically documented shifts run in parallel with correlative philosophical analyses of selfhood and privacy. Most important, in my view, are emerging understandings of relational autonomy. These understandings begin with especially feminist critiques of strongly individual conceptions of selfhood as "hyper-individualist" and overly "masculine" in their emphasis on reason as exclusive of emotions. At the same time, these theorists work to preserve modern understandings of individual rational autonomy as these undergird foundational normative commitments to emancipation and equality for women as well as the many Others previously excluded from the circles of personhood. The intention is thus to reconfigure autonomy "so as to be more sensitive to relations of care, interdependence, and mutual support that define our lives and which have traditionally marked the realm of the feminine" (Christman 2004: 143). The upshot is an understanding of self as both independent from and inextricably interdependent upon Others.

Thereby, these conceptions of relational autonomy explicitly interact with virtue ethics. Andrea Westlund, for example, highlights the skills and abilities—virtues—required for autonomy, noting that these "must be developed during a relatively long period of dependence on parents and other caregivers" (2009: 26). Relational autonomy thus means that "[s]ome social influences will not compromise, but instead enhance and improve the capacities we need for autonomous agency" (2009: 27). More broadly, Andrea Veltman and Mark Piper note that "autonomy is one primary good among others that a person needs to live a good life or to achieve human flourishing" (2014: 2). At the same time, Veltman explicitly conjoins virtue ethics with a Kantian deontological account of autonomy that grounds respect for persons as a primary value.

Lastly, Helen Nissenbaum (2010) has developed an account of privacy as "contextual integrity"—an account that is more accurate and fruitful with regard to contemporary practices of and attitudes towards privacy in online contexts. Nissenbaum's account begins with a squarely relational understanding of selfhood, as initially traced out by James Rachels (1975). Nissenbaum's account shifts our understanding of privacy as demarcating specific (and usually static) *spaces* and *kinds* of information, and as defined with regard to *individuals*; rather, she argues that what we consider as "private" depends first of all upon the given *relationship(s)* that define the context of a given bit of information. For example, a given bit of information, such as an important fact about my current health conditions, while clearly sensitive and personal, may be recognized as legitimately sharable with both my physician and the network of healthcare professionals responsible for diagnosis and treatment. On the other hand, we further recognize that this same bit of information is *not* legitimately shareable, e.g. with a pharmaceutical company for the sake of entering my name into a database for targeted advertising of its products (see Ess and Fossheim 2013: 44–6). "Privacy" is thus contextual and defined specifically by the given conjunction of relationships within which a bit of information is shared.

3.2 Relational selfhood and (inclusive) property

Just as these diverse developments circling around privacy index a shift towards more relational conceptions of selfhood (and thereby virtue ethics), so our changing attitudes towards and practices regarding *property*—especially in online contexts—can likewise be seen as indexing such a shift.

The most prominent examples here include the Free and Open Source Software (FOSS) or Free/Libre Open Source Software (FLOSS) movements.

Affiliated primarily with the work of Richard Stallman and the GNU project to develop first a freely sharable, Unix-like operating system, Free and Open Source software is consciously opposed to proprietary for-profit software—in our terms, software understood as *exclusive* property. Rather, FLOSS is defined by four basic freedoms, including the "freedom to redistribute copies so you can help your neighbor (freedom 2)" and the "freedom to improve the program, and release your improvements to the public, so that the whole community benefits (freedom 3)" (see Ess 2013: 94–5). This approach to software development and distribution thus exemplifies a clearly *inclusive* understanding of property (Ess 2013: 95). That is, while individuals may claim rights of recognition for development and distribution of a given component of code, precisely as this code is freely shareable with and manipulable by others, code is thereby accessible by the entire community.

These notions of *inclusive* property are spelled out in considerably more detail in various Creative Commons licenses. Explicitly invoking the notion of a commons, Creative Commons licenses help creators—we call them licensors if they use our tools—retain copyright while allowing others to copy, distribute, and make some uses of their work, at least non-commercially. Every Creative Commons license also ensures licensors get the credit for their work they deserve.[2]

While some of the licenses offered in the contemporary spectrum of choices are clearly more restrictive than others, broadly speaking, as the language of the commons suggests, the aim is to offer ways of articulating more inclusive understandings of property, while acknowledging (indeed, resting upon) the legitimacy of exclusive property rights as encoded in copyright law.

4. Hybrid selves at work: Norway

It may be of interest to note that these developments cohere with recent legislation and ethical guidelines in Norway. This is to say, these shifts and changes are not simply observable within philosophical theory or empirical analyses of online behaviors; in addition, in the Norwegian case, they take expression in important law and practical ethical guidelines.

We have already seen that Norwegian law (among others) preserves the premodern notion of a commons as inclusive property in terms of its protection of the *allmannsretten* —the "freedom to roam" (Outdoor Recreation Act, 1957). Consistent with this notion of inclusive property is an account of the human being as both an individual autonomy and a relational being, explicitly invoked in justification of the revised Article 100 of the Norwegian Constitution. This article defines, and dramatically expands, freedom of expression as a foundational right in a liberal-democratic society. It does so in part by invoking the principle of autonomy (Kant and Habermas would be pleased), but autonomy here is incorporated within a richer notion of the "mature human being":

> This is neither the collectivist concept of the individual, which states that the individual is subordinate to the community, nor the individualistic view, which states that regard for the individual takes precedence over regard for the community. The conception of "the mature human being" [...] transcends the other two and assumes that a certain competence (socialization or education) is required in order to function as an autonomous individual in the open society.
>
> There Shall Be Freedom of Expression: 18

While the term "relational autonomy" is not explicitly in play here, this mature human being functions as a relational autonomy in which relationships with others—including the virtues we acquire and practice through these relationships—enhance rather than detract from autonomy (Westlund 2009: 27).

Still more recently, §13 of the 2006 research ethics guidelines issued by the Norwegian National Committee for Research Ethics in the Social Sciences and the Humanities (NESH) articulates "[t]he obligation to respect individual's privacy [*privatliv*] and close relationships" (17). This code thus requires researchers to protect the privacy and confidentiality of not only a given individual research subject, but also the privacy and confidentiality of the subject's close relationships—the relationships that help constitute *privatlivet.* At the same time, we can recognize here an anticipation of Nissenbaum's account of privacy as contextual integrity, that is, as defined within the contexts of specific relationships (Ess and Fossheim 2013: 51–2).

5. The future of copyright?

If this broad account of changing selfhood and correlative changes in Western attitudes and practices concerning privacy and property is at least roughly correct, then what do these shifts and transformations suggest for emerging practices, guidelines, and laws?

At least one point seems clear: "traditional" notions of individual selfhood and thereby exclusive property rights are not going away anytime soon. This is apparent in the evolution of Creative Commons licensing, which now makes explicit that it operates *within* the framework of extant copyright law: "Every Creative Commons license works around the world and lasts as long as applicable copyright lasts (because they are built on copyright)."[3]

In this light, it may be instructive to explore ethical responses to contemporary copyright matters through three distinct frameworks—namely, utilitarianism, deontology, and then virtue ethics. Most briefly, while utilitarianism and deontology support (as they long have) largely exclusive conceptions of property and thus the continuation of extant copyright law, the integration of relational notions of autonomy in deontology correlates with a shift towards more inclusive forms of property, as articulated in Creative Commons licensing schemes. Finally, as two examples of "virtuous copying" make clear, virtue ethics complements utilitarianism and deontology with more relational understandings of selfhood and inclusive property.

5.1 What would a (act/rule) utilitarian say?

As we have seen above, copyright law in the United States' tradition is justified by a straightforward utilitarian calculus: as Burk (2007) shows, copyright protections are justified by their contributions to the greater public good. Briefly, the argument is that authors, inventors, etc. will bother to develop new inventions and create new cultural products only if they will be rewarded—first of all, in monetary terms. Such reward is safeguarded through exclusive property rights. Economic rewards through exclusive copyright (and patents) thus encourage the ongoing development and creation of new inventions, cultural products, and so on that thereby contribute to the greater public good (96; cf. Ess 2013, 93).

5.2 What would a (relationally autonomous) deontologist say?

As we saw, contemporary notions of relational autonomy sustain core emphases of more individual or atomistic conceptions of autonomy, precisely with the intention of maintaining many of the key features and consequences of modern deontology, beginning with emphasis on respect for persons and equality, and correlative demands for rights derived from our status as autonomies to be protected in a liberal-democratic society.

Sustaining this approach would then mean, first of all, an ongoing endorsement of copyright as grounded on the moral rights of the author. This would also entail, at least by default, copyright as oriented towards *exclusive* forms of property.

At the same time, however, if we take on board the emphases on relationality in relational autonomy, this would *prima facie* shift our understanding of property towards more *inclusive* or shared forms. Specifically, such relational autonomies are coherent with especially current versions of Creative Commons licensing. As we have seen, these current versions seek to extend premodern notions of the commons into the digital era, where such commons—as exemplified in the contemporary Norwegian *allmennsretten*—are premier examples of inclusive property. At the same time, by doing so within extant copyright law, Creative Commons licensing thus does so in ways directly coherent with strong notions of individual autonomy and exclusive property.

5.3 What would a virtue ethicist say?

We have already seen that virtue ethics is immediately implicated both generally by relational selfhood and more specifically in conjunction with emerging notions of relational autonomy (e.g. Veltman and Piper 2014). Before proceeding further, however, it is necessary to first review virtue ethics in broad outline, in order to see in greater detail how it can apply to questions of copying and copyright.

5.4 What is virtue ethics?

Virtue ethics has enjoyed a striking renaissance over the past fifty years, as manifest, for example, in the work of Martha Nussbaum (1997) and in the role of virtue ethics in shaping Information and Computing Ethics (ICE) from its very beginnings. Generally, virtue ethics comes to the fore (again) as we have come to recognize that for all of their advantages, neither utilitarianism nor deontology take up what we recognize as desirable, if not simply necessary, for a complete moral life: this includes "moral wisdom or discernment [*phronesis*], friendship and family relationships, a deep concept of happiness [*eudaimonia*], the role of the emotions in our moral life, and the questions of what sort of person I should be" (Hursthouse 1999: 3; cf. Ess 2013: 238–9). Broadly, virtue ethics serves as a strong candidate for a *global* ethics, as required especially in conjunction with internet-based and related technologies that increasingly interlink people and institutions across the world. Very simply, virtue ethics is globally ubiquitous, as it appears across a very wide array of global cultures and traditions, including

Buddhism, Hindu thought, Indigenous traditions, the Abrahamic religions, and most famously in Confucian and Socratic/Platonic/Aristotelian virtue ethics. More specifically, virtue ethics is embedded in the foundations of ICE—namely, in the work of Norbert Wiener ([1950] 1954). In particular, Wiener enjoins the design and appropriation of computing technologies in the service of a larger human project—namely, the human emancipation and liberation thematic of the Enlightenment and Western liberalism. Wiener specifically understands "liberty" to mean "the liberty of each human being to develop in his freedom the full measure of the human possibilities embodied in him" (1954: 106). The development and unfolding of this freedom is central to basic conceptions of *the good life*, as a life of *flourishing* (Bynum 2000; Volkman 2010).

Virtue ethics foregrounds that a good life depends on the acquisition, practice, and improvement of specific habits or abilities ("virtues")—e.g. those required for establishing and fostering deep friendships. So Shannon Vallor has applied Aristotle's understanding of virtues and friendship to social networking sites (SNSs), arguing first that friendship requires such virtues as empathy, trust, patience, and perseverance. Vallor makes clear that the contexts and affordances of social networking sites (SNSs) tend to work against our acquiring or practicing these virtues (Vallor 2012, 2015).

Perhaps most importantly, virtue ethics emphasizes the central necessity of our acquiring and practicing a specific form of ethical judgment: *phronesis*. In contrast with more determinative, "top-down," rule-based judgments, *phronesis* or reflective judgment works from the ground up, that is, starting precisely in the thick of specific contexts and their fine-grained details. As our common language and intuitions regarding "judgment calls" suggest, more than one good or justified judgment is possible in specific cases. More broadly, we acquire and practice judgment as a virtue first of all as (relational) members of larger communities; indeed, a primary focus in our development of especially relational autonomy is our experiences—over many years and in the face of wildly diverse situations—of appropriating the judgments, practices, and habits of our immediate communities. (This is in part what "enculturation" means, that is, learning how to *judge* in ways closely similar to the [best] representatives of our cultures and communities.) We further practice and improve on our own judgments through the difficult experiences of making judgments, only to find, occasionally but inevitably, that they are mistaken. This capacity for ethical self-correction is at the heart of Plato's account of the κυβερνήτης (*cybernetes*)—a steersman, helmsman, or pilot. In Plato's description: "An outstanding pilot or doctor is aware of the difference between what is impossible in his art and what is possible, and he attempts the one, and lets the other go; and if, after all, he should still trip up in any way, he is competent to set himself aright" (*Republic*, 360e–61a). As readers might suspect, the capacity for self-correction on the part of the ethical *cybernetes* is the central meaning of cybernetics as taken up by Wiener as "the science of messages" (1954 [1950]: 77).

Finally, it is important to note that the acquisition and practice of virtues, including the core virtue of *phronesis*, is intrinsically a matter of *embodied*, and thereby often *tacit* forms of learning and experience. Hubert Dreyfus provides a good description of the essential role of embodied and tacit learning in his examples of the medical students following a senior colleague on rounds, the novice chess player following the moves of a master player, and the younger musician "hanging out" (my phrase) with a more experienced one; much of what we learn in these experiences—including the place and direction of specific *judgments*—can *not* be articulated and thus learned, as it were, remotely, but is only learned within close quarters with another human being (Dreyfus 2001).

It is partly for these reasons that a primary way of instructing newcomers in the arts of *phronesis* and affiliated virtues is through narratives that present us with the *phronimos*—the good person, that is, the person who literally embodies and carries out the judgments, virtues, and actions that are taken to be exemplary within a given tradition or culture. This approach is explicit in the Confucian understanding of the *junzi*—the exemplary person, the one who excels in both striving and achievement, and thereby comes to embody human excellence (Ames and Rosemont 1998: 62–3).

In these contexts, the ultimate goal of becoming deeply familiar with, say, *The Analects*, a given set of Scriptures, primary texts such as *The Epic of Gilgamesh*, *The Odyssey*, the Platonic dialogues, and so on, is not simply to acquire an abstract understanding of rules, principles, or norms. It is rather to absorb an understanding of a specific example of the exemplary person and how s/he has behaved in specific situations, against which one can begin to practice and attune one's own *judgment* in contemporary contexts. Asking the questions, "What would Odysseus do?," "What would Confucius say?," etc. is a way of calling to mind the *phronimos* and attempting to discern what judgments she or he might make in a situation similar to one's own (a process formalized in part in the practices of casuistics, for example). Again, this is not simply for the sake of fulfilling a moral ideal or norm; still more fundamentally, the training and honing of such judgment is in the service of pursuing a good life, one marked by flourishing, contentment, and harmony.

5.5 Virtuous copying

With this as background, we are better prepared to understand how classical approaches to copying of texts (regarded first of all as *inclusive* property)—we have briefly examined Confucian and medieval traditions as first examples—are justified as fostering multiple virtues. This background will further help us understand two Western examples of virtuous copying: first, the tradition formalized in Renaissance Humanism of the commonplace book; and second, contemporary examples of copying digital materials.

5.6 Virtuous copying: The commonplace book

As Naomi Baron documents, Desiderius Erasmus, building on an older medieval tradition, encouraged individuals to "strengthen their minds through guided use of the written word" (Baron 2008: 196). Specifically, in his *On Copia of Words and Ideas*, Erasmus—echoing Cicero—encourages not only the reading of great works, but the further practice of copying out "important passages in to a commonplace book" (ibid.). These passages were in turn to be "organized into conceptual categories, committed to memory, and then incorporated through paraphrase into the young man's own thinking and writing" (ibid.). According to Baron, the use of such a commonplace book amounted to a movement in the Renaissance, and thrived through the nineteenth century (2008: 196–7).[4] Baron observes that this disciplined practice of copying resulted in a commonplace book that served "both as a vehicle for and a chronicle of one's intellectual development": specifically, "the scribal act [of copying] was a necessary component in this stepwise development in the life of the mind" (2008: 197).

Through the lens of virtue ethics, we can see that the practice of copying can foster a number of critical virtues, beginning with those basic to communication and friendship, such as patience and perseverance (cf. Vallor 2012). It also seems likely that the practice of copying by hand thus engages embodied learning and recollection—a point established in recent studies contrasting, for example, memory and comprehension as fostered by long-hand writing *vis-à-vis* typing at a keyboard (e.g. Mueller and Oppenheimer 2014). Perhaps most importantly, as the contemporary writer Nicholson Baker articulates, the (deliberately) slow process of handwriting a text offers a "great virtue" as compared to underlining and typing: "for in those secret interclausal tracts of cleared thought-space [enabled through undistracted focus and time devoted to each word and phrase] ... new quiet racemes will emerge from among the paving stones and foam greenly up in places they would never otherwise have prospered" (Baker 2000: 8, cited in Baron 2008: 197). In plainer language: in the quiet and focus on copying a text word for word, new insights and understandings emerge that otherwise seem unlikely to appear in conjunction with rapid typing of a text.

This form of copying thus offers close analogues to the virtues of copying as practiced in traditional painting instruction (e.g. Bäcklund 2016). More specifically, copying texts in a commonplace book, especially for the sake of the virtuous ends of cultivation of mind and character, is hence clearly justified from the standpoint of virtue ethics.[5] We can further note that such copying is by default non-problematic if we assume that the texts in question are regarded as *inclusive* property. But even in the case of more modern instances of text as copyrighted as *exclusive* property, including regimes intended to protect the moral rights of the author, it seems that such copying for one's personal interest and development is likewise non-problematic, at least if we assume that such texts will remain private and unpublished.[6]

5.7 Virtuous copying: Sampling, mixing, retweeting—copying for democracy?

In their comprehensive global survey of attitudes and practices regarding copying digital materials, Mark Latonero and Aram Sinnreich hint that part of the tension between traditional copyright norms and contemporary practices of sampling, remixing, retweeting, etc. indeed rest on the contrast we have explored above regarding more individual *vis-à-vis* more relational conceptions of selfhood: "the premise of intellectual property tends to presume a discrete individual author, while these new practices are often collaborative and collective in nature" (2014: 573). In this light, as we have seen, digital copying thereby invokes more premodern understandings of relational selfhood and correlative sensibilities of property as inclusive property. Again, such senses of selfhood and property implicate virtue ethics—and as now several examples make clear, copying inclusive property for the sake of virtuous purposes can be justified, for example, in terms of fostering new techniques and approaches to creativity and artistic expression (cf. Nieswandt 2016).

One might further argue that mirroring censored sites is a form of copying that can be justified as it supports emerging democracies. That is, such copying seeks to overcome censorship of sites regarded as threatening to authoritarian regimes by setting up copies, often in other countries and with different access routes, that thereby remain accessible, both to activists and the larger population. We can recall here that Western virtue ethics, both within the Enlightenment and in Information and Computing Ethics more specifically, focuses on freedom and emancipation as first of all enabling nothing less than the virtuous project of unfolding one's best capacities and abilities as a human being (cf. Wiener 1954: 106), where this project is core to a good life of flourishing and harmony (Bynum 2000). At the same time, it is the unfolding of the idea of autonomy as an essential characteristic of human beings, where such autonomy includes strong notions of rational as well as relational autonomy that further justify and require liberal-democratic states. These core components of virtue ethics thus provide further justification of digital copying aimed towards overcoming authoritarian censorship and thereby fostering democratic processes.

6. Concluding remarks

These two positive examples of copying are not meant to suggest that all forms of copying can be justified from a virtue ethics perspective. As a reminder, virtue ethics asks us to evaluate any potential practice or capacity by way of the questions, "What skills, practices, excellences, habits are brought into play and fostered?" and "How far do these foster or frustrate the development of aesthetic/ethical judgment, long-term contentment, and individual/social harmony?" It is not hard to find examples of copying—e.g. illegal downloading of copyrighted materials via a site such as Pirate Bay—along with other uses of digital technologies that are problematic from a virtue ethics perspective, and this for one or two reasons. One, a given technology or practice may of itself be relatively neutral in terms of whether or not it positively fosters important virtues; but even so, participation in and/or use of such a technology might be suspect insofar as it represents an "opportunity cost," that is, our *not* actively pursuing and fostering important virtues.[7] More negatively, it is straightforward to show how some practices and affordances foster the development of skills and abilities that are *not* conducive to long-term contentment, formation of judgment, practices of harmony. So, for example, Shannon Vallor has criticized certain affordances of SNSs as they either encourage or positively require the practice of deception; but if I practice deception for less than virtuous intentions, I become more skilled in deception, less empathic, less trustworthy, which, especially in online contexts, decreases our capacities for *practicing* and thereby enjoying friendship, trust-building, and community (Vallor 2012).

Especially if we foreground the emancipatory impulse of contemporary virtue ethics, we can approach issues of copying in the digital era by asking the question: Are there forms and practices of copying that, for example, *increase dependency* rather than *liberté*, that deskill us in important ways? (cf. Vallor 2015).

A first example of copying that works contrary to enhancing our freedom are those copying practices that solely serve our interests in consumption of entertainment goods—at least insofar as we allow such practices and consumption to trump our pursuit of those virtues requisite for our self-development as free human beings. Here it is helpful to recall that especially at the beginning, acquiring a new virtue is difficult: hence, it is always easier to reach instead for distraction and amusement. Worst-case, to recall Neil Postman, the pursuit of entertainment and consumerist interests thus risks a form of "[a]musing ourselves to death"—i.e. neglecting the virtues and capacities required for both self-development as an autonomous being and as a citizen engaged in democratic processes (Postman 1985).

Similarly, copying practices that contribute to the now well-documented and well-critiqued practices of *self-commodification* seem most directly contrary to our pursuing the virtues of freedom and citizenship (e.g. Fuchs and Dyer-Witherford 2012). Taken together, taking up copying practices that foster both self-commodification *and* ever greater distraction would thus constitute a perfect storm of practices that work to reduce, rather than enhance, our pursuit of the virtues that foster freedom and thereby engagement in democratic societies. In sum, what would an exemplary person say—i.e. one who most fully embodies and exemplifies such freedom and self-development for the sake of democratic processes as well as contentment and harmony?

Notes

1 See Grundgesetz für die Bundesrepublik Deutschland, Article 1, sec. 1: "The dignity of many is inviolable. To respect and protect it shall be the duty of all public authority."

2 https://creativecommons.org/licenses

3 https://creativecommons.org/licenses/. There is no space to document it here, but I discern a similar shift in the Ubuntu Linux community, as the more overtly FLOSS philosophy defining the community and its work in 2007 or so is now all but submerged in the more commercially oriented Open Source approach of Canonical.

4 In the U.S. experience, perhaps the best-known commonplace book is that of Thomas Jefferson; see e.g. Wilson 2014.

5 This focus on the development of one's self, we can note, is arguably part and parcel of traditional literacy and writing more broadly. So Foucault has developed an account of writing as a "technology of the self," one that entails the virtue of care for the self an "ethic of self-care" (*epimelēsthai sautou*: Foucault 1988: 19) beginning with Socrates and the Stoics, and extending from first-century Roman uses of diaries and letters, through Puritan prayer journals, to Freudian psychoanalysis.

6 In the case of publishing one's commonplace book, cf. Bently 2016, on self-copying.

7 Such concerns are specifically emphasized by the so-called perfectionist forms of virtue ethics. Happily, in my view, perfectionism is recognized as an important point of critique of virtue ethics—with the result that non-perfectionist forms are articulated and defended; see e.g. Christman 2014.

References

Ames, R. and H. Rosemont (1998), *The Analects of Confucius: A Philosophical Translation*, New York: Ballantine Books.

Bäcklund, J. (2016), "The Paradox of Style as a Concept of Art," in D. H. Hick and R. Schmücker (eds), *The Aesthetics and Ethics of Copying*, 211–23, London and New York: Bloomsbury.

Baker, N. (2000), "Narrow Ruled," *American Scholar* 69 (4): 5–8.

Baron, N. (2008), *Always On: Language in an Online and Mobile World*, Oxford: Oxford University Press.

Bently, L. (2016), "Self-Copying and Copyright," in D. H. Hick and R. Schmücker (eds), *The Aesthetics and Ethics of Copying*, 271–94, London and New York: Bloomsbury.

boyd, d. and A. Marwick (2011), "Social Privacy in Networked Publics: Teens' Attitudes, Practices, and Strategies," in *Proceedings of A Decade in Internet Time: Symposium on the Dynamics of the Internet and Society*, September 21–24, 2011, Oxford: Oxford University Press.

Burk, D. (2007), "Privacy and Property in the Global Datasphere," in S. Hongladarom and C. Ess (eds), *Information Technology Ethics: Cultural Perspectives*, 94–107, Hershey, PA: IGI Global.

Bynum, T. (2000), "A Very Short History of Computer Ethics," *Newsletter on Philosophy and Computers*. Available online: http://southernct.edu/organizations/rccs/a-very-short-history-of-computer-ethics

Christman, J. (2004), "Relational Autonomy, Liberal Individualism, and the Social

Constitution of Selves," *Philosophical Studies: An International Journal for Philosophy in the Analytic Tradition* 117 (1/2): 143–64.

Christman, J. (2014), "Coping or Oppression: Autonomy and Adaptation to Circumstance," in A. Veltman and M. Piper (eds), *Autonomy, Oppression and Gender*, 201–26, Oxford: Oxford University Press.

Dreyfus, H. (2001), *On the Internet*, New York: Routledge.

Ess, C. (2013), *Digital Media Ethics*, 2nd edn, Oxford: Polity.

Ess, C. and H. Fossheim (2013), "Personal Data: Changing Selves, Changing Privacy Expectations," in M. Hildebrandt, K. O'Hara, and M. Waidner (eds), *Digital Enlightenment Forum Yearbook 2013: The Value of Personal Data*, 40–55, Amsterdam: IOS Amsterdam.

Foucault, M. (1988), "Technologies of the Self," in L. Martin, H. Gutman, and P. Hutton (eds), *Technologies of the Self: A Seminar with Michel Foucault*, 16–49, Amherst, MA: University of Massachusetts Press.

Fuchs, C. and N. Dyer-Witheford (2013), "Karl Marx @ Internet Studies," *New Media & Society* 15 (5): 782–96. DOI: 10.1177/1461444812462854

Hursthouse, P. (1999), *On Virtue Ethics*, Oxford: Oxford University Press.

Lange, P. G. (2007), "Publicly Private and Privately Public: Social Networking on YouTube," *Journal of Computer-Mediated Communication* 13 (1), article 18. DOI: 10.1111/j.1083-6101.2007.00400.x

Latonero, M. and A. Sinnreich (2014), "The Hidden Demography of New Media Ethics," *Information, Communication & Society* 17 (5): 572–93. Available online: http://dx.doi.org/10.1080/1369118X.2013.808364

Lomborg, Stine (2012), "Negotiating Privacy through Phatic Communication: A Case Study of the Blogging Self," *Philosophy and Technology* 25: 415–34. DOI: 10.1007/s13347-011-0018-7.

Lü, Y.-H. (2005), "Privacy and Data Privacy Issues in Contemporary China," *Ethics and Information Technology* 7(1): 7–15.

Mueller, P. and D. Oppenheimer (2014), "The Pen Is Mightier Than the Keyboard: Advantages of Longhand Over Laptop Note Taking," *Psychological Science* 25 (6): 1159–68.

Nieswandt, H. (2016), "In Defence of Disco Edits," in D. H. Hick and R. Schmücker (eds), *The Aesthetics and Ethics of Copying*, 381–91, London and New York: Bloomsbury.

Nissenbaum, H. (2010), *Privacy in Context: Technology, Policy, and the Integrity of Social Life*, Stanford, CA: Stanford Law Books.

The [Norwegian] National Committee for Research Ethics in the Social Sciences and the Humanities (NESH) (2006). "Forskningsetiske retningslinjer for samfunnsvitenskap, humaniora, juss og teologi" ["Research Ethics Guidelines for Social Sciences, the Humanities, Law and Theology"]. Available online: https://www.etikkom.no/Aktuelt/publikasjoner/Guidelines-for-research-ethics-in-the-social-sciences-law-and-the-humanities/

[The Norwegian] Outdoor Recreation Act (1957), Available online: https://www.regjeringen.no/en/dokumenter/outdoor-recreation-act/id172932/

Nussbaum, M. C. (1997), *Cultivating Humanity: A Classical Defense of Reform in Liberal Education*, Cambridge, MA: Cambridge University Press.

Peukert, A. (2014), "Das Urheberrecht und die zwei Kulturen der Online-Kommunikation," *GRUR [Gewerblicher Rechtsschutz und Urheberrecht], Beilage*, 77–93.

Postman, N. (1985), *Amusing Ourselves to Death: Public Discourse in the Age of Show Business*, New York: Penguin.

Rachels, J. (1975), "Why Privacy Is Important," *Philosophy and Public Affairs* 4 (4): 323–33.

Tavani, H. (2013), *Ethics and Technology: Ethical Issues in an Age of Information and Communication Technology*, 4th edn, Hoboken, NJ: Wiley.

Taylor, C. (1989), *Sources of the Self: The Making of the Modern Identity*, Cambridge, MA: Harvard University Press.

"There Shall be Freedom of Expression": Proposed New Article 100 of the Norwegian Constitution: Report of Commission Appointed by Royal Decree on August 26, 1996: Submitted to the Ministry of Justice and the Police on September 22, 1999. Excerpts. Available online: www.uio.no/studier/emner/hf/imk/JOUR4330/v13/unesco-report.pdf

Vallor, S. (2012), "Flourishing on Facebook: Virtue Friendship & New Social Media," *Ethics and Information Technology* 14 (3): 185–99.

Vallor, S. (2015), "Moral Deskilling and Upskilling in a New Machine Age: Reflections on the Ambiguous Future of Character," *Philosophy and Technology* 28 (1): 107–24.

Veltman, A. and M. Piper (2014), "Introduction," in A. Veltman and M. Piper (eds), *Autonomy, Oppression and Gender*, 1–11, Oxford: Oxford University Press.

Volkman, R. (2010), "Why Information Ethics Must Begin with Virtue Ethics," *Metaphilosophy* 41 (3): 380–401.

Westlund, A. (2009), "Rethinking Relational Autonomy," *Hypatia* 24 (4): 26–49.

Wiener, N. (1954 [1950]), *The Human Use of Human Beings: Cybernetics and Society*, Garden City, NY: Doubleday Anchor.

Wilson, D. L. (ed.) (2014), *Jefferson's Literary Commonplace Book*, Princeton, NJ: Princeton University Press.

17

Ethics, Evolved: An International Perspective on Copying in the Networked Age

Aram Sinnreich

One of the defining characteristics of media cultures and industries in the past two decades has been the emergence and widespread adoption of new expressive forms and practices whose aesthetic logics echo and reproduce the organizational precepts of digital communications networks. These new cultural forms, such as mashups, remixes, mods, memes, and machinima, abandon the linearity inherent in mass-mediated communications and supply chains in favor of more modular, recursive aesthetic and economic models.

As cultural logics have evolved, so has our understanding of media producers and audiences. Perhaps most notably, the categorical distinction between producer and consumer itself appears to be eroding, a premise explored in terms ranging from "remix culture" (Lessig 2008) to "produsage" (Bruns 2008) to "prosumption" (Ritzer and Jurgenson 2010) to "configurability" (Sinnreich 2010) to "convergence" (Jenkins 2006). While these theoretical perspectives differ in terms of their nuances, foci, and conclusions, they point collectively to a fundamental paradigm shift regarding the role of cultural expression as a vector of power, identity, and ideology in the networked age. Broadly speaking, most theorists consider the new challenges to industrial models of cultural production to carry a resistant, critical, and/or democratizing capacity, though others have either questioned this assumption outright (Keen 2008), raised concerns that these new cultural logics and the sociotechnical platforms on which they rely will undermine traditional economies to the point where culture industries cease to function altogether (Levine 2011; Timberg 2015), or lamented that digital media may serve as a new mask for social and economic power, strengthening rather than weakening hegemonic forces and thereby consigning cultural laborers and audiences, or even citizens at large, to a more subservient position than they previously occupied (Andrejevic 2013; Morozov 2011).

Regardless of its net impact on the empowerment or subjugation of media audiences, nearly all scholarship agrees that the digital disruption of traditional media cultures and industries contributes to an increasing tension between the practices of media producers and consumers on the one hand, and the institutional environment in which those cultural practices occur on the other. Centuries of co-evolution between the aesthetic, legal, economic, and organizational structures governing creative expression have contributed to a normative isomorphism between these structures, which has historically been both challenged and reified by the work of avant-garde movements (Poggiolo 1981), "outsider" artists (Zolberg and Cherbo 1997), pranksters (McLeod 2014), pirates (Johns 2010), street performers (Mann 2016) and others. While the historical dialectic between cultural regulation and resistance has itself served as a vital engine for innovation in a variety of contexts, the structural incompatibility between new, digital network-based "configurable" cultural forms and practices and these legacy institutions is so great that it threatens to upend this dialectic altogether (Sinnreich 2010). Put simply, when a majority of media audiences are engaging in some form of expressive practice that violates the normative assumptions governing cultural exchange, it's no longer an avant-garde; it's a new era.

One of the greatest points of tension to develop within this context has been between the ethical frameworks that emerge from the widespread adoption of configurable culture and the legal frameworks within which cultural exchange continues to operate—specifically, copyright and intellectual property (IP) law. As Ess (2013) observes, both media ethics and IP law vary from nation to nation, and the delineations of these often conflicting codes reflect broader social philosophies regarding conceptions of the self, community, and society from place to place and era to era. Yet while laws and ethics have always come into some degree of conflict, scholars like Ess, Lessig (2005), and others document the extent to which emerging digital cultural practices have helped these long-simmering tensions to boil up and explode into public consciousness, and the extent to which their continuing incompatibility creates challenges for businesses, legislators, enforcers, creators, and citizens around the globe.

This chapter examines these tensions by analyzing qualitatively and quantitatively the results of a survey fielded in 2014 and 2015 to 1,397 English-speaking adults in eleven different nations in Europe, North America, Africa, and the Asia/Pacific region. The survey is substantially similar to earlier ones fielded by the author in 2006 (Sinnreich, Latonero, and Gluck 2009) and 2010 (Sinnreich and Latonero 2014; Latonero and Sinnreich 2014). The survey combines quantitative, multiple-choice questions regarding the prevalence of configurable cultural practices and attitudes with qualitative, open-ended questions in which respondents' write-in responses reflect their ethical beliefs regarding these practices. As I will argue below, configurable culture has emerged as a definitively mainstream global phenomenon in the past five years, and despite global efforts to "harmonize" IP laws (Sinnreich 2013), residents of different nations and regions continue to employ a variety of different ethical frameworks—most of which bear very little resemblance to the contours of the law—when evaluating the validity of these emerging cultural behaviors.

1. Configurable culture adoption by the numbers

One of the fundamental aims of this series of surveys is to document the continuing proliferation of new, configurable cultural practices, from their relative infancy (in 2006) to their broader adoption in more recent years. We may conceive of this proliferation in terms of three modalities: *awareness*, which reflects whether a respondent has heard of a given cultural practice or form; *consumption*, which reflects a traditional audience/end user relationship to a given cultural practice or form; and *engagement*, which suggests a deeper relationship in which the end user participates to some degree in the production as well as the consumption of the mediated cultural artifact. Of course, not all forms of engagement entail the same balance between productive and consumptive elements. Some practices, like creating a play list of favorite songs or videos, entail a low barrier to entry and resemble consumption more than production. Others, like producing a mashup or remix and sharing it online, entail a higher barrier to entry and resemble production more than consumption. Although it would be a challenge to demarcate specific points in the vast and ever-widening grey area between traditional notions of production and consumption, it is useful to conceive of the lower-barrier forms of engagement as "consumption-adjacent" and the higher-barrier ones as "production-adjacent" (Sinnreich, Latonero, and Gluck 2009).

Survey results show that, in the U.S. and elsewhere around the globe, measured in terms of awareness, consumption, and every level of engagement, configurable culture has become increasingly prevalent over the past decade.[1] As Figure 17.1 shows, awareness of a range of configurable cultural practices

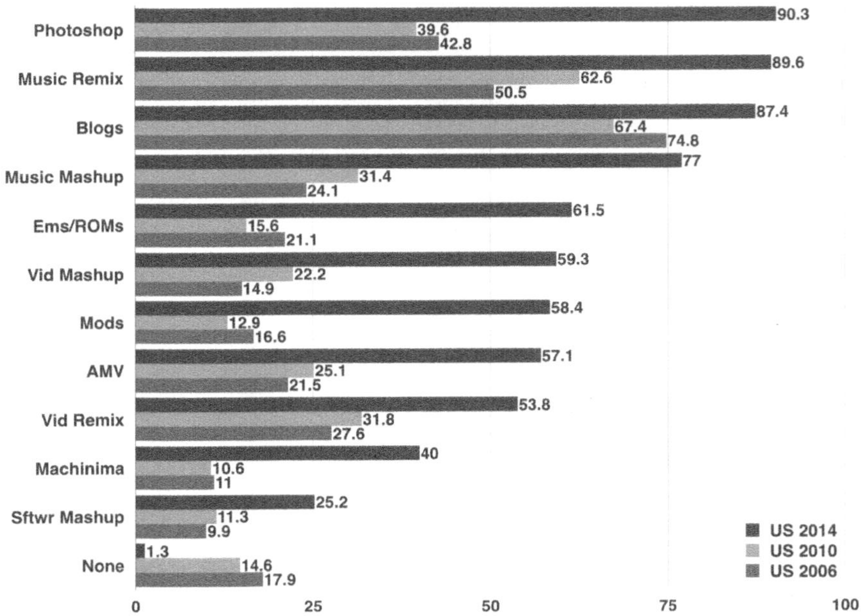

Figure 17.1 U.S. Awareness of Configurable Culture, 2006–14

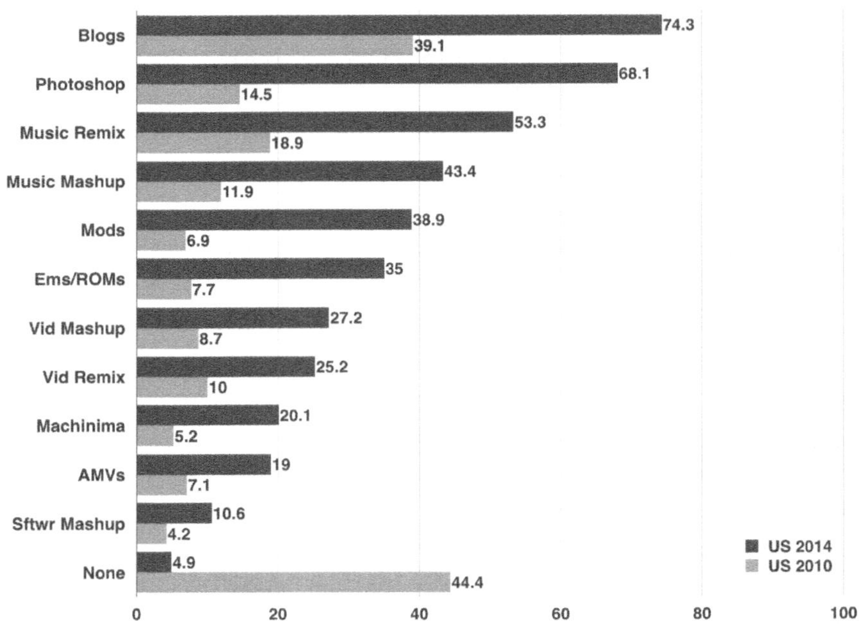

Figure 17.2 U.S. Consumption of Configurable Culture, 2010–14

within the U.S. mostly grew from 2006–10, but 2014 awareness levels[2] showed considerable growth relative to both earlier surveys. In the most recent survey, only 1.3 percent of respondents reported that they hadn't heard of any of the cultural practices mentioned on the survey, down from 14.6 percent and 17.9 percent in 2010 and 2006, respectively.

Consumption levels for configurable culture (see Figure 17.2) also grew dramatically between 2010 and 2014. For every category listed on the surveys, the percentage of respondents who reported consuming at least one of these cultural artifacts within the past year more than doubled. For over half the categories, consumption prevalence more than tripled. During the same period of time, the percentage of respondents saying they'd never consumed any media from these categories dropped from nearly half (44.4 percent) to fewer than one in twenty (4.9 percent).

Consumption levels grew elsewhere around the globe during the same years. As Figure 17.3 shows, configurable culture consumption levels (measured by the percentage of respondents who reported consuming at least one such cultural artifact within the previous twelve months) grew between 2010–15 in every nation for which each survey provided a representative sample. In half of those nations, consumption levels grew by 20 percent or more from one survey to the next.

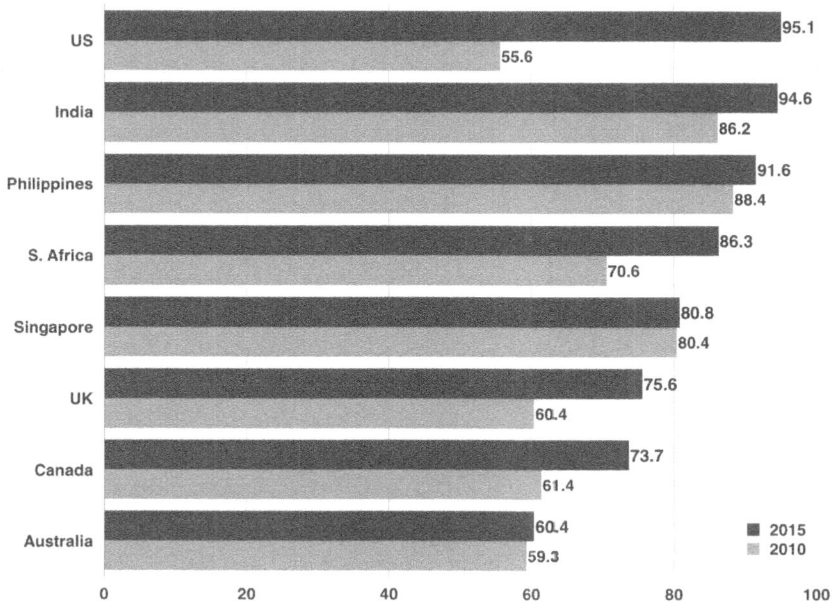

Figure 17.3 International Consumption of Configurable Culture, 2010–15

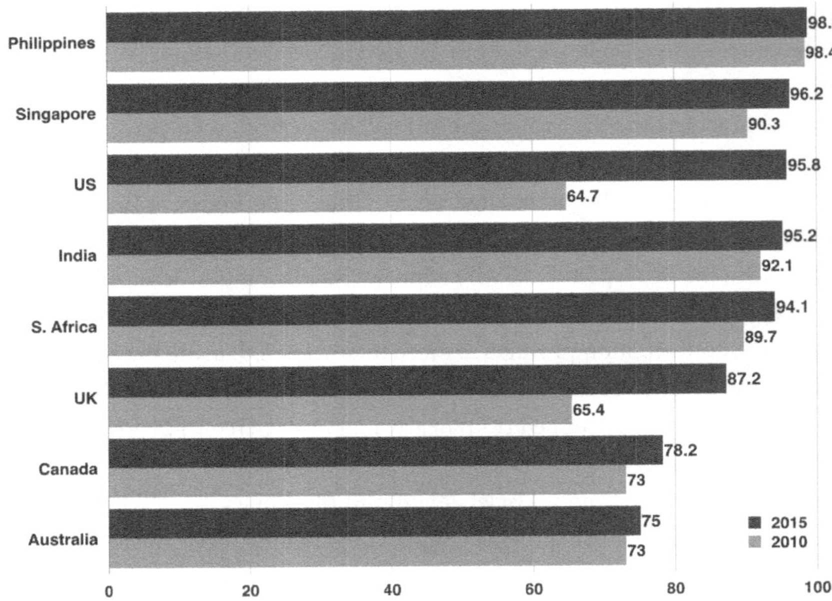

Figure 17.4 International Engagement With Musical Configurable Culture, 2010–15

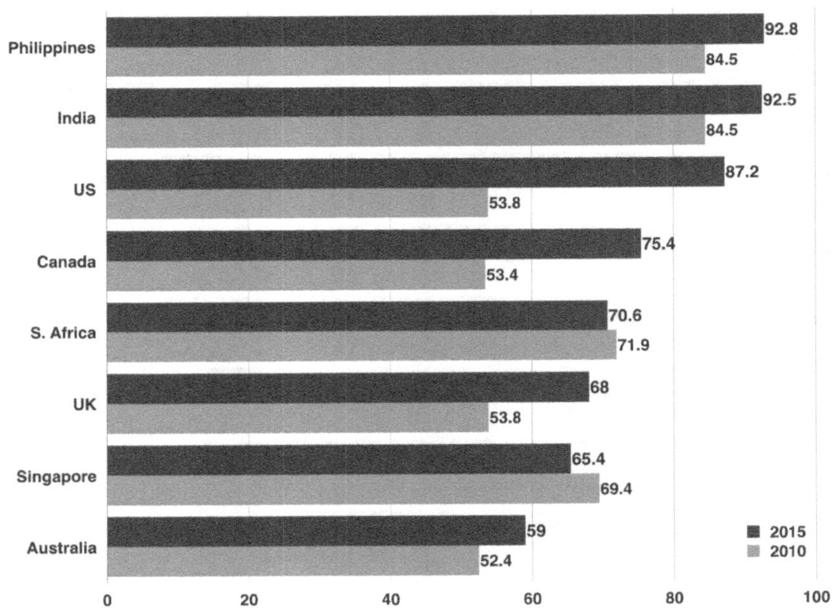

Figure 17.5 International Engagement With Video Configurable Culture, 2010–15

Just as with awareness and consumption, configurable culture engagement levels have grown considerably in recent years. For music-related forms of configurable culture (from consumption-adjacent practices like customized play lists and CD ripping to production-adjacent ones like producing mashups and remixes), overall engagement levels grew in every nation represented in both surveys (Figure 17.4). For video-related forms of configurable culture (from consumption-adjacent practices like accessing DVD bonus features and stream-ripping to production-adjacent ones like producing machinima and anime music videos), every nation except South Africa and Singapore saw gains in engagement during the same time frame (Figure 17.5). In the case of Singapore, where configurable video engagement levels dropped by over 5 percent from 2010–15, the government prosecution of online activists such as Roy Ngerng Yi Ling and Alex Au during the interim years may have had a chilling effect on actual or self-reported online activity.

2. Configurable culture ethics by the numbers

In addition to tracking adoption of configurable cultural practices, the surveys ask respondents to report their opinions regarding the ethics of appropriation and creative reuse. Because ethics can be a more nuanced and multifaceted subject than adoption, the survey addresses this issue via both quantitative, multiple-choice questions (geared toward longitudinal, empirical analyses) and qualitative, write-in questions (geared toward discursive analysis).

The first multiple-choice ethics question on the survey uses the language of "originality" as a proxy for ethical validity. As MacFarlane (2007) and others have argued, the discourse of originality in creative expression often serves a legitimizing function; creators and creations demonstrating a sufficient level of originality are granted the titles "artist" and "art" accordingly, but those deemed insufficiently original are consigned to secondary, inferior categories such as "derivative," "plagiarism," "counterfeit," "bootleg," "pirate," "ripoff," "knockoff," and so forth.

The 2006 survey included the following question: "To what extent do you consider mash-ups and remixes 'original'?" Respondents were required to choose between three responses: "I think that any use of pre-existing materials is unoriginal" (a categorical negative); "I think that all uses of pre-existing materials for remixes and mash-ups constitute original or innovative use" (a categorical positive); and "I think that some uses of pre-existing material are

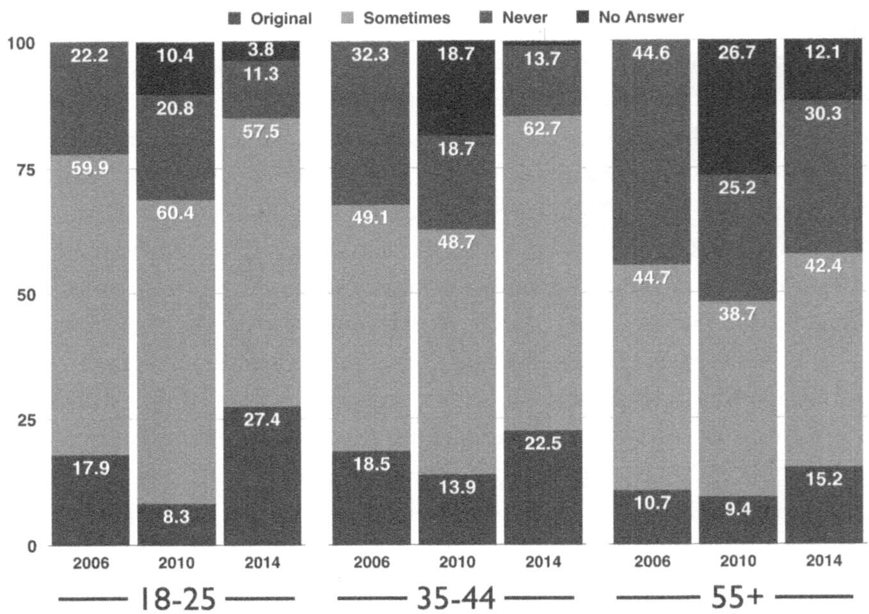

Figure 17.6 U.S. Opinions About Configurability and Originality by Age, 2006–14

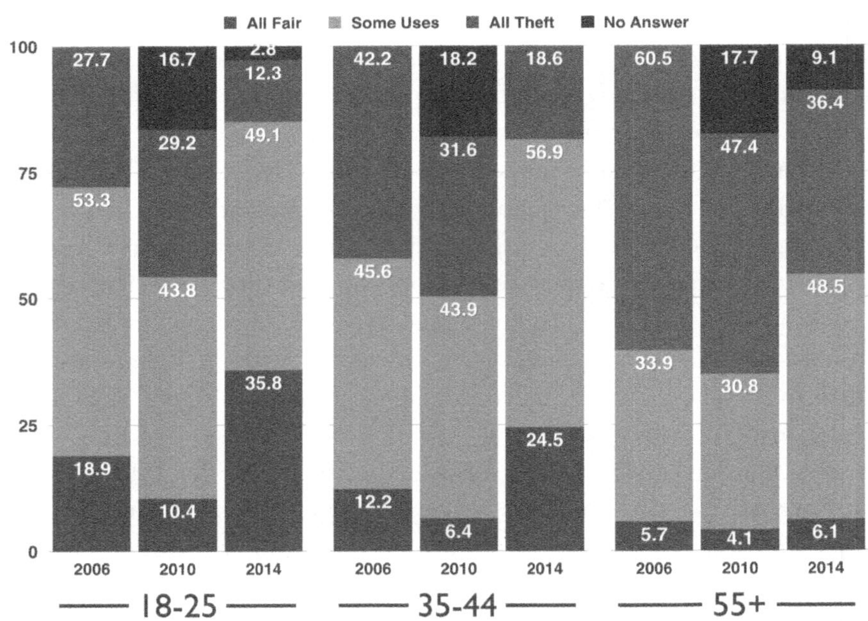

Figure 17.7 U.S. Opinions About Configurability and Permission by Age, 2006–14

unoriginal, but other uses constitute original or innovative use" (a middle ground).

Results of the first survey showed a strong relationship between age and ethical stance; more than three-quarters (77.8 percent) of respondents aged 18–25 acknowledged that configurable culture could be "original" at least some of the time, while only two-thirds (67.7 percent) of those aged 35–44 and little more than half (55.4 percent) of those aged 55 and above felt the same way (see Figure 17.6).

In subsequent surveys, a fourth possible response was added to this question: "prefer not to answer" (an opt-out). The addition of this option complicated the seemingly straightforward role of age in mediating ethics. While the 2010 survey still revealed a linear relationship between age and ethical stance, the delta between age cohorts was considerably lessened. The percentage of people 18–25 who categorically *supported* the "originality" of any and all configurable culture dropped by half, while the percentage of people fifty-five and over who categorically *rejected* it also dropped by nearly half. Analyzing these data, my co-author and I concluded that "younger respondents, forced to render a judgment regarding cultural practices about which they are unfamiliar," had erred on the side of accepting the validity of these practices in the earlier survey, while their elders had done the opposite (Sinnreich and Latonero 2014: 812). Once we gave respondents the opportunity to admit they lacked the expertise to make an ethical decision, those who remained opinionated differed to a lesser extent on the basis of age.

The 2014 survey also offered the opt-out response, but the recent rise in configurable culture adoption apparently has its corollary in a drastic drop in the number of respondents of any age choosing "prefer not to answer"—especially among those aged 35–44, none of whom selected it. This latest survey showed a considerable rise in the level of respondents of *any* age who are willing to accord configurable culture the mantle of originality at least some of the time. These figures were virtually identical for respondents aged 18–25 (84.9 percent) and those aged 35–44 (85.2 percent). Older respondents remain a bit more skeptical; only 57.6 percent of those aged 55 and above are willing to accord configurable culture a degree of originality, but this figure has climbed fairly steeply since 2010, when fewer than half (48.1 percent) did.

Another proxy for ethics is the legalistic binary between permission and theft. Beginning in 2006, respondents were asked the following question: "In your opinion, how should copyright apply to mash-ups and remixes?" Similar to the previous question, the earliest survey offered three answers: "I think that any use of copyrighted materials without permission of the owner should be treated as theft" (categorical negative); "I think that some uses of copyrighted materials should require permission, and other uses should not" (middle ground); and "I think that all uses of copyrighted materials for remixes and mash-ups should be allowed without permission" (categorical positive). The 2010 and 2014 surveys included a "prefer not to answer" response as well.

Response patterns to this question were very similar to those for the previous question. As with the concept of originality, younger people were far more likely than their elders to accept that at least some configurable reuses of third-party material should not necessarily require permission from the "original" creator. Again, the gap between younger (18-25) and middle-aged (35–44) respondents virtually disappeared between 2006 and 2010, and the two groups remained similar in 2014. Older respondents appear to be changing their opinions as well, albeit more slowly. In 2014, over half (54.6 percent) of respondents aged 55 and up acknowledged that some examples of configurable culture should not require permission, a fairly steep climb from the roughly one-third (34.9 percent) who selected this response in 2010.

3. Ethical frameworks employed by respondents

In addition to multiple-choice questions, the surveys also included open-ended questions intended to capture respondents' discursive approaches to evaluating the ethics of configurable culture. While this format lacks the ease of empirical analysis presented by multiple choice, it provides a far more nuanced view into the ethical frameworks employed by people throughout the world when confronted with new and innovative cultural practices that don't conform to established paradigms and lexicons.

Specifically, each survey followed its multiple-choice questions regarding awareness, consumption, engagement, and opinions of configurable culture with the following invitation: "We welcome your general thoughts about remixes and mash-ups, as well as any feedback about this survey." The qualitative data garnered in the responses were coded individually using an emergent open coding scheme (Denzin and Lincoln 2005; Strauss 1987). In the 2014 survey, 425 of the 1,397 total responses included language that conveyed an ethical judgment.[3]

In the 2006 survey, my co-authors and I identified seven specific ethical frameworks that emerged from the hundreds of write-in responses, each

Table 17.1 Twelve Emergent Ethical Criteria for Evaluating Configurable Culture

Unethical	Criterion	Ethical
For-Profit	*Commercial*	Non-profit
Unpermissioned	*Legal*	Permissioned
Pretension	*Authenticity*	Referenced
Unoriginal	*Innovation*	Original
Easy	*Labor*	Hard work
Bastardization	*Moral*	Homage
Rupture	*Continuity*	Evolution
Useless/Harmful	*Use Value**	Fun/Beneficial
Ugly	*Aesthetic**	Beautiful
Undermining	*Power Relations**	Empowering
Meaningless	*Self-Expression**	Expressive
Exploitative	*Industry Relations***	Promotional

conveying a different means of evaluating the validity of configurable cultural practices (Sinnreich, Latonero, and Gluck 2009). In the 2010 follow-up, my co-author and I again identified these seven strains of discourse, plus an additional four, which had likely emerged as a result of the intervening years in addition to the extension of the survey to an international respondent base (Latonero and Sinnreich 2014). In the 2014 survey, I again identified those eleven ethical frameworks in the write-in responses, plus an additional, twelfth rubric. The twelve ethical frameworks employed by respondents in their evaluations of configurable cultural practices are summarized in Table 17.1. Criteria with an asterisk first emerged in the 2010 data, while the criterion with two asterisks was first identified in the 2014 data.

While most respondents only relied on a single ethical criterion, some responses integrated multiple perspectives; all told, the 425 respondents who employed ethical language in their responses yielded 574 specific instances of ethical evaluation. In the 2014 survey, the most frequently invoked criteria were Innovation (121 cases), Use Value (112), and Legal (91). The least commonly invoked were Labor (7) and Moral (8).

What are these ethical criteria, and how do they appear in the qualitative data generated by the respondents themselves? Obviously, in the absence of direct prompts or easy-to-choose categories, responses were all over the map, idiosyncratically phrased, and at times maddeningly ambiguous. Yet the three sets of write-in responses submitted over the course of a decade, comprising thousands of individual opinions from diverse respondents around the globe, also demonstrate a compelling degree of consistency.

The *Commercial* criterion (37 instances in 2014) simply evaluates whether a remixer or mashup producer is profiting financially from his or her efforts. A typical response using this criterion in the most recent survey read as follows: "I think if done for fun, not a problem. If your making money, then you should pay the rights holder. [*sic*]"

The *Legal* criterion (91 instances in 2014) hinges on the question of whether someone gets permission to reuse a work, or whether copyright law is being violated. In the rather straightforward words of one respondent: "Any alteration to original content without permission I consider as theft."

Authenticity (24 instances in 2014) is a bit more of a subtle concept, but still a regular feature in write-in responses. The question at issue is whether a creative reuse of material acknowledges and references its sources, or obscures them, making a claim to originality. As one respondent opined: "Remixes are enjoyed by some people but those who are making it should consider crediting the owner of material." In these cases, the "original" can be another work of configurable culture; as another respondent wrote: "They're fine as long as they aren't blatantly ripping off other remixes."

The *Innovation* criterion—most frequently cited in 2014 (121 instances)—evaluates the ethics of copying based on whether the reuse adds something new. One often-referenced aspect of this analysis is whether a given remix is (or even whether it can be) "better than the original." Other respondents employing this criterion simply dismiss configurable culture in a single broad brush-stroke, based on the impossibility of innovation. To cite one succinct example: "Remixes and mashups are being creative in an unoriginal way."

The *Labor* criterion evaluates a work based on whether the respondent perceives that an adequate amount of work has gone into its creation. This was a more common refrain in the first survey results, but appeared only sporadically in 2010 (4 instances) and 2014 (7 instances). In a typical example, one respondent simply wrote: "Laziness and no imagination."

The *Moral* criterion (8 instances in 2014), another fairly subtle premise, stakes the ethics of configurability on the relationship between the "original" and the reuse. A use may be unethical if it's seen as "spoiling the original version" (in the words of several respondents), but ethical if it does justice to it. Along similar lines, some invoke the Moral criterion with more grandiose lamentations about the state of our species; in the words of one respondent: "Remix and Mashups are not acceptable because it will reduce humans craetivity. [*sic*]"

The *Continuity* criterion (17 instances in 2014) evaluates configurable culture based on whether it's seen as a disruption or a continuity of historical cultural forms and practices. As one respondent observed: "artists, writers and musicians have used existing works of others for hundreds of years." In the words of another: "Remixes and mashups are a great way to remind people of songs, but with a new twist."

The frequently cited *Use Value* criterion (112 instances in 2014) is fundamentally pragmatic in nature. Many positive responses echo the sentiments of this typical example: "remixes and mashups are good and fun." Several other negative ones cited concerns that configurable culture may be "unnecessary," "annoying," "boring," or even "more trouble than it's worth."

The *Aesthetic* criterion (69 instances in 2014) evaluates configurable culture based on its beauty, or on whether they can be perceived as "art" or "artistic." In the words of one respondent: "some mashups are OK, but I don't think of them as a major branch of art." "They are an art form, period," another wrote. "In general, I do not think of them as artistic," opined another.

The *Power Relations* criterion (37 instances in 2014) entails an evaluation by the end user about the social dynamics underlying copyright and other mechanisms of cultural regulation. These tend to number among the most thoughtful write-in responses. "I feel that technology has moved to a point where legislation can no longer keep up with controlling permissions on copyright materials etc." one respondent wrote. "Fair use is Fair use the DMCA system is corrupted and abused to hell and needs a reform, [sic]" another wrote. Generally speaking, respondents employing this framework describe a gap between their perception of the law's contours and the ethical calculus underpinning their own media behaviors.

Self-Expression (35 instances in 2014) evaluates the legitimacy of configurable culture based on whether a remixer or mashup artist is revealing something about himself or herself through the work. Some respondents made this point explicitly; as one wrote: "I think they are a good way for people to express their creative side." Others made the point more tacitly, simply observing that, as one respondent put it, "remixes and mashups are great to make."

The final ethical criterion, *Industry Relations*, appeared for the first time in the 2014 survey with 16 instances. Most of these respondents pointed out that remixes and mashups are actually beneficial to the culture industries, and should therefore be understood as ethical (or fair, or legitimate, or legal). In the words of one respondent: "It's a great way to promote the content that you're remixing."

4. Configurable culture ethics by nation

The 2014 survey garnered responses from online English-speaking adults in eleven nations: United States (n=452), United Kingdom (n=172), India (n=147), Australia (n=144), Canada (n=118), Philippines (n=83), Singapore (n=52), Ireland (n=52), New Zealand (n=52), South Africa (n=51), and Malaysia (n=47). As scholars such as Ess (2013) and Licht, Goldschmidt, and Schwartz (2007) have observed, both media ethics and media law vary from nation to nation, and they tend to covary (that is to say, the contours of each influences the other).

Data from the two international surveys reveal consistent variations in the way that respondents of various nationalities address the laws and ethics of copying. A good example is the disparity in the adoption of Creative Commons and other "open licenses," which were conceived explicitly as legal interventions rooted in the ethical rejection of copyright's normative role as an obstacle to the free sharing of knowledge (Lessig 2005; Williams 2002).

In both surveys, respondents from India, the Philippines, and Malaysia were by far the most likely to say they'd made their work available via Creative

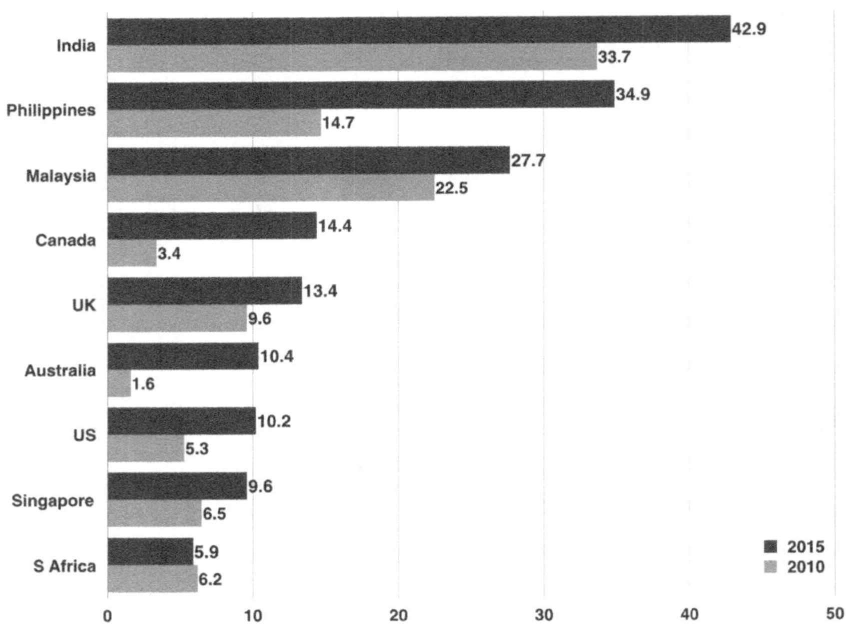

Figure 17.8 Open License Use Prevalence by Nation, 2010–15

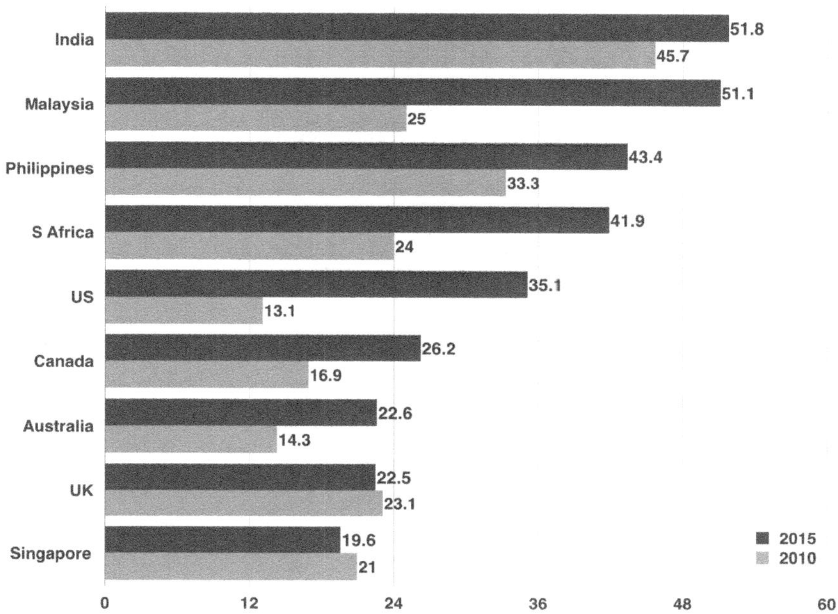

Figure 17.9 Open License Search Prevalence by Nation, 2010–15

Commons and open source licenses, and that they'd searched for other people's work made available via such licenses (see Figures 17.8 and 17.9). In both surveys, respondents in South Africa had a very low licensing-to-searching ratio (which may be understood broadly as an index of online cultural reciprocity), while those in the United Kingdom, despite a middling level of overall interest in open licensing, maintained a relatively high ratio. Both searching and licensing behaviors grew considerably from 2010 to 2015 in every nation surveyed except for Singapore and the United Kingdom, where searching levels decreased slightly, and South Africa, where licensing levels decreased slightly.

Attitudes regarding the validity of configurable culture have changed disproportionately in some nations relative to others over the past five years. In 2010, respondents in most nations surveyed had a similar likelihood of believing that some or all configurable reuses of content could be "original." By 2015, however, there was a far greater range and variance between nations, with the vast majority of respondents in the U.S. (84.1 percent) and Philippines (79.5 percent) demonstrating a willingness to accord creative reuse a degree of originality, but only roughly half of respondents in South Africa (58.8 percent) and Australia (44.4 percent) coming to the same conclusion.

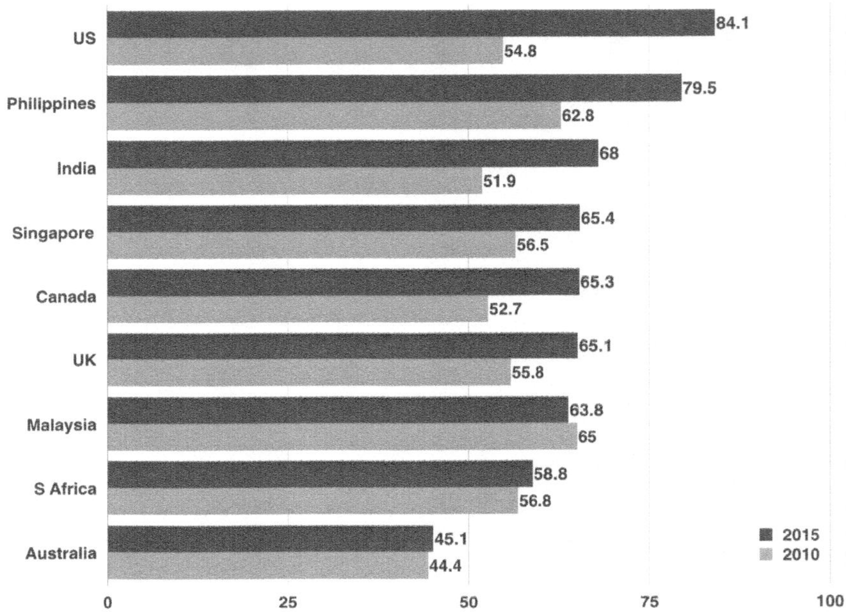

Figure 17.10 Opinions About Configurability and Originality by Nation, 2010–15

Similar figures apply to the questions of permission and copyright. The overall percentage of respondents who said that some or all configurable cultural works shouldn't be subject to permission from the original copyright holder was relatively similar across national boundaries in 2010. The variance between nations grew considerably by 2015, when large majorities of respondents in the U.S. (79.4 percent) and the Philippines (62.7 percent) supported some or all reuse without permission, but half or fewer did in nations like Singapore (51.9 percent), South Africa (49 percent), and Australia (38.9 percent). Not only do these figures directly echo those cited above regarding "originality," but they also echo the contours of the legal systems in these nations. The United States and the Philippines both have "fair use" exemptions in their copyright laws, specifically allowing users to transform works creatively without permission under certain circumstances. Singapore, South Africa, and Australia, by contrast, have "fair dealing" provisions in their laws, which, in the words of law scholar Michael Geist (2013), tend to be less "open-ended" and more "restrictive" than fair use provisions.

Finally, there are some intriguing distinctions between the ethical approaches to copying embraced by respondents from different nations in

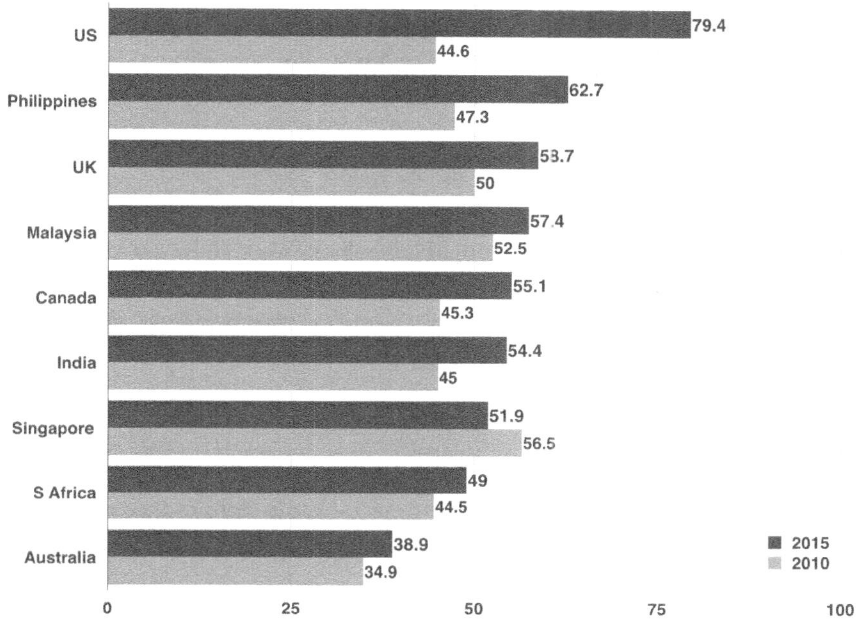

Figure 17.11 Opinions About Configurability and Permission by Nation, 2010–15

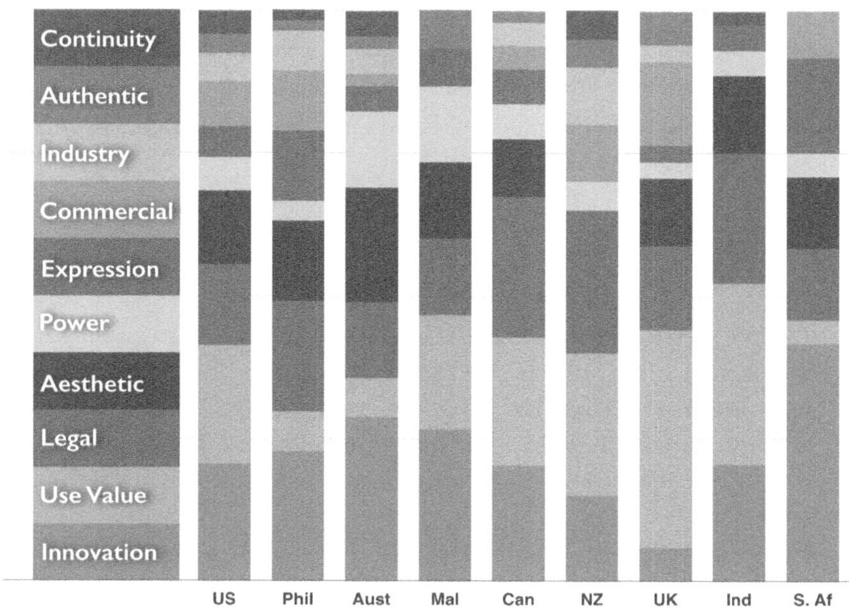

Figure 17.12 Distribution of Ethical Frameworks by Nation, 2015

their write-in responses. Overall, respondents from the U.S. (a relatively diverse and pluralistic nation) were the most ethically diverse, embracing all ten widely cited ethical criteria[4] in relatively equal number (see Figure 17.12). This doesn't necessarily mean that individual Americans espouse an ethical balance; in previous research (Latonero and Sinnreich 2014), my co-author and I have demonstrated that demographic factors like age, race, and gender may be highly determinative in the ethical stance embraced by a given respondent.

Other nations tended to exhibit more of an ethical bias relative to the general survey population. Respondents from the Philippines were far more likely to invoke the Commercial, Authenticity, and Self-Expression criteria, while Australians were more likely to invoke Aesthetic and Power Relations. Canadians were the most concerned with Legal permission-based ethics, South Africans tended to stress Innovation, and respondents from India and the U.K. were the most pragmatic, citing Use Value far more than other respondents. Given the relatively limited data set (551 ethical judgments distributed among eleven national subsets and the ten most frequently invoked criteria), these findings shouldn't be taken as empirically determinative analyses of the ethical fiber of these nations, but they do offer a glimpse into the deeper cultural divides underpinning the empirical differences noted above. They also suggest that further research, with a larger data set, would likely yield valuable data regarding the ethical tensions between nations, generations, classes, ethnicities, and genders as configurable culture continues to proliferate and as IP maximalists continue to push for the "harmonization" of copyright laws across national boundaries and around the globe.

Notes

1 The 2010 survey was only fielded to U.S. adults. Because of this fact, and because of changes in survey recruitment techniques from 2010 to 2014, I will only compare topline data from year to year within single nations. For data that rely on crosstabulation, in which age, gender, or some other demographic factor is the causal variable, comparisons of global-scale data are more feasible and meaningful.

2 Most U.S. responses to the third survey were fielded in the second half of 2014, while most responses outside of the U.S. were fielded in the first half of 2015. For the sake of clarity, I will refer to this as the "2014 survey" in the article text, but mark data as collected in 2015 where appropriate.

3 The remaining responses consisted of feedback on the survey, illegible or minimal text, or some variation on "no comment."

4 This discussion excludes the Labor and Moral criteria, which had too few instances in the most recent survey to warrant empirical analysis.

References

Andrejevic, M. (2013), "Estranged Free Labor," in T. Scholz (ed.), *Digital Labor: The Internet as Playground and Factory*, 149–64, New York: Routledge.

Bruns, A. (2008), *Blogs, Wikipedia, Second Life and Beyond: From the Production to Produsage*, New York: Peter Lang.

Denzin, N. K. and Y. S. Lincoln (2005), *The Sage Handbook of Qualitative Research*, 3rd edn, Thousand Oaks, CA: Sage.

Ess, C. (2013), *Digital Media Ethics*, Cambridge: Polity.

Geist, M. (2013), "Fairness Found: How Canada Quietly Shied from Fair Dealing to Fair Use," in M. Geist (ed.) *The Copyright Pentalogy: How the Supreme Court of Canada Shook the Foundations of Canadian Copyright Law*, 157–86, Ottawa: University of Ottawa Press.

Jenkins, H. (2006), *Convergence Culture: Where Old and New Media Collide*, New York: New York University Press.

Johns, A. (2010), *Piracy: The Intellectual Property Wars from Gutenberg to Gates*, Chicago: University of Chicago Press.

Keen, A. (2008), *The Cult of the Amateur: How Blogs, MySpace, YouTube, and the Rest of Today's User-Generated Media are Destroying Our Economy, Our Culture, and Our Values*, New York: Doubleday.

Latonero, M. and A. Sinnreich (2014), "The Hidden Demography of New Media Ethics," *Information, Communication & Society* 17 (5): 572–93.

Lessig, L. (2005), *Free Culture: The Nature and Future of Creativity*, New York: Penguin.

Lessig, L. (2008), *Remix: Making Art and Commerce Thrive in the Hybrid Economy*, New York: Penguin.

Levine, R. (2011), *Free Ride*, New York: Random House.

Licht, A. N., C. Goldschmidt, and S. H. Schwartz (2007), "Culture Rules: The Foundations of the Rule of Law and Other Norms of Governance," *Journal of Comparative Economics* 35(4), 659–88.

MacFarlane, R. (2007), *Original Copy: Plagiarism and Originality in Nineteenth-Century Literature*, New York: Oxford University Press.

Mann, L. K. (2016), "White Faces in Intimate Spaces: Jamaican Popular Music in Global Circulation," *Communication, Culture & Critique* 9(2): 266–83, DOI: 10.1111/cccr.12106.

McLeod, K. (2014), *Pranksters: Making Mischief in the Modern World*, New York: New York University Press.

Morozov, E. (2011), *The Net Delusion: The Dark Side of Internet Freedom*, New York: Public Affairs.

Poggioli, R. (1981), *The Theory of the Avant-Garde*, Cambridge, MA: Harvard University Press.

Ritzer, G. and N. Jurgenson (2010), "Production, Consumption, Presumption: The Nature of Capitalism in the Age of the Digital 'Prosumer'," *Journal of Consumer Culture* 10 (1): 13–36.

Sinnreich, A. (2010), *Mashed Up: Music, Technology and the Rise of Configurable Culture*, Amherst, MA: University of Massachusetts Press.

Sinnreich, A. (2013), *The Piracy Crusade: How the Music Industry's War on Sharing Destroys Markets and Erodes Civil Liberties*, Amherst, MA: University of Massachusetts Press.

Sinnreich, A. and M. Latonero (2014), "Tracking Configurable Culture From the Margins to the Mainstream," *Journal of Computer-Mediated Communication* 19 (4): 798–823.

Sinnreich, A., M. Latonero, and M. Gluck (2009), "Ethics Reconfigured: How Today's Media Consumers Evaluate the Role of Creative Reappropriation," *Information, Communication & Society* 12 (8): 1242–60.

Strauss, A. L. (1987), *Qualitative Analysis for Social Scientists*, Cambridge: Cambridge University Press.

Timberg, S. (2015), *Culture Crash: The Killing of the Creative Class*, New Haven, CT: Yale University Press.

Williams, S. (2002), *Free as in Freedom: Richard Stallman's Crusade for Free Software*, Sebastopol, CA: O'Reilly.

Zolberg, V. L. and J. M. Cherbo (1997), *Outsider Art: Contesting Boundaries in Contemporary Culture*, Cambridge: Cambridge University Press.

18

Online Piracy and the Transformation of the Audiences' Practices: The Case of the Czech Republic

Jakub Macek and Pavel Zahrádka

Digital information and communication technologies (ICTs) offer internet users a wide range of possibilities for easy and instant access to digital copies of cultural objects. Copying and distribution of content transmitted through analog media was always (with some exception of content distributed by broadcasting media) tied to duplication of the original material bearer and usually with a partial loss of information. In contrast, digital media enable loss-less copying and distribution of content. Moreover, digital media are impartial and convergent, carrying all manner of content without being tied to any particular type of material object or distribution channel (cf. Feldman 1999; Manovich 2001; Jenkins 2006). As a result of the dissemination and domestication of digital media, we witness in the Czech Republic—as well as worldwide—a clash between audiences' practices of obtaining content and legislation regulating access to content protected as "a unique outcome of the creative activity of the author" (Czech Copyright Act, vol. 1, art. 2). Employing Giddens's structuration theory (Giddens 1976, 1984), we approach the tension between audiences' practices and regulatory rules as a tension between agency and structures. We do not, however, reduce such structures simply to the legislative rules regulating the recirculation of cultural objects, but recognize and take into account other contextual influences including, on the one hand, social and cultural norms, economics and markets, technological and textual properties of the cultural objects (cf. Lessig 2006: 120–37), and, on the other, the contingencies of everyday life (cf. Bakardjieva 2005; Silverstone 1994).

The Czech music and film industries (represented by the Czech Anti-piracy Union and other organizations aiming to protect copyright law) and state agencies (such as the Industrial Property Office) aim for control over and penalization of non-authorized distribution of digital content using Czech copyright law. Despite their efforts, however, the content protected by the law continues to be spread via illegal peer-to-peer file sharing (P2P), streaming, and file-sharing services. It seems that the efforts to regulate content distribution through educational campaigns, legal and market regulations, and technological means (such as digital rights management [DRM]) do not come with sufficient power to transform common users' practices—especially when these measures are not compliant with other socio-cultural norms structuring audiences' practices. Our suggestion therefore is that understanding the sources of the lasting tension between one of the structures (law) and the practice (downloading digital content) has to be based on inquiry into the everyday content-related practices of the audiences, and therefore into the other structures that form their practices.

Tension between the law and audiences' practices was recently addressed by several sociological and criminological studies that can be divided into two groups. Studies in the first group assume copyright laws as default and obligatory norms and seek explanation for audiences' motivations for infringements, i.e. they treat the infringement primarily as deviant behavior. Their purpose is often to formulate recommendations for the industry in terms of effective measures preventing further illegal digital circulation of protected works. Ingram and Hinduja (2008), for instance, analyze so-called neutralizing rhetorical strategies (denial of responsibility, denial of injury, denial of victim, appeal to higher loyalties, condemnation of condemners) used to justify the actions of music pirates aware of the infringing or socially deviant character of their practices. Other studies (Freestone and Mitchell 2004; Lysonski and Durvasula 2008; Flores and James 2012) conclude that criminal practices are conditioned mainly by a lack of ethical or moral thinking[1] amplified by online anonymity, by spatial distance from the consequences of one's behavior, by the depersonalized or disinhibited nature of online communication, or by surfing the internet in the comfort of one's own home.

Methodologically these studies suffer from two things: from the a priori assumption that the agents' online practices are deviant; and from a theoretical notion of ethical or moral agency that does not take into account the normative standpoints of the social actors themselves. In general, this deductive approach neglects the "principle of charity" (Davidson 1984) as it approaches—contrary to what the social actors themselves think—the respondents' practices as deviant, and interprets motivations for the practices as mere attempts to explain away the misconduct. Therefore, we consider the approach of evaluating respondents' actions by employing hypothetical dilemmas deductively inferred from a priori ethical theory as methodologically inappropriate and biased for inquiry into audiences' practices and their social conditions.

The studies of the second type approach the online audiences from a value-neutral or interpretive standpoint, aiming to understand the normative frameworks that structure the practices related to the obtaining of non-authorized digital content which members of online audiences share with their peers. However, quantitative studies of this type usually do not enable a more thorough understanding of the motives linked with illicit downloading (Xanthidis and Aleisa 2012; Svensson and Larsson 2012). Moreover, the problem of consumption of non-authorized content is often reduced to a conflict between the copyright law and audiences' maximization of their own benefits (Rochelandet and Le Guel 2005; Hennig-Thurau et al. 2007).

Qualitative studies, on the other hand, could be at risk of idealizing the studied phenomenon—such as Jenkins's *Convergence Culture* (Jenkins 2006), offering a broader contextual picture of the transforming power relation between active, participatory audiences and broadcasters, or as the qualitative studies of creation of reconfigurable cultural forms where authors infringe copyright and do not accept the definition of a legal copy (Shiga 2007). However, this type of study primarily focuses on those who hold a reflexively oppositional stance towards the cultural industries and their business models, offering economically alternative models for the recirculation of cultural objects (cf. Lessig 1999, 2004; Vaidhyanathan 2001, 2004; Strangelove 2005). On the one hand, this results in an inappropriate and voluntaristic idealization of the recipient as an empowered, highly reflexive or horizontal-sharing actor intentionally challenging the capitalist system (Jenkins 2006; Bruns 2008). And, on the other hand, it easily opens a path to a similarly inaccurate techno-deterministic interpretation of, for example, decentralized P2P networks as revolutionary innovations undermining the current media industries (cf. Bauwens 2002).

In our research of audiences' practices of obtaining and recirculating non-authorized content, we avoid the methodological failures threatening both approaches to the topic. In this regard, we draw upon traditions of methodological relativism and on a context-oriented social-constructivist approach to social agency.[2] Methodological relativism (Najder 1975; Zahrádka 2015) rests on the assumption that it is the social actors and their practices—and not deductive theory—that should be conceived as the source of the notions of *right* and *wrong* practices. As researchers, we investigate, describe, and analyze the normative systems as they are experienced and reconstructed by the social actors within the contexts of their everyday lives; values, in other words, cannot be theoretically postulated—values are chosen and lived by the social actors. As we show below, we conceive of values (organized in normative systems) as contextual structures changeable in time, negotiated by the social actors, and, as such, culturally relative. Therefore, the topic of online piracy interests us in terms of the experience of the members of the audiences, not in terms of media industries, and not in terms of legal regulation. We do not intend to identify which of the respondents' practices are illegal—after all, our respondents themselves have a problem with determining the legality of their own practices. Instead of the legal status of the practices, we focus in this chapter on these questions: (1) How and why do the social actors choose particular content? What sources of content do the actors employ and why? And what technological interfaces do they use for reception of content and why? (2) What motivations do the actors have for receiving the (potentially) illegally distributed content? And, last but not least: (3) What evaluative criteria structure their content-related practices?

1. Theory and methods

This chapter builds upon a quantitative survey and two qualitative data collections connected to two distinct research projects, each led by one of the authors of the chapter. Both projects focus on current media-related practices of Czech audiences, and both suggest that one of the symptomatic features of the ongoing transformation of media environments and audiences' practices is a partial shift of the content reception from TV broadcasting to the discontinuous reception of online content. This trend is intertwined with multiplication of technological objects—PCs and laptops, smartphone and tablets—treated by audiences that use them as alternative screens for content reception. Therefore, we address the phenomenon of the Czech "online piracy" (or, broadly speaking, issues related to the obtaining of digital content from non-authorized sources) in relation to the wider context of audiences' reception of popular content. In the case of Czech media audiences, and with focus on their reception of popular content (i.e. films and TV series, music, books, and videogames) we investigate how new, convergent reception practices are distributed in the society and their position relative to the "traditional" reception practices.

Reception of downloaded audiovisual content is not a discrete, inherently generic practice. It is part of a bigger story framed by the whole set of audience members' practices, of what we call *media ensembles*.[3] Downloading films and TV series thus, in the first place, must be analyzed and understood as a textual practice, as one of the variations of what used to be called—maybe too simply, given its ongoing change—"watching television." Therefore we analyze the downloading of online content as contextualized intentional practice conditioned by choice of a particular type of text (content- or work-type: movie or TV series, comedy or drama, etc.) and particular reception interface, and structured by the choice—curation—of particular content. Downloading is thus approached in the whole context of recipients' everyday media-related practices, an approach we hope will forestall inappropriate overestimation of the studied phenomenon. Such overestimation—easily threatening the analysis when downloading is framed as the centre of the picture—could simply lead to misunderstanding why people do what they do when they download digital copies of popular content.

The context-based approach is, as we stated above, integral to the general theoretical model we employ in the chapter. We draw here upon the *structuration model of media* built on Giddens's theory of structuration with its recognition of mutual relations between agency and structures (Giddens 1976, 1984). The structuration model of media—originally formulated for purposes of holistic analysis of new media uses (Macek 2013)—addresses creation, distribution, and reception of media texts as practices that shall be analyzed as conditioned and formed in three mutually related dimensions of (1) intentions, internalized values, knowledge, and needs of social actors, (2) technological and textual affordances of the medium, and (3) contexts surrounding and structuring the media-related agency. Furthermore, the contexts include two layers of contextual structures. Immediate contexts of the first order, i.e. contexts of everyday life (spatiotemporal structures of private home or public spaces where media are used as means of reception and interaction) directly structure—and are restructured by—uses of media. Contexts of the second order have more general character: they are represented by systems of common cultural values and shared knowledge, by regulatory codes of law and technical norms, by the systems of the political sphere, systems of economic relations, and other systems beyond the direct reach of the common actors' agency.

All the data for the analysis were collected in the Czech Republic between 2012 and 2015, using both qualitative and quantitative techniques. The data were collected in three waves. The first and the second wave of data collection were organized by Jakub Macek and focused on media practices in general, providing us with a broader picture of media-related practices in the everyday

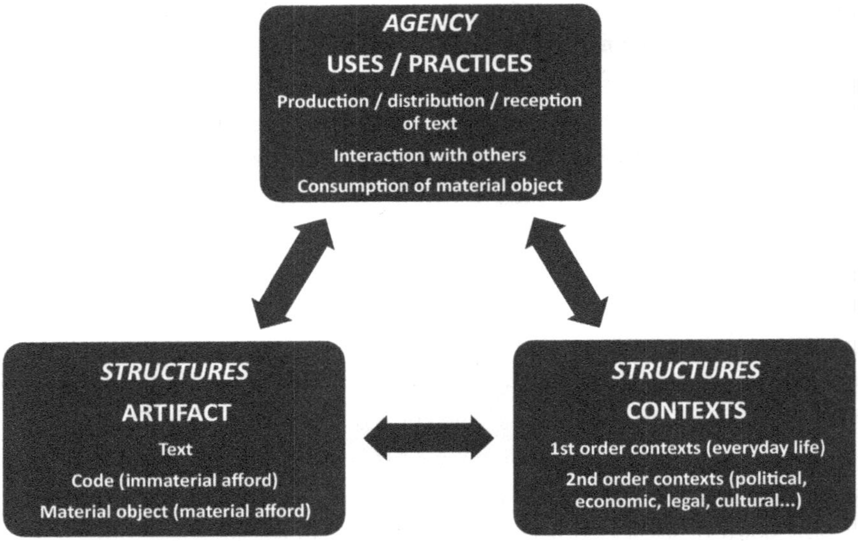

Figure 18.1 Structuration Model of Media (Source: Macek 2013)

lives of the respondents. The third data collection, organized by Pavel Zahrádka, focused more specifically on practices related to downloaded content.

Our aim was to avoid the romanticizing idealization of the creation, recirculation, and obtaining of non-authorized digital copies. Therefore, in the qualitative parts of the research, we focus on the general population; in the quantitative survey we used quota sampling representing the Czech population; and in the qualitative interviews we worked with ordinary members of audiences, excluding members of groups with pronounced and reflexively articulated interests related to copyright law (software and content creators, members of the Czech Anti-piracy Union or the Czech Pirate Party, etc.). The term "ordinary members of audiences" we use here in line with Maria Bakardjieva's notion of ordinary users (Bakardjieva 2005: 9), i.e. as an equivalent to what Latour describes as the "simple customer" (Latour 1987: 137)—a man or woman without technical expertise, hobbyist motives, or economic interests in relation to a novel technological artifact. In our research it is the actor that does not have, in relation to online recirculation of content, the explicit commercial or political interest in application or weakening of copyright law. Moreover, in order to meet our exploratory need for getting a complex picture of various consumer practices and attitudes towards the illegally distributed content, in sampling we emphasize socio-demographic heterogeneity of the respondents (in terms of age, gender, family or relationship status, education, occupation). At the same time, we hold to the interpretive, value-neutral approach both in the interviews and in the analysis; our aim was to minimize expression of our own normative and moralist standpoints that could eventually prevent the respondents from speaking openly, thus biasing the analytical process.

The first data collection was a qualitative one, taking place in the Czech Republic between 2012 and 2014. This began with ethnographic interviewing of four middle-class couples with children and continued with 48 semi-structured interviews with respondents with various characteristics. The aim of the qualitative inquiry was to provide a more thorough understanding of audiences' everyday media-related and communicative practices, and thus with sufficient inductive knowledge needed for the consequent quantitative survey.

The second data collection was a quantitative quota-sampling survey into the general Czech population (n=1998, 18+). The data were collected in October and November 2014 using CAPI and a highly structured questionnaire based on filters enabling us to map all the potential practices, textualities, and technological interfaces. The quantitative data serve us in this chapter as the main source of information on distribution of particular practices in the Czech population.[4]

The third, additional set of data was consequently collected in 2015 and built on the conclusions of the survey. It included 30 semi-structured qualitative interviews with age 18+ members of audiences and specifically focused on the informants' practices and opinions related to obtaining, using, and further recirculating of non-authorized popular online content that appeared as most important in the survey (films, TV shows, music, books, videogames).

2. Choices of textuality and interfaces

In Czech society, according to our quantitative survey, reception of films and TV series are among the most widespread practices related to popular content. Films are regularly—at least several times a week—watched by almost two-thirds of Czechs and TV series by more than half.

The qualitative interviews focusing on motivations structuring the practices suggest that choices of particular media content made by audiences are informed by what might be called textual motivations (related to "purely textual" preferences of particular genres, narrative structures, etc.) as well as by contextual motivations external to such pure textuality, such as those related

Table 18.1 Frequencies of Selected Media-Related Practices (% Overall) (Source: Macek et al. 2015)

	Never	**Less than once a month**	**Several times a month**	**Several times a week**	**Once a day**	**Several times a day**
reading magazines	25.6 %	14.8 %	25.3 %	22.7 %	8.0 %	2.8 %
reading books	35.1 %	21.1 %	13.4 %	13.1 %	11.8 %	5.5 %
watching TV series	**23.2 %**	**6.5 %**	**14.8 %**	**33.5 %**	**15.1 %**	**6.8 %**
watching films	**4.7 %**	**8.0 %**	**27.3 %**	**40.6 %**	**15.1 %**	**4.4 %**
listening to music	8.2 %	4.2 %	10.1 %	20.5 %	17.2 %	39.9 %
playing videogames	71.9 %	6.3 %	6.8 %	7.1 %	4.0 %	3.9 %

to respondents' everyday lives (available time, need for activities shared within couples, cultural capital forming the recipient's identity and taste). At the same time, the quantitative data show that despite the increasing role of reception from online sources and through computer screens and tablets, TV broadcasting remains the main source both of films and TV series.

Nevertheless, though still marginal in general comparison to the reception of TV broadcasting, "post-TV" practices are not insignificant. In the case of younger members of audiences, these practices are becoming as widespread as the reception of TV broadcasting. The data here unsurprisingly illustrate, first, that new media are still in the process of adoption and have not yet reached their peak, and second, that the age of adopters plays a crucial role as an independent variable. It seems possible to formulate an "innovation hypothesis" such that

Table 18.2 Where Respondents Watch Films and TV Series (Source: Macek et al. 2015)

	Films	**TV series**
On a TV set – via TV broadcasting/cable	90.4 %	92.4 %
On a TV set – from DVD, USB, other physical carrier or from connected PC	28.5 %	7.2 %
On a PC monitor	7.6 %	4.0 %
On a laptop or tablet	13.5 %	8.1 %
With a projector connected to a PC or other device	1.4 %	0.8 %
Else	0.2 %	0.4 %

Table 18.3 Watching Films in Ways Other than via TV Broadcasting—Age Groups (Source: Macek et al. 2015)

	TV broadcasting	Other than TV broadcasting
18–29 years	79.6 %	68.1 %
30–39	88.0 %	52.2 %
40–49	89.0 %	43.2 %
50–59	94.9 %	31.6 %
60–69	95.6 %	18.4 %
70+	100.0 %	11.5 %

the dominant position of TV broadcasting will further weaken in time, and that reception of popular content from TV broadcasting will be further supplemented or substituted with "post-TV" practices.

On the other hand, relying on age alone to explain the choice of technological interface and source of content (or, in other words, reducing explanation simply to the innovation hypothesis) would be short-sighted. The innovation hypothesis helps to show only the uneven distribution of the ownership of new media and therefore of the access to them. A more plausible explanation must take into account the key role played in "post-TV" practices by the intentions of the social actors—the motivations and needs that structure those practices.

Analysis of our qualitative interviews identifies clusters of main motivations, suggesting interface and content choice as aspects of active participation in the (re)construction of media ensembles. These motivations appear related to respondents' cultural capital (Bourdieu 1996), to the moral economy of their home (Silverstone et al. 1992; Silverstone 2006), to their need for organization and ritualization of domestic time and, ultimately, to other arbitrary instrumental needs and decisions.

Table 18.4 Watching TV Series in Ways Other than via TV Broadcasting—Age Groups (Source: Macek et al. 2015)

	TV broadcasting	Other than TV broadcasting
18–29 years	78.1 %	37.1 %
30–39	93.1 %	13.2 %
40–49	91.4 %	11.3 %
50–59	97.2 %	8.0 %
60–69	98.4 %	3.8 %
70+	97.9 %	1.9 %

The same relations between these motivations and audiences' choices of interface can be seen as weighing on the historically antecedent choice between watching films in movie theaters and buying or renting films on material media (videocassettes, DVDs, and today, Blu-ray).

The role of cultural capital—establishing consumption taste and fostering self-identity distinctions—is most conspicuously manifested in cases where respondents identify themselves as moviegoers in general, as art film fans, or, for instance, as science fiction movie buffs. For these respondents, watching films is one of the constitutive practices of their socio-cultural identity. As such, respondents suggest, it is better to do this in a *proper way*—a practice often more idealized than actually done. One respondent, Silva, identifying herself as a fan of art films, mentions several times that, before she had children, she used to regularly visit a small, art-oriented movie theater with her husband because she "grew up on that." Her husband, however, admits that these visits were rather infrequent, even in the past. The *proper way* is usually connected with *possession* of proper material media—with owning and watching the original DVD, for example. Jakub, a *Star Wars* fan, remarks: "In the case of *Star Wars*, I need to have them, I need to have the original [DVD], so I buy it." And Adam, a highbrow music listener, says even in relation to movies: "The original has a bit more value. When I like something a lot or when it is somehow significant for me, I buy the original."

Motivations drawing on respondents' moral economy rest on a sense of practical rationality. The notion of moral economy addresses the "alternative logic" of domestic economy arising from the interaction between the "inner" private space and the "outer" public (economic, cultural, political) space, and which is based on domestic negotiations over reasonability and adequacy of particular practices (Silverstone et al. 1992; Silverstone 2006). The "moral," as Jo Pierson notes, then "refers to the way that the meaning of public activities like work, relaxation or shopping is being negotiated through the knowledge, values, norms, assessment and the aesthetics within the household" (Pierson 2006: 213). With regard to watching films, the moral economy is apparent in weighing the reasonability of the financial and temporal costs of visiting movie theaters, buying original DVDs, or using online rental services. Anna, twenty-five years old and working in a food factory, suggests: "We have seen *X-Men* recently in the cinema. But I have to choose what film I really want to see in the cinema, for what movie I'm willing to pay that much money. Otherwise I download it, you know."

Respondents subordinate their choice of reception interface to their need for control over the temporal dimension of their everyday lives and to their need for ritualization of their time. The ritualization of time refers, on the one hand, to the repetitive and cyclical experience of the everyday activities (Silverstone 1994), and, on the other, to the Durkheimian distinction between profane and sacred time (Durkheim 2008). While the respondents' decision to download the content is—as we show below—often motivated by their will to control the time of reception and of their domestic rituals, the choice of cinema is usually framed as a special, festive event connected with both the unique experience of media content and the maintenance and reproduction of social ties. "Well, we usually combine it with some socializing," says Marta, forty-one years old, "so [we go to the cinema] because we can meet, we go with our friends."

Television is, in contrast to the cinema or physical DVDs, experienced as an inexpensive and taken-for-granted source of content[5]—and though TV is not connected with the "special event" of the cinema or the possession of a culturally prestigious object such as the original DVD, the TV set and TV broadcasting remain an important part of the everyday life. Television keeps its position at the centre of respondents' homes, given its role in mundane everyday rituals (Silverstone 1994).

However, despite the centrality of television in the majority of the Czech homes, the respondents employing "post-TV" practices repeatedly refer to problems they have with TV broadcasting. The first problem is linked with the need for control over domestic time—the flow of TV broadcasting pushes viewers to subordinate to the programming. Adam, in his thirties, married with two children, complains: "There's a lot of good stuff I'd like to watch on TV but it's too late for me. Or it's at completely the wrong time." Therefore he chooses other sources of content.

The second problem—despite Adam's opinion that "there's a lot of good stuff"—is dissatisfaction with the programming that Czech TV stations offer. Alena, forty-nine years old, notes that she simply does not watch TV frequently because "there's not much to choose"; one of the other respondents straightforwardly remarks, "What can I say? There's complete shit on TV."

The need for control over temporality of reception and over the content choice brings us back to the issue of downloading. The most influential affordance of television—the flow of broadcasting structuring the temporality of the domestic space and creating opportunities to relax, or serving as background for other domestic routines—is at the same time one of the most important reasons for some viewers to shift their reception to online sources.

3. Downloading online content: Practices and motivations

Among our respondents, 31.8 percent of the film viewers and 30.1 percent of the TV series viewers download the content for free, watch it online for free, or watch it for a fee.

The low percentages related to watching film and TV series online for a fee are—like the low frequency of buying music online—connected with the simple fact that the current portfolio of online services is (specifically in the case of films and TV series) limited in the Czech Republic. Audiences (as we show below) have thus had to rely on the limited offerings of TV broadcasting or else on non-authorized sources of content.

Table 18.5 Sources of Content Used by Film and TV Series Viewers (Other than TV Broadcasting) (Source: Macek et al. 2015)

	Films	**TV series**
Buying on DVDs or other media	13.7 %	1.4 %
Renting DVDs or other media in rentals	2.6 %	0.7 %
Borrowing DVDs or other media from friends	11.9 %	1.1 %
Downloading for free from the Internet	20.1 %	8.6 %
Having content downloaded by a partner	5.0 %	1.5 %
Having content downloaded by friends	6.7 %	1.4 %
Watching for free in a web browser (from YouTube or other online platforms offering the content)	12.6 %	8.2 %
Watching in a web browser for a fee	2.0 %	0.9 %

Table 18.6 Sources of Content Used by Music Listeners (Other than Radio and TV Broadcasting) (Source: Macek et al. 2015)

Buying on CDs, vinyl or other media	23.4 %
Renting CDs, vinyl or other media in the public library	1.8 %
Borrowing CDs, vinyl or other media from friends	13.6 %
Downloading for free from the Internet	27.8 %
Having downloaded content by partner	5.3 %
Having downloaded content by friends	10.1 %
Listening for free in web browser (from YouTube or other online platforms offering the content)	23.1 %
Listening online using authorized music services (Spotify, Deezer, Last FM etc.)	9.6 %
Buying online (iTunes etc.)	1.6 %

The decision to download content from online sources is actually an integral part of the choice of reception interface, and so downloading content is unsurprisingly related to the age of respondents.

Though data from the qualitative samples suggest that older respondents in particular do not treat downloading as an obvious and routine choice, the motivations for such decisions are mostly banal and instrumental, describable in terms of maximization of use value and minimization of transaction costs. As suggested above, the choice usually depends on (1) the respondent's unfulfilled expectations (unsatisfying TV programming or cinema offerings, unavailability of content on physical media), (2) unacceptable costs of cinema-going or physical media, and (3) contextual needs related to the structure of everyday routines. Online content sources simply serve these interests in many cases better than broadcasting media or officially distributed physical media: the content is instantly and easily available for no or low financial costs, the respondents have access to a wider and more up-to-date reservoir of content, and they have full control over the interface and as well as over the temporal dimension of the reception. To put it simply, the respondents practicing downloading conceive it as the easiest and most affordable way to satisfy their other cultural needs.

The financial costs—and here again we encounter the logic of moral economy—are not neglected by the respondents. Rather, the respondents see some pricing as unreasonable, given the limited variety and low quality of authorized online offerings in the Czech Republic, and availability of other online options for that content. One respondent reports: "[T]here is no single service that would be able to offer it, the movie, in the proper quality for realistic money. For me it's nonsense to spent six hundred [about $25] for a DVD, to watch it once and then to throw it into a drawer." By "proper quality," he refers (as do several others) to the fact that the officially distributed titles are mostly years out of date (both films and TV series) and, in the case of foreign titles, officially distributed content rarely comes with the option to

Table 18.7 Downloading and Age

	Downloading films or TV series	Downloading music
Age 18–39	45.70 %	54.20 %
40+	12.90 %	17.90 %
P	< 0.001	< 0.001
N	1998	1998

choose between Czech dubbing and Czech subtitles. The non-authorized online sources provided by grassroots efforts offer both: current films and TV content as well as Czech subtitles. In this regard, respondents usually suggest that they are prepared to pay some *reasonable* amount of money, lower than the price of a cinema ticket (suggestions are in the range of 50 cents to three dollars per film or episode, or in the form of monthly or annual fees), but would expect the proper quality and access to content as simply and comfortably as access to non-authorized online sources.

Obviously, the choice of content source is not necessarily or primarily driven by reasons of *minimizing financial costs*. This is especially apparent in the interviews from the second qualitative data collection, where we broadened our focus to include how respondents obtained videogames, books, and computer software. Paralleling the proper quality of films and TV series, respondents highlighted the comfort connected with official technical support, with regular software or OS updates or, in the case of videogames, with full access to online features and bugfixes. The difference is that, in this case, respondents are getting what they desire: "I aim to have a legal operating system, simply because of the upgrades, because I want to have the system secured and want to use the customer services, you know, the helpline and so on," said Milan, one of the older respondents.

It is important to emphasize that, with few exceptions, our data do *not* suggest that respondents—ordinary audience members—consider downloading as a revolt against the corporate industry or the capitalist market system. Nor do the data from the second qualitative sample—specifically focusing on the topic—suggest that respondents who engage in such downloading are "pathological nonconformists" deliberately breaking social norms. On the contrary, as we will show below, they largely conceive of their practices as complying with social norms, as a normatively acceptable and legitimate form of accessing content.

4. Curation of online content

Before discussing the ethical dimension of our respondents' experiences, we need to have a closer look at a final element in audiences' content decisions: the choice of particular film or TV series. Drawing upon Jiří Fiala's ethnographic study of Czech audiences' reception of content from non-authorized sources (Fiala 2012), we call this decision-making process *curation of content*. Fiala concludes that broadcasters are losing their monopoly over distribution of content, that audience members employ different tactics in the obtaining and reception of online content than they employ in choosing content from broadcasting media. Here, Fiala makes the distinction between *expert curation* and *social curation*.

Expert curation is typical for broadcasting media reception and is derived from broadcasters' program strategies, so that audiences' decision-making is limited to a content terrain pre-structured by the broadcast programming. Social curation, on the other hand, is based on viewers' own (push) activities. According to Fiala, when it comes to online reception, viewers and listeners employ curation tactics based primarily on trust in recommendations from their social peers (from friends and relatives, from contacts on Facebook, etc.).

However, the findings of Fiala's pilot study—based on interviews with relatively young and quite active online content consumers—do not cover the whole field of curation practices. Samples of our two qualitative inquiries were broadened to include a wider socio-demographic field, including both extensive and occasional viewers. Analysis of these interviews indicates that, besides the expert and social curation identified by Fiala, there is another distinct curation practice: *data-consultation curation*. Moreover, in the case of couples living together, the choice of content is inevitably negotiated between partners and reflects the dynamics of their relationships as well as compatibilities or dissonances of their individual cultural capital (however, these domestic negotiations we bracket here).

Data-consultation curation centrally involves the use of online databases such as IMDb, or its regional equivalents—Czech audience members mostly used the domestic databases ČSFD and FDB. "[W]hen we have no inspiration, we go to ČSFD," says thirty-three-year-old Tereza, "and we [she and her husband] check the premieres three months back." Tereza and other respondents use online databases as a routine consultation source because the databases allow access to a classification system organized by a reliable external authority and covering the whole reservoir of films and TV. Such databases thus serve as a resource of extratextual and intratextual knowledge, enabling viewers to contextualize received content. Moreover, databases are intentionally used as a tool for preliminary classification of the quality of content. Users employ folksonomies—social indexing—enabling them to evaluate the content included in the database using both scale measures and verbal evaluations. Another respondent, Vera, notes: "so he [Vera's husband] looks at the name of what he downloaded and then he checks the [other users'] reviews [laughing] at what it's about." Data consultation is, as such, one of the first and key decision filters preceding the final decision whether to consume the particular content or not.

Table 18.8 Distribution of Curation Practices—Differences Between the TV and Post-TV Viewers

	Not downloading films or TV series/ not watching online (n=1302)	**Downloading films or TV series/watching online (n=636)**
Expert curation	76.30 %	45.40 %
Social curation	26.40 %	61.00 %
Data-consultation curation	6.70 %	37.90 %

Viewers watching films and TV series downloaded from online sources usually do not reject expert curation but combine it with other curation styles. Table 18.8 displays distribution of all three modes of curation within Czech film and TV series audiences, comparing curation practices of the viewers who watch content from online sources with those who rely on TV broadcasting. The viewers watching films and TV shows obtained from online sources employ social curation and data-consultation curation more often than those watching the content conventionally, via TV broadcasting.

5. Downloading and ethics

In this last part of the chapter we take a closer look at how respondents reflect on illicit downloading from an ethical point of view. Since that topic was not covered by the questionnaire of the quantitative survey, we rely here on qualitative interviews and our conclusions are limited to interpretation, avoiding more general statements about the frequency of the phenomenon in the population.

As already mentioned, our respondents generally conceived of downloading audiovisual content as a normatively acceptable and legitimate practice, as mundane consumer practice not ordinarily subject to deeper reflection or ethical reconsideration. When those respondents taking part in the second qualitative data collection were confronted during the interview with an analogy comparing illicit downloading with theft from a store, they reacted in a variety of ways: some were surprised; many did not have an immediate or coherent answer; some intuitively rejected the analogy, unable to explain thoroughly their reasons for the rejection. Indeed, only a few individuals in either qualitative sample were able to offer a reflexive and pre-formulated position towards illicit downloading—notably in the form of hyperbole and self-irony, as in case of David and his wife Silva:

> Q: Where do you get these movies?
> David: [Ironically] Stealin'.
> Q: Who steals them? You? Your wife?
> David: I steal them. She's not that much into it.
> Q: Some people have a problem with downloading because they take it for free …
> Silva: We don't have this problem. Neh. This is how much of a crook I am. I even ride the tram without a ticket. [laughing]

This irony should be seen as a reaction to the normative public discourse ("downloading is stealing") confronted with lived experience: as a reflexive diminution of the conflict between the everyday routine practices and external normative rule experienced in everyday life as implausible.

However, this answer is unique in our samples. Most of the respondents did not have an instant answer or strong opinion because they have not yet faced the need to build such a reflection. When asked what they usually do when someone recommends some audiovisual product, the typical answer was similar to one fifty-two-year-old Iva told us: "If it was a movie, I would go to uloz.to [Czech file server]. Yes, I would try to look for it there and download it." Absent from these answers is any reflection of possibly problematic action.

Unsurprisingly in this regard, most of the respondents—when asked directly about the issue—were not able to make clear distinction between legal and illegal online sources of data. Michal, forty years old, openly admits: "I never thought about it, on this level. You know, I was never thinking about my downloading being legal or illegal." And Jiří, twenty-four, rejects any concern about the issue: "Look, I don't care if it's there legally or illegally." Moreover, those with some awareness of Czech copyright law had mostly limited and misleading knowledge about it. One of the respondents, for instance, symptomatically concludes that "Czech law says something like, you can download music and video but you can't offer it for download"; in fact, Czech copyright law allows for the downloading of non-authorized copies for non-commercial, personal needs "only if the use of a work in such special cases shall not conflict with the normal exploitation of the work and shall not unreasonably prejudice the legitimate interests of the author" (Czech Copyright Act, vol. 4, art. 29).

So, is it possible to conceive of practices of downloading content from mostly non-authorized online sources as a purely instrumental decision? Could we understand these practices as disinhibited agency, taking into account only the immediate context and ignoring the broader context represented here by law and social norms? Such a conclusion would be short-sighted. Despite respondents' low reflexivity on the topic, the interviews reveal several implicit moral intuitions that emerged when respondents were explicitly confronted with different views on the legitimacy of downloading and sharing of non-authorized copies of content, and with hypothetical scenarios.

(1) The respondents distinguish between downloading for one's own use and downloading for selling; from the ethical point of view, they reject downloading from the non-authorized source for purposes of further profit. Martin, twenty-eight, says: "[I prefer] to buy it from the author or to try it somewhere for free and then support the author retrospectively. But I don't approve much when there is some third person taking advantage from it." In other words, respondents mostly consider acquiring a non-authorized copy when motivated by profit rather than by use value as theft—as profiting at the expense of the author. The respondents at the same time reject the notion that downloading for their own use might be theft—some see it as an ethical offense, harmless in comparison to commercial downloading.

(2) Unsurprisingly, respondents expressing some positive relation towards a particular creator (based, for example, on personal knowledge of the author, or on strong preference for the author's work) express even higher willingness to choose more costly and time-consuming forms of acquiring the artist's work, e.g. buying the DVD instead of downloading an online copy. Our hypothesis is that—as with related motivations based on cultural capital—both an emotional tie to the artist and spatial proximity to the artist decrease the respondents' sense of disinhibition and increase the commitment to obtain the content in the *proper way*. Milan, sixty-one, in this regard remarked: "[When] I'm at some concert of my favorite band, for example, and they're selling their CDs and DVDs and [...] I buy it because I get the first-class quality and, at the same time, it is an immediate appreciation of a follower [...] that they deserve [...] to get paid by me for the product." However, this sort of position is typically linked with local or indie music production (where the geographic and social distance is experienced as low) and not with global music or audiovisual production.

(3) Yet, no matter how close or distant the author is, almost all our respondents implicitly employ the labor theory of value—in other words, they acknowledge that the author has ownership rights to the outcome of her work because her effort created a value that did not exist before. The respondents' recognition of the author's ownership of the work then explains why the respondents consider

the profit-oriented non-authorized sharing or downloading content as wrong: they see it as a violation of the author's potential legitimate profit.

Here, respondents face an apparent clash in their views: on the one hand they see the downloading of non-authorized content as a routine, mundane, and more-or-less unproblematic practice; on the other hand, they admit that downloading can be wrong as it could cause financial loss to the authors. The discrepancy between respondents' words and practices finds its reconciliation in some respondents' claims, well illustrated by Jaroslav's words: "I don't have a bad feeling about [downloading] films because I would not go to the cinema anyway so they don't lose anything. I just have it earlier [than it is on TV]. So, otherwise I would not have it." In other words, some of the respondents contend that they would not buy the content they download anyway, and so they cannot be blamed for causing any harm to anybody's profit. Some other respondents admit (at least implicitly) the incoherence by employing—as we have already seen above in a similar context—the self-ironic standpoint.

Is it possible to frame these responses as *post-hoc* justifications of the perceived misconduct, or as a neutralization preceding the actual misconduct (see Ingram and Hinduja 2008)? They could probably be interpreted both ways. However, to think here in terms of linear causality (implied both by the "post-hoc" and neutralization reasoning) is to ascribe to our respondents intentions not easily found in the qualitative interviews. We consider it more accurate to reject the "post-hoc justification" and "neutralization" explanations, instead interpreting such justification as symptomatic of the simple fact that some of the respondents experience their practices as problematic, but not unacceptable. After all, most of the other respondents do not consider the discrepancy a problem at all, and do not have any particular need for explanation or legitimation of their habits.

(4) Respondents considered it more reasonable to pay the market price for software and music, i.e. for content designed for repeated reception or use. However, they mostly expressed reluctance to buy films and TV shows—conceived, with exceptions mentioned above, as mundane content for one-time reception—for the current market prices. Martin, twenty-nine, does the calculation: "You know, when counting the use value, I watch the film once or twice but the program I use many times, so if I would make the mean [of the price of a single use] [...] I would get the final value." Here again we encounter the logic of moral economy: respondents usually describe the market prices as unreasonably high in comparison to "more durable" products or "more unique" content-related events (such as visiting a cinema or attending a concert), and therefore as illegitimate.

(5) Last but not least, several respondents expressed critical distrust of content distributors or copyright protection monopolies, blaming corporate or institutional actors for "robbing" the authors of their profit and for preventing the free circulation of information. "Indeed, they [OSA, one of the major Czech collective rights management societies] are the thieves, they are robbing the artists. Not us, but they are robbing the artists most," concludes one of the respondents. Nevertheless, for the same reasons as in case above, we hesitate to describe this critical stance as *post-hoc* justification.

6. Conclusion

Our quantitative data show that Czech film and TV audiences are moving from TV broadcasting to discontinuous and selective practices connected with uses of new digital media. Though TV broadcasting maintains its dominance as a source of content, primarily younger audience members increasingly employ "post-TV" practices connected with uses of films and TV series from online sources. Moreover, as analysis of our eighty-six qualitative interviews indicates, our respondents experience these practices as a mundane, more-or-less unproblematic part of their everyday media-related routines. But yet, the specific situation of the Czech distribution market—characterized by limited authorized sources of current content—creates a context in which most "post-TV" practices inevitably confront the boundaries of existing Czech copyright law.

The qualitative data suggest that this situation is accompanied by limited awareness of the copyright protection of online content and that even the better-informed respondents employ rather fragmentary and biased knowledge of the legal status of their practices. Nevertheless, when analyzing the reception of downloaded content in relation to the broader context of respondents' everyday lives and the whole ensemble of their media-related practices, we do not consider it appropriate to reduce the issue either to insufficient legal awareness of Czech audiences or to the problem of piracy.

First, we have shown that the decision to employ downloading as a source of audiovisual content is part of a wider set of intertwined decisions related to the choice of particular media technologies used for reception, of particular types of works, and of particular content. In this regard, the decision for downloading is structured by everyday contexts transformed by the presence and uses of new media, and by the broader contexts mainly represented by the system of media production and distribution. The respondents' need for control over the routine of their everyday lives meets here with their need to maintain their cultural capital, with their moral economy, with their desire to do things in the simplest and most effective ways, as well as within the limits of the authorized offerings of broadcasters and distributors. From this point of view, the "post-TV" practices we have discussed should be seen as symptomatic of the ongoing transformation of both media audiences and media industries—and to reduce the issues to a conflict between practice and legal regulation would prevent us from seeing the whole picture.

Secondly, we argue that despite their limited legal awareness, the respondents should not be seen as acting in an ethical vacuum. Although they have little urge to reflect on their practices from an ethical point of view (as they consider their practices normatively unproblematic), this hardly allows us to ethically blame them. They acknowledge the authors' rights to the content, although their conception of these rights and their recognition of authors legitimate claim for rewards do not fully correspond with copyright law, with respondents judging themselves as entitled to download the content for free under some circumstances. Furthermore, they obviously employ implicit and shared criteria for making the distinction between "legitimate" and "illegitimate" copies of content, and they employ ethical rules enabling them to frame the profit-oriented downloading and sharing of content as unfair to the authors of the content. In other words, the shared social norms expressed through downloading practices differ from the legal rules, but should be conceived of as ethical in nature—respondents operate on a notion of correct or acceptable practice, enabling them to think and act in terms of "being wrong" and "being right."

Finally, the broader contextual perspective applied to online piracy in the Czech Republic underlines the discrepancy between audiences' expectations regarding scope, quality, and price of content services and the actual offerings of authorized content distributors. Our conclusion is that the distributors have simply not yet been able to react satisfactorily to the transformation of audiences' "post-TV" needs and consumption habits. Audiences' need for affordable, comfortable, up-to-date, and—from the viewers' point of view—desirable online content accompanied by balanced roles for consumers and producers was nicely formulated by one of our respondents:

> I understand that some protection of the authors [is necessary] but I think that [...] if I would offer, as an author, in some scope, some product such as a game, music, film or whatever, that I would share online or even would aim to sell online, I would probably appreciate that, for instance, nine of ten people will buy it for some ridiculous[ly low] testing price and some of them will pay me

the full price later. Instead of one buying and nine just downloading it somehow illegally. Yes, I believe there must be some third way, not that harsh on one side or the other.
Martin, 28[6]

Notes

1 Flores and James define *moral thinking* as one's ability to recognize consequences of one's actions for known others, a capacity for empathy and adherence to the principles such as fairness, justice, and mutual respect in relation to known others, whereas *ethical thinking* is defined as an awareness of potential effects of one's actions for larger entities, reflection on one's roles and responsibilities in community, and consideration for the multiple interests of other stakeholders (Flores and James 2012).

2 Our chapter is in this regard similar to Schwarz's qualitative research on online file sharing (Schwarz 2014) or to Latonero's and Sinnreich's reseach on criteria applied by recipients in evaluation of legitimacy of new reconfigurable cultural forms (mashups), substituting unclear legal criteria (Latonero and Sinnreich 2014).

3 By "media ensembles" we mean the individually variable sets of media-related practices, media technologies, and textualities that could be seen as "more or less reflexively constructed classificatory systems structured by particular needs, by cultural, social and economic capital and impacted by the spatiotemporal organization of their everyday lives" (Macek 2015: 199).

4 A detailed technical report on the survey and the full collection basic descriptive data is available online; see Macek et al. 2015.

5 The Czech broadcasting system is organized in a way more or less similar to other European countries (e.g. Germany or the U.K.): every household owning a TV set (or functional equivalent) is supposed to pay an obligatory monthly fee (135 CZK, i.e. 6 US dollars). The fee is used for financing media of public service. Even in other aspects, the Czech media system does not differ substantially from the rest of Europe: the terrestrial broadcasting has been completely digitized since 2010, and the dual media system includes both commercial channels (making profit on advertising revenue or on cable subscriptions) and public service channels (financed mainly from the fee).

6 The chapter is built on two research projects: "New and old media in everyday life: Media audiences at the time of transforming media uses" (Czech Science Foundation, 13-15684P) and "Sociological research on ethics of copying" (Internal Grant Agency of Palacký University Olomouc, IGA-FF-2015-30).

References

Bakardjieva, M. (2005), *Internet Society: The Internet in Everyday Life*, London: Sage.

Bauwens, M. (2002), "Peer to Peer: From Technology to Politics to a New Civilisation." Available online: https://www.itu.int/osg/spu/wsis-themes/contributions/others/pEERNewP2P.pdf

Bourdieu, P. (2006), *Distinction: A Social Critique of the Judgement of Taste*, London: Routledge.

Bruns, A. (2008), *Blogs, Wikipedia, Second Life, and Beyond: From Production to Produsage*, New York: Peter Lang.

Davidson, D. (1984), "On the Very Idea of a Conceptual Scheme," in *Inquiries into Truth and Interpretation*, 183–98, Oxford: Clarendon Press.

Durkheim, E. (2008), *The Elementary Forms of Religious Life*, Oxford: Oxford University Press.

Feldman, T. (1999), *An Introduction to Digital Media*, New York: Routledge.

Fiala, J. (2012), "Nelegálně distribuované video z hlediska mediální etnografie," *Mediální studia* 6 (1): 60–75.

Flores, A. and C. James (2012), "Morality and Ethics behind the Screen: Young People's Perspectives on Digital Life," *New Media & Society* 15 (6): 834–52.

Freestone, O. and V. Mitchell (2004), "Generation Y Attitudes Towards E-ethics and Internet-related Misbehaviours," *Journal of Business Ethics* 54 (2): 121–8.

Giddens, A. (1976), *New Rules of Sociological Method*, London: Hutchinson.

Giddens, A. (1984), *The Constitution of Society: Outline of the Theory of Structuration*, Cambridge: Polity Press.

Hennig-Thurau, T., V. Henning, and H. Sattler (2007), "Consumer File Sharing of Motion Pictures," *Journal of Marketing* 71 (4): 1–18.

Ingram, J. R. and S. Hinduja (2008), "Neutralizing Music Piracy: An Empirical Examination," *Deviant Behavior* 29 (4): 334–66.

Jenkins, H. (2006), *Convergence Culture: Where Old and New Media Collide*, New York: New York University Press.

Latonero, M. and A. Sinnreich (2014), "The Hidden Demography of New Media Ethics," *Information, Communication & Society* 17 (5): 572–93.

Latour, B. (1987), *Science in Action: How to Follow Scientists and Engineers through Society*, Milton Keynes: Open University Press.

Lessig, L. (1999), *Code and Other Laws of Cyberspace*, New York: Basic Books.

Lessig, L. (2004), *Free Culture: How Big Media Uses Technology and the Law to Lock down Culture and Control Creativity*, New York: Penguin Press.

Lessig, L. (2006), *Code: Version 2.0*, New York: Basic Books.

Lysonski, S. and S. Durvasula (2008), "Digital Piracy of MP3s: Consumer and Ethical Predispositions," *Journal of Consumer Marketing* 25 (3): 167–78.

Macek, J. (2013), *Poznámky ke studiím nových médií* [*Notes on New Media Studies*]. Brno: MUNI Press.

Macek, J. (2015), "Social Media and Diffused Participation," in P. Lorentz, D. Šmahel, M. Metyková, and M. Wright (eds), *Living in the Digital Age: Self-presentation, Networking, Playing, and Participating in Politics*, 196–209, Brno: MUNI Press.

Macek, J., A. Macková, K. Škařupová, and L. Waschková Císařová (2015), *Old and New Media in Everyday Life of Czech Audiences. (Research Report.)*, Brno: Masaryk University.

Manovich, L. (2001), *Language of New Media*, Cambridge, MA: MIT Press.

Najder, Z. (1975), *Values and Evaluations*, Oxford: Clarendon Press.

Pierson, J. (2006), "Domestication at Work in Small Businesses," in T. Berker, M. Hartmann, Y. Punie, and K. Ward (eds), *Domestication of Media and Technology*, 205–25, Maidenhead: Open University Press.

Rochelandet, F. and F. Le Guel (2005), "P2P Music Sharing Networks: Why the Legal Fight Against Copiers May Be Inefficient," *Review of Economic Research on Copyright Issues* 2 (2): 69–82.

Schwarz, J. A. (2014), *Online File Sharing: Innovations in Media Consumption*. New York: Routledge.

Shiga, J. (2007), "Copy-and-Persist: The Logic of Mash-Up Culture," *Critical Studies in Media Communication* 24 (2): 93–114.

Silverstone, R. (1994), *Television in Everyday Life*, New York: Routledge.

Silverstone, R. (2006), "Domesticating Domestication: Reflections on the Life of a Concept," in T. Berker, M. Hartmann, Y. Punie, and K. Ward (eds), *Domestication of Media and Technology*, 229–48, Maidenhead: Open University Press.

Silverstone, R., E. Hirsch, and D. Morley (1992), "Information and Communication Technologies and the Moral Economy of the Household," in R. Silverstone and E. Hirsch (eds), *Consuming Technologies: Media and Information in Domestic Spaces*, 15–31, Routledge: London.

Strangelove, M. (2005), *The Empire of Mind: Digital Piracy and the Anti-capitalist Movement*, Toronto: University of Toronto Press.

Svensson, M. and S. Larsson (2012), "Intellectual Property Law Compliance in Europe: Illegal File Sharing and the Role of Social Norms," *New Media & Society* 14 (7): 1147–63.

Vaidhyanathan, S. (2001), *Copyrights and Copywrongs: The Rise of Intellectual Property and How It Threatens Creativity*, New York: New York University Press.

Vaidhyanathan, S. (2004), *The Anarchist in the Library: How the Clash Between Freedom and Control is Hacking the Real World and Crashing the System*, New York: Basic Books.

Xanthidis, D. and E. Aleisa (2012), "Internet Piracy from a Digital Consumer's Viewpoint," *International Journal of Communications* 6 (4): 153–65.

Zahrádka, P. (2015), *Heteronomie estetické hodnoty: Sociologická kritika filozofické estetiky*, Brno: Host.

19

Normative Resources and Domain-Specific Principles: Heading for an Ethics of Copying

Reinold Schmücker

1. The need for an ethics of copying

Copying has always been a widespread human practice. In which cases and to what degree it might or might not be permissible to copy an artifact is, however, a question that is more controversial today than ever. Of course, there are acts of copying whose moral wrongness is beyond dispute. This is true in particular for the production of copies made to deceive—as is the case with counterfeits, forgeries, and plagiarism: since deceiving is morally wrong, copies should neither be produced nor circulated in order to deceive. Copying, however, does not necessarily involve deception. And it is "mere" copying, i.e. copying that does not involve the intention to deceive, that raises difficult ethical questions which have become more and more urgent with advances in technology giving rise to entirely new modes of copying. Technical means for creating high-quality copies—in particular digital copying technologies and, even more recently, 3D printers—have become much more affordable, allowing for partial or complete copying with a hitherto unknown ease and (virtually) without any loss of quality. So, copying is today an activity that has become easily available for nearly everyone. The amount of copies that can be made of an object is limited only by the availability of the required resources.

Not surprisingly, then, restrictions on copying have an important cultural, economic, and socio-political significance. They not only regulate a society's cultural development and promote or prevent the economic success of industry; they also affect the social distribution of a great number of welfare-determining and cultural goods by making access to generally desirable artifacts more difficult than it could be, at least for some. Copying restrictions also safeguard the social status and economic capital of those who have produced or own original artifacts, including engineers, designers, artists, scientists, and sellers of originals that possess a sometimes enormous cultural or economic value due to their authenticity and carefully maintained scarcity. So the problem is: abolishing copying restrictions might weaken the motivation to create new, innovative objects and to conceive and establish new ways of disseminating goods. On the other hand, simple and unrestricted access to reproducible goods would, in many cases, be highly beneficial for many people. Beyond this, copying restrictions can stifle processes of democratization and political participation which, to a certain degree, depend on easy access to important goods for many people. Once more, it should be noted that the notion of "copying" is not limited to exact (1:1) duplicates, but also encompasses products that differ in shape and form from their respective originals, as well as imitation of behavior and acts of appropriating creative ideas. Against this background, it is clear that copying restrictions are a vital matter of social conflict and may be neither too strict nor too weak in order to obtain an appropriate level of social acceptance.

In modern societies, the medium for normatively restricting acts of copying is the law, particularly copyright law, patent and trademark law, and laws regulating unfair competition. These laws are—at least partially—concerned with acts of misappropriation and misrepresentation. However, the limits of regulating acts of copying by mere legal means have become obvious. Restricting copying by largely controlling the use of digital media is hardly compatible with the freedom of communication in a free and democratic state. Furthermore, effective technical copy protection and prevention tend to affect an owner's right of disposal of his property to a degree that is problematic both legally and morally. Present communication technologies allow for easy and hardly checkable sharing of copies of digitizable goods, and it becomes increasingly difficult to draw a line between private copying (allowed without the right holder's consent in every copyright system, though conceptualized differently in different legislations) and commercial copying activities. Although this has made some scholars appreciate the advent of a new "culture of sharing" (e.g. Sützl et al. 2012), the exercise of lawful private copying is "not shielded against technological or contractual restrictions" and so can be "rendered moot by technological protection measures or contractual clauses" (Karapapa 2012: 5).

Matters are further complicated, however. While many copyright holders (including both creators and exploiters) think that the law does not go far enough, the acceptance of existing laws imposing copying restrictions is limited and diminishing (see Sinnreich et al. 2009; Macek and Zahrádka 2016). Worldwide, many embrace the use of copying technology without a thought that there is anything wrong in what they are doing, even if they knowingly infringe existing copyright law, say, by illegally downloading music or movies from the internet. Some of them demand a liberalization or even the abolition of copyright law and intellectual property rights. Some of them contribute to the emergence of new ethical frameworks. Recent survey-based research on new media ethics has shown how and to what degree such new ethical frameworks "have arisen in the absence of a robust and adaptive legal regulatory apparatus, and often in contradistinction to the letter of copyright law itself" (Latonero and Sinnreich 2014: 590).

One factor adding to the growing discrepancy between the legal assessment of many copying processes and the widespread lack of a sense of guilt about copying in everyday life certainly is the ubiquitous availability of copying technology and the effortlessness of producing copies. Another factor might be that the law is often (and often rightly) perceived as being the result of lobbying pressure (from various parties, ranging from Hollywood to Google). The current shift from owning and copying physical things to merely having access to electronic data (streaming, cloud computing) further grows this discrepancy. While it is doubtful whether these factors can fully explain the remarkable gap between the current legal situation and common morality (a gap not limited to particular societies—see Sinnreich 2016), the divergence points to a normative deficit: major parts of the existing copyright laws, and of intellectual property law in general, are not regarded as normatively appropriate by a growing number of people.[1] It is primarily for this reason that we are in need of an ethics of copying. Although there exists a slew of articles and books preparing the grounds for an ethics of copying (predominantly written by lawyers transcending the horizon of the existing intellectual property law),[2] there isn't yet an ethics of copying that could be used as a normative framework for establishing a just balance of the interests of those affected by copying practices.

Of course, such an ethics can neither be carved in stone, nor be the result of scientific reflection alone. Being a contribution to the social discourse about the difference between legitimate and illegitimate acts of copying, an ethics of copying might, however, formulate specific rules for cases where current legal norms seem insufficient or unjust. Although it would be excessive to claim that these rules constitute the one definite catalogue or system of rules that should be internalized by everyone (or that would represent an objective ethics), an ethics of copying that offers well-argued proposals might influence future legislation and facilitate the formation as well as the intersubjective recognition of moral principles for distinguishing between legitimate and illegitimate forms of copying.

Such principles could also lead to best practice norms. Hence an ethics of copying will also have to attribute a heuristic value to existing best practice norms that have been formulated in science and the humanities, for example, as reactions to plagiarism cases. These might be candidates for the rules an ethics of copying is seeking (or at least hint towards them). However, it may be the case that there are restrictions of copying that are domain-specific—relative perhaps to what Max Weber termed "cultural value spheres" (see Weber 1988: I, 541), such as technology, economy, art, law, and the sciences, each with its own specific structure and peculiarity—and an ethics of copying should account for these.

An ethics of copying is also necessary from a legal point of view. If the law is supposed to shape reality in a way that can be normatively justified, lawmakers should seek to avoid a deep gap between positive law and common morality. This, however, requires reflection about the rationality and justifiability of normative attitudes that contradict the law, but which manifest in common practices and, in particular, in ongoing developments in the arts (sampling, remixing, digital art, appropriation art) or in social expectations and habits concerning the access to and use of information (the use of computer programs, information contained in databases, or internet-based social networks). The law might also benefit from an ethics of copying insofar as the latter can expose the implicit normative premises of the law and, at the same time, question them. For instance, Locke's justification of property has offered a universalistic foundation for copyright law in natural law, which has facilitated restrictions of copying across borders and states. But the limits of this paradigm also become visible: an ethics of copying may raise, among other things, the question of whether this paradigm prioritizes certain rights of copyright owners over justified claims for access and use made by third parties. This prioritization might no longer be generally acceptable.

Ultimately, the value of an ethics of copying can also be seen in bridging another gap between the legal situation and public opinion. We can observe public disapproval of traditional and legally permitted practices—such as branding the republication of a text by its author as "self-plagiarism"—promoted by today's means of discovering congruencies between artifacts. An ethics of copying will have to assess whether the partial appropriation of an artifact's elements could be legitimate in certain contexts and for certain purposes, even if it does not comply with the established norms for quoting and borrowing. Should we really expect that, for instance, opinions of the court, references, and exam questions must not contain any unquoted use of previous texts? Should a carpenter not be allowed to copy the standing desk that he has seen somewhere? Is the prestige of an expensive designer dress (and, perhaps, of some works of art) not also due to the fact that it is copied many times?

2. A normative basis for an ethics of copying

The reasons for being skeptical about an ethics of copying are many and understandable. Of course, the mere existence of moral norms—or the simple fact that some people assume some norms to be moral—does not guarantee that they will be respected, just as the existence of legal norms does not guarantee that people keep with them. Moral norms might even be less respected than legal norms, since ignoring them will, at most, be sanctioned informally, perhaps by contempt or exclusion from a social group. Ignoring moral norms (where these do not overlap with legal rules) will not be sanctioned by forms of punishment that affect the physical integrity of a person, such as a prison sentence. But the fact that norms cannot guarantee compliance is neither an argument against the need for norms, nor does it exclude the possibility of morally justified but widely deplored norms. Nevertheless, the question remains what the normative foundations of an ethics of copying might be, what areas it would apply to, and which kinds of normative statements it could make.

If we were to understand an ethics of copying literally as an applied ethics, we would delve into a quagmire. Simply applying rules and principles that some ethical theory prescribes—such as Kant's deontology, or Mill's or Sidgwick's utilitarianism—will surely not suffice to establish an ethics of copying. All of the well-known ethical theories are far too problematic and disputed even within Western cultures, and so we can put aside any question of how they could function as the basis of a *globally* convincing ethics. The idea that an ethics of copying could be developed by deriving concrete rules from the general principles of an ethical theory is also untenable: there is no well-known ethical theory from which sufficiently concrete rules could be derived for an ethics of copying. The subject is simply too heterogeneous and too specific to allow us to derive a workable rule from any general theory without additional normative assumptions. An ethics of copying cannot reasonably be derived; rather, it must be *built*.

We should therefore drop the common term "applied ethics" and rather consider the ethics of copying in terms of a *domain-specific ethics* (Nida-Rümelin 2005): an open set of assumptions or moral judgments that specifically refer to acts of copying. A domain-specific ethics of copying will be a set of normative intuitions, beliefs, and rules based on the attempt to critically reconstruct and systematize those moral intuitions and beliefs that we already have concerning the regulation of acts of copying. This is why an ethics of copying has to take empirical data about given moral beliefs into account and can therefore only be achieved in an interdisciplinary approach.

For a critical reconstruction, it is important to investigate whether the intuitions and beliefs of any individual person, group, or culture can be traced back to particular interests of that group or culture—and, perhaps, to its particular skills. These interests, however, may not matter from a moral point of view. We must investigate whether moral intuitions and beliefs about copying are compatible with other fundamental moral intuitions and beliefs—especially those that many people, or even cultures, share. And, of course, moral beliefs can be questioned—some of them might be justified, others might have to be refuted. Carrying out these investigations from a moral point of view most basically means assessing actions and beliefs impartially (see Hume 1751) and based on the criterion of fairness (see Rawls 2001).

The reconstruction and systematization that an ethics of copying is concerned with should not only be critical, but also constructive—which means spelling out rules and norms that should apply in regulating of acts of copying. These are rules that can be justified from a moral point of view. Since nobody has exclusive access to the moral point of view, however, an ethics of copying that is constructive in this sense can of course only develop theses and suggestions as contributions to the social discourse about regulating such acts. One will have to see whether they are in fact as convincing as they might seem *prima facie* and whether others will regard them as an adequate reconstruction of their own moral intuitions.

3. The main focus of an ethics of copying

When we judge an actual or possible action, we sort this action into a certain category. The basic categories of moral judgments are what is morally required, permissible, and prohibited, plus certain subcategories (see Schmücker 2011). The categories are basic, because moral judgments always presuppose that we can distinguish between what is morally prohibited and what is required, independently of which ethical theory we endorse. Regarding these categories as the basic categories of moral judgments of actions is therefore compatible with a pluralistic and even relativistic meta-ethics, because it does not presuppose a specific justification of moral duties or a specific ethical theory. The basic categories of moral judgments are rather the framework of categories that are at our disposal for morally assessing actions.

With regard to acts of copying, the following can be stated: (1) Normative conflicts about acts of copying rarely concern the question of whether an act of copying is morally required or not. In an emergency situation, such as a dangerous epidemic, copying the drugs that are needed to fight the epidemic might be morally required, even if the owner of the respective patent does not agree. It might also be morally required to copy the prescription for a vital drug that the pharmacist will not provide without a prescription. So we can say: acts of copying may be morally required in an emergency situation, where ignoring certain norms—which would hold in a normal situation—is morally permissible. The definition of an emergency situation, however, is the task of an ethics of emergencies (see Schmücker 2014) and not of an ethics of copying. (2) Normative conflicts about acts of copying rarely concern the question of whether an act of copying is morally condemnable and therefore strictly prohibited or not. Of course, an act of copying can be a central element of a deed that we consider to be morally condemnable. But what we consider to be morally condemnable is *this* action—which might be a capital crime, treason, deliberate deception (as in scientific plagiarism), or fraud—and not the act of copying itself that is part of the action. (3) In many cases of copying, the question of whether an act is morally permissible is a matter of dispute. However, even those who think that illegally downloading software or movies is morally prohibited do not seem to think that this is as strictly condemnable as burglary or capital crimes. We can take this fact into account by adding an intermediate category to the basic categories for the moral judgment of actions, that is, the category of *morally objectionable actions*, located somewhere between the category of morally permissible and morally prohibited actions (see Figure 19.1). This allows us to specify the main focus of moral judgments relevant for an ethics of copying. In many or maybe even most cases, normative conflicts regarding acts of copying concern the question of whether a non-authorized act of copying should be considered morally acceptable—and therefore morally permissible—or morally objectionable.

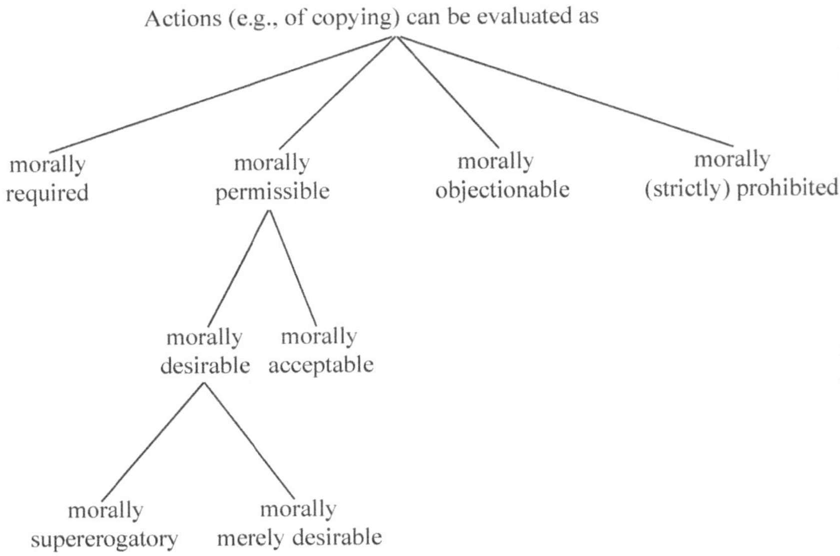

Figure 19.1 Basic Categories of Moral Evaluation

4. Some examples for domain-specific rules of an ethics of copying

In order to give an idea of what domain-specific rules might look like that an ethics of copying might propose, I shall suggest five principles that I think most of us could agree upon. These are akin to the midlevel principles established in medical ethics (Beauchamp and Childress 2013: esp. Ch. 6)[3], and their persuasiveness depends upon whether they can be regarded as plausible consequences of a systematization of common moral intuitions and considerations.

1. Our meta-ethical considerations so far suggest a first principle. It follows from a general moral principle that can be called the *principle of limited legal strictness: the legal evaluation of acts of copying should not be stricter than their moral evaluation.* This sounds like a very abstract principle and armchair philosophy. But the impression is misleading. If you agree with my diagnosis that normative conflicts about acts of copying mostly concern the question of whether an action is morally (still) acceptable or (already) objectionable, then you will be skeptical about criminalizing non-authorized acts of copying. If it were clear that, for instance, acts of illegally downloading music are at most

morally objectionable, but not strictly prohibited actions,[4] we would merely consider such actions to be minor offenses. In contrast to that, section 106 of the German Copyright Law (*Urheberrechtsgesetz*), for instance, states that the duplication, dissemination, and public playback of a copyrighted work will be punished by a prison sentence of up to three years or a fine, unless it takes place in certain contexts specified by the law as contexts of legal copying, or is authorized by the copyright holder. If you recognize the principle of limited legal strictness as a moral principle and agree that it is relevant in the given context, you will not think that this law can be morally justified. In fact, it seems to be morally required that acts of copying of this kind should be decriminalized, though many might consider them to be harmful and therefore morally objectionable. As acts of illicit copying would seem to belong to the same moral category as mere speeding (not resulting in any serious bodily harm), it is unreasonable that we should judge the former more harshly than the latter. We can, I believe, state the following: *since the legal evaluation of acts of copying should not be stricter than their moral evaluation, illegitimate acts of copying should legally only be sanctioned as minor offenses.*

How about the objection that there are also illegitimate acts of copying that are morally strictly prohibited—maybe copying the "biscuit": the card containing the American president's nuclear launch codes? I am not convinced by this objection. For what is morally strictly prohibited in such a case is not an act of copying as such, but rather the dissemination of a document that should remain secret for very good reasons—something different from the act of copying. Section 106 of the German copyright law, however, prohibits the mere duplication of a copyright-protected work and includes the dissemination of copies, even without financial gain, if it is not covered by the right to own a private copy or another barrier limit of the right holder's copyright. A protection of the rights of authors and exploiters that is this far-reaching cannot be morally justified by the fact that acts of copying can be part of offenses that we consider to be morally prohibited. The prevention of morally objectionable actions that involve acts of copying does not require a criminalization of acts of copying as such. Such prevention is already covered by criminalizing the respective morally objectionable action.

2. A second principle I would like to suggest is that *acts of copying that do not result in an entity that could substitute the template with regard to at least one of its principal purposes should be permissible, as long as there is no particular reason to protect the template against possible damages caused by the copying.* We

could call this the *principle of permissible non-substitutional copying*. It seems to me that this principle is supported by common intuitions and beliefs. The moral rights or claims of the copyright holders can only be violated if the act of copying leads to the production of one or more objects that could substitute the template with regard to whichever of its principal purposes—for instance, as the template for further copies, or as an exemplar of a multiply instantiable artifact. (Of course this only applies if we assume that the mere wish of the creator or others that there should be no copies does not constitute a sufficient justification for a moral demand to refrain from copying. But there are good reasons for this assumption.)

It is worth noting that the principle of permissible non-substitutional copying does in fact imply some moral restrictions of copying. It not only bans copying that would damage the template; it only allows for producing copies which cannot substitute the template at all, i.e. with regard to one of its principal purposes. However, this does not imply that the production of copies that could be used to substitute the copied object—in whichever respect—is altogether morally forbidden. There might be other reasons for allowing the production of copies that could be used instead of the template.

Acknowledging the principle of permissible non-substitutional copying would allow for implementing a law that prescribes the right to produce partial copies, with the exceptions mentioned above. It is clear that not all conflicts about copyrights that concern the use of partial copies or, for instance, reappearances of a fictional character (Young 2016) could be mitigated this way. However, acknowledging the principle of permissible non-substitutional copying would, for instance, avoid the absurdity that digital art as such would have to be regarded as a violation of copyright law for the very fact only that it involves copying pixels—even if the pixels copied obviously constitute a completely different entity (see e.g. Dreier 2016).

3. A third principle is a close relative of the second, and should make us skeptical about the results of software that detects instances of plagiarism. We should not automatically regard these results as cases of illegitimate acts of copying, for the vast majority of cases of so-called *self*-plagiarism are covered by a principle that can be called the *principle of permissible partial copying by the author. It should be allowed in principle (and not be subject to the disposition of contracting parties) that an author may copy parts of her own previously published works.* It does not seem morally objectionable if an author takes over parts of her own work—even if she has sold the copyright to an exploiter. For

there is no deception about the actual authorship, and no reputation of an original author is harmed. One could argue, however, that such self-repetitions by an author who has sold the copyright to someone else harms the copyright holder (for instance, the publishing house) because it might compromise the sales of the previous work. But note that the principle only allows for partial copying. Of course, even partial copying may under certain circumstances affect the sales of a work. But the risk that partial copying will cause this effect seems not only negligible (since in most cases a partial copy is not a substitute for the template), but from a moral point of view it rather seems to be outbalanced in principle by the positive effects to be expected by the acknowledgment of the principle of permissible partial copying by the author, namely that an author is generally entitled to re-present parts of her own works (specific formulations or visualizations, for instance) in a new context or to another audience, thereby enabling new insights. For if the principle of permissible partial copying by the author is acknowledged, an exploiter could calculate the expected sales by taking this right of the author into account, and there would be no harm done to the exploiter.

Reusing parts of one's own texts could only seem morally objectionable with respect to readers' attention. If I seem to say (at least partly) the same thing in two different texts without pointing this out explicitly to the reader, she might feel annoyed for having spent time reading a passage that she was already familiar with. Indeed, I was once told that self-plagiarism must not be permitted, else an appointment committee in medicine could not trust the calculation of the impact factor of an applicant's publications—meaning the committee would have to actually read them! However, even if we assume that a different context in which a certain passage appears will not lead to new insights, it is hard to see how a waste of the reader's attention resources would constitute a morally objectionable act. Do we want to suggest that *any* act that wastes another's time is immoral? This would be absurd. The repeated use of parts of an already published text can be illegal if one assumes—as, for example, British copyright law does—that authorship constitutes a mere right of control over the use of certain forms of expression that can be transferred to a third person with the effect that it will then be theirs. So, if I have transferred the copyright to a publishing house, the use of parts of my own text can be a copyright violation. It makes more sense to hold to the conception of a copyright as an author's right that cannot be transferred, as codified in the European *droit d'auteur* tradition. The morally well-justified idea that an author can use her own thoughts and phrasing as often as she wants—without having to note that she has already uttered them elsewhere—is better reflected by the *droit d'auteur* than by the copyright tradition.

One might object that the principle of permissible partial copying by the author should not exclude the waiving of permission to partial self-copying by contract. Given the generally prevailing imbalance of power between authors and exploiters, however, this exclusion seems necessary to assure the principle's efficacy. The principle itself is further validated by the fact that an author might need to partially copy her own works in order to continue authoring works at all. It could be the case that without the partial copying of (some of) her earlier works, she could no longer create works *in her style* at all: creating works in her style may require the reuse of an already developed idea, character, definition, formula, drawing, diagram, design, or whatever (see Bently 2016).

4. A fourth principle is suggested by the results of empirical research on people's normative attitudes with regard to copying, since it has been shown that people motivate their opinion that illegally downloading from the internet is at worst a minor offense with the alleged illegitimacy of the market prices they would have to pay otherwise (see Macek and Zahrádka 2016). This result suggests a principle that can be called the *principle of the illegitimacy of copying restrictions primarily achieving exorbitant prices: the restriction of acts of copying is illegitimate (i.e. morally forbidden) if it would result primarily in the establishment, retention or enhancement of someone's chances to benefit from an exchange of inequivalent goods*, as would be the case if someone were enabled by copying restrictions to achieve exorbitant prices, i.e. to obtain payment without rendering an adequate equivalent. This principle is validated by the deep-rooted moral intuition that it cannot be morally allowable to restrict others' valuable actions (as we might describe copying—see Alfino 2016; Houkes 2016) for the sake of facilitating exorbitant profits or other unfair material advantages. Its importance should not be underestimated: according to this principle, it is illegitimate to restrict copying by law for the primary purpose of providing someone with an unfair material advantage. Of course, one might object that it is difficult to determine whether a certain price should be recognized as exorbitant. The principle of the illegitimacy of copying restrictions primarily achieving exorbitant prices provides us, however, with a quite suitable criterion for this. Economists would have no great difficulty calculating the difference between the actual market price for a copyrighted work and the notional market price that the respective work would have if others were allowed to copy it without the author's permission, and it can be assumed that in a certain society, there is a

certain—albeit vague—social consensus about what market price is acceptable and which would count as an exorbitant price. If it can be supposed that, for instance, 200 percent of the notional market price is regarded as the maximum acceptable, it could be concluded that copying restrictions are illegitimate if they primarily result in the enabling of the achievement of a higher market price than this 200 percent.

5. A fifth principle should be uncontroversial, because most copyright legislations are explicitly or implicitly based on it: *the regulation of acts of copying should be governed by rules that establish a fair and impartial balance between the interests of authors, exploiters, users or consumers, people who potentially copy works, and the general public.* We could call this the *principle of a fair and impartial balance.*

Of course, details can be tricky. The principle itself might be uncontroversial, but what the concrete regulations are that should follow from it has been a matter of dispute throughout the history of copyright law. To this day, discussions about reforming copyright legislation mostly center around this point. The following aspects seem to be particularly relevant here.

Acknowledging the principle of a fair and impartial balance will require paying attention to the heterogeneity of interests between the parties mentioned above. This is currently a very important matter owing to the strongly diverging interests of first-order exploiters—that is, traditional publishing houses, the holders of image rights, the film and music industries—and second-order exploiters like Google. These conflicts of interest are also frequently taken to court.

The principle is also important because of the diverging interests of groups that usually gain less attention. For people working in a field that is not very profitable, it is important to be able to make copies without running the risk of the high costs that a lawsuit would entail. Those who can expect high profits from their copyrighted work, on the other hand, will usually be interested in maximizing that profit.

It is obviously important to strengthen the interests of authors, compared with those of exploiters, in order to adjust existing unfair imbalances. Anyone who has tried to remove the clauses about far-reaching ancillary rights from the contract for a scientific book will know what I mean. But an unfair advantage of second-order exploiters, such as Google, over first-order exploiters has to be avoided. This requires, first of all, explicit acknowledgment of the fact that the use of published material by databank-based online platforms is also a form of exploiting texts in the sense of the copyright law, even if there is no corresponding agreement between the authors or first-order exploiters and such second-order exploiters. The next step would be to discuss how the interests of authors and first-order exploiters can be protected by copy restrictions.

How can an ethics of copying acknowledge the principle of a fair and impartial balance so that the interests of the public as well as those of authors and exploiters are equally taken into account (while recognizing the diverging interests of different groups of authors)? Surely, a further extension of copyright terms is not the right solution. In Germany, until 1934, protection lasted for the lifetime of the author plus thirty years. Now, since 1965, it lasts for seventy years from the death of the author. The revised Berne Convention established fifty years after the author's death as the international minimum. Many critics of current copyright policy think that is too much. Seventy years *post mortem auctoris* is far too long. The life-plus-seventy-year period means that authors, their heirs, and contractual partners (like publishers and possibly a collecting society) can restrict a great many uses of the work and thus limit the creativity of artists who want to refer to the work for two generations after the original author's lifetime. And, thanks to the progress of modern medicine, the life expectancy even of authors has increased considerably. A prominent example might be Ernst Jünger, who published his first bestseller, *In Stahlgewittern*, in 1920 and lived another seventy-eight years before passing away in 1998. The copyright in his works will not expire before 2069, 149 years after the publication of *In Stahlgewittern*. There is no reason to think that the interests of the public today are less important relative to those of authors and exploiters than they were in the nineteenth century. On the contrary: the fact that many works today can be utilized globally, without any problems, and in countless ways, rather recommends a shortening of the copyright protection term. It is implausible that the ideal interests of an author should be protected longer than her mortal remains, which are protected for between fifteen and thirty years in Germany.

Given the general interests of a society that grants far-reaching artistic freedom (and promotes artists and other persons engaged in the cultural sector as well as scientists in manifold ways, not least by supporting them financially either directly or indirectly), authors can be expected to accept a shorter protection period for their works. The potential financial losses that this would entail would hardly affect the large majority of authors who are not commercially successful anyway, but only a small minority of successful authors and their heirs. According to our moral intuitions, this would be unproblematic. The advantages that commercially successful authors gain from their activities are considerable and need to be restricted to a certain degree in favor of the public's interest in having open access to works. I would go even further and suggest that the protection of promptly successful works should be limited to a shorter term than that of the works of less immediately successful authors, since even those authors who are not immediately successful should, ideally, have a chance to reap the benefits of their work. Since the promptness of commercial success does not seem to be revealing of the quality of a work, it would be only fair to give those authors who failed to have prompt economic success an additional chance to reap the benefits of their work (or at least to get reimbursed for their investments) by offering them an option for an extended copyright term.

A consequence of the principle of a fair and impartial balance would be a shorter copyright term of, say, thirty years after the date of publication that could be extended, perhaps even several times. The extension should only be possible in such cases where the authors and exploiters can show that the income generated by the work has, so far, not exceeded a certain threshold that should be determined for different kinds of works. (Since the income generated by copyrighted works has to be taxed in every country known to me, it should not be too difficult to determine the respective sum without bellying bureaucracy.) This model would turn highly successful works into the public domain much earlier than less successful works. This effect would be desirable for several reasons: it would ensure that authors and exploiters of works who failed to have prompt economic success are given an additional break to reap the benefits of their work. At the same time, the success and popularity of a work prove that the respective work has become part of the cultural (or technical) "vocabulary" of a community (perhaps even the global community). This vocabulary, however, should be accessible to everyone, unless there are particularly grave reasons against it, because it is needed by everyone either in order to express herself in a contemporary way or to contribute to the further development of culture as well as technology.

Notes

1 Many who copy without thinking that there is anything wrong in what they are doing not only unknowingly infringe copyright norms but do not even seem able

to imagine there could be a law that contradicts their actions (see e.g. Macek and Zahrádka 2016).

2 Bringsjord 1989; Alfino 1996; Bently and Maniatis 1998; Vaidhyanathan 2001; Palmer 2002; Garon 2003; Halpern 2003; Weil 2003; Hilton, Choi, and Chen 2004; Torremans 2004; Gosseries, Marciano, and Strowel 2008; Cohen 2009; Ess 2009; Hick 2009; Sabanna 2009; Sinnreich, Latonero, and Gluck 2009; Helfer and Austin 2011; Lever 2012; Pattanaik 2012; Theisohn 2012; Bahr 2013; Fiorentino 2013; and, in particular, Geiger 2015.

3 Robert P. Merges, in his very inspiring book *Justifying Intellectual Property*, has already offered four midlevel principles—developed by "starting in the middle, with the actual principles of law" (Coleman 2001: 6) and common morality—to bridge the gap between normative foundations and specific practices in order to justify intellectual property. These are (1) "efficiency," (2) "nonremoval," (3) "proportionality," and (4) "dignity" (Merges 2011: 8). Although the aim of an ethics of copying is at least partly different from the justification of intellectual property and so we can assume that it is in need of some further and different (and perhaps less abstract) principles, and even though I am skeptical regarding the possibility of grounding an ethics of copying on "truly foundational concept[s]" (Merges 2011: 6), I would like to draw attention to Merges's "nonremoval principle." This midlevel principle "says that information and ideas in the public domain must not be taken away or privatized" (Merges 2011: 7). I think that an ethics of copying should include this principle or a quite exact equivalent of it.

4 It is worth noting that empirical research confirms the assumption that illegally downloading music or films is broadly regarded as being at most morally objectionable, but not a strictly prohibited action; see Macek and Zahrádka 2016.

References

Alfino, M. (1996), "Intellectual Property and Copyright Ethics" [1991], in R. A. Larmer (ed.), *Ethics in the Workplace. Selected Readings in Business Ethics*, 278–93, Minneapolis, MN: West Publishing.

Alfino, M. (2016), "Deep Copy Culture," in D. H. Hick and R. Schmücker (eds), *The Aesthetics and Ethics of Copying*, 19–37, London and New York: Bloomsbury.

Bahr, A. (2013), "Was heißt 'ein Artefakt illegitim kopieren'? Grundlagen einer artefaktbezogenen Ethik des Kopierens," *Deutsche Zeitschrift für Philosophie* 61 (2): 283–99.

Beauchamp, T. L. and J. F. Childress (2013), *Principles of Biomedical Ethics*, 7th edn, New York: Oxford University Press.

Bently, L. (2016), "Self-Copying and Copyright," in D. H. Hick and R. Schmücker (eds), *The Aesthetics and Ethics of Copying*, 271–94, London and New York: Bloomsbury.

Bently, L. and S. Maniatis (eds) (1998), *Intellectual Property and Ethics*, London: Sweet & Maxwell.

Bringsjord, S. (1989), "In Defense of Copying," *Public Affairs Quarterly* 3 (1): 1–9.

Cohen, H. (2009), "'Moral Copyright': Indigenous People and Contemporary Film," in L. Gross, J. Katz, and J. Ruby (eds), *Image Ethics in the Digital Age*, 313–25, Minneapolis, MN: University of Minnesota Press.

Coleman, J. (2001), *The Practice of Principle. In Defence of a Pragmatist Approach to Legal Theory*, New York: Oxford University Press.

Dreier, T. (2016), "The Ethics of Copyright and *droit d'auteur* – An Outline," in D. H. Hick and R. Schmücker (eds), *The Aesthetics and Ethics of Copying*, 251–69, London and New York: Bloomsbury.

Ess, C. (2009), "The Ethics of Copying: Is it Theft, Open Source, or Confucian Homage to the Master?" in *Digital Media Ethics*, 73–103, Cambridge and Malden, MA: Polity Press.

Fiorentino, S. (2013), *Intellectual Property and Human Rights: Is a Balance Possible?* Oisterwijk: Wolf Legal Publishers.

Garon, J. (2003), "Normative Copyright. A Conceptual Framework for Copyright Philosophy and Ethics," *Cornell Law Review* 88: 1278–360.

Geiger, C. (ed.) (2015), *Research Handbook on Human Rights and Intellectual Property*, Northampton, MA: Edward Elgar.

Gosseries, A., A. Marciano, and A. Strowel (eds) (2008), *Intellectual Property and Theories of Justice*, Basingstoke: Palgrave Macmillan.

Halpern, S. W. (2003), "Copyright Law and the Challenge of Digital Technology," in L. Gross, J. Katz, and J. Ruby (eds), *Image Ethics in the Digital Age*, 143–70, Minneapolis, MN: University of Minnesota Press.

Helfer, L. R. and G. W. Austin (2011), *Human Rights and Intellectual Property*, New York: Cambridge University Press.

Hick, D. H. (2009), "Finding a Foundation: Copyright and the Creative Act," *Texas Intellectual Property Law Journal* 17 (3): 363–83.

Hilton, B., C. J. Choi, and S. Chen (2004), "The Ethics of Counterfeiting in the Fashion Industry. Quality, Credence and Profit Issues," *Journal of Business Ethics* 55 (4): 345–54.

Houkes, W. (2016), "Imitation and Replication of Technologies: The Prospects for an Evolutionary Ethics of Copying," in D. H. Hick and R. Schmücker (eds), *The Aesthetics and Ethics of Copying*, 39–57, London and New York: Bloomsbury.

Hume, D. (1751), *An Enquiry Concerning the Principles of Morals*, London: Millar.

Karapapa, S. (2012), *Private Copying*, London: Routledge.

Latonero, M. and A. Sinnreich (2014), "The Hidden Demography of New Media Ethics," *Information, Communication & Society* 17 (5): 572–93.

Lever, A. (ed.) (2012), *New Frontiers in the Philosophy of Intellectual Property*, New York: Cambridge University Press.

Macek, J. and P. Zahrádka (2016), "Online Piracy and the Transformation of the Audiences' Practices: The Case of the Czech Republic," in D. H. Hick and R. Schmücker (eds), *The Aesthetics and Ethics of Copying*, 335–58, London and New York: Bloomsbury.

Merges, R. P. (2011), *Justifying Intellectual Property*, Cambridge, MA and London: Harvard University Press.

Nida-Rümelin, J. (ed.) (2005), *Angewandte Ethik. Die Bereichsethiken und ihre theoretische Fundierung. Ein Handbuch*, 2nd edn, Stuttgart: Kröner.

Palmer, T. (2002), "Are Patents and Copyrights Morally Justified? The Philosophy of Property Rights and Ideal Objects" [1990], in A. Thierer and W. Crews (eds), *Copy Fights. The Future of Intellectual Property in the Information Age*, 43–93, Washington, DC: Cato Institute.

Pattanaik, M. K. (ed.) (2012), *Human Rights and Intellectual Property*, West Tripura: Icfai University Press.

Rawls, J. (2001), *Justice as Fairness. A Restatement*, Cambridge, MA: Harvard University Press.

Sabanna, T. (2009), *Intellectual Property Rights and Human Development in India*, New Delhi: Serials Publications.

Schmücker, R. (2011), "Grundkategorien moralischer Bewertung," in R. Stoecker, C. Neuhäuser, M.-L. Raters, and F. Koberling (eds), *Handbuch Angewandte Ethik*, 13–17, Stuttgart and Weimar: J. C. B. Metzler.

Schmücker, R. (2014), "Wozu berechtigt Not? Ein Plädoyer für eine Notethik," *Deutsche Zeitschrift für Philosophie* 62 (6): 1090–105.

Sinnreich, A. (2016), "Ethics, Evolved: An International Perspective on Copying in the Networked Age," in D. H. Hick and R. Schmücker (eds), *The Aesthetics and Ethics of Copying*, 315–34, London and New York: Bloomsbury.

Sinnreich, A., M. Latonero, and M. Gluck (2009), "Ethics Reconfigured. How Today's Media Consumers Evaluate the Role of Creative Reappropriation," *Information, Communication & Society* 12 (8): 1242–60.

Sützl, W., F. Stalder, R. Maier, and T. Hug (eds) (2012), *Cultures and Ethics of Sharing: Media, Knowledge and Education/Kulturen und Ethiken des Teilens: Medien—Wissen—Bildung*, Innsbruck: Innsbruck University Press.

Theisohn, P. (2012), *Literarisches Eigentum. Zur Ethik geistiger Arbeit im digitalen Zeitalter*, Stuttgart: Kröner.

Torremans, P. L. C. (ed.) (2004), *Copyright and Human Rights. Freedom of Expression—Intellectual Property—Privacy*, The Hague: Kluwer Law International.

Vaidhyanathan, S. (2001), *Copyrights and Copywrongs. The Rise of Intellectual Property and How It Threatens Creativity*, New York: New York University Press.

Weber, M. (1988), *Gesammelte Aufsätze zur Religionssoziologie*, 2 vols, Tübingen: J. C. B. Mohr (Paul Siebeck).

Weil, S. E. (2003), "Fair Use and the Visual Arts: Please Leave Some Room for Robin Hood," in L. Gross, J. Katz, and J. Ruby (eds), *Image Ethics in the Digital Age*, 171–82, Minneapolis, MN: University of Minnesota Press.

Young, J. O. (2016), "Appropriating Fictional Characters," in D. H. Hick and R. Schmücker (eds), *The Aesthetics and Ethics of Copying*, 153–72, London and New York: Bloomsbury.

Coda

20

In Defense of Disco Edits[1]

Hans Nieswandt

1. What exactly is an edit?

An edit is the product of an editing process, which is (very generally) a means of altering the shape, form, or content of media objects or data, physical or non-physical.

The term "edit" is used in many different ways. Many things can be edited—text, for example, by an editor. But mostly the term refers to tape—specifically to video or audio tape. Of course, nowadays, sound and other digital files get edited, too, but the term itself refers back to non-digital techniques people once executed with their hands—with razor blades, glue, and other cutting and pasting devices.

In this chapter, the term "edit" will specifically be used in connection to its meaning in audio treatment. More precisely, the perspective on the edit issue here is that of the DJ—someone who works with and makes edits himself.

2. So, what is an edit, then, in the DJ context?

Edits are customized versions of songs. Sometimes they are commissioned by record labels, but nowadays are mostly made without permission. And here we can find the difference between the edit and the edit's younger cousin, the remix: remixes are usually made from the original multitrack recordings. These days, when you create a remix, you mostly work with what are called "stem files." Remixers have access to all of the separate tracks that make up a song—8, 16, 24, or whatever (these numbers, of course, come from tape-machine times and have no more real relevance today). But you can still only get this type of working material directly from the record company, the agency, or the artist.

Making remixes is always a legal process, a deal, a job, at least a favor. You get asked: can you do me a remix?

Edits, on the contrary, are mostly made by those who have not been asked by anybody. They just have this idea and they go for it. The reason that this is possible at all is that edits are traditionally derived from the original stereo master—the full song just the way you hear it on the radio, find it on a record, buy it in a shop, download it at wherever, put it on a stick at a friend's house. Anybody with interest, passion, and a (hard) drive can have access to that gigantic mountain of recorded material and the software tools to climb it. At least nowadays.

3. Quick edit of edit history, Part 1

This was not always the case. The history of the edit begins with the history of the magnetic tape which—at least in our given field of interest—begins more or less (and similar to many other pop-cultural processes) with the end of the Second World War, when Jack Mullin, a U.S. Army Signal Corps soldier, brought home two AEG "Magnetophon" high-fidelity recording machines and fifty reels of "Farben" magnetic audio tape from Germany (Hammar 1994). By that time, Germany had the most advanced technology in audio recording, using it primarily for propaganda. Soon, Mullin realized the potential for entertainment purposes, eventually being hired by Bing Crosby, who was very impressed by the sound quality of the magnetic tape—much better than the shellac discs that were used until then to record audio material. Very quickly, tapes became the recording standard for radio and music companies around the world.

And naturally, these tapes had to be edited all the time—to cut out mistakes, to trim and shorten them to fit timings and prepare the recordings for use. And inventive people were at work here, to fool around with the tapes, to play them backwards, speed them up or down, creating then-unheard-of novelty audio effects. Different cutting angles created different kinds of attacks and decays; leaving blank spots in the right places on the adhesive tape generated nice tremoloes—there was a lot to be found out about the potential of tape editing from the late forties on.

French avant-garde composer Pierre Schaeffer was one of the key pioneers in such techniques, adapting and exploring them in the field of serious post-war experimental composition, recording and editing *études* for found objects not traditionally used in music composition, like (most famously) locomotives and other everyday sound sources. The name for this technique is *musique concrète*, and it has a firm place in the music history of the twentieth century. In Germany, Karlheinz Stockhausen ventured very early into tape experimentation, creating tape loops as sound sources. That their highbrow approaches were not a big success with wider audiences is negligible for our purposes here; what sets them apart from the modern idea of edits is that you cannot really recognize them as such. There was not yet an "edit aesthetic" detectable. To truly appreciate something as an edit today, it is necessary to hear the difference—the treatment done to the source material. It must be identifiable that something has happened to it.

Because of this, the credit for the edit—for the first true recognizable-as-such cut-up record—probably goes to two comedians, collectively credited as "Buchanan and Goodman," for their 1956 piece, "Flying Saucer," in which they intercut between reports on alien attacks and (sometimes very short) sections of rock 'n' roll hits of the day, commenting on this threat. In 1956, it must have sounded amazingly modern.

4. Quick edit of edit history, Part 2

Experimentation in edits continued and expanded into the sixties, both on the artsy and the gimmicky sides. The prices for the tape machines sank as their operability grew, turning them into sophisticated household items for tasteful home listeners of jazz and classics with higher lifestyle requirements for their listening pleasure. Soon, every member of the Beatles had a Revox machine at home, and their records offer many examples of their wild and joyful explorations. Experimental composer Terry Riley created a tape edit in 1967 that could have easily been the first disco edit ever, had it not been made by an experimental composer. His version of Harvey Averne's "You're No Good" keeps the funky soul groove of the original quite tight for a little while, until it starts to shift and warp to a psychedelically exhausting extent, which was the intention. Pieces like this were, of course, rarely under some mind-altering twenty minutes in length, so you needed some nerve and readiness to listen all the way through for the sake of research (never mind playing them at a club). But it's fascinating that the idea of tailoring finished songs for dance-floor use by extending certain parts and cutting out others could have easily been established five years earlier. It took the rise of disco in the early seventies—a culture with very specific musical needs—to really push the edit aesthetic in the direction it has taken up to this day: make the song—any song—work for you (and your crowd). You bought it, you got it; in a way it's your song now. You can customize it the way you can customize a car, a jacket, or a meal. Push the potatoes aside and go just for the meat.

This, of course, creates a problem. First of all, it's obviously not really your song: it's just a piece of plastic (or a bag of bytes) that you own. With the jacket, you can cut the arms off, sew your name in silver studs on the back, and walk around in your creation, but you cannot sell that product, let alone mass-produce it. You can, however, sell the *performance* of walking around like that. This is where DJs come in: they can actually do both. DJs soon started to customize the music, creating special, private versions so as to increase the impact of a song on their crowds, and essentially sold the exclusive listening and dancing pleasure at the clubs where they played. Initially not much appreciated (especially by the original artists, but realized as having big potential and picked up very soon by on-the-spot New York record companies, many of them independent and specialized), edit-making became a new small business in the early seventies in the highly inventive New York disco scene.

First, there were the acetates. DJs and engineers with a good sense for timing and a calm hand for the razor blade started to make reel-to-reel edits of certain hot tracks, extending the tribalistic drum parts, inserting effects, creating tension, tailor-making versions to hype up their crowds, to get maximum effect from the strongest parts of the song—usually a brand new, up-tempo disco song. Pretty soon, they realized that sections of other songs could be edited in as well, and the master mix was born. These creations were taken to small cutting studios, where the sound was cut directly into the acetate disc in real time. Thus, a single copy was made that the DJ could play the same night at his club. Only there could you hear this super-special derivative version of, let's say, "Instant Replay" or "Another One Bites The Dust." In the creation of early disco edits, among the most famous names are Walter Gibbons, John Morales, the company Sunshine Sound, and DJ Danny Krivit, and their edits can easily be found online nowadays. Edit-works by Gibbons, Morales, and Krivit are also available on properly licensed vinyl compilations. Original acetates (and dubplates, a different name for essentially the same thing), however, are extremely expensive. Should you get hold of one, digitize it on first play—these acetates only have a life of about thirty plays, and most are well worn out today.

These improved-for-dance-floor-use derivates proved to be a big success, especially as seamlessly beatmixed music (the synchronized playing of two records at once) became standard at the clubs (a standard not much changed today). Every club wanted the seamless mix, but not every suburban disco DJ was able to beatmix. As well, fans of the music wanted this never-stop style available at home. The discrete cassette-tape-copy market blossomed, and the larger labels stepped in, cashing in with Stars On 45 and other horrors of the disco gold rush.[2]

A lot of this was throwaway stuff, but still important. Influential masterpieces were edited together, even while unconscious of their future effect. In 1980, the bootleg label Remix Records released "On & On" by Mach, the B-Side of "Funky Mix," a relentless sequence of then-current club favorites, cut and pasted over a looped beat. Pretty good, actually, but *very* relentless: the basic tape loop just never stops. The same is true for "On & On," which uses the same loop ("Funky Town" by Lipps Inc.) as its backbone, adding a few more layers as it loops along, evolving into what many today consider the very first house track. Chicago's DJ Jesse Saunders made extensive use of "On & On" as his trademark intro until his copy was stolen. Saunders decided to try re-recording it himself, releasing his version on his own Jes Say label.[3] Back then, this was just a little story on the South Side of Chicago; today, it is a key myth in the old testament of house music.

Although disco edits played a key role in the development of house music and modern DJ approaches, be it as acetates, bootleg vinyl or reel-to-reel-machines set up in the DJ booth, by the time house music gained full momentum, the making of edits quickly lost popularity. The reason for this was the rise (or rather the fall of prices) of the digital sampler. By the late eighties, these were affordable for most DJs, who now started to get fully into music production.

5. Quick edit of edit history, Part 3

By the eighties, DJs (as the holders of dance-floor wisdom) were being hired to assist productions or commissioned to do remixes. Remixes became hip and everybody wanted one. More and more DJs started to develop their own styles or trademark sounds, and their fame and proven power as taste- and hit-makers led to ever more adventurous approaches to remixes, sometimes making the original version almost disappear. Still, proper studios with trained engineers were needed to operate mixing consoles and even sampling machines well into the digital era. In their funny little book, *The Manual (How To Have A Number One The Easy Way)* (1999), Bill Drummond and Jimmy Cauty (together, the U.K. pop prankster duo, the KLF) describe this basically curatorial approach to production very precisely: take a bunch of records you want to sample to the studio, tell the operator what to do, and don't forget to make him tea and sandwiches, and to give him compliments about his place. Soon after, by the beginning of the nineties, a lot of the smaller studios doing productions like that had to close, because now the DJs were turning their bedrooms into their studios (by the time of this writing, my studio and my typewriter have become the same, and I can take them everywhere I go).

Since DJs are all about repertoire, the new sampling devices turned out to be an ideal access-giver to the sonic archive of recorded music history. But for many years to come, samplers were of limited memory capacity. As is often the case, technical limitations led to new aesthetic solutions. Short, sampled loops—musical quotes—became the new backbone of productions. Ten years earlier, hip-hop DJs had taken great pains in mixing famous funk breaks back and forth on two turntables to create a steady backbeat for a rapper. Now, these could easily be looped-up and endlessly repeated without fuss. Records were plundered both for the obscure and the obvious. An early peak of the sample craze was De La Soul's 1989 debut album, *Three Feet High And Rising*, which not only showed the artistic potential of sampled collages, but also the legal problems you can get yourself into by doing them. It took months of legal negotiating until the album—now a cornerstone not only of hip-hop but of sample-based music history in general—could be properly released (see Okpaluba 2014).

At that time, nobody in the business had really anticipated a development like this. Copying parts of others' recordings to make new music was not a top-to-bottom-decision, something that had been thought out, planned, or decided on the management floors of big record companies. Rather, the opposite: making music with turntables and samplers was for the underprivileged, for musicians without money and no access to expensive gear. So, while the big companies quickly developed ways to get compensated for sampling (there were rarely samples prohibited outright, as did Gilbert O'Sullivan to Biz Markie;[4] mostly deals were being made, and some old drummers got good licensing money for it while others did not), underneath the radar of the big market, sampling culture flourished in underground clubs. The basic house formula of the steady pulse of a four-to-the-floor beat turned out to be a brilliant canvas for all kinds of sample-arranging inventiveness. "Filter disco" became a catchphrase in the nineties, as various bits of disco tracks were repeated ad nauseam while being filtered open and closed, thereby creating tension and trance at the same time. The original bit—the sampled source material—more and more became just a seed of inspiration that grew in whatever direction the DJ producer wished to take it. This was a movement not about celebrating any original; it was about using it as raw source material—the more it got twisted and masked, the better.

6. Quick edit of edit history, Part 4

That started to change after the year 2000. Not only had hard-disk recording achieved new, unheard-of memory capacities; additionally, after years of forward-pushing innovation in the huge field of sample-based or -assisted electronic music production (ranging from hip-hop to house, from drum and bass to techno, and way beyond), escorted by an overall astonishing commercial success and global impact, some underground producers started to take a look at the heritage, basically looking for a way ahead by taking a look backwards, reconsidering the by now old-fashioned art form of the edit, finding a new way to make limitations lead to solutions. Instead of sampling just a break or any usable section of a record, whole songs could now be loaded into the computer and edited right there, with no glue and no razor. Modern software for equalizing and compressing made it instead possible to let old songs pump and shine like they were just made last week, with a bottom nobody ever knew they had in them. Additional kickdrums gave them a punch that was impossible before. These days, the lines between new productions that sound like old ones and old productions that sound like new can become very blurred (as Pharrell Williams and Robin Thicke can attest, having been sued over their 2013 groove quotation of Marvin Gaye's "Got to Give It Up").[5]

So edits came back, but something had changed in the attitude towards making them, and also in the range of material considered to be editable. While the basic reason for making them was still to make something work (for certain dance floors), a big portion of the new school of editors was less interested in *using* a song than in *adoring* a song—in bringing out its hidden potential. Where the first wave of edits was all about customizing the latest music, the new wave of edits is, first, all about digging out stuff—be it obscure or very popular (like Fleetwood Mac or Bruce Springsteen)—and, second, about making music work for DJ purposes which was never intended to be danced to at clubs (Bruce Springsteen, again).

This has to do with the liquid nature sound acquires in the digital state. Tempo and pitch used to be obstacles that, in the old edits, sometimes produced harsh transitions. This is especially true of recordings that were made before the use of click tracks became common (not only in dance music), and which tended to shift in speed, sometimes wildly. As a DJ, you needed to know their nature inside out to be able to integrate them in club mixes, and well-trained skills were necessary to avoid creating so-called "trainwreck mixes." As digital audio files, shifts in such songs—say, old soul numbers—can be fixed in minutes by grabbing single beats in the waveform with the mouse and relocating them to the nearest correct place in the arrangement grid. This way, ballads can become up-tempo stompers, swing numbers get reggaefied, and even Phil Collins songs can become cool underground disco tracks. Often, the true song gets held back for a long time to enhance the joy of recognizing the release. There is an edit around of Toto's "Africa" that loops up half of the initial bars seemingly forever—nobody recognizes the nice groove they all are dancing to (though it might sound familiar) until, after five minutes, the chorus comes in, and everybody over forty starts to sing along.

This observation leads to another effect that modern-day disco edits have on a societal level: delivered in a production aesthetic that both fits the listening habits of the young and the desire for familiarity of the old, originally boring Chris Rea songs are suddenly able to unite generations of dancers. And by being rhythmically tightened through processing, they can be mixed with any new production, making possible very exciting transitions and juxtapositions between different ages of dance music, from the very beginnings (there are edits of Slim Gaillard jams from the forties around) to just-made-it-this-morning, from hippie dance to hard techno, all in the time it takes to make a crossfade.

7. Edit economy

Naturally, creating those edits is not a serious business. Artistically, yes, of course—it cannot get much more serious than in disco-edit nerd-circles. But economically, no: you cannot run a real label releasing edits of other people's music—there are only a few willing to take on the labor of tracking down rights-holders, sealing deals, and releasing beautiful, theme-oriented centerfold packages with rich liner notes on legendary editors like John Morales or Walter Gibbons, or certain scenes like "The Real Sound of Chicago" on mostly British labels like BBE or Strut. Much more often, the labels are only imaginary. It's like playing at being a label. Since a big part of the appeal of edit culture has to do with a love for vinyl records and the hunt for them, the round paper label in the middle of the record is a very important detail for the feel of the product. It's not so much about the printed information given there (many times, it's a lot of sweet lies and disguises to avoid legal trouble—in the seventies, they often used the term "Canadian Mix" for that purpose); it is more a visual platform for eclectic aesthetic statements. A lot of them look fake-vintage, even with fake stains on them. They are made by romantics who want to continue the tradition, or ensure the existence, of a fetish-object that you can go digging for—something that mp3 files can hardly ever be. These edits on tiny fantasy labels with names like Star Time, Disco Deviance, Super Value, Discolexic, Bearded Science, Hidden History, Titanic Ballroom, Mindless Boogie, Editainment, Copycat, Razor 'n' Tape, Tuff Cut, or Flashback (this list could be extended endlessly) crop up in very small numbers in the most specialist vinyl stores, just like obscure import records in the heydays of vinyl. Besides these fantasy labels, there are loads of white labels too, with handwritten or stamped information (of the same hazy nature).

Many of these "labels" come from England. This might have to do with a certain sense for passionate, piratic romanticism that pervaded U.K. pop culture for a long time and in various places. The idea of the honorable corsair or Robin Hood, who steals, yes, not to get rich, but rather for the good cause, for the benefit of the underprivileged (who don't have access to certain tunes they need). The northern soul tradition of "keepin' the faith," the so-called "hardcore continuum," the pirate stations story, the travelers, and all those other U.K. rebel lifestyle manifestations breed into the perception of those edits—music you could consider withheld from the people and freed by the editors.

Then there is the spiritual side. British writers like Simon Reynolds and Marc Fisher have elaborated at great lengths about terms like "hauntology," which is perfectly applicable to the makings of the world of modern edits (see e.g. Reynolds 2006; Fisher 2013). There is a great and widespread desire throughout the finer minds of club and DJ culture to go back, to visit and hang out with the ghosts of the innocent disco past, to the times before superclubs and weekend packages in Ibiza, to a more dedicated time, when disco was not just fun and business, but really the festive expression, the celebration of a liberation that had just happened (of gays, of blacks, of hippies). Or to more guilty times, at legendary clubs in New York, northern Italy, or northern England, which live on only in the imagination of editmakers.

The fact that editmaking—or at least the manufacturing of even a small amount of vinyl copies (300 to 500)—is not exactly legal raises many questions from copyright infringement to artistic freedom. Some of those guerilla labels make a point out of it, a stance for the case of appropriation art. There's a compilation series called "Gema" after the German version of BMI, ASCAP, and so on—the association that collects money for and from the artists. For the tracklistings of these compilations of wildly and rawly slammed-together mash-ups (another subcategory of editing: instead of one track, two or more are mashed together, often to very funny, funky, touching, or satirical effect), the producers use the original reporting sheet that artists have to fill out when registering a piece at GEMA. In between the mash-ups, there are sound bytes of pro-copyright lobbyists and politicians, put to ridicule. The most famous example of politically motivated appropriation art in music is the 1986 album, *Tacky Souvenirs of Pre-Revolutionary America*, by the Houston, Texas punk band, Culturecide. For the album, they just played original recordings of the Beach Boys, USA for Africa, etc. through their board, adding effects and singing anti-corporate lyrics over it. The album gained them minor cult status and huge legal problems.

But situationist actions like this (or by the KLF) hint at an underlying question: How far must property control go? Whose property really is a song anyway, once released? As Diedrich Diederichsen points out in his book, *Über Pop-Musik* (*On Pop Music*, 2014), pop is put together—very complexly—of many things, a very crucial one being the role of the listener, who is looking for a way of integrating it into his own life. This is what makes the song complete: only then it is truly pop. This may sound heavy for the artist, who seems to have lost control over his own creation, but never really had it in the first place—control over how her or his music has to be enjoyed, has to be used. This is essentially why pop music has been so successful for so long, this is what it's really made for: to be used individually in individual lives.

Doing this, by means of edits, is very common practice now. Apart from the ideal-driven, vinyl-fetish-fixated editors, the web is full of homemade versions of just about anything. This is pure prosumerism. When Metallica released an album together with Lou Reed a few years ago,[6] quickly there were versions on the web where "this horrible old guy," who no one seemed to know, was edited out. Cruel to late Lou Reed, but you can't help smiling at this case of self-empowerment, this move from passive consumption to active customizing. Even some of my own songs are around as edits. Do I care? Do I feel robbed? Well, as long as there is no profit being made and no heavy abuse is going on—like big advertising or right-wing propaganda videos decorated with my music—I rather feel flattered about the attention I get. As long as it does not interfere with my own set of ethical ideas, which is part of the basis of my work in general, I like the idea of art as an offering for further interpreting—but that's a very subjective perspective. In my mind, at least, editmaking can and should be a way of honoring the original; I take it as a compliment. Obviously I inspired somebody to do something—for this, I don't have to charge.

Notes

1 The title of this text is sampled from the brilliant, highly inspirational essay, "In Defence of Disco" (1979) by Richard Dyer, for the magazine *Gay Left*, where he takes a pro-disco stance from a gay Marxist perspective.
2 For a sense of the volume of edits and master mixes produced on acetate, bootleg, or legal vinyl between 1973 and 1986 alone, Lejeune and Vogt (2007) is a rich source.
3 Saunders tells the story in Chapter 5 of his (2007).
4 See *Grand Upright Music Limited v. Warner Brothers Records, Inc. et al.*, 780 F. Supp. 182 (S.D.N.Y. 1991).
5 See *Williams v. Bridgeport Music, Inc.*, 2014 U.S. Dist. LEXIS 182240 (C.D. Cal., Oct. 30, 2014); see also Ortland 2016.
6 *Lulu*, 2011.

References

Cauty, J. and B. Drummond (1999), *The Manual (How To Have A Number One The Easy Way)*, London: Ellipsis.

Diederichsen, D. (2014), *Über Pop-Musik*, Cologne: Kiepenheuer & Witsch.

Dyer, R. (1979), "In Defence of Disco," *Gay Left* 8: 20–3.

Fisher, M. (2013), "The Metaphysics of Crackle: Afrofuturism and Hauntology," *Dancecult: Journal of Electronic Dance Music Culture* 5 (2): 42–55.

Hammar, P. (1994), "In Memoriam: John T. (Jack) Mullin," *Journal of the Audio Engineering Society* 47 (9): 776–7.

Lejeune, P. and P. Vogt (2007), *Disco Patrick Presents: The Bootleg Guide to Disco, Acetates, Funk, Rap and Disco Medleys*, Netherlands: Patrick Lejeune and Patrick Vogt.

Okpaluba, J. (2014), "Digital Sampling and Music Industry Practices, Re-spun," in K. Bowrey and M. Handler (eds), *Law and Creativity in the Age of the Entertainment Franchise*, 75–100, Cambridge: Cambridge University Press.

Ortland, E. (2016), "Blurred Lines: A Case Study on the Ethics and Aesthetics of Copying," in D. H. Hick and R. Schmücker (eds), *The Aesthetics and Ethics of Copying*, London and New York: Bloomsbury.

Reynolds, S. (2006), "Haunted Audio," *The Wire* 273: 26–33.

Saunders, J. and J. Cummins (2007), *House Music … The Real Story*, Baltimore: PublishAmerica.

Index of Names

Index of Subjects

Made in United States
Cleveland, OH
22 July 2026

40895724R00240